The Desire of Ages

BOOK I

E. G. White

FH₿

Family Heritage Books
Thomaston, GA 30286

The bracketed numbers at the foot of each page coordinate this edition with the pagination of the standard hardback printings published under the title, *The Desire of Ages*.

Cover design by Kim Justinen and Merwin Stewart
Interior design by Gena Cowen, Dan Willett, & C. David Wingate
All photographs & artwork supplied by Pacific Press Publishing Association
Type set: 10/11.5 Times Roman
Printed on acid free paper

Printed in U.S.A. by Pacific Press Publishing Association

FHB Cataloging Service

White, Ellen G., 1827-1915
  The Desire of Ages, Book 1

  1. History, Christ   2. Jesus' Ministry
I. Title

ISBN 0-8163-1016-5

Contents

Section IV. Days of Promise

Section V. Falling Shadows.

"God With Us"

His name shall be called Immanuel, . . . God with us." "The light of the knowledge of the glory of God" is seen "in the face of Jesus Christ." From the days of eternity the Lord Jesus Christ was one with the Father; He was "the image of God," the image of His greatness and majesty, "the outshining of His glory." It was to manifest this glory that He came to our world. To this sin-darkened earth He came to reveal the light of God's love, — to be "God with us." Therefore it was prophesied of Him, "His name shall be called Immanuel."

By coming to dwell with us, Jesus was to reveal God both to men and to angels. He was the Word of God, — God's thought made audible. In His prayer for His disciples He says, "I have declared unto them Thy name," — "merciful and gracious, longsuffering, and abundant in goodness and truth," — "that the love wherewith Thou hast loved Me may be in them, and I in them." But not alone for His earth-born children was this revelation given. Our little world is the lesson-book of the universe. God's wonderful purpose of grace, the mystery of redeeming love, is the theme into which "angels desire to look," and it will be their study throughout endless ages. Both the redeemed and the unfallen beings will find in the cross of Christ their science and their song. It will be seen that the glory shining in the face of Jesus is the glory of self-sacrificing love. In the light from Calvary it will be seen, that the law of self-renouncing love is the law of life for earth and heaven; that the love which "seeketh not her own" has its source in the heart of God; and that in the meek and lowly One is manifested the character of Him who dwelleth in the light which no man can approach unto.

In the beginning, God was revealed in all the works of creation. It was Christ that spread the heavens, and laid the foundations of the earth. It was His hand that hung the worlds in space, and fashioned the flowers of the field. "His strength setteth fast the mountains." "The sea is His, and He made it." Psalms 65:6; 95:5. It was He that filled the earth with beauty, and the air with song. And upon all things in earth, and air, and sky, He wrote the message of the Father's love.

Now sin has marred God's perfect work, yet that handwriting remains. Even now all created things declare the glory of His excellence. There is nothing, save the selfish heart of man, that lives unto itself. No bird that cleaves the air, no animal that moves upon the ground, but ministers to some other life. There is no leaf of the forest, or lowly blade of grass, but has its ministry. Every tree and shrub and leaf pours forth that element of life, without which neither man nor animal could live; and man and animal, in turn, minister to the life of tree and shrub and leaf. The flowers breathe fragrance and unfold their beauty in blessing to the world. The sun sheds its light to gladden a thousand worlds. The ocean, itself the source of all our springs and fountains, receives the streams from every land, but takes to give. The mists ascending from its bosom fall in showers to water the earth, that it may bring forth and bud.

The angels of glory find their joy in giving, — giving love and tireless watch-care to souls that are fallen and unholy. Heavenly beings woo the hearts of men; they bring to this dark world light from the courts above; by gentle and patient ministry they move upon the human spirit, to bring the lost into a fellowship with Christ which is even closer than they themselves can know.

But turning from all lesser representations, we behold God in Jesus. Looking unto Jesus we see that it is the glory of our God to give. "I do nothing of Myself," said Christ; "the living Father hath sent Me, and I live by the Father." "I seek not Mine own glory," but the glory of Him that sent Me. John 8:28; 6:57; 8:50; 7:18. In these words is set forth the great principle which is the law of life for the universe. All things Christ received from God, but He took to give. So in the heavenly courts, in His ministry for all created beings; through the beloved Son, the Father's life flows out to all; through the Son it returns, in praise and joyous service, a tide of love, to the great Source of all. And thus through Christ the circuit of beneficence is complete, representing the character of the great Giver, the law of life.

In heaven itself this law was broken. Sin originated in self-seeking. Lucifer, the covering cherub, desired to be first in heaven. He sought to gain control of heavenly beings, to draw them away from their Creator, and to win their homage to himself. Therefore he misrepresented God, attributing to Him the desire for self-exaltation. With his own evil characteristics he sought to invest the loving Creator. Thus he deceived angels. Thus he deceived men. He led them to doubt the word of God, and to distrust His goodness. Because God is a God of justice and terrible majesty, Satan caused them to look upon Him as severe and unforgiving. Thus he drew men to join him in rebellion against God, and the night of woe settled down upon the world.

The earth was dark through misapprehension of God. That the gloomy shadows might be lightened, that the world might be brought back to God, Satan's deceptive power was to be broken. This could not be done by force. The exercise of force is contrary to the principles of God's government; he desires only the service of love; and love cannot be commanded; it cannot be won by force or authority. Only by love is love awakened. To know God is to love Him; His character must be manifested in contrast to the character of Satan. This work only one Being in all the universe could do. Only He who knew the height and depth of the love of God, could make it known. Upon the world's dark night the Sun of Righteousness must rise, "with healing in His wings." Malachi 4:2.

The plan for our redemption was not an after-thought, a plan formulated after the fall of Adam. It was a revelation of "the mystery which hath been kept in silence through times eternal." Romans 16:25, R.V. It was an unfolding of the principles that from eternal ages have been the foundation of God's throne. From the beginning, God and Christ knew of the apostasy of Satan, and of the fall of man through the deceptive power of the apostate. God did not ordain that sin should exist, but He foresaw its existence, and made provision to meet the terrible emergency. So great was His love for the world, that He covenanted to give His only begotten Son, "that whosoever believeth in Him should not perish, but have everlasting life. John 3:16.

Lucifer had said, "I will exalt my throne above the stars of God; . . . I will be like the Most High." Isaiah 14:13, 14.

But Christ, "being in the form of God, counted it not a thing to be grasped to be on an equality with God, but emptied Himself, taking the form of a servant, being made in the likeness of men." Phil. 2:6, 7, R.V., margin.

This was a voluntary sacrifice. Jesus might have remained at the Father's side. He might have retained the glory of heaven, and the homage of the angels. But He chose to give back the scepter into the Father's hands, and to step down from the throne of the universe, that He might bring light to the benighted, and life to the perishing.

Nearly two thousand years ago, a voice of mysterious import was heard in heaven, from the throne of God, "Lo, I come." "Sacrifice and offering Thou wouldst not, but a body hast Thou prepared Me. . . . Lo, I come (in the volume of the book it is written of Me,) to do Thy will, O God." Heb. 10:5-7. In these words is announced the fulfillment of the purpose that had been hidden from eternal ages. Christ was about to visit our world, and to become incarnate. He says, "A body hast Thou prepared Me." Had He appeared with the glory that was His with the Father before the world was, we could not have endured the light of His presence. That we might behold it and not be destroyed, the manifestation of His glory was shrouded. His divinity was veiled with humanity,—the invisible glory in the visible human form.

This great purpose had been shadowed forth in types and symbols. The burning bush, in which Christ appeared to Moses, revealed God. The symbol chosen for the representation of the Deity was a lowly shrub, that seemingly had no attractions. This enshrined the Infinite. The all-merciful God shrouded His glory in a most humble type, that Moses could look upon it and live. So in the pillar of cloud by day and the pillar of fire by night, God communicated with Israel, revealing to men His will, and imparting to them His grace. God's glory was subdued, and His majesty veiled, that the weak vision of finite men might behold it. So Christ was to come in "the body of our humiliation," Phil. 3:21, R.V. "in the likeness of men." In the eyes of the world He possessed no beauty that they should desire Him; yet He was the incarnate God, the light of heaven and earth. His glory was veiled, His greatness and majesty were hidden, that He might draw near to sorrowful, tempted men.

God commanded Moses for Israel, "Let them make Me a sanctuary, that I may dwell among them," Exodus 25:8. and He abode in the sanctuary, in the midst of His people. Through all their weary wandering in the desert, the symbol of His presence was with them. So Christ set up His tabernacle in the midst of our human encampment. He pitched His tent by the side of the tents of men, that He might dwell among us, and make us familiar with His divine character and life. "The Word became flesh, and tabernacled among us (and we beheld His glory, glory as of the only begotten from the Father) full of grace and truth. John 1:14, R.V., margin.

Since Jesus came to dwell with us, we know that God is acquainted with our trials, and sympathizes with our griefs. Every son and daughter of Adam may understand that our Creator is the friend of sinners. For in every doctrine of grace, every promise of joy, every deed of love, every divine attraction presented in the Saviour's life on earth, we see "God with us."

Satan represents God's law of love as a law of selfishness. He declares that it is impossible for us to obey its precepts. The fall of our first parents, with all the woe that has resulted, he charges upon the Creator, leading men to look upon God as the author of sin, and suffering, and death. Jesus was to unveil this deception. As one of us He was to give an example of obedience. For this He took upon Himself our nature, and passed through our experiences. "In all things it behooved Him to be made like unto His brethren." Hebrews 2:17. If we had to bear anything which Jesus did not endure, then upon this point Satan would represent the power of God as insufficient for us. Therefore Jesus was "in all points tempted like as we are." Hebrews 4:15. He endured every trial to which we are subject. And He exercised in His own behalf no power that is not freely offered to us. As man, He met temptation, and overcame in the strength given Him from God. He says, "I delight to do Thy will, O My God; yea, Thy law is within My heart." Psalms 40:8. As He went about doing good, and healing all who were afflicted by Satan, He made plain

> **"Christ was treated as we deserve, that we might be treated as He deserves. He was condemned for our sins, in which He had no share, that we might be justified by His righteousness, in which we had no share. He suffered the death which was ours, that we might receive the life which was His. 'With His stripes we are healed.'"**

to men the character of God's law and the nature of His service. His life testifies that it is possible for us also to obey the law of God.

By His humanity, Christ touched humanity; by His divinity, He lays hold upon the throne of God. As the Son of man, He gave us an example of obedience; as the Son of God, He gives us power to obey. It was Christ who from the bush of Mount Horeb spoke to Moses saying, "I Am That I Am. . . . Thus shalt thou say unto the children of Israel, I Am hath sent me unto you." Exodus 3:14. This was the pledge of Israel's deliverance. So when He came "in the likeness of men," He declared Himself the I Am. The Child of Bethlehem, the meek and lowly Saviour, is God "manifest in the flesh." 1 Timothy 3:16. And to us He says, "I Am the Good Shepherd. I Am the living Bread. I Am the Way, the Truth, and the Life. All power is given unto Me in heaven and in earth." John 10:11; 6:51; 14:6; Matthew 28:18. "I Am the assurance of every promise. I Am; be not afraid." "God with us" is the surety of our deliverance from sin, the assurance of our power to obey the law of heaven.

In stooping to take upon Himself humanity, Christ revealed a character the opposite of the character of Satan. But He stepped still lower in the path of humiliation. "Being found in fashion as a man, He humbled Himself, and became obedient unto death, even the death of the cross." Philippians 2:8. As the high priest laid aside his gorgeous pontifical robes, and officiated in the white linen dress of the common priest, so Christ took the form of a servant, and offered sacrifice, Himself the priest, Himself the victim. "He was wounded for our transgressions, He was bruised for our iniquities; the chastisement of our peace was upon Him." Isaiah 53:5.

Christ was treated as we deserve, that we might be treated as He deserves. He was condemned for our sins, in which He had no share, that we might be justified by His righteousness, in which we had no share. He suffered the death which was ours, that we might receive the life which was His. "With His stripes we are healed."

By His life and His death, Christ has achieved even more than recovery from the ruin wrought through sin. It was Satan's purpose to bring about an eternal separation between God and man; but in Christ we become more closely united to God than if we had never fallen. In taking our nature, the Saviour has bound Himself to humanity by a tie that is never to be broken. Through the eternal ages He is linked with us. "God so loved the world, that He gave His only begotten Son." John 3:16. He gave Him not only to bear our sins, and to die as our sacrifice; He gave Him to the fallen race. To assure us of His immutable counsel of peace, God gave His only begotten Son to become one of the human family, forever to retain His human nature. This is the pledge that God will fulfil His word. "Unto *us* a child is born; unto *us* a son is given; and the government shall be upon His shoulder." God has adopted human nature in the person of His Son, and has carried the same into the highest heaven. It is the "Son of man" who shares the throne of the universe It is the "Son of man" whose name shall be called, "Wonderful, Counselor, the mighty God, the everlasting Father, the Prince of Peace." Isaiah 9:6. The I Am is the Daysman between God and humanity, laying His hand upon both. He who is "holy, harmless, undefiled, separate from sinners," is not ashamed to call us brethren. Hebrews 7:26; 2:11. In Christ the family of earth and the family of heaven are bound together. Christ glorified is our brother. Heaven is enshrined in humanity, and humanity is enfolded in the bosom of Infinite Love.

Of His people God says, "They shall be as the stones of a crown, lifted up as an ensign upon His land. For how great is His goodness, and how great is His beauty!" Zechariah 9:16, 17. The exaltation of the redeemed will be an eternal testimony to God's mercy. "In the ages to come," He will "show the exceeding riches of His grace in His kindness toward us through Christ Jesus." "To the intent that . . . unto the principalities and the powers in the heavenly places might be made known . . . the manifold wisdom of God, according to the eternal purpose which He purposed in Christ Jesus our Lord." Ephesians 2:7; 3:10, 11, R. V.

Through Christ's redeeming work the government of God stands justified. The Omnipotent One is made known as the God of love. Satan's charges are refuted, and his character unveiled. Rebellion can never again arise. Sin can never again enter the universe. Through eternal ages all are secure from apostasy. By love's self-sacrifice, the inhabitants of earth and heaven are bound to their Creator in bonds of indissoluble union.

The work of redemption will be complete. In the place where sin abounded, God's grace much more abounds. The earth itself, the very field that Satan claims as his, is to be not only ransomed but exalted. Our little world, under the curse of sin the one dark blot in His glorious creation, will be honored above all other worlds in the universe of God. Here, where the Son of God tabernacled in humanity; where the King of Glory lived and suffered and died, — here, when He shall make all things new, the tabernacle of God shall be with men, "and He shall dwell with them, and they shall be His people, and God Himself shall be with them, and be their God." And through endless ages as the redeemed walk in the light of the Lord, they will praise Him for His unspeakable Gift, —

Immanuel, "God with us."

The Chosen People

For more than a thousand years the Jewish people had awaited the Saviour's coming. Upon this event they had rested their brightest hopes. In song and prophecy, in temple rite and household prayer, they had enshrined His name. And yet at His coming, they knew Him not. The Beloved of heaven was to them "as a root out of a dry ground;" He had "no form nor comeliness;" and they saw in Him no beauty that they should desire Him. "He came unto His own, and His own received Him not." Isaiah 53:2; John 1:11.

Yet God had chosen Israel. He had called them to preserve among men the knowledge of His law, and of the symbols and prophecies that pointed to the Saviour. He desired them to be as wells of salvation to the world. What Abraham was in the land of his sojourn, what Joseph was in Egypt, and Daniel in the courts of Babylon, the Hebrew people were to be among the nations. They were to reveal God to men.

In the call of Abraham the Lord had said, "I will bless thee, . . . and thou shalt be a blessing, . . . and in thee shall all families of the earth be blessed." Genesis 12:2, 3. The same teaching was repeated through the prophets. Even after Israel had been wasted by war and captivity, the promise was theirs, "The remnant of Jacob shall be in the midst of many people as a dew from the Lord, as the showers upon the grass, that tarrieth not for man, nor waiteth for the sons of men." Micah 5:7. Concerning the temple at Jerusalem, the Lord declared through Isaiah, "Mine house shall be called an house of prayer for all peoples." Isaiah 56:7, R.V.

But the Israelites fixed their hopes upon worldly greatness. From the time of their entrance to the land of Canaan, they departed from the commandments of God, and followed the ways of the heathen. It was in vain that God sent them warning by His prophets. In vain they suffered the chastisement of heathen oppression. Every reformation was followed by deeper apostasy.

Had Israel been true to God, He could have accomplished His purpose through their honor and exaltation. If they had walked in the ways of obedience, He would have made them "high above all nations which He hath made, in praise, and in name, and in honor." "All people of the earth," said Moses, "shall see that thou art called by the name of Jehovah; and they shall be afraid of thee." "The nations which shall hear all these statutes" shall say, "Surely this great nation is a wise and understanding people." Deuteronomy 26:19; 28:10; 4:6. But because of their unfaithfulness, God's purpose could be wrought out only through continued adversity and humiliation.

They were brought into subjection to Babylon, and scattered through the lands of the heathen. In affliction many renewed their faithfulness to His covenant. While they hung their harps upon the willows, and mourned for the holy temple that was laid waste, the light of truth shone out through them, and a knowledge of God was spread among the nations. The heathen systems of sacrifice were a perversion of the system that God had appointed; and many a sincere observer of heathen rites learned from the Hebrews the meaning of the service divinely ordained, and in faith grasped the promise of a Redeemer.

Many of the exiles suffered persecution. Not a few lost their lives because of their refusal to disregard the Sabbath and to observe the heathen festivals. As idolaters were roused to crush out the truth, the Lord brought His servants face to face with kings and rulers, that they and their people might receive the light. Time after time the greatest monarchs were led to proclaim the supremacy of the God whom their Hebrew captives worshiped.

By the Babylonish captivity the Israelites were effectually cured of the worship of graven images. During the centuries that followed, they suffered from the oppression of heathen foes, until the conviction became fixed that their prosperity depended upon their obedience to the law of God. But with too many of the people, obedience was not prompted by love. The motive was selfish. They rendered outward service to God as the means of attaining to national greatness. They did not become the light of the world, but shut themselves away from the world in order to escape temptation to idolatry. In the instruction given through Moses, God had placed restrictions upon their association with idolaters; but this teaching had been misinterpreted. It was intended to prevent them from conforming to the practises of the heathen. But it was used to build up a wall of separation between Israel and all other nations. The Jews looked upon Jerusalem as their heaven, and they were actually jealous lest the Lord should show mercy to the Gentiles.

After the return from Babylon, much attention was given to religious instruction. All over the country, synagogues were erected, where the law was expounded by the priests and scribes. And schools were established, which, together with the arts and sciences, professed to teach the principles of righteousness. But these agencies became corrupted. During the captivity, many of the people had received heathen ideas and customs, and these were brought into their religious service. In many things they conformed to the practices of idolaters.

As they departed from God, the Jews in a great degree lost sight of the teaching of the ritual service. That service had been instituted by Christ Himself. In every part it was a symbol of Him; and it had been full of vitality and spiritual beauty. But the Jews lost the spiritual life from their ceremonies, and clung to the dead forms. They trusted to the sacrifices and ordinances themselves, instead of resting upon Him to whom they pointed. In order to supply the place of that which they had lost, the priests and rabbis multiplied requirements of their own; and the more rigid they grew, the less of the love of God was manifested. They measured their holiness by the multitude of their ceremonies, while their hearts were filled with pride and hypocrisy.

With all their minute and burdensome injunctions, it was an impossibility to keep the law. Those who desired to serve God, and who tried to observe the rabbinical precepts, toiled under a heavy burden. They could find no rest from the accusings of a troubled conscience. Thus Satan worked to discourage the people, to lower their conception of the character of God, and to bring the faith of Israel into contempt. He hoped to establish the claim put forth when he rebelled in heaven, — that the requirements of God were unjust, and could not be obeyed. Even Israel, he declared, did not keep the law.

While the Jews desired the advent of the Messiah, they had no true conception of His mission. They did not seek redemption from sin, but deliverance from the Romans. They looked for the Messiah to come as a conqueror, to break the oppressor's power, and exalt Israel to universal dominion. Thus the way was prepared for them to reject the Saviour.

At the time of the birth of Christ the nation was chafing under the rule of her foreign masters, and racked with internal strife. The Jews had been permitted to maintain the form of a separate government; but nothing could disguise the fact that they were under the Roman yoke, or reconcile them to the restriction of their power. The Romans claimed the right of appointing and removing the high priest, and the office was often secured by fraud, bribery, and even murder. Thus the priesthood became more and more corrupt. Yet the priests still possessed great power, and they employed it for selfish and mercenary ends. The people were subjected to their merciless demands, and were also heavily taxed by the Romans. This state of affairs caused wide-spread discontent. Popular outbreaks were frequent. Greed and violence, distrust and spiritual apathy, were eating out the very heart of the nation.

Hatred of the Romans, and national and spiritual pride, led the Jews still to adhere rigorously to their forms of worship. The priests tried to maintain a reputation for sanctity by scrupulous attention to the ceremonies of religion. The people, in their darkness and oppression, and the rulers, thirsting for power, longed for the coming of One who would vanquish their enemies and restore the kingdom of Israel. They had studied the prophecies, but without spiritual insight. Thus they overlooked those scriptures that point to the humiliation of Christ's first advent, and misapplied those that speak of the glory of His second coming. Pride obscured their vision. They interpreted prophecy in accordance with their selfish desires.

"The Fullness of the Time"

When the fullness of the time was come, God sent forth His Son . . . to redeem them that were under the law, that we might receive the adoption of sons." Galatians 4:4, 5.

The Saviour's coming was foretold in Eden. When Adam and Eve first heard the promise, they looked for its speedy fulfilment. They joyfully welcomed their first-born son, hoping that he might be the Deliverer. But the fulfilment of the promise tarried. Those who first received it, died without the sight. From the days of Enoch the promise was repeated through patriarchs and prophets, keeping alive the hope of His appearing, and yet He came not. The prophecy of Daniel revealed the time of His advent, but not all rightly interpreted the message. Century after century passed away; the voices of the prophets ceased. The hand of the oppressor was heavy upon Israel, and many were ready to exclaim, "The days are prolonged, and every vision faileth." Ezekiel 12:22.

But like the stars in the vast circuit of their appointed path, God's purposes know no haste and no delay. Through the symbols of the great darkness and the smoking furnace, God had revealed to Abraham the bondage of Israel in Egypt, and had declared that the time of their sojourning should be four hundred years. "Afterward," He said, "shall they come out with great substance." Genesis 15:14. Against that word, all the power of Pharaoh's proud empire battled in vain. On "the selfsame day" appointed in the divine promise, "it came to pass that all the hosts of the Lord went out from the land of Egypt." Exodus 12:41. So in heaven's council the hour for the coming of Christ had been determined. When the great clock of time pointed to that hour, Jesus was born in Bethlehem.

"When the fullness of the time was come, God sent forth His Son." Providence had directed the movements of nations, and the tide of human impulse and influence, until the world was ripe for the coming of the Deliverer. The nations were united under one government. One language was widely spoken, and was everywhere recognized as the language of literature. From all lands the Jews of the dispersion gathered to Jerusalem to the annual feasts. As these returned to the places of their sojourn, they could spread throughout the world the tidings of the Messiah's coming.

At this time the systems of heathenism were losing their hold upon the people. Men were weary of pageant and fable. They longed for a religion that could satisfy the heart. While the light of truth seemed to have departed from among men, there were souls who were looking for light, and who were filled with perplexity and sorrow. They were thirsting for a knowledge of the living God, for some assurance of a life beyond the grave.

As the Jews had departed from God, faith had grown dim, and hope had well-nigh ceased to illuminate the future. The words of the prophets were uncomprehended. To the masses of the people, death was a dread mystery; beyond was uncertainty and gloom. It was not alone the wailing of the mothers of Bethlehem, but the cry from the great heart of humanity, that was borne to the prophet across the centuries, — the voice heard in Ramah, "lamentation, and weeping, and great mourning, Rachel weeping for her children, and would not be comforted, because they are not." Matthew 2:18. In "the region and shadow of death," men sat unsolaced. With longing eyes they looked for the coming of the Deliverer, when the darkness should be dispelled, and the mystery of the future should be made plain.

Outside of the Jewish nation there were men who foretold the appearance of a divine instructor. These men were seeking for truth, and to them the Spirit of inspiration was imparted. One after another, like stars in the darkened heavens, such teachers had arisen. Their words of prophecy had kindled hope in the hearts of thousands of the Gentile world.

For hundreds of years the Scriptures had been translated into the Greek language, then widely spoken throughout the Roman empire. The Jews were scattered everywhere, and their expectation of the Messiah's coming was to some extent shared by the Gentiles. Among those whom the Jews styled heathen, were men who had a better understanding of the Scripture prophecies concerning the Messiah than had the teachers in Israel. There were some who hoped for His coming as a deliverer from sin. Philosophers endeavored to study into the mystery of the Hebrew economy. But the bigotry of the Jews hindered the spread of the light. Intent of maintaining the separation between themselves and other nations, they were unwilling to impart the knowledge they still possessed concerning the symbolic service. The true Interpreter must come. The One whom all these types prefigured, must explain their significance.

Through nature, through types and symbols, through patriarchs and prophets, God had spoken to the world. Lessons must be given to humanity in the language of humanity. The Messenger of the covenant must speak. His voice must be heard in His own temple. Christ must come to utter words which should be clearly and definitely understood. He, the author of truth, must separate truth from the chaff of man's utterance, which had made it of no effect. The principles of God's government and the plan of redemption must be clearly defined. The lessons of the Old Testament must be fully set before men.

Among the Jews there were yet steadfast souls, descendants of that holy line through whom a knowledge of God had been preserved. These still looked for the hope of the promise made unto the fathers. They strengthened their faith by dwelling upon the assurance given through Moses, "A prophet shall the Lord your God raise up unto you of your brethren, like unto me; Him shall ye hear in all things whatsoever He shall say unto you." Acts 3:22. Again, they read how the Lord would anoint One "to preach good tidings unto the meek," "to bind up the broken-hearted, to proclaim liberty to the captives," and to declare the "acceptable year of the Lord." Isaiah 61:1, 2. They read how He would "set judgment in the earth," how the isles should "wait for His law," how the Gentiles should come to His light, and kings to the brightness of His rising. Isaiah 42:4; 60:3.

The dying words of Jacob filled them with hope: "The scepter shall not depart from Judah, nor a lawgiver from between his feet, until Shiloh come." Genesis 49:10. The

waning power of Israel testified that the Messiah's coming was at hand. The prophecy of Daniel pictured the glory of His reign over an empire which should succeed all earthly kingdoms; and, said the prophet, "It shall stand forever." Daniel 2:44. While few understood the nature of Christ's mission, there was a wide-spread expectation of a mighty prince who should establish his kingdom in Israel, and who should come as a deliverer of the nations.

The fullness of the time had come. Humanity, becoming more degraded through ages of transgression, called for

---

"None but Christ can fashion anew the character that has been ruined by sin. He came to expel the demons that had controlled the will. He came to lift us up from the dust, to reshape the marred character after the pattern of His divine character, and to make it beautiful with His own glory."

---

the coming of the Redeemer. Satan had been working to make the gulf deep and impassable between earth and heaven. By his falsehoods he had emboldened men in sin. It was his purpose to wear out the forbearance of God, and to extinguish His love for man, so that He would abandon the world to Satanic jurisdiction.

Satan was seeking to shut out from men a knowledge of God, to turn their attention from the temple of God, and to establish his own kingdom. His strife for supremacy had seemed to be almost wholly successful. It is true that in every generation God had His agencies. Even among the heathen there were men through whom Christ was working to uplift the people from their sin and degradation. But these men were despised and hated. Many of them suffered a violent death. The dark shadow that Satan had cast over the world grew deeper and deeper.

Through heathenism, Satan had for ages turned men away from God; but he won his great triumph in perverting the faith of Israel. By contemplating and worshiping their own conceptions, the heathen had lost a knowledge of God, and had become more and more corrupt. So it was with Israel. The principle that man can save himself by his own works, lay at the foundation of every heathen religion; it had now become the principle of the Jewish religion. Satan had implanted this principle. Wherever it is held, men have no barrier against sin.

The message of salvation is communicated to men through human agencies. But the Jews had sought to make a monopoly of the truth which is eternal life. They had hoarded the living manna, and it had turned to corruption. The religion which they tried to shut up to themselves became an offense. They robbed God of his glory, and defrauded the world by counterfeit of the gospel. They had refused to surrender themselves to God for the salvation of the world, and they became agents of Satan for its destruction.

The people whom God had called to be the pillar and ground of the truth, had become representatives of Satan. They were doing the work that he desired them to do, taking a course to misrepresent the character of God, and cause the world to look upon Him as a tyrant. The very priests who ministered in the temple had lost sight of the significance of the service they performed. They had ceased to look beyond the symbol to the thing signified. In presenting the sacrificial offerings they were as actors in a play. The ordinances which God Himself had appointed were made the means of blinding the mind and hardening the heart. God could do no more for man through these channels. The whole system must be swept away.

The deception of sin had reached its height. All the agencies for depraving the souls of men had been put in operation. The Son of God, looking upon the world, beheld suffering and misery. With pity He saw how men had become victims of Satanic cruelty. He looked with compassion upon those who were being corrupted, murdered, and lost. They had chosen a ruler who chained them to his car as captives. Bewildered and deceived, they were moving on in gloomy procession toward eternal ruin,—to death in which is no hope of life, toward night to which comes no morning. Satanic agencies were incorporated with men. The bodies of human beings, made for the dwelling-place of God, had become the habitation of demons. The senses, the nerves, the passions, the organs of men, were worked by supernatural agencies in the indulgence of the vilest lust. The very stamp of demons was impressed upon the countenances of men. Human faces reflected the expression of the legions of evil with which they were possessed. Such was the prospect upon which the world's Redeemer looked. What a spectacle for Infinite Purity to behold!

Sin had become a science, and vice was consecrated as a part of religion. Rebellion had struck its roots deep into the heart, and the hostility of man was most violent against heaven. It was demonstrated before the universe that, apart from God, humanity could not be uplifted. A new element of life and power must be imparted by Him who made the world.

With intense interest the unfallen worlds had watched to see Jehovah arise, and sweep away the inhabitants of the earth. And if God should do this, Satan was ready to carry out his plan for securing to himself the allegiance of heavenly beings. He had declared that the principles of God's government make forgiveness impossible. Had the world been destroyed, he would have claimed that his accusations were proved true. He was ready to cast blame upon God, and to spread his rebellion to the worlds above. But instead of destroying the world, God sent His Son to save it. Though corruption and defiance might be seen in every part of the alien province, a way for its recovery was provided. At the very crisis, when Satan seemed about to triumph, the Son of God came with the embassage of divine grace. Through every age, through every hour, the love of God had been exercised toward the fallen race. Notwithstanding the perversity of men, the signals of mercy had been continually exhibited. And when the fullness of the time had come, the Deity was glorified by pouring upon the world a flood of healing grace that was never to be obstructed or withdrawn till the plan of salvation should be fulfilled.

Satan was exulting that he had succeeded in debasing the image of God in humanity. Then Jesus came to restore in man the image of his Maker. None but Christ can fashion anew the character that has been ruined by sin. He came to expel the demons that had controlled the will. He came to lift us up from the dust, to reshape the marred character after the pattern of His divine character, and to make it beautiful with His own glory.

Unto You a Saviour

The King of Glory stooped low to take humanity. Rude and forbidding were His earthly surroundings. His glory was veiled, that the majesty of His outward form might not become an object of attraction. He shunned all outward display. Riches, worldly honor, and human greatness can never save a soul from death; Jesus proposed that no attraction of an earthly nature should call men to His side. Only the beauty of heavenly truth must draw those who would follow Him. The character of the Messiah had long been foretold in prophecy, and He desired men to accept Him upon the testimony of the word of God.

The angels had wondered at the glorious plan of redemption. They watched to see how the people of God would receive His Son, clothed in the garb of humanity. Angels came to the land of the chosen people. Other nations were dealing in fables and worshiping false gods. To the land where the glory of God had been revealed, and the light of prophecy had shone, the angels came. They came unseen to Jerusalem, to the appointed expositors of the Sacred Oracles, and the ministers of God's house. Already to Zacharias the priest, as he ministered before the altar, the nearness of Christ's coming had been announced. Already the forerunner was born, his mission attested by miracle and prophecy. The tidings of his birth and the wonderful significance of his mission had been spread abroad. Yet Jerusalem was not preparing to welcome her Redeemer.

With amazement the heavenly messengers beheld the indifference of that people whom God had called to communicate to the world the light of sacred truth. The Jewish nation had been preserved as a witness that Christ was to be born of the seed of Abraham and of David's line; yet they knew not that His coming was now at hand. In the temple the morning and the evening sacrifice daily pointed to the Lamb of God; yet even here was no preparation to receive Him. The priests and teachers of the nation knew not that the greatest event of the ages was about to take place. They rehearsed their meaningless prayers, and performed the rites of worship to be seen by men, but in their strife for riches and worldly honor they were not prepared for the revelation of the Messiah. The same indifference pervaded the land of Israel. Hearts selfish and world-engrossed were untouched by the joy that thrilled all heaven. Only a few were longing to behold the Unseen. To these heaven's embassy was sent.

Angels attend Joseph and Mary as they journey from their home in Nazareth to the city of David. The decree of imperial Rome for the enrollment of the peoples of her vast dominion, has extended to the dwellers among the hills of Galilee. As in old time Cyrus was called to the throne of the world's empire that he might set free the captives of the Lord, so Caesar Augustus is made the agent for the fulfilment of God's purpose in bringing the mother of Jesus to Bethlehem. She is of the lineage of David, and the Son of David must be born in David's city. Out of Bethlehem, said the prophet, "shall He come forth . . . that is to be ruler in Israel; whose goings forth have been from of old, from the days of eternity." Micah 5:2, margin. But in the city of their royal line, Joseph and Mary are unrecognized and unhonored. Weary and homeless, they traverse the entire length of the narrow street, from the gate of the city to the eastern extremity of the town, vainly seeking a resting-place for the night. There is no room for them at the crowded inn. In a rude building where the beasts are sheltered, they at last find refuge, and here the Redeemer of the world is born.

14   This chapter is based on Luke 2:1-20.   (43-47)

Men know it not, but the tidings fill heaven with rejoicing. With a deeper and more tender interest the holy beings from the world of light are drawn to the earth. The whole world is brighter for His presence. Above the hills of Bethlehem are gathered an innumerable throng of angels. They wait the signal to declare the glad news to the world. Had the leaders in Israel been true to their trust, they might have shared the joy of heralding the birth of Jesus. But now they are passed by.

God declares, "I will pour water upon him that is thirsty, and floods upon the dry ground." "Unto the upright there ariseth light in the darkness." Isaiah 44:3; Psalms 112:4. To those who are seeking for light, and who accept it with gladness, the bright rays from the throne of God will shine.

In the fields where the boy David had led his flock, shepherds were still keeping watch by night. Through the silent hours they talked together of the promised Saviour, and prayed for the coming of the King to David's throne. "And, lo, the angel of the Lord came upon them, and the glory of the Lord shone round about them; and they were sore afraid. And the angel said unto them, Fear not; for, behold, I bring you good tidings of great joy, which shall be to all people. For unto you is born this day in the city of David a Saviour, which is Christ the Lord."

At these words, visions of glory fill the minds of the listening shepherds. The Deliverer has come to Israel! Power, exaltation, triumph, are associated with His coming. But the angel must prepare them to recognize their Saviour in poverty and humiliation. "This shall be a sign unto you," he says; "ye shall find the babe wrapped in swaddling clothes, lying in a manger."

The heavenly messenger had quieted their fears. He had told them how to find Jesus. With tender regard for their human weakness, he had given them time to become accustomed to the divine radiance. Then the joy and glory could no longer be hidden. The whole plain was lighted up with the bright shining of the hosts of God. Earth was hushed, and heaven stooped to listen to the song, —

"Glory to God in the highest,
And on earth peace, good will toward men."

O that to-day the human family could recognize that song! The declaration then made, the note then struck, will swell to the close of time, and resound to the ends of the earth. When the Sun of Righteousness shall arise, with healing in his wings, that song will be re-echoed by the voice of a great multitude, as the voice of many waters, saying, "Alleluia, for the Lord God omnipotent reigneth." Revelation 19:6.

As the angels disappeared, the light faded away, and the shadows of night once more fell on the hills of Bethlehem. But the brightest picture ever beheld by human eyes remained in the memory of the shepherds. "And it came to pass, as the angels were gone away from them into heaven, the shepherds said one to another, Let us now go even unto Bethlehem, and see this thing which is come to pass, which the Lord hath made known unto us. And they came with haste, and found Mary, and Joseph, and the babe lying in a manger."

Departing with great joy, they made known the things they had seen and heard. "And all they that heard it wondered at those things which were told them by the shepherds. But Mary kept all these things, and pondered them in her heart. And the shepherds returned, glorifying and praising God."

Heaven and earth are no wider apart today than when shepherds listened to the angels' song. Humanity is still as much the object of heaven's solicitude as when common men of common occupations met angels at noonday, and talked with the heavenly messengers in the vineyards and the fields. To us in the common walks of life, heaven may be very near. Angels from the courts above will attend the steps of those who come and go at God's command.

The story of Bethlehem is an exhaustless theme. In it is hidden "the depth of the riches both of the wisdom and knowledge of God." Romans 11:33. We marvel at the Saviour's sacrifice in exchanging the throne of heaven for the manger, and the companionship of adoring angels for the beasts of the stall. Human pride and self-sufficiency stand rebuked in His presence. Yet this was but the beginning of His wonderful condescension. It would have been an almost infinite humiliation for the Son of God to take man's nature, even when Adam stood in his innocence in Eden. But Jesus accepted humanity when the race had been weakened by four thousand years of sin. Like every child of Adam He accepted the results of the working of the great law of heredity. What these results were is shown in the history of His earthly ancestors. He came with such a heredity to share our sorrows and temptations, and to give us the example of a sinless life.

Satan in heaven had hated Christ for His position in the courts of God. He hated Him the more when he himself was dethroned. He hated Him who pledged Himself to redeem a race of sinners. Yet into the world where Satan claimed dominion God permitted His Son to come, a helpless babe, subject to the weakness of humanity. He permitted Him to meet life's peril in common with every human soul, to fight the battle as every child of humanity must fight it, at the risk of failure and eternal loss.

The heart of the human father yearns over his son. He looks into the face of his little child, and trembles at the thought of life's peril. He longs to shield his dear one from Satan's power, to hold him back from temptation and conflict. To meet a bitterer conflict and a more fearful risk, God gave His only begotten Son, that the path of life might be made sure for our little ones. "Herein is love." Wonder, O heavens! and be astonished, O earth!

The Dedication

About forty days after the birth of Christ, Joseph and Mary took Him to Jerusalem, to present Him to the Lord, and to offer sacrifice. This was according to the Jewish law, and as man's substitute Christ must conform to the law in every particular. He had already been subjected to the rite of circumcision, as a pledge of His obedience to the law.

As an offering for the mother, the law required a lamb of the first year for a burnt offering, and a young pigeon or a turtle dove for a sin offering. But the law provided that if the parents were too poor to bring a lamb, a pair of turtle doves or two young pigeons, one for a burnt offering, the other for a sin offering, might be accepted.

The offerings presented to the Lord were to be without blemish. These offerings represented Christ, and from this it is evident that Jesus Himself was free from physical deformity. He was the "lamb without blemish and without spot." 1 Peter 1:19. His physical structure was not marred by any defect; His body was strong and healthy. And throughout His lifetime He lived in conformity to nature's laws. Physically as well as spiritually, He was an example of what God designed all humanity to be through obedience to His laws.

The dedication of the first-born had its origin in the earliest times. God had promised to give the First-born of heaven to save the sinner. This gift was to be acknowledged in every household by the consecration of the first-born son. He was to be devoted to the priesthood, as a representative of Christ among men.

In the deliverance of Israel from Egypt, the dedication of the first-born was again commanded. While the children of Israel were in bondage to the Egyptians, the Lord directed Moses to go to Pharaoh, king of Egypt, and say,

"Thus saith the Lord, Israel is My son, even My first-born; and I say unto thee, Let My son go, that he may serve Me: and if thou refuse to let him go, behold, I will slay thy son, even thy first-born." Exodus 4:22,23.

Moses delivered his message; but the proud king's answer was , "Who is the Lord, that I should obey His voice to let Israel go? I know not the Lord, neither will I let Israel go." Exodus 5:2. The Lord worked for His people by signs and wonders, sending terrible judgments upon Pharaoh. At length the destroying angel was bidden to slay the first-born of man and beast among the Egyptians. That the Israelites might be spared, they were directed to place upon their door posts the blood of a slain lamb. Every house was to be marked, that when the angel came on his mission of death, he might pass over the homes of the Israelites.

After sending this judgment upon Egypt, the Lord said to Moses, "Sanctify unto Me all the first-born, . . . both of man and of beast; it is Mine;" "for on the day that I smote all the first-born in the land of Egypt, I hallowed unto Me all the first-born in Israel, both man and beast: Mine shall they be; I am the Lord." Exodus 13:2; Numbers 3:13. After the tabernacle service was established, the Lord chose the tribe of Levi in the place of the first-born of all Israel to minister in the sanctuary. But the first-born were still to be regarded as the Lord's, and were to be bought back by a ransom.

Thus the law for the presentation of the first-born was made particularly significant. While it was a memorial of the Lord's wonderful deliverance of the children of Israel, it prefigured a greater deliverance, to be wrought out by the only begotten Son of God. As the blood sprinkled on

This chapter is based on Luke 2:21-38.

the door posts had saved the first-born of Israel, so the blood of Christ has power to save the world.

What meaning then was attached to Christ's presentation. But the priest did not see through the veil; he did not read the mystery beyond. The presentation of infants was a common scene. Day after day the priest received the redemption money as the babes were presented to the Lord. Day after day he went through the routine of his work, giving little heed to the parents or children, unless he saw some indication of the wealth or high rank of the parents. Joseph and Mary were poor; and when they came with their child, the priests saw only a man and woman dressed as Galileans, and in the humblest garments. There was nothing in their appearance to attract attention, and they presented only the offering made by the poorer classes.

The priest went through the ceremony of his official work. He took the child in his arms, and held it up before the altar. After handling it back to its mother, he inscribed the name "Jesus" on the roll of the first-born. Little did he think, as the babe lay in his arms, that it was the Majesty of Heaven, the King of Glory. The priest did not think that this babe was the One of whom Moses had written, "A prophet shall the Lord your God raise up unto you of your brethren, like unto me; Him shall ye hear in all things whatsoever He shall say unto you." Acts 3:22. He did not think that this babe was He whose glory Moses had asked to see. But One greater than Moses lay in the priest's arms; and when he enrolled the child's name, he was enrolling the name of One who was the foundation of the whole Jewish economy. That name was to be its death warrant; for the system of sacrifices and offerings was waxing old; the type had almost reached its antitype, the shadow its substance.

The Shekinah had departed from the sanctuary, but in the Child of Bethlehem was veiled the glory before which angels bow. This unconscious babe was the promised seed, to whom the first altar at the gate of Eden pointed. This was Shiloh, the peace giver. It was He who declared Himself to Moses as the I AM. It was He who in the pillar of cloud and of fire, had been the guide of Israel. This was He whom seers had long foretold. He was the Desire of all nations, the Root and the Offspring of David, and the Bright and Morning Star. The name of that helpless little babe, inscribed in the roll of Israel, declaring Him our brother, was the hope of fallen humanity. The child for whom the redemption money had been paid was He who was to pay the ransom for the sins of the whole world. He was the true "high priest over the house of God," the head of "an unchangeable priesthood," the intercessor at "the right hand of the Majesty on high." Hebrews 10:21; 7:24; 1:3.

Spiritual things are spiritually discerned. In the temple the Son of God was dedicated to the work He had come to do. The priest looked upon Him as he would upon any other child. But though he neither saw nor felt anything

unusual, God's act in giving His Son to the world was acknowledged. This occasion did not pass without some recognition of Christ. "There was a man in Jerusalem whose name was Simeon; and the same man was just and devout, waiting for the Consolation of Israel; and the Holy Ghost was upon him. And it was revealed unto him by the Holy Ghost that he should not see death, before he had seen the Lord's Christ."

As Simeon enters the temple, he sees a family presenting their first-born son before the priest. Their appearance bespeaks poverty; but Simeon understands the warnings of the Spirit, and he is deeply impressed that the infant being presented to the Lord is the Consolation of Israel, the One he has longed to see. To the astonished priest, Simeon appears like a man enraptured. The child has been returned to Mary, and he takes it in his arms and presents it to God, while a joy that he has never before felt enters his soul. As he lifts the infant Saviour toward heaven, he says, "Lord, now lettest Thou Thy servant depart in peace, according to Thy word; for mine eyes have seen Thy salvation, which Thou hast prepared before the face of all people; a light to lighten the Gentiles, and the glory of Thy people Israel."

The spirit of prophecy was upon this man of God, and while Joseph and Mary stood by, wondering at his words, he blessed them, and said unto Mary, "Behold, this child is set for the fall and rising again of many in Israel; and for a sign which shall be spoken against (yea, a sword shall pierce through thy own soul also,); that the thoughts of many hearts may be revealed."

Anna also, a prophetess, came in and confirmed Simeon's testimony concerning Christ. As Simeon spoke, her face lighted up with the glory of God, and she poured out her heartfelt thanks that she had been permitted to behold Christ the Lord.

These humble worshipers had not studied the prophecies in vain. But those who held positions as rulers and priests in Israel, though they too had before them the precious utterances of prophecy, were not walking in the way of the Lord, and their eyes were not open to behold the Light of life.

So it is still. Events upon which the attention of all heaven is centered, are undiscerned, their very occurrence is unnoticed, by religious leaders, and worshipers in the house of God. Men acknowledge Christ in history, while they turn away from the living Christ. Christ in His word calling to self-sacrifice, in the poor and suffering who plead for relief, in the righteous cause that involves poverty and toil and reproach, is no more readily received today than He was eighteen hundred years ago.

Mary pondered the broad and far-reaching prophecy of Simeon. As she looked upon the child in her arms, and recalled the words spoken by the shepherds of Bethlehem, she was full of grateful joy and bright hope. Simeon's words called to her mind the prophetic utterances of Isaiah: "There shall come forth a rod out of the stem of

Jesse, and a Branch shall grow out of his roots: and the Spirit of the Lord shall rest upon Him, the spirit of wisdom and understanding, the spirit of counsel and might, the spirit of knowledge and of the fear of the Lord. . . . And righteousness shall be the girdle of His loins, and faithfulness the girdle of His reins." "The people that walked in darkness have seen a great light; they that dwell in the land of the shadow of death, upon them hath the light shined. . . . For unto us a child is born, unto us a son is given: and the government shall be upon His shoulder: and His name shall be called Wonderful, Counselor, the mighty God, the everlasting Father, the Prince of Peace." Isaiah 11:1-5; 9:2-6.

Yet Mary did not understand Christ's mission. Simeon had prophesied of Him as a light to lighten the Gentiles, as well as a glory to Israel. Thus the angels had announced the Saviour's birth as tidings of joy to all peoples. God was seeking to correct the narrow, Jewish conception of the Messiah's work. He desired men to behold Him, not merely as the deliverer of Israel, but as the Redeemer of the world. But many years must pass before even the mother of Jesus would understand His mission.

Mary looked forward to the Messiah's reign on David's throne, but she saw not the baptism of suffering by which it must be won. Through Simeon it is revealed that the Messiah is to have no unobstructed passage through the world. In the words to Mary, "A sword shall pierce through thy own soul also," God in His tender mercy gives to the mother of Jesus an intimation of the anguish that already for His sake she had begun to bear.

"Behold," Simeon had said, "this child is set for the fall and rising again of many in Israel; and for a sign which shall be spoken against." They must fall who would rise again. We must fall upon the Rock and be broken, before we can be uplifted in Christ. Self must be dethroned, pride must be humbled, if we would know the glory of the spiritual kingdom. The Jews would not accept the honor that is reached through humiliation. Therefore they would not receive their Redeemer. He was a sign that was spoken against.

"That the thoughts of many hearts may be revealed." In the light of the Saviour's life, the hearts of all, even from the Creator to the prince of darkness, are revealed. Satan has represented God as selfish and oppressive, as claiming all, and giving nothing, as requiring the service of His creatures for His own glory, and making no sacrifice for their good. But the gift of Christ reveals the Father's heart. It testifies that the thoughts of God toward us are "thoughts of peace, and not of evil." Jeremiah 29:11. It declares that

while God's hatred of sin is as strong as death, His love for the sinner is stronger than death. Having undertaken our redemption, He will spare nothing, however dear, which is necessary to the completion of His work. No truth essential to our salvation is withheld, no miracle of mercy is neglected, no divine agency is left unemployed. Favor is heaped upon favor, gift upon gift. The whole treasury of heaven is open to those He seeks to save. Having collected the riches of the universe, and laid open the resources of infinite power, He gives them all into the hands of Christ, and says, All these are for man. Use these gifts to convince him that there is no love greater than Mine in earth or heaven. His greatest happiness will be found in loving Me.

At the cross of Calvary, love and selfishness stood face to face. Here was their crowning manifestation. Christ had lived only to comfort and bless, and in putting Him to death, Satan manifested the malignity of his hatred against God. He made it evident that the real purpose of his rebellion was to dethrone God, and to destroy Him through whom the love of God was shown.

By the life and the death of Christ, the thoughts of men also are brought to view. From the manger to the cross, the life of Jesus was a call to self-surrender, and to fellowship in suffering. It unveiled the purposes of men. Jesus came with the truth of heaven, and all who were listening to the voice of the Holy Spirit were drawn to Him. The worshipers of self belonged to Satan's kingdom. In their attitude toward Christ, all would show on which side they stood. And thus every one passes judgment on himself.

In the day of final judgment, every lost soul will understand the nature of his own rejection of truth. The cross will be presented, and its real bearing will be seen by every mind that has been blinded by transgression. Before the vision of Calvary with its mysterious Victim, sinners will stand condemned. Every lying excuse will be swept away. Human apostasy will appear in its heinous character. Men will see what their choice has been. Every question of truth and error in the long-standing controversy will then have been made plain. In the judgment of the universe, God will stand clear of blame for the existence or continuance of evil. It will be demonstrated that the divine decrees are not accessory to sin. There was no defect in God's government, no cause for disaffection. When the thoughts of all hearts shall be revealed, both the loyal and the rebellious will unite in declaring, "Just and true are Thy ways, Thou King of saints. Who shall not fear Thee, O Lord, and glorify Thy name? . . . For Thy judgments are made manifest." Revelation 15:3, 4.

"We Have Seen His Star"

Now when Jesus was born in Bethlehem of Judea in the days of Herod the king, behold, there came wise men from the East to Jerusalem, saying, Where is He that is born King of the Jews? for we have seen His star in the East, and are come to worship Him."

The wise men from the East were philosophers. They belonged to a large and influential class, that included men of noble birth, and comprised much of the wealth and learning of their nation. Among these were many who imposed on the credulity of the people. Others were upright men who studied the indications of Providence in nature, and who were honored for their integrity and wisdom. Of this character were the wise men who came to Jesus.

The light of God is ever shining amid the darkness of heathenism. As these magi studied the starry heavens, and sought to fathom the mystery hidden in their bright paths, they beheld the glory of the Creator. Seeking clearer knowledge, they turned to the Hebrew Scriptures. In their own land were treasured prophetic writings that predicted the coming of a divine teacher. Balaam belonged to the magicians, though at one time a prophet of God; by the Holy Spirit he had foretold the prosperity of Israel and the appearing of the Messiah; and his prophecies had been handed down by tradition from century to century. But in the Old Testament the Saviour's advent was more clearly revealed. The magi learned with joy that His coming was near, and that the whole world was to be filled with a knowledge of the glory of the Lord.

The wise men had seen a mysterious light in the heavens upon that night when the glory of God flooded the hills of Bethlehem. As the light faded, a luminous star appeared, and lingered in the sky. It was not a fixed star nor a planet, and the phenomenon excited the keenest interest. That star was a distant company of shining angels, but of this the wise men were ignorant. Yet they were impressed that the star was of special import to them. They consulted priests and philosophers, and searched the scrolls of the ancient records. The prophecy of Balaam had declared, "There shall come a star out of Jacob, and a scepter shall rise out of Israel." Numbers 24:17. Could this strange star have been sent as a harbinger of the Promised One? The magi had welcomed the light of heaven-sent truth; now it was shed upon them in brighter rays. Through dreams they were instructed to go in search of the newborn Prince.

As by faith Abraham went forth at the call of God, "not knowing whither he went" Hebrews 11:8; as by faith Israel followed the pillar of cloud to the promised land, so did these Gentiles go forth to find the promised Saviour. The Eastern country abounded in precious things, and the magi did not set out empty-handed. It was the custom to offer presents as an act of homage to princes or other personages of rank, and the richest gifts the land afforded were borne as an offering to Him in whom all the families of the earth were to be blessed. It was necessary to journey by night in order to keep the star in view; but the travelers beguiled the hours by repeating traditional sayings and prophetic utterances concerning the One they sought. At every pause for rest they searched the prophecies; and the conviction deepened that they were divinely guided. While they had the star before them as an outward sign, they had also the inward evidence of the Holy Spirit, which was impressing their hearts, and inspiring them with hope. The journey, though long, was a happy one to them.

They have reached the land of Israel, and are descending the Mount of Olives, with Jerusalem in sight, when lo, the

20   This chapter is based on Matthew 2.   (59-60)

star that has guided them all the weary way rests above the temple, and after a season fades from their view. With eager steps they press onward, confidently expecting the Messiah's birth to be the joyful burden of every tongue. But their inquiries are in vain. Entering the holy city, they repair to the temple. To their amazement they find none who seem to have a knowledge of the newborn king. Their questions call forth no expressions of joy, but rather of surprise and fear, not unmingled with contempt.

The priests are rehearsing traditions. They extol their religion and their own piety, while they denounce the Greeks and Romans as heathen, and sinners above others. The wise men are not idolaters, and in the sight of God they stand far higher than do these, His professed worshipers; yet they are looked upon by the Jews as heathen. Even among the appointed guardians of the Holy Oracles their eager questionings touch no chord of sympathy.

The arrival of the magi was quickly noised throughout Jerusalem. Their strange errand created an excitement among the people, which penetrated to the palace of King Herod. The wily Edomite was aroused at the intimation of a possible rival. Countless murders had stained his pathway to the throne. Being of alien blood, he was hated by the people over whom he ruled. His only security was the favor of Rome. But this new prince had a higher claim. He was born to the kingdom.

Herod suspected the priests of plotting with the strangers to excite a popular tumult and unseat him from the throne. He concealed his mistrust, however, determined to thwart their schemes by superior cunning. Summoning the chief priests and the scribes, he questioned them as to the teaching of their sacred books in regard to the place of the Messiah's birth.

This inquiry from the usurper of the throne, and made at the request of strangers, stung the pride of the Jewish teachers. The indifference with which they turned to the rolls of prophecy enraged the jealous tyrant. He thought them trying to conceal their knowledge of the matter. With an authority they dared not disregard, he commanded them to make close search, and to declare the birthplace of their expected King. "And they said unto him, In Bethlehem of Judea; for thus it is written by the prophet, —

"And thou Bethlehem, land of Judah,
Art in no wise least among the princes of Judah;
For out of thee shall come forth a governor,
Which shall be shepherd of My people Israel." R.V.

Herod now invited the magi to a private interview. A tempest of wrath and fear was raging in his heart, but he preserved a calm exterior, and received the strangers courteously. He inquired at what time the star had appeared, and professed to hail with joy the intimation of the birth of Christ. He bade his visitors, "Search diligently for the young child; and when ye have found Him, bring me word again, that I may come and worship Him also." So saying, he dismissed them to go on their way to Bethlehem.

The priests and elders of Jerusalem were not as ignorant concerning the birth of Christ as they pretended. The report of the angels' visit to the shepherds had been brought to Jerusalem, but the rabbis had treated it as unworthy of their notice. They themselves might have found Jesus, and might have been ready to lead the magi to His birthplace; but instead of this, the wise men came to call their attention to the birth of the Messiah. "Where is He that is born King of the Jews?" they said; "for we have seen His star in the East, and are come to worship Him."

Now pride and envy closed the door against the light. If the reports brought by the shepherds and the wise men were credited, they would place the priests and rabbis in a most unenviable position, disproving their claim to be the exponents of the truth of God. These learned teachers would not stoop to be instructed by those whom they termed heathen. It could not be, they said, that God had passed them by, to communicate with ignorant shepherds or uncircumcised Gentiles. They determined to show their contempt for the reports that were exciting King Herod and all Jerusalem. They would not even go to Bethlehem to see whether these things were so. And they led the people to regard the interest in Jesus as a fanatical excitement. Here began the rejection of Christ by the priests and rabbis. From this point their pride and stubbornness grew into a settled hatred of the Saviour. While God was opening the door to the Gentiles, the Jewish leaders were closing the door to themselves.

The wise men departed alone from Jerusalem. The shadows of night were falling as they left the gates, but to their great joy they again saw the star, and were directed to Bethlehem. They had received no such intimation of the lowly estate of Jesus as was given to the shepherds. After the long journey they had been disappointed by the indifference of the Jewish leaders, and had left Jerusalem less confident than when they entered the city. At Bethlehem they found no royal guard stationed to protect the newborn King. None of the world's honored men were in attendance. Jesus was cradled in a manger. His parents, uneducated peasants, were His only guardians. Could this be He of whom it was written, that He should "raise up the tribes of Jacob," and "restore the preserved of Israel;" that He should be "a light to the Gentiles," and for "salvation unto the end of the earth?" Isaiah 49:6.

"When they were come into the house, they saw the young child with Mary His mother, and fell down and worshipped Him." Beneath the lowly guise of Jesus, they recognized the presence of Divinity. They gave their hearts to Him as their Saviour, and then poured out their gifts, — "gold, and frankincense, and myrrh." What a faith was theirs! It might have been said of the wise men from the East, as afterward of the Roman centurion, "I have not found so great faith, no, not in Israel." Matthew 8:10.

The wise men had not penetrated Herod's design toward Jesus. When the object of their journey was accomplished, they prepared to return to Jerusalem, intending to acquaint him with their success. But in a dream they received a divine message to hold no further communication with him. Avoiding Jerusalem, they set out for their own country by another route.

In like manner Joseph received warning to flee into Egypt with Mary and the child. And the angel said, "Be thou there until I bring thee word; for Herod will seek the young child to destroy Him." Joseph obeyed without delay, setting out on the journey by night for greater security.

Through the wise men, God has called the attention of the Jewish nation to the birth of His Son. Their inquiries in Jerusalem, the popular interest excited, and even the jealousy of Herod, which compelled the attention of the priests and rabbis, directed minds to the prophecies concerning the Messiah, and to the great event that had just taken place.

Satan was bent on shutting out the divine light from the world, and he used his utmost cunning to destroy the Saviour. But He who never slumbers nor sleeps, was watching over His beloved Son. He who had rained manna from heaven for Israel, and had fed Elijah in the time of famine, provided in a heathen land a refuge for Mary and the child Jesus. And through the gifts of the magi from a heathen country, the Lord supplied the means for the journey into Egypt and the sojourn in a land of strangers.

The magi had been among the first to welcome the Redeemer. Their gift was the first that was laid at His feet. And through that gift, what privilege of ministry was theirs! The offering from the heart that loves, God delights to honor, giving it highest efficiency in service for Him. If we have given our hearts to Jesus, we also shall bring our gifts to Him. Our gold and silver, our most precious earthly possessions, our highest mental and spiritual endowments, will be freely devoted to Him who loved us, and gave Himself for us.

Herod in Jerusalem impatiently awaited the return of the wise men. As time passed, and they did not appear, his suspicions were roused. The unwillingness of the rabbis to point out the Messiah's birthplace seemed to indicate that they had penetrated his design, and that the magi had purposely avoided him. He was maddened at the thought. Craft had failed, but there was left the resort to force. He would make an example of this Child-king. Those haughty Jews should see what they might expect in their attempts to place a monarch on the throne.

Soldiers were at once sent to Bethlehem, with orders to put to death all the children of two years and under. The quiet homes of the city of David witnessed those scenes of horror that, six hundred years before, had been opened to the prophet. "In Ramah was there a voice heard, lamentation, and weeping, and great mourning, Rachel weeping for her children, and would not be comforted, because they are not."

This calamity the Jews had brought upon themselves. If they had been walking in faithfulness and humility before God, He would in a signal manner have made the wrath of the king harmless to them. But they had separated themselves from God by their sins, and had rejected the Holy Spirit, which was their only shield. They had not studied the Scriptures with a desire to conform to the will of God. They had searched for prophecies which could be interpreted to exalt themselves, and to show how God despised all other nations. It was their proud boast that the Messiah was to come as a king, conquering His enemies, and threading down the heathen in His wrath. Thus they had excited the hatred of their rulers. Through their misrepresentation of Christ's mission, Satan had purposed to compass the destruction of the Saviour; but instead of this, it returned upon their own heads.

This act of cruelty was one of the last that darkened the reign of Herod. Soon after the slaughter of the innocents, he was himself compelled to yield to that doom which none can turn aside. He died a fearful death.

Joseph, who was still in Egypt, was now bidden by an angel of God to return to the land of Israel. Regarding Jesus as the heir of David's throne, Joseph desired to make his home in Bethlehem; but learning that Archelaus reigned in Judea in his father's stead, he feared that the father's designs against Christ might be carried out by the son. Of all the sons of Herod, Archelaus most resembled him in character. Already his succession to the government had been marked by a tumult in Jerusalem, and the slaughter of thousands of Jews by the Roman guards.

Again Joseph was directed to a place of safety. He returned to Nazareth, his former home, and here for nearly thirty years Jesus dwelt, "that it might be fulfilled which was spoken by the prophets, He shall be called a Nazarene." Galilee was under the control of a son of Herod, but it had a much larger admixture of foreign inhabitants than Judea. Thus there was less interest in matters relating especially to the Jews, and the claims of Jesus would be less likely to excite the jealousy of those in power.

Such was the Saviour's reception when He came to the earth. There seemed to be no place of rest or safety for the infant Redeemer. God could not trust His beloved Son with men, even while carrying forward His work for their salvation. He commissioned angels to attend Jesus and protect Him till He should accomplish His mission on earth, and die by the hands of those whom He came to save.

As a Child

The childhood and youth of Jesus were spent in a little mountain village. There was no place on earth that would not have been honored by His presence. The palaces of kings would have been privileged in receiving Him as a guest. But He passed by the homes of wealth, the courts of royalty, and the renowned seats of learning, to make His home in obscure and despised Nazareth.

Wonderful in its significance is the brief record of His early life: "The child grew, and waxed strong in spirit, filled with wisdom; and the grace of God was upon Him." In the sunlight of His Father's countenance, Jesus "increased in wisdom and stature, and in favor with God and man." Luke 2:52. His mind was active and penetrating, with a thoughtfulness and wisdom beyond His years. Yet His character was beautiful in its symmetry. The powers of mind and body developed gradually, in keeping with the laws of childhood.

As a child, Jesus manifested a peculiar loveliness of disposition. His willing hands were ever ready to serve others. He manifested a patience that nothing could disturb, and a truthfulness that would never sacrifice integrity. In principle firm as a rock, His life revealed the grace of unselfish courtesy.

With deep earnestness the mother of Jesus watched the unfolding of His powers, and beheld the impress of perfection upon His character. With delight she sought to encourage that bright, receptive mind. Through the Holy Spirit she received wisdom to co-operate with the heavenly agencies in the development of this child, who could claim only God as His Father.

From the earliest times the faithful in Israel had given much care to the education of the youth. The Lord had directed that even from babyhood the children should be taught of His goodness and His greatness, especially as revealed in His law, and shown in the history of Israel. Song and prayer and lessons from the Scriptures were to be adapted to the opening mind. Fathers and mothers were to instruct their children that the law of God is an expression of His character, and that as they received the principles of the law into the heart, the image of God was traced on mind and soul. Much of the teaching was oral; but the youth also learned to read the Hebrew writings; and the parchment rolls of the Old Testament Scriptures were open to their study.

In the days of Christ the town or city that did not provide for the religious instruction of the young was regarded as under the curse of God. Yet the teaching had become formal. Tradition had in a great degree supplanted the Scriptures. True education would lead the youth to "seek the Lord, if haply they might feel after Him, and find Him." Acts 17:27. But the Jewish teachers gave their attention to matters of ceremony. The mind was crowded with material that was worthless to the learner, and that would not be recognized in the higher school of the courts above. The experience which is obtained through a personal acceptance of God's word, had no place in the educational system. Absorbed in the round of externals, the students found no quiet hours to spend with God. They did not hear His voice speaking to the heart. In their search after knowledge, they turned away from the Source of wisdom. The great essentials of the service of God were neglected. The principles of the law were obscured. That which was regarded as superior education, was the greatest hindrance to real development. Under the training of the rabbis the powers of the youth were repressed. Their minds became cramped and narrow.

*Train up a child in the way he should go; and
when he is old, he will not depart from it.*
Proverbs 22:6

*Verily I say unto you, Except ye be converted, and become as
little children, ye shall not enter into the kingdom of heaven.
Whosoever therefore shall humble himself as this little child,
the same is greatest in the kingdom of heaven.*
Matthew 18:3, 4

*Wives, submit yourselves unto your own husbands, as it is
fit in the Lord. Husbands, love your wives, and be
not bitter against them. Children, obey
your parents in all things: for
this is well pleasing unto
the Lord.*
Colossians 3:18-20

The child Jesus did not receive instruction in the synagogue schools. His mother was His first human teacher. From her lips and from the scrolls of the prophets, He learned of heavenly things. The very words which He Himself had spoken to Moses for Israel, He was now taught at His mother's knee. As He advanced from childhood to youth, He did to seek the schools of the rabbis. He needed not the education to be obtained from such sources; for God was His instructor.

The question asked during the Saviour's ministry, "How knoweth this man letters, having never learned?" John 7:15; does not indicate that Jesus was unable to read, but merely that He had not received a rabbinical education. Since He gained knowledge as we may do, His intimate acquaintance with the Scriptures shows how diligently His early years were given to the study of God's word. And spread out before Him was the great library of God's created works. He who had made all things studied the lessons which His own hand had written in earth and sea and sky. Apart from the unholy ways of the world, He gathered stores of scientific knowledge from nature. He studied the life of plants and animals, and the life of man. From His earliest years He was possessed of one purpose; He lived to bless others. For this He found resources in nature; new ideas of ways and means flashed into His mind as He studied plant life and animal life. Continually He was seeking to draw from things seen illustrations by which to present the living oracles of God. The parables by which, during His ministry, He loved to teach His lessons of truth, show how open His spirit was to the influences of nature, and how He had gathered the spiritual teaching from the surroundings of His daily life.

Thus to Jesus the significance of the word and the works of God was unfolded, as He was trying to understand the reason of things. Heavenly beings were His attendants, and the culture of holy thoughts and communings was His. From the first dawning of intelligence He was constantly growing in spiritual grace, and knowledge of truth.

Every child may gain knowledge as Jesus did. As we try to become acquainted with our Heavenly Father through His word, angels will draw near, our minds will be strengthened, our characters will be elevated and refined. We shall become more like our Saviour. And as we behold the beautiful and grand in nature, our affections go out after God. While the spirit is awed, the soul is invigorated by coming in contact with the Infinite through His works. Communion with God through prayer develops the mental and moral faculties, and the spiritual powers strengthen as we cultivate thoughts upon spiritual things.

The life of Jesus was a life in harmony with God. While He was a child, He thought and spoke as a child; but no trace of sin marred the image of God within Him. Yet He was not exempt from temptation. The inhabitants of Nazareth were proverbial for their wickedness. The low estimate in which they were generally held is shown by Nathanael's question, "Can there any good thing come out of Nazareth?" John 1:46. Jesus was placed where His character would be tested. It was necessary for Him to be constantly on guard in order to preserve His purity. He was subject to all the conflicts which we have to meet, that He might be an example to us in childhood, youth, and manhood.

Satan was unwearied in his efforts to overcome the Child of Nazareth. From His earliest years Jesus was guarded by heavenly angels, yet His life was one long struggle against the powers of darkness. That there should be upon the earth one life free from the defilement of evil, was an offense and a perplexity to the prince of darkness. He left no means untried to ensnare Jesus. No child of humanity will ever be called to live a holy life amid so fierce a conflict with temptation as was our Saviour.

The parents of Jesus were poor, and dependent upon their daily toil. He was familiar with poverty, self-denial, and privation. This experience was a safeguard to Him. In His industrious life there were no idle moments to invite temptation. No aimless hours opened the way for corrupting associations. So far as possible, He closed the door to the tempter. Neither gain nor pleasure, applause nor censure, could induce Him to consent to a wrong act. He was wise to discern evil, and strong to resist it.

Christ was the only sinless one who ever dwelt on earth; yet for nearly thirty years He lived among the wicked inhabitants of Nazareth. This fact is a rebuke to those who think themselves dependent upon place, fortune, or prosperity, in order to live a blameless life. Temptation, poverty, adversity, is the very discipline needed to develop purity and firmness.

Jesus lived in a peasant's home, and faithfully and cheerfully acted His part in bearing the burdens of the household. He had been the Commander of heaven, and angels had delighted to fulfill His word; now He was a willing servant, a loving, obedient son. He learned a trade, and with His own hands worked in the carpenter's shop with Joseph. In the simple garb of a common laborer He walked the streets of the little town, going to and returning from His humble work. He did not employ His divine power to lessen His burdens or to ligthen His toil.

As Jesus worked in childhood and youth, mind and body were developed. He did not use His physical powers recklessly, but in such a way as to keep them in health, that He might do the best work in every line. He was not willing to be defective, even in the handling of tools. He was perfect as a workman, as He was perfect in character. By His own example He taught that it is our duty to be industrious, that our work should be performed with exactness and thoroughness, and that such labor is honorable. The exercise that teaches the hands to be useful, and trains the young to bear their share of life's burdens, gives physical strength, and develops every faculty. All should find something to do that will be beneficial to themselves and helpful to others. God appointed work as a blessing, and only the diligent worker finds the true glory and joy of life. The approval of God rests with loving assurance upon children and youth who cheerfully take their part in the duties of the household, sharing the burdens of father and mother. Such children will go out from the home to be useful members of society.

Throughout His life on earth, Jesus was an earnest and constant worker. He expected much; therefore He attempted much. After He had entered on His ministry, He said, "I must work the works of Him that sent Me while it is day; the night cometh, when no man can work." John 9:4. Jesus did not shirk care and responsibility, as do many who profess to be His followers. It is because they seek to evade this discipline that so many are weak and inefficient. They may possess precious and amiable traits, but they are nerveless and almost useless when difficulties are to be met or obstacles surmounted. The positiveness and energy, the solidity and strength of character manifested in Christ, are to be developed in us, through the same discipline that He endured. And the grace that He received is for us.

So long as He lived among men, our Saviour shared the lot of the poor. He knew by experience their cares and hardships, and He could comfort and encourage all humble workers. Those who have a true conception of the teaching of His life, will never feel that a distinction must be made between classes, that the rich are to be honored above the worthy poor.

Jesus carried into His labor cheerfulness and tact. It requires much patience and spirituality to bring Bible religion into the home life and into the workshop, to bear the strain of worldly business, and yet keep the eye single to the glory of God. This is where Christ was a helper. He was never so full of worldly care as to have no time or thought for heavenly things. Often He expressed the gladness of His heart by singing psalms and heavenly songs. Often the dwellers in Nazareth heard His voice raised in praise and thanksgiving to God. He held communion with heaven in song; and as His companions complained of weariness from labor, they were cheered by the sweet melody from His lips. His praise seemed to banish the evil angels, and, like incense, fill the place with fragrance. The minds of His hearers were carried away from their earthly exile, to the heavenly home.

Jesus was the fountain of healing mercy for the world; and through all those secluded years at Nazareth, His life flowed out in currents of sympathy and tenderness. The aged, the sorrowing, and the sin-burdened, the children at play in their innocent joy, the little creatures of the groves, the patient beasts of burden,—all were happier for His presence. He whose word of power upheld the worlds, would stoop to relieve a wounded bird. There was nothing beneath His notice, nothing to which He disdained to minister.

Thus as He grew in wisdom and stature, Jesus increased in favor with God and man. He drew the sympathy of all hearts by showing Himself capable of sympathizing with all. The atmosphere of hope and courage that surrounded Him made Him a blessing in every home. And often in the synagogue on the Sabbath day He was called upon to read the lesson from the prophets, and the hearts of the hearers thrilled as a new light shone out from the familiar words of the sacred text.

Yet Jesus shunned display. During all the years of His stay in Nazareth, He made no exhibition of His miraculous power. He sought no high position and assumed no titles. His quiet and simple life, and even the silence of the Scriptures concerning His early years, teach an important lesson. The more quiet and simple the life of the child,—the more free from artificial excitement, and the more in harmony with nature,—the more favorable is it to physical and mental vigor and to spiritual strength.

Jesus is our example. There are many who dwell with interest upon the period of his public ministry, while they pass unnoticed the teaching of His early years. But it is in His home life that He is the pattern for all children and youth. The Saviour condescended to poverty, that He might teach how closely we in a humble lot may walk with God. He lived to please, honor, and glorify His Father in the common things of life. His work began in consecrating the lowly trade of the craftsmen who toil for their daily bread. He was doing God's service just as much when laboring at the carpenter's bench as when working miracles for the multitude. And every youth who follows Christ's example of faithfulness and obedience in His lowly home, may claim those words spoken of Him by the Father through the Holy Spirit, "Behold My servant, whom I uphold; Mine elect, in whom My soul delighteth." Isaiah 42:1.

The Passover Visit

Among the Jews the twelfth year was the dividing line between childhood and youth. On completing this year a Hebrew boy was called a son of the law, and also a son of God. He was given special opportunities for religious instruction, and was expected to participate in the sacred feasts and observances. It was in accordance with this custom that Jesus in His boyhood made the Passover visit to Jerusalem. Like all devout Israelites, Joseph and Mary went up every year to attend the Passover; and when Jesus had reached the required age, they took Him with them.

There were three annual feasts, the Passover, the Pentecost, and the Feast of Tabernacles, at which all the men of Israel were commanded to appear before the Lord at Jerusalem. Of these feasts the Passover was the most largely attended. Many were present from all countries where the Jews were scattered. From every part of Palestine the worshipers came in great numbers. The journey from Galilee occupied several days, and the travelers united in large companies for companionship and protection. The women and aged men rode upon oxen or asses over the steep and rocky roads. The stronger men and the youth journeyed on foot. The time of the Passover corresponded to the close of March or the beginning of April, and the whole land was bright with flowers, and glad with the song of birds. All along the way were spots memorable in the history of Israel, and fathers and mothers recounted to their children the wonders that God had wrought for His people in ages past. They beguiled their journey with song and music, and when at last the towers of Jerusalem came into view, every voice joined in the triumphant strain, —

"Our feet shall stand
Within thy gates, O Jerusalem.

Peace be within thy walls,
And prosperity within thy palaces." Psalms 122:2, 7.

The observance of the Passover began with the birth of the Hebrew nation. On the last night of their bondage in Egypt, when there appeared no token of deliverance, God commanded them to prepare for an immediate release. He had warned Pharaoh of the final judgment on the Egyptians, and He directed the Hebrews to gather their families within their own dwellings. Having sprinkled the door posts with the blood of the slain lamb, they were to eat the lamb, roasted, with unleavened bread and bitter herbs. "And thus shall ye eat it," He said, "with your loins girded, your shoes on your feet, and your staff in your hand; and ye shall eat it in haste; it is the Lord's passover." Exodus 12:11. At midnight all the first-born of the Egyptians were slain. Then the king sent to Israel the message, "Rise up, and get you forth from among my people; ... and go, serve the Lord, as ye have said." Exodus 12:31. The Hebrews went out from Egypt an independent nation. The Lord had commanded that the Passover should be yearly kept. "It shall come to pass," He said, "when your children shall say unto you, What mean ye by this service? that ye shall say, It is the sacrifice of the Lord's passover, who passed over the houses of the children of Israel when He smote the Egyptians." Thus from generation to generation the story of this wonderful deliverance was to be repeated.

The Passover was followed by the seven days' feast of unleavened bread. On the second day of the feast, the first fruits of the year's harvest, a sheaf of barley, was presented before the Lord. All the ceremonies of the feast were types of the work of Christ. The deliverance of Israel from Egypt was an object lesson of redemption, which the Passover was intended to keep in memory. The slain lamb, the

This chapter is based on Luke 2:41-51.

unleavened bread, the sheaf of first fruits, represented the Saviour.

With most of the people in the days of Christ, the observance of this feast had degenerated into formalism. But what was its significance to the Son of God!

For the first time the child Jesus looked upon the temple. He saw the white-robed priests performing their solemn ministry. He beheld the bleeding victim upon the altar of sacrifice. With the worshipers He bowed in prayer, while the cloud of incense ascended before God. He witnessed the impressive rites of the paschal service. Day by day He saw their meaning more clearly. Every act seemed to be bound up with His own life. New impulses were awakening within Him. Silent and absorbed, He seemed to be studying out a great problem. The mystery of His mission was opening to the Saviour.

Rapt in the contemplation of these scenes, He did not remain beside His parents. He sought to be alone. When the paschal services were ended, He still lingered in the temple courts; and when the worshipers departed from Jerusalem, He was left behind.

In this visit to Jerusalem, the parents of Jesus wished to bring Him in connection with the great teachers in Israel. While He was obedient in every particular to the word of God, He did not conform to the rabbinical rites and usages. Joseph and Mary hoped that He might be led to reverence the learned rabbis, and give more diligent heed to their requirements. But Jesus in the temple had been taught by God. That which He had received, He began at once to impart.

At that day an apartment connected with the temple was devoted to a sacred school, after the manner of the schools of the prophets. Here leading rabbis with their pupils assembled, and hither the child Jesus came. Seating Himself at the feet of these grave, learned men, He listened to their instruction. As one seeking for wisdom, He questioned these teachers in regard to the prophecies, and to events then taking place that pointed to the advent of the Messiah.

Jesus presented Himself as one thirsting for a knowledge of God. His questions were suggestive of deep truths which had long been obscured, yet which were vital to the salvation of souls. While showing how narrow and superficial was the wisdom of the wise men, every question put before them a divine lesson, and placed truth in a new aspect. The rabbis spoke of the wonderful elevation which the Messiah's coming would bring to the Jewish nation; but Jesus presented the prophecy of Isaiah, and asked them the meaning of those scriptures that point to the suffering and death of the Lamb of God.

The doctors turned upon Him with questions, and they were amazed at His answers. With the humility of a child He repeated the words of Scripture, giving them a depth of meaning that the wise men had not conceived of. If followed, the lines of truth He pointed out, would have worked a reformation in the religion of the day. A deep interest in spiritual things would have been awakened; and when Jesus began His ministry, many would have been prepared to receive Him.

The rabbis knew that Jesus had not been instructed in their schools; yet His understanding of the prophecies far exceeded theirs. In this thoughtful Galilean boy they discerned great promise. They desired to gain Him as a student, that He might become a teacher in Israel. They wanted to have charge of His education, feeling that a mind so original must be brought under their molding.

The words of Jesus had moved their hearts as they had never before been moved by words from human lips. God was seeking to give light to those leaders in Israel, and He used the only means by which they could be reached. In their pride they would have scorned to admit that they could receive instruction from any one. If Jesus had appeared to be trying to teach them, they would have disdained to listen. But they flattered themselves that they were teaching Him, or at least testing His knowledge of the Scriptures. The youthful modesty and grace of Jesus disarmed their prejudices. Unconsciously their minds were opened to the word of God, and the Holy Spirit spoke to their hearts.

They could not but see that their expectation in regard to the Messiah was not sustained by prophecy; but they would not renounce the theories that had flattered their ambition. They would not admit that they had misapprehended the Scriptures they claimed to teach. From one to another passed the inquiry, How hath this youth knowledge, having never learned? The light was shining in darkness; but "the darkness apprehended it not." John 1:5, R. V.

Meanwhile Joseph and Mary were in great perplexity and distress. In the departure from Jerusalem they had lost sight of Jesus, and they knew not that He had tarried behind. The country was then densely populated, and the caravans from Galilee were very large. There was much confusion as they left the city. On the way the pleasure of traveling with friends and acquaintances absorbed their attention, and they did not notice His absence till night came on. Then as they halted for rest, they missed the helpful hand of their child. Supposing Him to be with their company, they had felt no anxiety. Young as He was, they had trusted Him implicitly, expecting that when needed, He would be ready to assist them, anticipating their wants as He had always done. But now their fears were roused. They searched for Him throughout their company, but in vain. Shuddering they remembered how Herod had tried to destroy Him in His infancy. Dark forebodings filled their hearts. They bitterly reproached themselves.

Returning to Jerusalem, they pursued their search. The next day, as they mingled with the worshipers in the temple, a familiar voice arrested their attention. They could not mistake it; no other voice was like His, so serious and earnest, yet so full of melody.

28

In the school of the rabbis they found Jesus. Rejoiced as they were, they could not forget their grief and anxiety. When He was with them again, the mother said, in words that implied reproof, "Son, why hast Thou thus dealt with us? Behold, Thy father and I have sought Thee sorrowing."

"How is it that ye sought Me?" answered Jesus. "Wist ye not that I must be about My Father's business?" And as they seemed not to understand His words, He pointed upward. On His face was a light at which they wondered. Divinity was flashing through humanity. On finding Him

---

"For the first time the child Jesus looked upon the temple. . . . He beheld the bleeding victim upon the altar of sacrifice. . . . Every act seemed to be bound up with His own life. . . . Silent and absorbed, He seemed to be studying out a great problem. The mystery of His mission was opening to the Saviour."

---

in the temple, they had listened to what was passing between Him and the rabbis, and they were astonished at His questions and answers. His words started a train of thought that would never be forgotten.

And His question to them had a lesson. "Wist ye not," He said, "that I must be about My Father's business?" Jesus was engaged in the work that He had come into the world to do; but Joseph and Mary had neglected theirs. God had shown them high honor in committing to them His Son. Holy angels had directed the course of Joseph in order to preserve the life of Jesus. But for an entire day they had lost sight of Him whom they should not have forgotten for a moment. And when their anxiety was relieved, they had not censured themselves, but had cast the blame upon Him.

It was natural for the parents of Jesus to look upon Him as their own child. He was daily with them, His life in many respects was like that of other children, and it was difficult for them to realize that He was the Son of God.

They were in danger of failing to appreciate the blessing granted them in the presence of the world's Redeemer. The grief of their separation from Him, and the gentle reproof which His words conveyed, were designed to impress them with the sacredness of their trust.

In the answer to His mother, Jesus showed for the first time that He understood His relation to God. Before His birth the angel had said to Mary, "He shall be great, and shall be called the Son of the Highest; and the Lord God shall give unto Him the throne of His father David, and He shall reign over the house of Jacob forever." Luke 1:32, 33. These words Mary had pondered in her heart; yet while she believed that her child was to be Israel's Messiah, she did not comprehend His mission. Now she did not understand His words; but she knew that He had disclaimed kinship to Joseph, and had declared His Sonship to God.

Jesus did not ignore His relation to His earthly parents. From Jerusalem He returned home with them, and aided them in their life of toil. He hid in His own heart the mystery of His mission, waiting submissively for the appointed time for Him to enter upon His work. For eighteen years after He had recognized that He was the Son of God, He acknowledged the tie that bound Him to the home at Nazareth, and performed the duties of a son, a brother, a friend, and a citizen.

As His mission had opened to Jesus in the temple, He shrank from contact with the multitude. He wished to return from Jerusalem in quietness, with those who knew the secret of His life. By the paschal service, God was seeking to call His people away from their worldly cares, and to remind them of His wonderful work in their deliverance from Egypt. In this work He desired them to see a promise of deliverance from sin. As the blood of the slain lamb sheltered the homes of Israel, so the blood of Christ was to save their souls; but they could be saved through Christ only as by faith they should make His life their own. There was virtue in the symbolic service, only as it directed the worshipers to Christ as their personal Saviour. God desired that they should be led to prayerful study and meditation in regard to Christ's mission. But as the multitudes left Jerusalem, the excitement of travel and social intercourse too often absorbed their attention, and the service they had witnessed was forgotten. The Saviour was not attracted to their company.

As Joseph and Mary should return from Jerusalem alone with Jesus, He hoped to direct their minds to the prophecies of the suffering Saviour. Upon Calvary He sought to lighten His mother's grief. He was thinking of her now. Mary was to witness His last agony, and Jesus desired her to understand His mission, that she might be strengthened to endure, when the sword should pierce through her soul. As Jesus had been separated from her, and she had sought Him sorrowing three days, so when He should be offered up for the sins of the world, He would again be lost to her for three days. And as He should come forth from the tomb, her sorrow would again be turned to joy. But how much better she could have borne the anguish of His death if she had understood the scriptures to which He was now trying to turn her thoughts.

If Joseph and Mary had stayed their minds upon God by meditation and prayer, they would have realized the sacredness of their trust, and would not have lost sight of Jesus. By one day's neglect they lost the Saviour; but it cost them three days of anxious search to find Him. So with us; by idle talk, evil-speaking, or neglect of prayer, we may in one day lose the Saviour's presence, and it may take many days of sorrowful search to find Him, and regain the peace that we have lost.

In our association with one another, we should take heed lest we forget Jesus, and pass along unmindful that He is not with us. When we become absorbed in worldly things so that we have no thought for Him in whom our hope of eternal life is centered, we separate ourselves from Jesus and from the heavenly angels. These holy beings cannot remain where the Saviour's presence is not desired, and His absence is not marked. This is why discouragement so often exists among the professed followers of Christ.

Many attend religious services, and are refreshed and comforted by the word of God; but through neglect of meditation, watchfulness, and prayer, they lose the blessing, and find themselves more destitute than before they received it. Often they feel that God has dealt hardly with them. They do not see that the fault is their own. By separating themselves from Jesus, they have shut away the light of His presence.

It would be well for us to spend a thoughtful hour each day in contemplation of the life of Christ. We should take it point by point, and let the imagination grasp each scene, especially the closing ones. As we thus dwell upon His great sacrifice for us, our confidence in Him will be more constant, our love will be quickened, and we shall be more deeply imbued with His spirit. If we would be saved at last, we must learn the lesson of penitence and humiliation at the foot of the cross.

As we associate together, we may be a blessing to one another. If we are Christ's, our sweetest thoughts will be of Him. We shall love to talk of Him; and as we speak to one another of His love, our hearts will be softened by divine influences. Beholding the beauty of His character, we shall be "changed into the same image from glory to glory." 2 Corinthians 3:18.

Days of Conflict

From its earliest years the Jewish child was surrounded with the requirements of the rabbis. Rigid rules were prescribed for every act, down to the smallest details of life. Under the synagogue teachers the youth were instructed in the countless regulations which as orthodox Israelites they were expected to observe. But Jesus did not interest Himself in these matters. From childhood He acted independently of the rabbinical laws. The Scriptures of the Old Testament were His constant study, and the words, "Thus saith the Lord," were ever upon His lips.

As the condition of the people began to open to His mind, He saw that the requirements of society and the requirements of God were in constant collision. Men were departing from the word of God, and exalting theories of their own invention. They were observing traditional rites that possessed no virtue. Their service was a mere round of ceremonies; the sacred truths it was designed to teach, were hidden from the worshipers. He saw that in their faithless services they found no peace. They did not know the freedom of spirit that would come to them by serving God in truth. Jesus had come to teach the meaning of the worship of God, and He could not sanction the mingling of human requirements with the divine precepts. He did not attack the precepts or practices of the learned teachers; but when reproved for His own simple habits, He presented the word of God in justification of His conduct.

In every gentle and submissive way, Jesus tried to please those with whom He came in contact. Because He was so gentle and unobtrusive, the scribes and elders supposed that He would be easily influenced by their teaching. They urged Him to receive the maxims and traditions that had been handed down from the ancient rabbis, but He asked for their authority in Holy Writ. He would hear every word that proceeds from the mouth of God; but He could not obey the inventions of men. Jesus seemed to know the Scriptures from beginning to end, and He presented them in their true import. The rabbis were ashamed to be instructed by a child. They claimed that it was their office to explain the Scriptures, and that it was His place to accept their interpretation. They were indignant that He should stand in opposition to their word.

They knew that no authority could be found in Scripture for their traditions. They realized that in spiritual understanding Jesus was far in advance of them. Yet they were angry because He did not obey their dictates. Failing to convince Him, they sought Joseph and Mary, and set before them His course of noncompliance. Thus He suffered rebuke and censure.

At a very early age, Jesus had begun to act for Himself in the formation of His character, and not even respect and love for His parents could turn Him from obedience to God's word. "It is written" was His reason for every act that varied from the family customs. But the influence of the rabbis made His life a bitter one. Even in His youth He had to learn the hard lesson of silence and patient endurance.

His brothers, as the sons of Joseph were called, sided with the rabbis. They insisted that the traditions must be heeded, as if they were the requirements of God. They even regarded the precepts of men more highly than the word of God, and they were greatly annoyed at the clear penetration of Jesus in distinguishing between the false and the true. His strict obedience to the law of God they condemned as stubbornness. They were surprised at the knowledge and wisdom He showed in answering the rabbis. They knew that He had not received instruction from

(84-86)

the wise men, yet they could not but see that He was an instructor to them. They recognized that His education was of a higher type than their own. But they did not discern that He had access to the tree of life, a source of knowledge of which they were ignorant.

Christ was not exclusive, and He had given special offense to the Pharisees by departing in this respect from their rigid rules. He found the domain of religion fenced in by high walls of seclusion, as too sacred a matter for everyday life. These walls of partition He overthrew. In His contact with men He did not ask, What is your creed? To what church do you belong? He exercised His helping power in behalf of all who needed help. Instead of secluding Himself in a hermit's cell in order to show His heavenly character, He labored earnestly for humanity. He inculcated the principle that Bible religion does not consist in the mortification of the body. He taught that pure and undefiled religion is not meant only for set times and special occasions. At all times and in all places He manifested a loving interest in men, and shed about Him the light of a cheerful piety. All this was a rebuke to the Pharisees. It showed that religion does not consist in selfishness, and that their morbid devotion to personal interest was far from being true godliness. This had roused their enmity against Jesus, so that they tried to enforce His conformity to their regulations.

Jesus worked to relieve every case of suffering that He saw. He had little money to give, but He often denied Himself of food in order to relieve those who appeared more needy than He. His brothers felt that His influence went far to counteract theirs. He possessed a tact which none of them had, or desired to have. When they spoke harshly to poor, degraded beings, Jesus sought out these very ones, and spoke to them words of encouragement. To those who were in need He would give a cup of cold water, and would quietly place His own meal in their hands. As He relieved their sufferings, the truths He taught were associated with His acts of mercy, and were thus riveted in the memory.

All this displeased His brothers. Being older than Jesus, they felt that He should be under their dictation. They charged Him with thinking Himself superior to them, and reproved Him for setting Himself above their teachers, and the priests and rulers of the people. Often they threatened and tried to intimidate Him; but He passed on, making the Scriptures His guide.

Jesus loved His brothers, and treated them with unfailing kindness; but they were jealous of Him, and manifested the most decided unbelief and contempt. They could not understand His conduct. Great contradictions presented themselves in Jesus. He was the divine Son of God, and yet a helpless child. The Creator of the worlds, the earth was His possessions, and yet poverty marked His life experience at every step. He possessed a dignity and individuality wholly distinct from earthly pride and assumption; He did not strive for worldly greatness, and in even the lowliest position He was content. This angered His brothers. They could not account for His constant serenity under trial and deprivation. They did not know that for our sake He had become poor, that we "through His poverty might be rich." 2 Corinthians 8:9. They could understand the mystery of His mission no more than the friends of Job could understand his humiliation and suffering.

Jesus was misunderstood by His brothers because He was not like them. His standard was not their standard. In looking to men they had turned away from God, and they had not His power in their lives. The forms of religion which they observed, could not transform the character. They paid "tithe of mint and anise and cummin," but omitted "the weightier matters of the law, judgment, mercy, and faith." Matthew 23:23. The example of Jesus was to them a continual irritation. He hated but one thing in the world, and that was sin. He could not witness a wrong act without pain which it was impossible to disguise. Between the formalists, whose sanctity of appearance concealed the love of sin, and a character in which zeal for God's glory was always paramount, the contrast was unmistakable. Because the life of Jesus condemned evil, He was opposed, both at home and abroad. His unselfishness and integrity were commented on with a sneer. His forbearance and kindness were termed cowardice.

Of the bitterness that falls to the lot of humanity, there was no part which Christ did not taste. There were those who tried to cast contempt upon Him because of His birth, and even in His childhood He had to meet their scornful looks and evil whisperings. If He had responded by an impatient word or look, if He had conceded to His brothers by even one wrong act, He would have failed of being a perfect example. Thus He would have failed of carrying out the plan for our redemption. Had He even admitted that there could be an excuse for sin, Satan would have triumphed, and the world would have been lost. This is why the tempter worked to make His life as trying as possible, that He might be led to sin.

But to every temptation He had one answer, "It is written." He rarely rebuked any wrongdoing of His brothers, but He had a word from God to speak to them. Often He was accused of cowardice for refusing to unite with them in some forbidden act; but His answer was, It is written, "The fear of the Lord, that is wisdom; and to depart from evil is understanding." Job 28:28.

There were some who sought His society, feeling at peace in His presence; but many avoided Him, because they were rebuked by His stainless life. Young companions urged Him to do as they did. He was bright and cheerful; they enjoyed His presence, and welcomed His ready suggestions; but they were impatient at His scruples, and pronounced Him narrow and strait-laced. Jesus answered, It is written, "Wherewithal shall a young man cleanse his way? By taking heed thereto according to Thy

word." "Thy word have I hid in mine heart, that I might not sin against Thee." Psalms 119:9, 11.

Often He was asked, Why are you bent on being so singular, so different from us all? It is written, He said, "Blessed are the undefiled in the way, who walk in the law of the Lord. Blessed are they that keep His testimonies, and that seek Him with the whole heart. They also do no iniquity; they walk in His ways." Psalms 119:1-3.

"Through childhood, youth, and manhood, Jesus walked alone. . . . He knew that unless there was a decided change in the principles and purposes of the human race, all would be lost. This was the burden of His soul, and none could appreciate the weight that rested upon Him. Filled with intense purpose, He carried out the design of His life that He Himself should be the light of men."

When questioned why He did not join in the frolics of the youth of Nazareth, He said, It is written, "I have rejoiced in the way of Thy testimonies, as much as in all riches. I will meditate in Thy precepts, and have respect unto Thy ways. I will delight myself in Thy statutes; I will not forget Thy word." Psalms 119:14-16.

Jesus did not contend for His rights. Often His work was made unnecessarily severe because He was willing and uncomplaining. Yet He did not fail nor become discouraged. He lived above these difficulties, as if in the light of God's countenance. He did not retaliate when roughly used, but bore insult patiently.

Again and again He was asked, Why do you submit to such despiteful usage, even from your brothers? It is written, He said, "My son, forget not My law; but let thine heart keep My commandments; for length of days, and long life, and peace, shall they add to thee. Let not mercy and truth forsake thee; bind them about thy neck; write them upon the table of thine heart: so shalt thou find favor and good understanding in the sight of God and man." Proverbs 3:1-4.

From the time when the parents of Jesus found Him in the temple, His course of action was a mystery to them. He would not enter into controversy, yet His example was a constant lesson. He seemed as one who was set apart. His hours of happiness were found when alone with nature and with God. Whenever it was His privilege, He turned aside from the scene of His labor, to go into the fields, to meditate in the green valleys, to hold communion with God on the mountainside or amid the trees of the forest. The early morning often found Him in some secluded place, meditating, searching the Scriptures, or in prayer. From these quiet hours He would return to His home to take up His duties again, and to give an example of patient toil.

The life of Christ was marked with respect and love for His mother. Mary believed in her heart that the holy child born of her was the long-promised Messiah, yet she dared not express her faith. Throughout His life on earth she was a partaker in His sufferings. She witnessed with sorrow the trials brought upon Him in His childhood and youth. By her vindication of what she knew to be right in His conduct, she herself was brought into trying positions. She looked upon the associations of the home, and the mother's tender watchcare over her children, as of vital importance in the formation of character. The sons and daughters of Joseph knew this, and by appealing to her anxiety, they tried to correct the practices of Jesus according to their standard.

Mary often remonstrated with Jesus, and urged Him to conform to the usages of the rabbis. But He could not be persuaded to change His habits of contemplating the works of God and seeking to alleviate the suffering of men or even of dumb animals. When the priests and teachers required Mary's aid in controlling Jesus, she was greatly troubled; but peace came to her heart as He presented the statements of Scripture upholding His practices.

At times she wavered between Jesus and His brothers, who did not believe that He was the Sent of God; but evidence was abundant that His was a divine character. She saw Him sacrificing Himself for the good of others. His presence brought a purer atmosphere into the home, and His life was as leaven working amid the elements of society. Harmless and undefiled, He walked among the thoughtless, the rude, the uncourteous; amid the unjust publicans, the reckless prodigals, the unrighteous Samaritans, the heathen soldiers, the rough peasants, and the mixed multitude. He spoke a word of sympathy here and a word there, as He saw men weary, yet compelled to bear heavy burdens. He shared their burdens, and repeated to them the lessons He had learned from nature, of the love, the kindness, the goodness of God.

He taught all to look upon themselves as endowed with precious talents, which if rightly employed would secure for them eternal riches. He weeded all vanity from life, and by His own example taught that every moment of time is fraught with eternal results; that it is to be cherished as a treasure, and to be employed for holy purposes. He passed by no human being as worthless, but sought to apply the saving remedy to every soul. In whatever company He found Himself, He presented a lesson that was appropriate to the time and the circumstances. He sought to inspire with hope the most rough and unpromising, setting before them the assurance that they might become blameless and harmless, attaining such a character as would make them manifest as the children of God. Often He met those who had drifted under Satan's control, and who had no power to break from his snare. To such a one, discouraged, sick, tempted, and fallen, Jesus would speak words of tenderest pity, words that were needed and could be understood. Others He met who were fighting a hand-to-hand battle with the adversary of souls. These He encouraged to persevere, assuring them that they would win; for angels of God were on their side, and would give them the victory.

Those whom He thus helped were convinced that here was One in whom they could trust with perfect confidence. He would not betray the secrets they poured into His sympathizing ear.

Jesus was the healer of the body as well as of the soul. He was interested in every phase of suffering that came under His notice, and to every sufferer He brought relief, His kind words having a soothing balm. None could say that He had worked a miracle; but virtue — the healing power of love — went out from Him to the sick and distressed. Thus in an unobtrusive way He worked for the people from His very childhood. And this was why, after His public ministry began, so many heard Him gladly.

Yet through childhood, youth, and manhood, Jesus walked alone. In His purity and His faithfulness, He trod the wine-press alone, and of the people there was none with Him. He carried the awful weight of responsibility for the salvation of men. He knew that unless there was a decided change in the principles and purposes of the human race, all would be lost. This was the burden of His soul, and none could appreciate the weight that rested upon Him. Filled with intense purpose, He carried out the design of His life that He Himself should be the light of men.

The Voice in the Wilderness

From among the faithful in Israel, who had long waited for the coming of the Messiah, the forerunner of Christ arose. The aged priest Zacharias and his wife Elizabeth were "both righteous before God;" and in their quiet and holy lives the light of faith shone out like a star amid the darkness of those evil days. To this godly pair was given the promise of a son, who should "go before the face of the Lord to prepare His ways."

Zacharias dwelt in "the hill country of Judea," but he had gone up to Jerusalem to minister for one week in the temple, a service required twice a year from the priests of each course. "And it came to pass, that while he executed the priest's office before God in the order of his course, according to the custom of the priest's office, his lot was to burn incense when he went into the temple of the Lord."

He was standing before the golden altar in the holy place of the sanctuary. The cloud of incense with the prayers of Israel was ascending before God. Suddenly he became conscious of a divine presence. An angel of the Lord was "standing on the right side of the altar." The position of the angel was an indication of favor, but Zacharias took no note of this. For many years he had prayed for the coming of the Redeemer; now heaven had sent its messenger to announce that these prayers were about to be answered; but the mercy of God seemed too great for him to credit. He was filled with fear and self-condemnation.

But he was greeted with the joyful assurance: "Fear not, Zacharias; for thy prayer is heard; and thy wife Elizabeth shall bear thee a son, and thou shalt call his name John. And thou shalt have joy and gladness, and many shall rejoice at his birth. For he shall be great in the sight of the Lord, and shall drink neither wine nor strong drink; and he shall be filled with the Holy Ghost. . . . And many of the children of Israel shall he turn to the Lord their God. And he shall go before Him in the spirit and power of Elias, to turn the hearts of the fathers to the children, and the disobedient to the wisdom of the just; to make ready a people prepared for the Lord. And Zacharias said unto the angel, Whereby shall I know this? for I am an old man, and my wife well stricken in years."

Zacharias well knew how to Abraham in his old age a child was given because he believed Him faithful who had promised. But for a moment the aged priest turns his thought to the weakness of humanity. He forgets that what God has promised, He is able to perform. What a contrast between this unbelief, and the sweet, childlike faith of Mary, the maiden of Nazareth, whose answer to the angel's wonderful announcement was, "Behold the handmaid of the Lord; be it unto me according to thy word." Luke 1:38.

The birth of a son to Zacharias, like the birth of the child of Abraham, and that of Mary, was to teach a great spiritual truth, a truth that we are slow to learn and ready to forget. In ourselves we are incapable of doing any good thing; but that which we cannot do, will be wrought by the power of God in every submissive and believing soul. It was through faith that the child of promise was given. It is through faith that spiritual life is begotten, and we are enabled to do the works of righteousness.

To the question of Zacharias, the angel said, "I am Gabriel, that stand in the presence of God; and am sent to speak unto thee, and to show thee these glad tidings." Five hundred years before, Gabriel had made known to Daniel the prophetic period which was to extend to the coming of Christ. The knowledge that the end of this period was near, had moved Zacharias to pray for the Messiah's advent.

This chapter is based on Luke 1:5-23, 57-80; 3:1-18; Matt. 3:1-12; Mark 1:1-8.

Now the very messenger through whom the prophecy was given, had come to announce its fulfilment.

The words of the angel, "I am Gabriel, that stand in the presence of God," show that he holds a position of high honor in the heavenly courts. When he came with a message to Daniel, he said, "There is none that holdeth with me in these things, but Michael [Christ] your prince." Daniel 10:21. Of Gabriel the Saviour speaks, in the Revelation, saying that "He sent and signified it by His angel unto His servant John." Revelation 1:1. And to John the angel declared, "I am a fellow servant with thee, and with thy brethren the prophets." Revelation 22:9, R. V. Wonderful thought — that the angel who stands next in honor to the Son of God, is the one chosen to open the purposes of God to sinful men.

Zacharias had expressed doubt of the angel's words. He was not to speak again until they were fulfilled. "Behold," said the angel, "thou shalt be dumb, . . until the day that these things shall be performed, because thou believest not my words, which shall be fulfilled in their season." It was the duty of the priest in this service to pray for the pardon of public and national sins, and for the coming of the Messiah; but when Zacharias attempted to do this, he could not utter a word.

Coming forth to bless the people, "he beckoned unto them, and remained speechless." They had waited long, and had begun to fear, lest he had been cut down by the judgment of God. But as he came forth from the holy place, his face was shining with the glory of God, "and they perceived that he had seen a vision in the temple." Zacharias communicated to them what he had seen and heard; and "as soon as the days of his ministration were accomplished, he departed to his own house."

Soon after the birth of the promised child, the father's tongue was loosed, "and he spake and praised God. And fear came on all that dwelt round about them; and all these sayings were noised abroad throughout all the hill country of Judea. And all they that heard them laid them up in their hearts, saying, What manner of child shall this be?" All this tended to call attention to the Messiah's coming, for which John was to prepare the way.

The Holy Spirit rested upon Zacharias, and in these beautiful words he prophesied of the mission of his son: —

"Thou, child, shalt be called the prophet of the Highest;
For thou shalt go before the face of the Lord
to prepare His ways;
To give knowledge of salvation unto His people
By the remission of their sins,
Through the tender mercy of our God,
Whereby the dayspring from on high hath visited us,
To give the light to them that sit in darkness
and in the shadow of death;
To guide our feet into the way of peace."

"And the child grew, and waxed strong in spirit, and was in the deserts till the day of his showing unto Israel." Before the birth of John, the angel had said, "He shall be great in the sight of the Lord, and shall drink neither wine nor strong drink; and he shall be filled with the Holy Ghost." God had called the son of Zacharias to a great work, the greatest ever committed to men. In order to accomplish this work, he must have the Lord to work with him. And the Spirit of God would be with him if he heeded the instruction of the angel.

John was to go forth as Jehovah's messenger, to bring to men the light of God. He must give a new direction to their thoughts. He must impress them with the holiness of God's requirements, and their need of His perfect righteousness. Such a messenger must be holy. He must be a temple for the indwelling Spirit of God. In order to fulfil his mission, he must have a second physical constitution, and mental and spiritual strength. Therefore it would be necessary for him to control the appetites and passions. He must be able so to control all his powers that he could stand among men as unmoved by surrounding circumstances as the rocks and mountains of the wilderness.

In the time of John the Baptist, greed for riches, and the love of luxury and display, had become widespread. Sensuous pleasures, feasting and drinking, were causing physical disease and degeneracy, benumbing the spiritual perceptions, and lessening the sensibility to sin. John was to stand as a reformer. By his abstemious life and plain dress he was to rebuke the excesses of his time. Hence the directions given to the parents of John, — a lesson of temperance by an angel from the throne of heaven.

In childhood and youth the character is most impressible. The power of self-control should then be acquired. By the fireside and at the family board, influences are exerted whose results are as enduring as eternity. More than any natural endowment, the habits established in early years decide whether a man will be victorious or vanquished in the battle of life. Youth is the sowing time. It determines the character of the harvest, for this life and for the life to come.

As a prophet, John was "to turn the hearts of the fathers to the children, and the disobedient to the wisdom of the just; to make ready a people prepared for the Lord." In preparing the way for Christ's first advent, he was a representative of those who are to prepare a people for our Lord's second coming. The world is given to self-indulgence. Errors and fables abound. Satan's snares for destroying souls are multiplied. All who would perfect holiness in the fear of God, must learn the lessons of temperance and self-control. The appetites and passions must be held in subjection to the higher powers of the mind. This self-discipline is essential to that mental strength and spiritual insight which will enable us to understand and to practice the sacred truths of God's word. For this reason temperance finds its place in the work of preparation for Christ's second coming.

In the natural order of things, the son of Zacharias would have been educated for the priesthood. But the training of the rabbinical schools would have unfitted him for his work. God did not end him to the teachers of theology to learn how to interpret the Scriptures. He called him to the desert, that he might learn of nature, and nature's God.

It was a lonely region where he found his home, in the midst of barren hills, wild ravines, and rocky caves. But it was his choice to forego the enjoyments and luxuries of life for the stern discipline of the wilderness. Here his surroundings were favorable to habits of simplicity and self-denial. Uninterrupted by the clamor of the world, he could here study the lessons of nature, of revelation, and of Providence. The words of the angel to Zacharias had been often repeated to John by his God-fearing parents. From childhood his mission had been kept before him, and he had accepted the holy trust. To him the solitude of the desert was a welcome escape from society in which suspicion, unbelief, and impurity had become well-nigh all-pervading. He distrusted his own power to withstand temptation, and shrank from constant contact with sin, lest he should lose the sense of its exceeding sinfulness.

Dedicated to God as a Nazarite from his birth, he made the vow his own in a lifelong consecration. His dress was that of the ancient prophets, a garment of camel's hair, confined by a leather girdle. He ate the "locusts and wild honey" found in the wilderness, and drank the pure water from the hills.

But the life of John was not spent in idleness, in ascetic gloom, or in selfish isolation. From time to time he went forth to mingle with men; and he was ever an interested observer of what was passing in the world. From his quiet retreat he watched the unfolding of events. With vision illuminated by the divine Spirit he studied the characters of men, that he might understand how to reach their hearts with the message of heaven. The burden of his mission was upon him. In solitude, by meditation and prayer, he sought to gird up his soul for the lifework before him.

Although in the wilderness, he was not exempt from temptation. So far as possible, he closed every avenue by which Satan could enter, yet he was still assailed by the tempter. But his spiritual perceptions were clear; he had developed strength and decision of character, and through the aid of the Holy Spirit he was able to detect Satan's approaches, and to resist his power.

John found in the wilderness his school and his sanctuary. Like Moses amid the mountains of Midian, he was shut in by God's presence, and surrounded by the evidences of His power. It was not his lot to dwell, as did Israel's great leader, amid the solemn majesty of the mountain solitudes; but before him were the heights of Moab, beyond Jordan, speaking of Him who had set fast the mountains, and girded them with strength. The gloomy and terrible aspect of nature in his wilderness home, vividly pictured the condition of Israel. The fruitful vineyard of the Lord had become a desolate waste. But above the desert the heavens bent bright and beautiful. The clouds that gathered, dark with tempest, were arched by the rainbow of promise. So above Israel's degradation shone the promised glory of the Messiah's reign. The clouds of wrath were spanned by the rainbow of His covenant-mercy.

Alone in the silent night he read God's promise to Abraham of a seed numberless as the stars. The light of dawn, gilding the mountains of Moab, told of Him who should be as "the light of the morning, when the sun riseth, even a morning without clouds." 2 Samuel 23:4. And in the brightness of noontide he saw the splendor of His manifestation, when "the glory of the Lord shall be revealed, and all flesh shall see it together" Isaiah 40:5.

With awed yet exultant spirit he searched in the prophetic scrolls the revelations of the Messiah's coming,—the promised seed that should bruise the serpent's head; Shiloh, "the peace giver," who was to appear before a king

---

❝As a prophet, John was 'to turn . . . the disobedient to the wisdom of the just; to make ready a people prepared for the Lord.' In preparing the way for Christ's first advent, he was a representative of those who are to prepare a people for our Lord's second coming.❞

---

should cease to reign on David's throne. Now the time had come. A Roman ruler sat in the palace upon Mount Zion. By the sure word of the Lord, already the Christ was born.

Isaiah's rapt portrayals of the Messiah's glory were his study by day and by night,—the Branch from the root of Jesse; a King to reign in righteousness, judging "with equity for the meek of the earth;" "a covert from the tempest, . . . the shadow of a great rock in a weary land;" Israel no longer to be termed "Forsaken," nor her land "Desolate," but to be called of the Lord, "My Delight," and her land "Beulah." Isaiah 11:4; 32:2; 62:4, margin. The heart of the lonely exile was filled with the glorious vision.

He looked upon the King in His beauty, and self was forgotten. He beheld the majesty of holiness, and felt himself to be inefficient and unworthy. He was ready to go forth as Heaven's messenger, unawed by the human, because he had looked upon the Divine. He could stand erect and fearless in the presence of earthly monarchs, because he had bowed low before the King of kings.

John did not fully understand the nature of the Messiah's kingdom. He looked for Israel to be delivered from her national foes; but the coming of a King in righteousness, and the establishment of Israel as a holy nation, was the great object of his hope. Thus he believed would be accomplished the prophecy given at his birth, —

"To remember His holy covenant; . . .

That we being delivered out of the hand of our enemies

Might serve Him without fear,

In holiness and righteousness before Him

all the days of our life."

He saw his people deceived, self-satisfied, and asleep in their sins. He longed to rouse them to a holier life. The message that God had given him to bear was designed to startle them from their lethargy, and cause them to tremble because of their great wickedness. Before the seed of the gospel could find lodgment, the soil of the heart must be broken up. Before they would seek healing from Jesus, they must be awakened to their danger from the wounds of sin.

God does not send messengers to flatter the sinner. He delivers no message of peace, to lull the unsanctified into fatal security. He lays heavy burdens upon the conscience of the wrongdoer, and pierces the soul with arrows of conviction. The ministering angels present to him the fearful judgments of God to deepen the sense of need, and prompt the cry, "What must I do to be saved?" Then the hand that has humbled in the dust, lifts up the penitent. The voice that has rebuked sin, and put to shame pride and ambition, inquires with tenderest sympathy, "What wilt thou that I shall do unto thee?"

When the ministry of John began, the nation was in a state of excitement and discontent verging on revolution. At the removal of Archelaus, Judea had been brought directly under the control of Rome. The tyranny and extortion of the Roman governors, and their determined efforts to introduce the heathen symbols and customs kindled revolt, which had been quenched in the blood of thousands of the bravest of Israel. All this intensified the national hatred against Rome, and increased the longing to be freed from her power.

Amid discord and strife, a voice was heard from the wilderness, a voice startling and stern, yet full of hope: "Repent ye; for the kingdom of heaven is at hand." With a new, strange power it moved the people. Prophets had foretold the coming of Christ as an event far in the future; but here was an announcement that it was at hand. John's singular appearance carried the minds of his hearers back to the ancient seers. In his manner and dress he resembled the prophet Elijah. With the spirit and power of Elijah he denounced the national corruption, and rebuked the pre-

vailing sins. His words were plain, pointed, and convincing. Many believed him to be one of the prophets risen from the dead. The whole nation was stirred. Multitudes flocked to the wilderness.

John proclaimed the coming of the Messiah, and called the people to repentance. As a symbol of cleansing from sin, he baptized them in the waters of the Jordan. Thus by a significant object lesson he declared that those who claimed to be the chosen people of God were defiled by sin, and that without purification of heart and life they could have no part in the Messiah's kingdom.

Princes and rabbis, soldiers, publicans, and peasants came to hear the prophet. For a time the solemn warning from God alarmed them. Many were brought to repentance, and received baptism. Persons of all ranks submitted to the requirement of the Baptist, in order to participate in the kingdom he announced.

Many of the scribes and Pharisees came confessing their sins, and asking for baptism. They had exalted themselves as better than other men, and had led the people to entertain a high opinion of their piety; now the guilty secrets of their lives were unveiled. But John was impressed by the Holy Spirit that many of these men had no real conviction of sin. They were timeservers. As friends of the prophet, they hoped to find favor with the coming Prince. And by receiving baptism at the hands of this popular young teacher, they thought to strengthen their influence with the people.

John met them with the scathing inquiry, "O generation of vipers, who hath warned you to flee from the wrath to come? Bring forth therefore fruits meet for repentance; and think not to say within yourselves, We have Abraham to our father; for I say unto you, that God is able of these stones to raise up children unto Abraham."

The Jews had misinterpreted God's promise of eternal favor to Israel: "Thus saith the Lord, which giveth the sun for a light by day, and the ordinances of the moon and of the stars for a light by night, which divideth the sea when the waves thereof roar; The Lord of hosts is His name: If those ordinances depart from before Me, saith the Lord, then the seed of Israel also shall cease from being a nation before Me forever. Thus saith the Lord: If heaven above can be measured, and the foundations of the earth searched out beneath, I will also cast off all the seed of Israel for all that they have done, saith the Lord." Jeremiah 31:35-37. The Jews regarded their natural descent from Abraham as giving them a claim to this promise. But they overlooked the conditions which God had specified. Before giving the promise, He had said, "I will put My law in their inward parts, and write it in their hearts; and will be their God, and they shall be My people. . . . For I will forgive their iniquity, and I will remember their sin no more." Jeremiah 31:33,34.

To a people in whose hearts His law is written, the favor of God is assured. They are one with Him. But the Jews had separated themselves from God. Because of their sins they were suffering under His judgments. This was the cause of their bondage to a heathen nation. Their minds were darkened by transgression, and because in times past the Lord had shown them so great favor, they excused their sins. They flattered themselves that they were better than other men, and entitled to His blessings.

These things "are written for our admonition, upon whom the ends of the world are come." 1 Corinthians 10:11. How often we misinterpret God's blessings, and flatter ourselves that we are favored on account of some goodness in us. God cannot do for us that which He longs to do. His gifts are used to increase our self-satisfaction, and to harden our hearts in unbelief and sin.

John declared to the teachers of Israel that their pride, selfishness, and cruelty showed them to be a generation of vipers, a deadly curse to the people, rather than the children of just and obedient Abraham. In view of the light they had received from God, they were even worse than the heathen, to whom they felt so much superior. They had forgotten the rock whence they were hewn, and the hole of the pit from which they had been digged. God was not dependent upon them for the fulfilling of His purpose. As He had called Abraham out from a heathen people, so He could call others to His service. Their hearts might now appear as lifeless as the stones of the desert, but His Spirit could quicken them to do His will, and receive the fulfillment of His promise.

"And now also," said the prophet, "the ax is laid unto the root of the trees: therefore every tree which bringeth not forth good fruit, is hewn down, and cast into the fire." Not by its name, but by its fruit, is the value of a tree determined. If the fruit is worthless, the name cannot save the tree from destruction. John declared to the Jews that their standing before God was to be decided by their character and life. Profession was worthless. If their life and character were not in harmony with God's law, they were not His people.

Under his heart-searching words, his hearers were convicted. They came to him with the inquiry, "What shall we do then?" He answered, "He that hath two coats, let him impart to him that hath none; and he that hath meat, let him do likewise." And he warned the publicans against injustice, and the soldiers against violence.

All who became the subjects of Christ's kingdom, he said, would give evidence of faith and repentance. Kindness, honesty, and fidelity would be seen in their lives.

They would minister to the needy, and bring their offerings to God. They would shield the defenseless, and give an example of virtue and compassion. So the followers of Christ will give evidence of the transforming power of the Holy Spirit. In the daily life, justice, mercy, and the love of God, will be seen. Otherwise they are like the chaff, that is given to the fire.

"I indeed baptize you in water unto repentance," said John; "but He that cometh after me is mightier than I, whose shoes I am not worthy to bear: He shall baptize you with the Holy Ghost, and with fire." Matthew 3:11, R.V., margin. The prophet Isaiah had declared that the Lord would cleanse His people from their iniquities "by the spirit of judgment, and by the spirit of burning." The word of the Lord to Israel was, "I will turn My hand upon thee, and purely purge away thy dross, and take away all thy tin." Isaiah 4:4; 1:25. To sin, wherever found, "our God is a consuming fire." Hebrews 12:29. In all who submit to His power, the Spirit of God will consume sin. But if men cling to sin, they become identified with it. Then the glory of God, which destroys sin, must destroy them. Jacob, after his night of wrestling with the angel, exclaimed, "I have seen God face to face, and my life is preserved." Genesis 32: 30. Jacob had been guilty of a great sin in his conduct toward Esau; but he had repented. His transgression had been forgiven, and his sin purged; therefore he could endure the revelation of God's presence. But wherever men came before God while wilfully cherishing evil, they were destroyed. At the second advent of Christ the wicked shall be consumed "with the Spirit of His mouth," and destroyed "with the brightness of His coming." 2 Thessalonians 2:8. The light of the glory of God, which imparts life to the righteous, will slay the wicked.

In the time of John the Baptist, Christ was about to appear as the revealer of the character of God. His very presence would make manifest to men their sin. Only as they were willing to be purged from sin could they enter into fellowship with Him. Only the pure in heart could abide in His presence.

Thus the Baptist declared God's message to Israel. Many gave heed to his instruction. Many sacrificed all, in order to obey. Multitudes followed this new teacher from place to place, and not a few cherished the hope that he might be the Messiah. But as John saw the people turning to him, he sought every opportunity of directing their faith to Him who was to come.

The Baptism

Tidings of the wilderness prophet, and his wonderful announcement, spread throughout Galilee. The message reached the peasants in the remotest hill towns, and the fisherfolk by the sea, and in these simple, earnest hearts found its truest response. In Nazareth it was told in the carpenter shop that had been Joseph's, and One recognized the call. His time had come. Turning from His daily toil, He bade farewell to His mother, and followed in the steps of His countrymen who were flocking to the Jordan.

Jesus and John the Baptist were cousins, and closely related by the circumstances of their birth; yet they had had no direct acquaintance with each other. The life of Jesus had been spent at Nazareth in Galilee; that of John, in the wilderness of Judea. Amid widely different surroundings, they had lived in seclusion, and had had no communication with each other. Providence had ordered this. No occasion was to be given for the charge that they had conspired together to support each other's claims.

John was acquainted with the events that had marked the birth of Jesus. He had heard of the visit to Jerusalem in His boyhood, and of what had passed in the school of the rabbis. He knew of His sinless life, and believed Him to be the Messiah; but of this he had no positive assurance. The fact that Jesus had for so many years remained in obscurity, giving no special evidence of His mission, gave occasion for doubt as to whether He could be the Promised One. The Baptist, however, waited in faith, believing that in God's own time all would be made plain. It had been revealed to him that the Messiah would seek baptism at his hands, and that a sign of His divine character should then be given. Thus he would be enabled to present Him to the people.

When Jesus came to be baptized, John recognized in Him a purity of character that he had never before perceived in any man. The very atmosphere of His presence was holy and awe-inspiring. Among the multitudes that had gathered about him at the Jordan, John had heard dark tales of crime, and had met souls bowed down with the burden of myriad sins; but never had he come in contact with a human being from whom there breathed an influence so divine. All this was in harmony with what had been revealed to John regarding the Messiah. Yet he shrank from granting the request of Jesus. How could he, a sinner, baptize the Sinless One? And why should He who needed no repentance submit to a rite that was a confession of guilt to be washed away?

As Jesus asked for baptism, John drew back, exclaiming, "I have need to be baptized of Thee, and comest Thou to me?" With firm yet gentle authority, Jesus answered, "Suffer it to be so now; for thus it becometh us to fulfill all righteousness." And John, yielding, led the Saviour down into the Jordan, and buried Him beneath the water. "And straightway coming up out of the water," Jesus "saw the heavens opened, and the Spirit like a dove descending upon Him."

Jesus did not receive baptism as a confession of guilt on His own account. He identified Himself with sinners, taking the steps that we are to take, and doing the work that we must do. His life of suffering and patient endurance after His baptism was also an example to us.

Upon coming up out of the water, Jesus bowed in prayer on the river bank. A new and important era was opening before Him. He was now, upon a wider stage, entering on the conflict of His life. Though He was the Prince of Peace, His coming must be as the unsheathing of a sword. The kingdom He had come to establish was the opposite of that which the Jews desired. He who was the foundation of the ritual and economy of Israel, would be looked upon as its enemy and destroyer. He who had proclaimed the law upon Sinai would be condemned as a transgressor. He who had come to break the power of Satan would be denounced as Beelzebub. No one upon earth had understood Him, and during His ministry He must still walk alone. Throughout His life His mother and His brothers did not comprehend His mission. Even His disciples did not understand Him. He had dwelt in eternal light, as one with God, but His life on earth must be spent in solitude.

> **"The light which fell from the open portals upon the head of our Saviour will fall upon us as we pray for help to resist temptation. The voice which spoke to Jesus says to every believing soul, This is My beloved child, in whom I am well pleased."**

As one with us, He must bear the burden of our guilt and woe. The Sinless One must feel the shame of sin. The peace lover must dwell with strife, the truth must abide with falsehood, purity with vileness. Every sin, every discord, every defiling lust that transgression had brought, was torture to His spirit.

Alone He must tread the path; alone He must bear the burden. Upon Him who had laid off His glory, and accepted the weakness of humanity, the redemption of the world must rest. He saw and felt it all, but His purpose remained steadfast. Upon His arm depended the salvation of the fallen race, and He reached out His hand to grasp the hand of Omnipotent Love.

The Saviour's glance seems to penetrate heaven as He pours out His soul in prayer. Well He knows how sin has hardened the hearts of men, and how difficult it will be for them to discern His mission, and accept the gift of salvation. He pleads with the Father for power to overcome their unbelief, to break the fetters with which Satan has en-thralled them, and in their behalf to conquer the destroyer. He asks for the witness that God accepts humanity in the person of His Son.

Never before have the angels listened to such a prayer. They are eager to bear to their loved Commander a message of assurance and comfort. But no; the Father Himself will answer the petition of His Son. Direct from the throne issue the beams of His glory. The heavens are opened, and upon the Saviour's head descends a dovelike form of purest light, — fit emblem of Him, the meek and lowly One.

Of the vast throng at the Jordan, few except John discerned the heavenly vision. Yet the solemnity of the divine presence rested upon the assembly. The people stood silently gazing upon Christ. His form was bathed in the light that ever surrounds the throne of God. His upturned face was glorified as they had never before seen the face of man. From the open heavens a voice was heard saying, "This is My beloved Son, in whom I am well pleased."

These words of confirmation were given to inspire faith in those who witnessed the scene, and to strengthen the Saviour for His mission. Notwithstanding that the sins of a guilty world were laid upon Christ, notwithstanding the humiliation of taking upon Himself our fallen nature, the voice from heaven declared Him to be the Son of the Eternal.

John had been deeply moved as he saw Jesus bowed as a suppliant, pleading with tears for the approval of the Father. As the glory of God encircled Him, and the voice from heaven was heard, John recognized the token which God had promised. He knew that it was the world's Redeemer whom he had baptized. The Holy Spirit rested upon him, and with outstretched hand pointing to Jesus, he cried, "Behold the Lamb of God, which taketh away the sin of the world."

None among the hearers, and not even the speaker himself, discerned the import of these words, "the Lamb of God." Upon Mount Moriah, Abraham had heard the question of his son, "My father, . . . where is the lamb for a burnt offering?" The father answered, "My son, God will provide Himself a lamb for a burnt offering." Genesis 22:7, 8. And in the ram divinely provided in the place of Isaac, Abraham saw a symbol of Him who was to die for the sins of men. The Holy Spirit through Isaiah, taking up the illustration, prophesied of the Saviour, "He is brought as a lamb to the slaughter," "and the Lord hath laid on Him the iniquity of us all" (Isaiah 53:7, 6); but the people of Israel had not understood the lesson. Many of them regarded the sacrificial offerings much as the heathen looked upon their sacrifices, — as gifts by which they themselves might propitiate the Deity. God desired to teach them that from His own love comes the gift which reconciles them to Himself.

And the word that was spoken to Jesus at the Jordan, "This is My beloved Son, in whom I am well pleased," embraces humanity. God spoke to Jesus as our representative. With all our sins and weaknesses, we are not cast aside as worthless. "He hath made us accepted in the Beloved." Ephesians 1:6. The glory that rested upon Christ is a pledge of the love of God for us. It tells us of the power of prayer, — how the human voice may reach the ear of God, and our petitions find acceptance in the courts of heaven. By sin, earth was cut off from heaven, and alienated from its communion; but Jesus has connected it again with the sphere of glory. His love has encircled man, and reached the highest heaven. The light which fell from the open portals upon the head of our Saviour, will fall upon us as we pray for help to resist temptation. The voice which spoke to Jesus says to every believing soul, "This is My beloved child, in whom I am well pleased."

"Beloved, now are we the sons of God, and it doth not yet appear what we shall be; but we know that, when He shall appear, we shall be like Him; for we shall see Him as He is." 1 John 3:2. Our Redeemer has opened the way, so that the most sinful, the most needy, the most oppressed and despised, may find access to the Father. All may have a home in the mansions which Jesus has gone to prepare. "These things saith He that is holy, He that is true, He that hath the key of David, He that openeth, and no man shutteth; and shutteth, and no man openeth; . . . behold, I have set before thee an open door, and no man can shut it." Revelation 3:7, 8.

The Temptation

"And Jesus, being full of the Holy Ghost, returned from Jordan, and was led by the Spirit into the wilderness." The words of Mark are still more significant. He says, "Immediately the Spirit driveth Him into the wilderness. And He was there in the wilderness forty days, tempted of Satan; and was with the wild beasts." "And in those days He did eat nothing."

When Jesus was led into the wilderness to be tempted, He was led by the Spirit of God. He did not invite temptation. He went to the wilderness to be alone, to contemplate His mission and work. By fasting and prayer He was to brace Himself for the bloodstained path He must travel. But Satan knew that the Saviour had gone into the wilderness, and he thought this the best time to approach Him.

Mighty issues for the world were at stake in the conflict between the Prince of Light and the leader of the kingdom of darkness. After tempting man to sin, Satan claimed the earth as his, and styled himself the prince of this world. Having conformed to his own nature the father and mother of our race, he thought to establish here his empire. He declared that men had chosen him as their sovereign. Through his control of men, he held dominion over the world. Christ had come to disprove Satan's claim. As the Son of man, Christ would stand loyal to God. Thus it would be shown that Satan had not gained complete control of the human race, and that his claim to the world was false. All who desired deliverance from his power would be set free. The dominion that Adam had lost through sin would be recovered.

Since the announcement to the serpent in Eden, "I will put enmity between thee and the woman, and between thy seed and her seed," Genesis 3:15. Satan had known that he did not hold absolute sway over the world. There was seen in men the working of a power that withstood his dominion. With intense interest he watched the sacrifices offered by Adam and his sons. In these ceremonies he discerned a symbol of communion between earth and heaven. He set himself to intercept this communion. He misrepresented God, and misinterpreted the rites that pointed to the Saviour. Men were led to fear God as one who delighted in their destruction. The sacrifices that should have revealed His love, were offered only to appease His wrath. Satan excited the evil passions of men, in order to fasten his rule upon them. When God's written word was given, Satan studied the prophecies of the Saviour's advent. From generation to generation he worked to blind the people to these prophecies, that they might reject Christ at His coming.

At the birth of Jesus, Satan knew that One had come with a divine commission to dispute his dominion. He trembled at the angel's message attesting the authority of the new-born King. Satan well knew the position that Christ had held in heaven as the Beloved of the Father. That the Son of God should come to this earth as a man, filled him with amazement and with apprehension. He could not fathom the mystery of this great sacrifice. His selfish soul could not understand such love for the deceived race. The glory and peace of heaven, and the joy of communion with God, were but dimly comprehended by men; but they were well known to Lucifer, the covering cherub. Since he had lost heaven, he was determined to find revenge by causing others to share his fall. This he would do by causing them to undervalue heavenly things, and to set the heart upon things of earth.

Not without hindrance was the Commander of heaven to win the souls of men to His kingdom. From the time when

44   This chapter is based on Matt. 4:1-11; Mark 1:12, 13; Luke 4:1-13.   (114-116)

He was a babe in Bethlehem, He was continually assailed by the evil one. The image of God was manifest in Christ, and in the councils of Satan it was determined that He should be overcome. No human being had come into the world, and escaped the power of the deceiver. The forces of the confederacy of evil were set upon His track to engage in warfare against Him, and if possible to prevail over Him.

At the Saviour's baptism, Satan was among the witnesses. He saw the Father's glory overshadowing His son. He heard the voice of Jehovah testifying to the divinity of Jesus. Ever since Adam's sin, the human race had been cut off from direct communion with God; the intercourse between heaven and earth had been through Christ; but now that Jesus had come "in the likeness of sinful flesh," the Father Himself spoke. He had before communicated with humanity *through* Christ; now He communicated with humanity *in* Christ. Satan had hoped that God's abhorrence of evil would bring an eternal separation between heaven and earth. But now it was manifest that the connection between God and man had been restored.

Satan saw that he must either conquer or be conquered. The issues of the conflict involved too much to be entrusted to his confederate angels. He must personally conduct the warfare. All the energies of apostasy were rallied against the Son of God. Christ was made the mark of every weapon of hell.

Many look on this conflict between Christ and Satan as having no special bearing on their own life; and for them it has little interest. But within the domain of every human heart this controversy is repeated. Never does one leave the ranks of evil for the service of God without encountering the assaults of Satan. The enticements which Christ resisted, were those that we find it so difficult to withstand. They were urged upon Him in as much greater degree as His character is superior to ours. With the terrible weight of the sins of the world upon Him, Christ withstood the test upon appetite, upon the love of the world, and upon that love of display which leads to presumption. These were the temptations that overcame Adam and Eve, and that so readily overcome us.

Satan had pointed to Adam's sin as proof that God's law was unjust, and could not be obeyed. In our humanity, Christ was to redeem Adam's failure. But when Adam was assailed by the tempter, none of the effects of sin were upon him. He stood in the strength of perfect manhood, possessing the full vigor of mind and body. He was surrounded with the glories of Eden, and was in daily communion with heavenly beings. It was not thus with Jesus when He entered the wilderness to cope with Satan. For four thousand years the race had been decreasing in physical strength, in mental power, and in moral worth; and Christ took upon Him the infirmities of degenerate humanity. Only thus could He rescue man from the lowest depths of his degradation.

Many claim that it was impossible for Christ to be overcome by temptation. Then He could not have been placed in Adam's position; He could not have gained the victory that Adam failed to gain. If we have in any sense a more trying conflict than had Christ, then He would not be able to succor us. But our Saviour took humanity, with all its liabilities. He took the nature of man, with the possibility of yielding to temptation. We have nothing to bear which He has not endured.

With Christ, as with the holy pair in Eden, appetite was the ground of the first great temptation. Just where the ruin began, the work of our redemption must begin. As by the indulgence of appetite Adam fell, so by the denial of appetite Christ must overcome. "And when He had fasted forty days and forty nights, He was afterward an hungered. And when the tempter came to Him, he said, If Thou be the Son of God, command that these stones be made bread. But He answered and said, It is written, Man shall not live by bread alone, but by every word that proceedeth out of the mouth of God."

From the time of Adam to that of Christ, self-indulgence had increased the power of the appetites and passions, until they had almost unlimited control. Thus men had become debased and diseased, and of themselves it was impossible for them to overcome. In man's behalf, Christ conquered by enduring the severest test. For our sake He exercised a self-control stronger than hunger or death. And in this first victory were involved other issues that enter into all our conflicts with the powers of darkness.

When Jesus entered the wilderness, He was shut in by the Father's glory. Absorbed in communion with God, He was lifted above human weakness. But the glory departed, and He was left to battle with temptation. It was pressing upon Him every moment. His human nature shrank for the conflict that awaited Him. For forty days He fasted and prayed. Weak and emaciated from hunger, worn and haggard with mental agony, "His visage was so marred more than any man, and His form more than the sons of men." Isaiah 52:14. Now was Satan's opportunity. Now he supposed that he could overcome Christ.

There came to the Saviour, as if in answer to His prayers, one in the guise of an angel from heaven. He claimed to have a commission from God to declare that Christ's fast was at an end. As God had sent an angel to stay the hand of Abraham from offering Isaac, so, satisfied with Christ's willingness to enter the bloodstained path, the Father had sent an angel to deliver Him; this was the message brought to Jesus. The Saviour was faint from hunger, He was craving for food, when Satan came suddenly upon Him. Pointing to the stones which strewed the desert, and which had the appearance of loaves, the tempter said, "If Thou be the Son of God, command that these stones be made bread."

Though he appears as an angel of light, these first words betray his character. "If Thou be the Son of God." Here is the insinuation of distrust. Should Jesus do what Satan suggests, it would be an acceptance of the doubt. The tempter plans to overthrow Christ by the same means that were so successful with the human race in the beginning. How artfully had Satan approached Eve in Eden! "Yea, hath God said, Ye shall not eat of every tree of the garden?" Genesis 3:1. Thus far the tempter's words were truth; but in his manner of speaking them, there was a disguised contempt for the words of God. There was a covert negative, a doubt of the divine truthfulness. Satan sought to instill into the mind of Eve the thought that God would not do as He had said; that the withholding of such beautiful fruit was a contradiction of His love and compassion for man. So now the tempter seeks to inspire Christ with his own sentiments. "If Thou be the Son of God." The words rankle with bitterness in his mind. In the tones of his voice is an expression of utter incredulity. Would God treat His own Son thus? Would He leave Him in the desert with wild beasts, without food, without companions, without comfort? He insinuates that God never meant His Son to be in such a state as this. "If Thou be the Son of God," show Thy power by relieving Thyself of this pressing hunger. Command that this stone be made bread.

The words from heaven, "This is My beloved Son, in whom I am well pleased," Matthew 3:17, were still sounding in the ears of Satan. But he was determined to make Christ disbelieve this testimony. The word of God was Christ's assurance of His divine mission. He had come to live as a man among men, and it was the word that declared His connection with heaven. It was Satan's purpose to cause Him to doubt that word. If Christ's confidence in God could be shaken, Satan knew that the victory in the whole controversy would be his. He could overcome Jesus. He hoped that under the force of despondency and extreme hunger, Christ would lose faith in His Father, and work a miracle in His own behalf. Had He done this, the plan of salvation would have been broken.

When Satan and the Son of God first met in conflict, Christ was the commander of the heavenly hosts; and Satan, the leader of revolt in heaven, was cast out. Now their condition is apparently reversed, and Satan makes the most of his supposed advantage. One of the most powerful of the angels, he says, has been banished from heaven. The appearance of Jesus indicates that He is that fallen angel, forsaken by God, and deserted by man. A divine being would be able to sustain his claim by working a miracle; "if Thou be the Son of God, command this stone that it be made bread." Such an act of creative power, urges the tempter, would be conclusive evidence of divinity. It would bring the controversy to an end.

Not without a struggle could Jesus listen in silence to the arch-deceiver. But the Son of God was not to prove His divinity to Satan, or to explain the reason of His humiliation. By conceding to the demands of the rebel, nothing for the good of man or the glory of God would be gained. Had Christ complied with the suggestion of the enemy, Satan would still have said, "Show me a sign that I may believe you to be the Son of God." Evidence would have been worthless to break the power of rebellion in his heart. And Christ was not to exercise divine power for His own benefit. He had come to bear trial as we must do, leaving us an example of faith and submission. Neither here nor at any subsequent time in His earthly life did He work a miracle in His own behalf. His wonderful works were all for the good of others. Though Jesus recognized Satan from the beginning, He was not provoked to enter into controversy with him. Strengthened with the memory of the voice from heaven, He rested in His Father's love. He would not parley with temptation.

> "In our own strength it is impossible for us to deny the clamors of our fallen nature. . . . Christ knew that the enemy would come to every human being, to take advantage of hereditary weakness . . . And by passing over the ground which man must travel, our Lord has prepared the way for us to overcome."

Jesus met Satan with the words of Scripture. "It is written," He said. In every temptation the weapon of His warfare was the word of God. Satan demanded of Christ a miracle as a sign of His divinity. But that which is greater than all miracles, a firm reliance upon a "thus saith the Lord," was a sign that could not be controverted. So long as Christ held to this position, the tempter could gain no advantage.

It was in the time of greatest weakness that Christ was assailed by the fiercest temptations. Thus Satan thought to prevail. By this policy he had gained the victory over men. When strength failed, and the will power weakened, and faith ceased to repose in God, then those who had stood long and valiantly for the right, were overcome. Moses was wearied with the forty years' wandering of Israel, when for the moment his faith let go its hold upon infinite power. He failed just upon the borders of the promised land. So with Elijah, who had stood undaunted before King Ahab; who had faced the whole nation of Israel, with the four hundred and fifty prophets of Baal at their head. After that terrible day upon Carmel, when the false prophets had been slain, and the people had declared their allegiance to God, Elijah fled for his life before the threats of the idolatrous Jezebel. Thus Satan has taken advantage of the weakness of humanity. And he will still work in the same way. Whenever one is encompassed with clouds, perplexed by circumstances, or afflicted by poverty or distress, Satan is at hand to tempt and annoy. He attacks our weak points of character. He seeks to shake our confidence in God, who suffers such a condition of things to exist. We are tempted to distrust God, to question His love. Often the tempter comes to us as he came to Christ, arraying before us our weakness and infirmities. He hopes to discourage the soul, and to break our hold on God. Then he is sure of his prey. If we would meet him as Jesus did, we should escape many a defeat. By parleying with the enemy, we give him an advantage.

When Christ said to the tempter, "Man shall not live by bread alone, but by every word that proceedeth out of the mouth of God," He repeated the words that, more than fourteen hundred years before, He had spoken to Israel: "The Lord thy God led thee these forty years in the wilderness, . . . and He humbled thee, and suffered thee to hunger, and fed thee with manna, which thou knewest not, neither did thy fathers know; that He might make thee know that man doth not live by bread only, but by every word that proceedeth out of the mouth of the Lord doth man live." Deuteronomy 8:2, 3. In the wilderness, when all means of sustenance failed, God sent His people manna from heaven; and a sufficient and constant supply was given. This provision was to teach them that while they trusted in God, and walked in His ways, He would not forsake them. The Saviour now practiced the lesson He had taught to Israel. By the word of God, succor had been given to the Hebrew host, and by the same word it would be given to Jesus. He awaited God's time to bring relief. He was in the wilderness in obedience to God, and He would not obtain food by following the suggestions of Satan. In the presence of the witnessing universe, He testified that it is a less calamity to suffer whatever may befall, than to depart in any manner from the will of God.

"Man shall not live by bread alone, but by every word of God." Often the follower of Christ is brought where he cannot serve God and carry forward his worldly enterprises. Perhaps it appears that obedience to some plain requirement of God will cut off his means of support. Satan would make him believe that he must sacrifice his conscientious convictions. But the only thing in our world upon which we can rely, is the word of God. "Seek ye first the kingdom of God, and His righteousness; and all these things shall be added unto you." Matthew 6:33. Even in

this life it is not for our good to depart from the will of our Father in heaven. When we learn the power of His word, we shall not follow the suggestions of Satan in order to obtain food or to save our lives. Our only questions will be, What is God's command? and what His promise? Knowing these, we shall obey the one, and trust the other.

In the last great conflict of the controversy with Satan those who are loyal to God will see every earthly support cut off. Because they refuse to break His law in obedience to earthly powers, they will be forbidden to buy or sell. It will finally be decreed that they shall be put to death. (See Revelation 13:11-17.) But to the obedient is given the promise, "He shall dwell on high; his place of defense shall be the munitions of rocks, bread shall be given him; his waters shall be sure." Isaiah 33:16. By this promise the children of God will live. When the earth shall be wasted with famine, they shall be fed. "They shall be ashamed in the evil time; and in the days of famine they shall be satisfied." Psalms 37:19. To that time of distress the prophet Habakkuk looked forward, and his words express the faith of the church: "Although the fig tree shall not blossom, neither shall fruit be in the vines; the labor of the olive shall fail, and the fields shall yield no meat; the flock shall be cut off from the fold, and there shall be no herd in the stalls; yet I will rejoice in the Lord, I will joy in the God of my salvation." Habakkuk 3:17,18.

Of all the lessons to be learned from our Lord's first great temptation, none is more important than that bearing upon the control of the appetites and passions. In all ages, temptations appealing to the physical nature have been most effectual in corrupting and degrading mankind. Through intemperance, Satan works to destroy the mental and moral powers that God gave to man as a priceless endowment. Thus it becomes impossible for men to appreciate things of eternal worth. Through sensual indulgence, Satan seeks to blot from the soul every trace of likeness to God.

The uncontrolled indulgence and consequent disease and degradation that existed at Christ's first advent, will again exist, with intensity of evil, before His second coming. Christ declares that the condition of the world will be as in the days before the flood, and as in Sodom and Gomorrah. Every imagination of the thoughts of the heart will be evil continually. Upon the very verge of that fearful time we are now living, and to us should come home the lesson of the Saviour's fast. Only by the inexpressible anguish which Christ endured, can we estimate the evil of unrestrained indulgence. His example declares that our only hope of eternal life is through bringing the appetites and passions into subjection to the will of God.

In our own strength it is impossible for us to deny the clamors of our fallen nature. Through this channel Satan will bring temptation upon us. Christ knew that the enemy would come to every human being, to take advantage of hereditary weakness, and by his false insinuations to ensnare all whose trust is not in God. And by passing over the ground which man must travel, our Lord has prepared the way for us to overcome. It is not His will that we should be placed at a disadvantage in the conflict with Satan. He would not have us intimidated and discouraged by the assaults of the serpent. "Be of good cheer," He says; "I have overcome the world." John 16:33.

Let him who is struggling against the power of appetite, look to the Saviour in the wilderness of temptation. See Him in His agony upon the cross, as He exclaimed, "I thirst." He has endured all that it is possible for us to bear. His victory is ours.

Jesus rested upon the wisdom and strength of His Heavenly Father. He declares, "The Lord God will help Me; therefore shall I not be confounded, . . . and I know that I shall not be ashamed. . . . Behold, the Lord God will help Me." Pointing to His own example, He says to us, "Who is among you that feareth the Lord, . . . that walketh in darkness, and hath no light? Let him trust in the name of the Lord, and stay upon his God." Isaiah 50:7-10.

"The prince of this world cometh," said Jesus, "and hath nothing in Me." John 14:30. There was in Him nothing that responded to Satan's sophistry. He did not consent to sin. Not even by a thought did He yield to temptation. So it may be with us. Christ's humanity was united with divinity; He was fitted for the conflict by the indwelling of the Holy Spirit. And He came to make us partakers of the divine nature. So long as we are united to Him by faith, sin has no more dominion over us. God reaches for the hand of faith in us to direct it to lay fast hold upon the divinity of Christ, that we may attain to perfection of character.

And how this is accomplished, Christ has shown us. By what means did He overcome in the conflict with Satan? — By the word of God. Only by the word could He resist temptation. "It is written," He said. And unto us are given "exceeding great and precious promises, that by these ye might be partakers of the divine nature, having escaped the corruption that is in the world through lust." 2 Peter 1:4. Every promise in God's word is ours. "By every word that proceedeth out of the mouth of God" are we to live. When assailed by temptation, look not to circumstances or to the weakness of self, but to the power of the word. All its strength is yours. "Thy word," says the psalmist, "have I hid in mine heart, that I might not sin against Thee." "By the word of Thy lips I have kept me from the paths of the destroyer." Psalms 119:11; 17:4.

The Victory

Then the devil taketh Him up into the holy city, and setteth Him on a pinnacle of the temple, and saith unto Him, If Thou be the Son of God, cast Thyself down; for it is written, —

"He shall give His angels charge concerning Thee;
And in their hands they shall bear Thee up,
Lest at any time Thou dash Thy foot against a stone."

Satan now supposes that he has met Jesus on His own ground. The wily foe himself presents words that proceeded from the mouth of God. He still appears as an angel of light, and he makes it evident that he is acquainted with the Scriptures, and understands the import of what is written. As Jesus before used the word of God to sustain His faith, the tempter now uses it to countenance his deception. He claims that he has been only testing the fidelity of Jesus, and he now commends His steadfastness. As the Saviour has manifested trust in God, Satan urges Him to give still another evidence of His faith.

But again the temptation is prefaced with the insinuation of distrust, "*If* Thou be the Son of God." Christ was tempted to answer the "if;" but He refrained from the slightest acceptance of the doubt. He would not imperil His life in order to give evidence to Satan.

The tempter thought to take advantage of Christ's humanity, and urge Him to presumption. But while Satan can solicit, he cannot compel to sin. He said to Jesus, "Cast Thyself down," knowing that he could not cast Him down; for God would interpose to deliver Him. Nor could Satan force Jesus to cast Himself down. Unless Christ should consent to temptation, He could not be overcome. Not all the power of earth or hell could force Him in the slightest degree to depart from the will of His Father.

The tempter can never compel us to do evil. He cannot control minds unless they are yielded to his control. The will must consent, faith must let go its hold upon Christ, before Satan can exercise his power upon us. But every sinful desire we cherish affords him a foothold. Every point in which we fail of meeting the divine standard, is an open door by which he can enter to tempt and destroy us. And every failure or defeat on our part gives occasion for him to reproach Christ.

When Satan quoted the promise, "He shall give His angels charge over Thee," he omitted the words, "to keep Thee in all Thy ways;" that is, in all the ways of God's choosing. Jesus refused to go outside the path of obedience. While manifesting perfect trust in His Father, He would not place Himself, unbidden, in a position that would necessitate the interposition of His Father to save Him from death. He would not force Providence to come to His rescue, and thus fail of giving man an example of trust and submission.

Jesus declared to Satan, "It is written again, Thou shalt not tempt the Lord thy God." These words were spoken by Moses to the children of Israel when they thirsted in the desert, and demanded that Moses should give them water, exclaiming, "Is the Lord among us, or not?" Exodus 17:7. God had wrought marvelously for them; yet in trouble they doubted Him, and demanded evidence that He was with them. In their unbelief they sought to put Him to the test. And Satan was urging Christ to do the same thing. God had already testified that Jesus was His Son; and now to ask for proof that He was the Son of God, would be putting God's word to the test, — tempting Him. And the same would be true of asking for that which God had not promised. It would manifest distrust, and be really proving or tempting Him. We should not present our petitions to God to *prove* whether He will fulfill His word, but *because* He will fulfill it; not to prove that He loves us, but because He loves us. "Without faith it is impossible to please Him; for he that cometh to God must believe that He is, and that He is a rewarder of them that diligently seek Him." Hebrews 11:6.

But faith is in no sense allied to presumption. Only he who has true faith is secure against presumption. For presumption is Satan's counterfeit of faith. Faith claims God's promises, and brings forth fruit in obedience. Presumption also claims the promises, but uses them as Satan did, to excuse transgression. Faith would have led our first parents to trust the love of God, and to obey His commands. Presumption led them to transgress His law, believing that His great love would save them from the consequence of their sin. It is not faith that claims the favor of Heaven without complying with the conditions on which mercy is to be granted. Genuine faith has its foundation in the promises and provisions of the Scriptures.

Often when Satan has failed of exciting distrust, he succeeds in leading us to presumption. If he can cause us to place ourselves unnecessarily in the way of temptation, he knows that the victory is his. God will preserve all who walk in the path of obedience; but to depart from it is to venture on Satan's ground. There we are sure to fall. The Saviour has bidden us, "Watch ye and pray, lest ye enter into temptation." Mark 14:38. Meditation and prayer would keep us from rushing unbidden into the way of danger, and thus we should be saved from many a defeat.

Yet we should not lose courage when assailed by temptation. Often when placed in a trying situation we doubt that the Spirit of God has been leading us. But it was the Spirit's leading that brought Jesus into the wilderness to be tempted by Satan. When God brings us into trial, He has a purpose to accomplish for our good. Jesus did not presume on God's promises by going unbidden into temptation, neither did He give up to despondency when temptation came upon Him. Nor should we. "God is faithful, who will not suffer you to be tempted above that ye are able; but will with the temptation also make a way to escape, that ye may be able to bear it." He says, "Offer unto God thanksgiving; and pay thy vows unto the Most High; and call upon Me in the day of trouble; I will deliver thee, and thou shalt glorify Me." 1 Corinthians 10:13; Psalms 50:14, 15.

Jesus was victor in the second temptation, and now Satan manifests himself in his true character. But he does not appear as a hideous monster, with cloven feet and bats' wings. He is a mighty angel, though fallen. He avows himself the leader of rebellion and the god of this world.

Placing Jesus upon a high mountain, Satan caused the kingdoms of the world, in all their glory, to pass in panoramic view before Him. The sunlight lay on templed cities, marble palaces, fertile fields, and fruit-laden vineyards. The traces of evil were hidden. The eyes of Jesus, so lately greeted by gloom and desolation, now gazed upon a scene of unsurpassed loveliness and prosperity. Then the tempter's voice was heard: "All this power will I give Thee, and the glory of them; for that is delivered unto me; and to whomsoever I will I give it. If Thou therefore wilt worship me, all shall be Thine."

Christ's mission could be fulfilled only through suffering. Before Him was a life of sorrow, hardship, and conflict, and an ignominious death. He must bear the sins of

---

"Now Satan manifests himself in his true character. But he does not appear as a hideous monster, with cloven feet and bat's wings. He is a mighty angel, though fallen. He avows himself the leader of rebellion and the god of this world."

---

the whole world. He must endure separation from His Father's love. Now the tempter offered to yield up the power he had usurped. Christ might deliver Himself from the dreadful future by acknowledging the supremacy of Satan. But to do this was to yield the victory in the great controversy. It was in seeking to exalt himself above the Son of God, that Satan had sinned in heaven. Should he prevail now, it would be the triumph of rebellion.

When Satan declared to Christ, The kingdom and glory of the world are delivered unto me, and to whomsoever I will I give it, he stated what was true only in part, and he declared it to serve his own purpose of deception. Satan's dominion was that wrested from Adam, but Adam was the vicegerent of the Creator. His was not an independent rule. The earth is God's, and He has committed all things to His Son. Adam was to reign subject to Christ. When Adam betrayed his sovereignty into Satan's hands, Christ still remained the rightful King. Thus the Lord had said to King Nebuchadnezzar, "The Most High ruleth in the kingdom of men, and giveth it to whomsoever He will." Daniel 4:17. Satan can exercise his usurped authority only as God permits.

When the tempter offered to Christ the kingdom and glory of the world, he was proposing that Christ should yield up the real kingship of the world, and hold dominion subject to Satan. This was the same dominion upon which the hopes of the Jews were set. They desired the kingdom of this world. If Christ had consented to offer them such a kingdom, they would gladly have received Him. But the curse of sin, with all its woe, rested upon it. Christ declared to the tempter, "Get thee behind Me, Satan; for it is written, Thou shalt worship the Lord thy God, and Him only shalt thou serve."

By the one who had revolted in heaven, the kingdoms of this world were offered Christ, to buy His homage to the principles of evil; but He would not be bought; He had come to establish a kingdom of righteousness, and He would not abandon His purpose. With the same temptation Satan approaches men, and here he has better success than with Christ. To men he offers the kingdom of this world on condition that they will acknowledge his supremacy. He requires that they sacrifice integrity, disregard conscience, indulge selfishness. Christ bids them seek first the kingdom of God, and His righteousness; but Satan walks by their side and says, "Whatever may be true in regard to life eternal, in order to make a success in this world you must serve me. I hold your welfare in my hands. I can give you riches, pleasures, honor, and happiness. Hearken to my counsel. Do not allow yourselves to be carried away with whimsical notions of honesty or self-sacrifice. I will prepare the way before you." Thus multitudes are deceived. They consent to live for the service of self, and Satan is satisfied. While he allures them with the hope of worldly dominion, he gains dominion over the soul. But he offers that which is not his to bestow, and which is soon to be wrested from him. In return he beguiles them of their title to the inheritance of the sons of God.

Satan had questioned whether Jesus was the Son of God. In his summary dismissal he had proof that he could not gainsay. Divinity flashed through suffering humanity. Satan had no power to resist the command. Writhing with humiliation and rage, he was forced to withdraw from the presence of the world's Redeemer. Christ's victory was as complete as had been the failure of Adam.

So we may resist temptation, and force Satan to depart from us. Jesus gained the victory through submission and faith in God, and by the apostle He says to us, "Submit yourselves therefore to God. Resist the devil, and he will flee from you. Draw nigh to God, and He will draw nigh to you." James 4:7, 8. We cannot save ourselves from the tempter's power; he has conquered humanity, and when we try to stand in our own strength, we shall become a prey to his devices; but "the name of the Lord is a strong tower; the righteous runneth into it, and is safe." Proverbs 18:10. Satan trembles and flees before the weakest soul who finds refuge in that mighty name.

After the foe had departed, Jesus fell exhausted to the earth, with the pallor of death upon His face. The angels of heaven had watched the conflict, beholding their loved Commander as He passed through inexpressible suffering to make a way of escape for us. He had endured the test, greater than we shall ever be called to endure. The angels now ministered to the Son of God, as He lay like one dying. He was strengthened with food, comforted with the message of His Father's love, and the assurance that all heaven triumphed in His victory. Warming to life again, His great heart goes out in sympathy for man, and He goes forth to complete the work He has begun; to rest not until the foe is vanquished, and our fallen race redeemed.

Never can the cost of our redemption be realized until the redeemed shall stand with the Redeemer before the throne of God. Then as the glories of the eternal home burst upon our enraptured senses, we shall remember that Jesus left all this for us, that He not only became an exile from the heavenly courts, but for us took the risk of failure and eternal loss. Then we shall cast our crowns at His feet, and raise the song, "Worthy is the Lamb that was slain to receive power, and riches, and wisdom, and strength, and honor, and glory, and blessing." Revelation 5:12.

"We Have Found the Messias"

John the Baptist was now preaching and baptizing at Bethabara, beyond Jordan. It was not far from this spot that God had stayed the river in its flow until Israel had passed over. A little distance from here the stronghold of Jericho had been overthrown by the armies of heaven. The memory of these events was at this time revived, and gave a thrilling interest to the Baptist's message. Would not He who had wrought so wonderfully in ages past, again manifest His power for Israel's deliverance? Such was the thought stirring the hearts of the people who daily thronged the banks of the Jordan.

The preaching of John had taken so deep a hold on the nation as to demand the attention of the religious authorities. The danger of insurrection caused every popular gathering to be looked upon with suspicion by the Romans, and whatever pointed toward an uprising of the people excited the fears of the Jewish rulers. John had not recognized the authority of the Sanhedrim by seeking their sanction for his work; and he had reproved rulers and people, Pharisees and Sadducees alike. Yet the people followed him eagerly. The interest in his work seemed to be continually increasing. Though he had not deferred to them, the Sanhedrim accounted that, as a public teacher, he was under their jurisdiction.

This body was made up of members chosen from the priesthood, and from the chief rulers and teachers of the nation. The high priest was usually the president. All its members were to be men advanced in years, though not aged; men of learning, not only versed in Jewish religion and history, but in general knowledge. They were to be without physical blemish, and must be married men, and fathers, as being more likely than others to be humane and considerate. Their place of meeting was an apartment connected with the temple at Jerusalem. In the days of Jewish independence the Sanhedrim was the supreme court of the nation, possessing secular as well as ecclesiastical authority. Though now subordinated by the Roman governors, it still exercised a strong influence in civil as well as religious matters.

The Sanhedrim could not well defer an investigation of John's work. There were some who recalled the revelation made to Zacharias in the temple, and the father's prophecy, that had pointed to his child as the Messiah's herald. In the tumults and changes of thirty years, these things had in a great measure been lost sight of. They were now called to mind by the excitement concerning the ministry of John.

It was long since Israel had had a prophet, long since such a reformation as was now in progress had been witnessed. The demand for confession of sin seemed new and startling. Many among the leaders would not go to hear John's appeals and denunciations, lest they should be led to disclose the secrets of their own lives. Yet his preaching was a direct announcement of the Messiah. It was well known that the seventy weeks of Daniel's prophecy, covering the Messiah's advent, were nearly ended; and all were eager to share in that era of national glory which was then expected. Such was the popular enthusiasm that the Sanhedrim would soon be forced either to sanction or to reject John's work. Already their power over the people was waning. It was becoming a serious question how to maintain their position. In the hope of arriving at some conclusion, they dispatched to the Jordan a deputation of priests and Levites to confer with the new teacher.

A multitude were gathered, listening to his words, when the delegates approached. With an air of authority designed to impress the people, and to command the defer-

This chapter is based on John 1:19-51.

ence of the prophet, the haughty rabbis came. With a movement of respect, almost of fear, the crowd opened to let them pass. The great men, in their rich robes, in the pride of rank and power, stood before the prophet of the wilderness.

"Who art thou?" they demanded.

Knowing what was in their thoughts, John answered, "I am not the Christ."

"What then? Art thou Elias?"

"I am not."

"Art thou that prophet?"

"No."

"Who art thou? that we may give an answer to them that sent us. What sayest thou of thyself?"

"I am the voice of one crying in the wilderness, Make straight the way of the Lord, as said the prophet Esaias."

The scripture to which John referred is that beautiful prophecy of Isaiah: "Comfort ye, comfort ye My people, saith your God. Speak ye comfortably to Jerusalem, and cry unto her, that her appointed time is accomplished, that her iniquity is pardoned. . . . The voice of him that crieth in the wilderness, Prepare ye the way of the Lord, make straight in the desert a highway for our God. Every valley shall be exalted, and every mountain and hill shall be made low; and the crooked shall be made straight, and the rough places plain; and the glory of the Lord shall be revealed, and all flesh shall see it together." Isaiah 40: 1-5, margin.

Anciently, when a king journeyed through the less frequented parts of his dominion, a company of men was sent ahead of the royal chariot to level the steep places and to fill up the hollows, that the king might travel in safety and without hindrance. This custom is employed by the prophet to illustrate the work of the gospel. "Every valley shall be exalted, and every mountain and hill shall be made low" When the Spirit of God, with its marvelous awakening power, touches the soul, it abases human pride. Worldly pleasure and position and power are seen to be worthless. "Imaginations, and every high thing that exalteth itself against the knowledge of God," (2 Corinthians 10:5.) are cast down; every thought is brought into captivity "to the obedience of Christ." Then humility and self-sacrificing love, so little valued among men, are exalted as alone of worth. This is the work of the gospel, of which John's message was a part.

The rabbis continued their questioning: "Why baptizest thou then, if thou be not that Christ, nor Elias, neither that prophet?" The words "that prophet" had reference to Moses. The Jews had been inclined to the belief that Moses would be raised from the dead, and taken to heaven. They did not know that he had already been raised. When the Baptist began his ministry, many thought that he might be the prophet Moses risen from the dead; for he seemed to have a thorough knowledge of the prophecies and of the history of Israel.

It was believed also that before the Messiah's advent, Elijah would personally appear. This expectation John met

in his denial; but his words had a deeper meaning. Jesus afterward said, referring to John, "If ye are willing to receive it, this is Elijah, which is to come." Matthew 11:14, R. V. John came in the spirit and power of Elijah, to do such a work as Elijah did. If the Jews had received him, it would have been accomplished for them. But they did not receive his message. To them he was not Elijah. He could not fulfill for them the mission he came to accomplish.

Many of those gathered at the Jordan had been present at the baptism of Jesus; but the sign then given had been manifest to but few among them. During the preceding months of the Baptist's ministry, many had refused to heed the call to repentance. Thus they had hardened their hearts and darkened their understanding. When Heaven bore testimony to Jesus at His baptism, they perceived it not. Eyes that had never been turned in faith to Him that is invisible, beheld not the revelation of the glory of God; ears that had never listened to His voice, heard not the words of witness. So it is now. Often the presence of Christ and the ministering angels is manifest in the assemblies of the people, and yet there are many who know it not. They discern nothing unusual. But to some the Saviour's presence is revealed. Peace and joy animate their hearts. They are comforted, encouraged, and blessed.

The deputies from Jerusalem had demanded of John, "Why baptizest thou?" and they were awaiting his answer. Suddenly, as his glance swept over the throng, his eye kindled, his face was lighted up, his whole being was stirred with deep emotion. With outstretched hands he cried, "I baptize in water; in the midst of you standeth One whom ye know not; even He that cometh after me, the latchet of whose shoe I am not worthy to unloose." John 1:27, R. V., Margin.

The message was distinct and unequivocal, to be carried back to the Sanhedrim. The words of John could apply to no other than the long-promised One. The Messiah was among them! In amazement priests and rulers gazed about them, hoping to discover Him of whom John had spoken. But He was not distinguishable among the throng.

When at the baptism of Jesus, John pointed to Him as the Lamb of God, a new light was shed upon the Messiah's work. The prophet's mind was directed to the words of Isaiah, "He is brought as a lamb to the slaughter." Isaiah 53:7. During the weeks that followed, John with new interest studied the prophecies and the teaching of the sacrificial service. He did not distinguish clearly the two phases of Christ's work, — as a suffering sacrifice and a conquering king, — but he saw that His coming had a deeper significance than priests or people had discerned. When he beheld Jesus among the throng, on His return from the desert, he confidently looked for Him to give the people some sign of His true character. Almost impatiently he waited to hear the Saviour declare His mission; but no word was spoken, no sign given. Jesus did not respond to the Baptist's announcement of Him, but mingled with the disciples of John, giving no outward evidence of His special work, and taking no measures to bring Himself to notice.

The next day John sees Jesus coming. With the light of the glory of God resting upon him, the prophet stretches out his hands, declaring, "Behold the Lamb of God, which taketh away the sin of the world. This is He of whom I said, After me cometh a man which is become before me; . . . and I knew Him not; but that He should be made manifest to Israel, for this cause came I baptizing in water. . . . I have beheld the Spirit descending as a dove out of

---

> **"Was this the Christ? . . . Every glance of the eye, every feature of the countenance, was marked with humility, and expressive of unutterable love. He seemed to be surrounded by an atmosphere of spiritual influence. . . . Was this the One for whom Israel had so long waited?"**

---

heaven; and it abode upon Him. And I knew Him not; but He that sent me to baptize in water, He said unto me, Upon whomsoever thou shalt see the Spirit descending, and abiding upon Him, the same is He that baptizeth with the Holy Spirit. And I have seen, and have borne witness that this is the Son of God." John 1:29-34, R.V., margin

Was this the Christ? With awe and wonder the people looked upon the One just declared to be the Son of God. They had been deeply moved by the words of John. He had spoken to them in the name of God. They had listened to him day after day as he reproved their sins, and daily the conviction that he was sent of Heaven had strengthened. But who was this One greater than John the Baptist? In His dress and bearing there was nothing that betokened rank. He was apparently a simple personage, clad like themselves in the humble garments of the poor.

There were in the throng some who at Christ's baptism had beheld the divine glory, and had heard the voice of God. But since that time the Saviour's appearance had greatly changed. At His baptism they had seen His countenance transfigured in the light of heaven; now, pale, worn, and emaciated, He had been recognized only by the prophet John.

But as the people looked upon Him, they saw a face where divine compassion was blended with conscious power. Every glance of the eye, every feature of the countenance, was marked with humility, and expressive of unutterable love. He seemed to be surrounded by an atmosphere of spiritual influence. While His manners were gentle and unassuming, He impressed men with a sense of power that was hidden, yet could not be wholly concealed. Was this the One for whom Israel had so long waited?

Jesus came in poverty and humiliation, that He might be our example as well as our Redeemer. If He had appeared with kingly pomp, how could He have taught humility? how could He have presented such cutting truths as in the sermon on the mount? Where would have been the hope of the lowly in life, had Jesus come to dwell as a king among men?

To the multitude, however, it seemed impossible that the One designated by John should be associated with their lofty anticipations. Thus many were disappointed, and greatly perplexed.

The words which the priests and rabbis so much desired to hear, that Jesus would now restore the kingdom to Israel, had not been spoken. For such a king they had been waiting and watching; such a king they were ready to receive. But one who sought to establish in their hearts a kingdom of righteousness and peace, they would not accept.

On the following day, while two disciples were standing near, John again saw Jesus among the people. Again the face of the prophet was lighted up with glory from the Unseen, as he cried, "Behold the Lamb of God!" The words thrilled the hearts of the disciples. They did not fully understand them. What meant the name that John had given Him, — "the Lamb of God"? John himself had not explained it.

Leaving John, they went to seek Jesus. One of the two was Andrew, the brother of Simon; the other was John the evangelist. These were Christ's first disciples. Moved by an irresistible impulse, they followed Jesus, — anxious to speak with Him, yet awed and silent, lost in the overwhelming significance of the thought, "Is this the Messiah?"

Jesus knew that the disciples were following Him. They were the first fruits of His ministry, and there was joy in the heart of the divine Teacher as these souls responded to His grace. Yet turning, He asked only, "What seek ye?" He would leave them free to turn back, or to speak of their desire.

Of one purpose only were they conscious. One presence filled their thought. They exclaimed, "Rabbi, where dwellest *Thou?*" In a brief interview by the wayside they could not receive that for which they longed. They desired to be alone with Jesus, to sit at His feet, and hear His words.

"He saith unto them, Come and see. They came, and saw where He dwelt, and abode with Him that day."

If John and Andrew had possessed the unbelieving spirit of the priests and rulers, they would not have been found as learners at the feet of Jesus. They would have come to Him as critics, to judge His words. Many thus close the door to the most precious opportunities. But not so did these first disciples. They had responded to the Holy Spirit's call in the preaching of John the Baptist. Now they recognized the voice of the heavenly Teacher. To them the words of Jesus were full of freshness and truth and beauty. A divine illumination was shed upon the teaching of the Old Testament Scriptures. The many-sided themes of truth stood out in new light.

It is contrition and faith and love that enable the soul to receive wisdom from heaven. Faith working by love is the key of knowledge, and every one that loveth "knoweth God." 1 John 4:7.

The disciple John was a man of earnest and deep affection, ardent, yet contemplative. He had begun to discern the glory of Christ, — not the worldly pomp and power for which he had been taught to hope, but "the glory as of the Only begotten of the Father, full of grace and truth." John 1:14. He was absorbed in contemplation of the wondrous theme.

Andrew sought to impart the joy that filled his heart. Going in search of his brother Simon, he cried, "We have found the Messias" Simon waited for no second bidding. He also had heard the preaching of John the Baptist, and he hastened to the Saviour. The eye of Christ rested upon him, reading his character and his life history. His impulsive nature, his loving, sympathetic heart, his ambition and self-confidence, the history of his fall, his repentance, his labors and his martyr death, — the Saviour read it all, and He said, "Thou art Simon the son of Jona; thou shalt be called Cephas, which is by interpretation, A stone."

"The day following Jesus would go forth into Galilee, and findeth Philip, and saith unto him, Follow Me." Philip obeyed the command, and straightway he also became a worker for Christ.

Philip called Nathanael. The latter had been among the throng when the Baptist pointed to Jesus as the Lamb of God. As Nathanael looked upon Jesus, he was disappointed. Could this man, who bore the marks of toil and poverty, be the Messiah? Yet Nathanael could not decide to reject Jesus; for the message of John had brought conviction to his heart.

At the time when Philip called him, Nathanael had withdrawn to a quiet grove to meditate upon the announcement of John, and the prophecies concerning the Messiah. He prayed that if the one announced by John was the deliverer, it might be made known to him, and the Holy Spirit rested upon him with assurance that God had visited His people and raised up a horn of salvation for them.

Philip knew that his friend was searching the prophecies, and while Nathanael was praying under a fig tree, Philip discovered his retreat. They had often prayed together in this secluded spot, hidden by the foliage.

The message, "We have found Him, of whom Moses in the law, and the prophets, did write," seemed to Nathanael a direct answer to his prayer. But Philip had yet a trembling faith. He added doubtfully, "Jesus of Nazareth, the son of Joseph." Again prejudice arose in Nathanael's heart. He exclaimed, "Can there any good thing come out of Nazareth?"

Philip entered into no controversy. He said, "Come and see. Jesus saw Nathanael coming to Him, and saith of him, Behold an Israelite indeed, in whom is no guile!" In surprise Nathanael exclaimed, "Whence knowest Thou me? Jesus answered and said unto him, Before that Philip called thee, when thou wast under the fig tree, I saw thee."

It was enough. The divine Spirit that had borne witness to Nathanael in his solitary prayer under the fig tree, now spoke to him in the words of Jesus. Though in doubt, and yielding somewhat to prejudice, Nathanael had come to Christ with an honest desire for truth, and now his desire was met. His faith went beyond that of the one who had brought him to Jesus. He answered and said, "Rabbi, Thou art the Son of God; Thou art the King of Israel."

If Nathanael had trusted to the rabbis for guidance, he would never have found Jesus. It was by seeing and judging for himself that he became a disciple. So in the case of many today whom prejudice withholds from good. How different would be the result, if they would "come and see."

While they trust to the guidance of human authority, none will come to a saving knowledge of the truth. Like Nathanael, we need to study God's word for ourselves, and pray for the enlightenment of the Holy Spirit. He who saw Nathanael under the fig tree, will see us in the secret place of prayer. Angels from the world of light are near to those who in humility seek for divine guidance.

With the calling of John and Andrew and Simon, of Philip and Nathanael, began the foundation of the Christian church. John directed two of his disciples to Christ. Then one of these, Andrew, found his brother, and called him to the Saviour. Philip was then called, and he went in search of Nathanael. These examples should teach us the importance of personal effort, of making direct appeals to our kindred, friends, and neighbors. There are those who for a lifetime have professed to be acquainted with Christ, yet who have never made a personal effort to bring even one soul to the Saviour. They leave all the work for the minister. He may be well qualified for his calling, but he cannot do that which God has left for the members of the church.

There are many who need the ministration of loving Christian hearts. Many have gone down to ruin who might have been saved, if their neighbors, common men and women, had put forth personal effort for them. Many are waiting to be personally addressed. In the very family, the neighborhood, the town where we live, there is work for us to do as missionaries for Christ. If we are Christians, this work will be our delight. No sooner is one converted than there is born within him a desire to make known to others what a precious friend he has found in Jesus. The saving and sanctifying truth cannot be shut up in his heart.

All who are consecrated to God will be channels of light. God makes them His agents to communicate to others the riches of His grace. His promise is, "I will make them and the places round about My hill a blessing; and I will cause the shower to come down in his season; there shall be showers of blessing." Ezekiel 34:26.

Philip said to Nathanael, "Come and see." He did not ask him to accept another's testimony, but to behold Christ for himself. Now that Jesus has ascended to heaven, His disciples are His representatives among men, and one of the most effective ways of winning souls to Him is in exemplifying His character in our daily life. Our influence upon others depends not so much upon what we say, as upon what we are. Men may combat and defy our logic, they may resist our appeals; but a life of disinterested love is an argument they cannot gainsay. A consistent life, characterized by the meekness of Christ, is a power in the world.

The teaching of Christ was the expression of an in-wrought conviction and experience, and those who learn of Him become teachers after the divine order. The word of God, spoken by one who is himself sanctified through it, has a life-giving power that makes it attractive to the hearers, and convicts them that it is a living reality. When one has received the truth in the love of it, he will make this manifest in the persuasion of his manner and the tones of his voice. He makes known that which he himself has heard, seen, and handled of the word of life, that others may have fellowship with him through the knowledge of Christ. His testimony, from lips touched with a live coal from off the altar, is truth to the receptive heart, and works sanctification upon the character.

And he who seeks to give light to others, will himself be blessed. "There shall be showers of blessing." "He that watereth shall be watered also himself." Proverbs 11:25. God could have reached His object in saving sinners without our aid; but in order for us to develop a character like Christ's, we must share in His work. In order to enter into His joy,— the joy of seeing souls redeemed by His sacrifice,—we must participate in His labors for their redemption.

Nathanael's first expression of his faith, so full and earnest and sincere, fell like music on the ears of Jesus. And He "answered and said unto him, Because I said unto thee, I saw thee under the fig tree, believest thou? Thou shalt see greater things than these." The Saviour looked forward with joy to His work in preaching good tidings to the meek, binding up the brokenhearted, and proclaiming liberty to the captives of Satan. At thought of the precious blessings He had brought to men, Jesus added, "Verily, verily, I say unto you, Hereafter ye shall see heaven open, and the angels of God ascending and descending upon the Son of man."

Here Christ virtually says, On the bank of the Jordan the heavens were opened, and the Spirit descended like a dove upon Me. That scene was but a token that I am the Son of God. If you believe on Me as such, your faith shall be quickened. You shall see that the heavens are opened, and are never to be closed. I have opened them to you. The angels of God are ascending, bearing the prayers of the needy and distressed to the Father above, and descending, bringing blessing and hope, courage, help, and life, to the children of men.

The angels of God are ever passing from earth to heaven, and from heaven to earth. The miracles of Christ for the afflicted and suffering were wrought by the power of God through the ministration of the angels. And it is through Christ, by the ministration of His heavenly messengers, that every blessing comes from God to us. In taking upon Himself humanity, our Saviour unites His interests with those of the fallen sons and daughters of Adam, while through His divinity He grasps the throne of God. And thus Christ is the medium of communication of men with God, and of God with men.

At the Marriage Feast

Jesus did not begin His ministry by some great work before the Sanhedrim at Jerusalem. At a household gathering in a little Galilean village, His power was put forth to add to the joy of a wedding feast. Thus He showed His sympathy with men, and His desire to minister to their happiness. In the wilderness of temptation He Himself had drank the cup of woe. He came forth to give to men the cup of blessing, by His benediction to hallow the relations of human life.

From the Jordan, Jesus had returned to Galilee. There was to be a marriage at Cana, a little town not far from Nazareth; the parties were relatives of Joseph and Mary; and Jesus, knowing of this family gathering, went to Cana, and with His disciples was invited to the feast.

Again He met His mother, from whom He had for some time been separated. Mary had heard of the manifestation at the Jordan, at His baptism. The tidings had been carried to Nazareth, and had brought to her mind afresh the scenes that for so many years had been hidden in her heart. In common with all Israel, Mary was deeply stirred by the mission of John the Baptist. Well she remembered the prophecy given at his birth. Now his connection with Jesus kindled her hopes anew. But tidings had reached her also of the mysterious departure of Jesus to the wilderness, and she was oppressed with troubled forebodings.

From the day when she heard the angel's announcement in the home at Nazareth, Mary had treasured every evidence that Jesus was the Messiah. His sweet, unselfish life assured her that He could be no other than the Sent of God. Yet there came to her also doubts and disappointments, and she had longed for the time when His glory should be revealed. Death had separated her from Joseph, who had shared her knowledge of the mystery of the birth of Jesus.

Now there was no one to whom she could confide her hopes and fears. The past two months had been very sorrowful. She had been parted from Jesus, in whose sympathy she found comfort; she pondered upon the words of Simeon, "A sword shall pierce through thy own soul also;" (Luke 2:35.) she recalled the three days of agony when she thought Jesus lost to her forever; and with an anxious heart she awaited His return.

At the marriage feast she meets Him, the same tender, dutiful son. Yet He is not the same. His countenance is changed. It bears the traces of His conflict in the wilderness, and a new expression of dignity and power gives evidence of His heavenly mission. With Him is a group of young men, whose eyes follow Him with reverence, and who call Him Master. These companions recount to Mary what they have seen and heard at the baptism and elsewhere. They conclude by declaring, "We have found Him, of whom Moses in the law, and the prophets, did write." John 1:45.

As the guests assemble, many seem to be preoccupied with some topic of absorbing interest. A suppressed excitement pervades the company. Little groups converse together in eager but quiet tones, and wondering glances are turned upon the Son of Mary. As Mary had heard the disciples' testimony in regard to Jesus, she had been gladdened with the assurance that her long-cherished hopes were not in vain. Yet she would have been more than human if there had not mingled with this holy joy a trace of the fond mother's natural pride. As she saw the many glances bent upon Jesus, she longed to have Him prove to the company that He was really the Honored of God. She hoped there might be opportunity for Him to work a miracle before them.

This chapter is based on John 2:1-11.

It was the custom of the times for marriage festivities to continue several days. On this occasion, before the feast ended it was found that the supply of wine had failed. This discovery caused much perplexity and regret. It was unusual to dispense with wine on festive occasions, and its absence would seem to indicate a want of hospitality. As a relative of the parties, Mary had assisted in the arrangements for the feast, and she now spoke to Jesus saying, "They have no wine." These words were a suggestion that He might supply their need. But Jesus answered, "Woman, what have I to do with thee? Mine hour is not yet come."

This answer, abrupt as it seems to us, expressed no coldness or discourtesy. The Saviour's form of address to His mother was in accordance with oriental custom. It was used toward persons to whom it was desired to show respect. Every act of Christ's earthly life was in harmony with the precept He Himself had given, "Honor thy father and thy mother." Exodus 20:12. On the cross, in His last act of tenderness toward His mother, Jesus again addressed her in the same way, as He committed her to the care of His best-loved disciple. Both at the marriage feast and upon the cross, the love expressed in tone and look and manner, interpreted His words.

At His visit to the temple in His boyhood, as the mystery of His lifework opened before Him, Christ had said to Mary, "Wist ye not that I must be about My Father's business?" Luke 2:49. These words struck the keynote of His whole life and ministry. Everything was held in abeyance to His work, the great work of redemption which He had come into the world to accomplish. Now He repeated the lesson. There was danger that Mary would regard her relationship to Jesus as giving her a special claim upon Him, and the right, in some degree, to direct Him in His mission. For thirty years He had been to her a loving and obedient son, and His love was unchanged; but He must now go about His Father's work. As Son of the Most High, and Saviour of the world, no earthly ties must hold Him from His mission, or influence His conduct. He must stand free to do the will of God. This lesson is also for us. The claims of God are paramount even to the ties of human relationship. No earthly attraction should turn our feet from the path in which He bids us walk.

The only hope of redemption for our fallen race is in Christ; Mary could find salvation only through the Lamb of God. In herself she possessed no merit. Her connection with Jesus placed her in no different spiritual relation to Him from that of any other human soul. This is indicated in the Saviour's words. He makes clear the distinction between His relation to her as the Son of man and as the Son of God. The tie of kinship between them in no way placed her on an equality with Him.

The words, "Mine hour is not yet come," point to the fact that every act of Christ's life on earth, was in fulfillment of the plan that had existed from the days of eternity. Before He came to earth, the plan lay out before Him, perfect in all its details. But as He walked among men, He was guided, step by step, by the Father's will. He did not hesitate to act at the appointed time. With the same submission He waited until the time had come.

In saying to Mary that His hour had not yet come, Jesus was replying to her unspoken thought, — to the expectation she cherished in common with her people. She hoped that He would reveal Himself as the Messiah, and take the throne of Israel. But the time had not come. Not as a King, but as a Man of sorrows, and acquainted with grief, had Jesus accepted the lot of humanity.

But though Mary had not a right conception of Christ's mission, she trusted Him implicitly. To this faith Jesus responded. It was to honor Mary's trust, and to strengthen the faith of His disciples, that the first miracle was performed. The disciples were to encounter many and great temptations to unbelief. To them the prophecies had made it clear beyond all controversy, that Jesus was the Messiah. They looked for the religious leaders to receive Him with confidence even greater than their own. They declared among the people the wonderful works of Christ and their own confidence in His mission, but they were amazed and bitterly disappointed by the unbelief, the deep-seated prejudice, and the enmity to Jesus, displayed by the priests and rabbis. The Saviour's early miracles strengthened the disciples to stand against this opposition.

In no wise disconcerted by the words of Jesus, Mary said to those serving at table, "Whatsoever He saith unto you, do it." Thus she did what she could to prepare the way for the work of Christ.

Beside the doorway stood six large stone water jars, and Jesus bade the servants fill these with water. It was done. Then as the wine was wanted for immediate use, He said, "Draw out now, and bear unto the governor of the feast." Instead of the water with which the vessels had been filled, there flowed forth wine. Neither the ruler of the feast nor the guests generally were aware that the supply of wine had failed. Upon tasting that which the servants brought, the ruler found it superior to any he had ever before drank, and very different from that served at the beginning of the feast. Turning to the bridegroom he said, "Every man at the beginning doth set forth good wine; and when men have well drunk, then that which is worse; but thou hast kept the good wine until now."

As men set forth the best wine first, then afterward that which is worse, so does the world with its gifts. That which it offers may please the eye and fascinate the senses, but it proves to be unsatisfying. The wine turns to bitterness, the gaiety to gloom. That which was begun with songs and mirth, ends in weariness and disgust. But the gifts of Jesus are ever fresh and new. The feast that He provides for the soul, never fails to give satisfaction and joy. Each new gift increases the capacity of the receiver to appreciate and enjoy the blessings of the Lord. He gives grace for grace. There can be no failure of supply. If you abide in Him, the fact that you receive a rich gift today, insures the reception of a richer gift tomorrow. The words of Jesus to Nathanael express the law of God's dealing with the children of faith. With every fresh revelation of His love, He declares to the receptive heart, "Believest thou? thou shalt see greater things than these." John 1:50.

The gift of Christ to the marriage feast was a symbol. The water represented baptism into His death; the wine, the shedding of His blood for the sins of the world. The water to fill the jars was brought by human hands, but the word of Christ alone could impart to it life-giving virtue. So with the rites which point to the Saviour's death. It is only by the power of Christ, working through faith, that they have efficacy to nourish the soul.

The word of Christ supplied ample provision for the feast. So abundant is the provision of His grace to blot out the iniquities of men, and to renew and sustain the soul.

At the first feast He attended with His disciples, Jesus gave them the cup that symbolized His work for their salvation. At the last supper He gave it again, in the institution of that sacred rite by which His death was to be shown forth "till He come." 1 Corinthians 11:26. And the sorrow of the disciples at parting from their Lord, was comforted with the promise of reunion, as He said, "I will not drink henceforth of this fruit of the vine, until that day when I drink it new with you in My Father's kingdom." Matthew 26:29.

The wine which Christ provided for the feast, and that which He gave to the disciples as a symbol of His own blood, was the pure juice of the grape. To this the prophet Isaiah refers when he speaks of the new wine "in the cluster," and says, "Destroy it not; for a blessing is in it." Isaiah 65:8.

It was Christ who in the Old Testament gave the warning to Israel, "Wine is a mocker, strong drink is raging; and whosoever is deceived thereby is not wise." Proverbs 20:1. And He Himself provided no such beverage. Satan tempts men to indulgence that will becloud reason and benumb the spiritual perceptions, but Christ teaches us to bring the lower nature into subjection. His whole life was an example of self-denial. In order to break the power of appetite, He suffered in our behalf the severest test that humanity could endure. It was Christ who directed that John the Baptist should drink neither wine nor strong drink. It was He who enjoined similar abstinence upon the wife of Manoah. And He pronounced a curse upon the man who should put the bottle to his neighbor's lips. Christ did not contradict His own teaching. The unfermented wine which He provided for the wedding guests was a wholesome and refreshing drink. Its effect was to bring the taste into harmony with a healthful appetite.

As the guests at the feast remarked upon the quality of the wine, inquiries were made that drew from the servants an account of the miracle. The company were for a time too much amazed to think of Him who had performed the wonderful work. When at length they looked for Him, it was found that He had withdrawn so quietly as to be unnoticed even by His disciples.

The attention of the company was now turned to the disciples. For the first time they had the opportunity of acknowledging their faith in Jesus. They told what they had seen and heard at the Jordan, and there was kindled in many hearts the hope that God had raised up a deliverer for His people. The news of the miracle spread through all that region, and was carried to Jerusalem. With new interest the priests and elders searched the prophecies pointing to Christ's coming. There was eager desire to learn the mission of this new teacher, who appeared among the people in so unassuming a manner.

The ministry of Christ was in marked contrast to that of the Jewish elders. Their regard for tradition and formalism had destroyed all real freedom of thought or action. They lived in continual dread of defilement. To avoid contact with the "unclean," they kept aloof, not only from the Gentiles, but from the majority of their own people, seeking neither to benefit them nor to win their friendship. By dwelling constantly on these matters, they had dwarfed their minds and narrowed the orbit of their lives. Their example encouraged egotism and intolerance among all classes of the people.

Jesus began the work of reformation by coming into close sympathy with humanity. While He showed the greatest reverence for the law of God, He rebuked the pretentious piety of the Pharisees, and tried to free the people from the senseless rules that bound them. He was seeking to break down the barriers which separated the different classes of society, that He might bring men together as children of one family. His attendance at the marriage feast was designed to be a step toward effecting this.

God had directed John the Baptist to dwell in the wilderness, that he might be shielded from the influence of the priests and rabbis, and be prepared for a special mission. But the austerity and isolation of his life were not an example for the people. John himself had not directed his hearers to forsake their former duties. He bade them give evidence of their repentance by faithfulness to God in the place where He had called them.

Jesus reproved self-indulgence in all its forms, yet He was social in His nature. He accepted the hospitality of all classes, visiting the homes of the rich and the poor, the learned and the ignorant, and seeking to elevate their thoughts from questions of commonplace life to those things that are spiritual and eternal. He gave no license to dissipation, and no shadow of worldly levity marred His conduct; yet He found pleasure in scenes of innocent happiness, and by His presence sanctioned the social gathering. A Jewish marriage was an impressive occasion, and its joy was not displeasing to the Son of man. By attending this feast, Jesus honored marriage as a divine institution.

In both the Old and the New Testament, the marriage relation is employed to represent the tender and sacred union that exists between Christ and His people. To the mind of Jesus the gladness of the wedding festivities pointed forward to the rejoicing of that day when He shall bring home His bride to the Father's house, and the redeemed with the Redeemer shall sit down to the marriage supper of the Lamb. He says, "As the bridegroom rejoiceth over the bride, so shall thy God rejoice over thee." "Thou shalt no more be termed Forsaken; . . . but thou shalt be called My Delight; . . . for the Lord delighteth in thee." "He will rejoice over thee with joy; He will rest in His love, He will joy over thee with singing." Isaiah 62: 5, 4, margin; Zephaniah 3:17. When the vision of heavenly things was granted to John the apostle, he wrote, "I heard as it were the voice of a great multitude, and as the voice of many waters, and as the voice of mighty thunderings, saying, Alleluia; for the Lord God omnipotent reigneth. Let us be glad and rejoice, and give honor to Him; for the marriage of the Lamb is come, and His wife hath made herself ready." "Blessed are they which are called unto the marriage supper of the Lamb." Revelation 19:6, 7, 9.

Jesus saw in every soul one to whom must be given the call to His kingdom. He reached the hearts of the people by going among them as one who desired their good. He sought them in the public streets, in private houses, on the boats, in the synagogue, by the shores of the lake, and at the marriage feast. He met them at their daily vocations, and manifested an interest in their secular affairs. He carried His instruction into the household, bringing families in their own homes under the influence of His divine presence. His strong personal sympathy helped to win hearts. He often repaired to the mountains for solitary prayer, but this was a preparation for His labor among men in active life. From these seasons He came forth to relieve the sick, to instruct the ignorant, and to break the chains from the captives of Satan.

It was by personal contact and association that Jesus trained His disciples. Sometimes He taught them, sitting among them on the mountain side; sometimes beside the sea, or walking with them by the way, He revealed the mysteries of the kingdom of God. He did not sermonize, as men do today. Wherever hearts were open to receive the divine message, He unfolded the truths of the way of salvation. He did not command His disciples to do this or that, but said, "Follow Me." On His journeys through country and cities He took them with Him, that they might see how He taught the people. He linked their interest with His, and they united with Him in the work.

The example of Christ in linking Himself with the interests of humanity should be followed by all who preach His word, and by all who have received the gospel of His grace. We are not to renounce social communion. We should not seclude ourselves from others. In order to reach all classes, we must meet them where they are. They will seldom seek us of their own accord. Not alone from the pulpit are the hearts of men touched by divine truth. There is another field of labor, humbler, it may be, but fully as promising. It is found in the home of the lowly, and in the mansion of the great; at the hospitable board, and in gatherings for innocent social enjoyment.

As disciples of Christ we shall not mingle with the world from a mere love of pleasure, to unite with them in folly. Such associations can result only in harm. We should never give sanction to sin by our words or our deeds, our silence or our presence. Wherever we go, we are to carry Jesus with us, and to reveal to others the preciousness of our Saviour. But those who try to preserve their religion by hiding it within stone walls, lose precious opportunities of doing good. Through the social relations, Christianity comes in contact with the world. Every one who has received the divine illumination, is to brighten the pathway of those who know not the Light of life.

We should all become witnesses for Jesus. Social power, sanctified by the grace of Christ, must be improved in winning souls to the Saviour. Let the world see that we are not selfishly absorbed in our own interests, but that we desire others to share our blessings and privileges. Let them see that our religion does not make us unsympathetic or exacting. Let all who profess to have found Christ, minister as He did for the benefit of men.

We should never give to the world the false impression that Christians are a gloomy, unhappy people. If our eyes are fixed on Jesus, we shall see a compassionate Redeemer, and shall catch light from His countenance. Wherever His spirit reigns, there peace abides. And there will be joy also, for there is a calm, holy trust in God.

Christ is pleased with His followers when they show that, though human, they are partakers of the divine nature. They are not statues, but living men and women. Their hearts, refreshed by the dews of divine grace, open and expand to the Sun of Righteousness. The light that shines upon them they reflect upon others in works that are luminous with the love of Christ.

In His Temple

A fter this He went down to Capernaum, He, and His mother, and His brethren, and His disciples; and they continued there not many days. And the Jews' Passover was at hand and Jesus went up to Jerusalem."

In this journey, Jesus joined one of the large companies that were making their way to the capital. He had not yet publicly announced His mission, and He mingled unnoticed with the throng. Upon these occasions, the coming of the Messiah, to which such prominence had been given by the ministry of John, was often the theme of conversation. The hope of national greatness was dwelt upon with kindling enthusiasm. Jesus knew that this hope was to be disappointed, for it was founded on a misinterpretation of the Scriptures. With deep earnestness He explained the prophecies, and tried to arouse the people to a closer study of God's word.

The Jewish leaders had instructed the people that at Jerusalem they were to be taught to worship God. Here during the Passover week large numbers assembled, coming from all parts of Palestine, and even from distant lands. The temple courts were filled with a promiscuous throng. Many were unable to bring with them the sacrifices that were to be offered up as typifying the one great Sacrifice. For the convenience of these, animals were bought and sold in the outer court of the temple. Here all classes of people assembled to purchase their offerings. Here all foreign money was exchanged for the coin of the sanctuary.

Every Jew was required to pay yearly a half shekel as "a ransom for his soul;" (Exodus 30:12-16.) and the money thus collected was used for the support of the temple. Besides this, large sums were brought as freewill offerings, to be deposited in the temple treasury. And it was required that all foreign coin should be changed for a coin called the temple shekel, which was accepted for the service of the sanctuary. The money changing gave opportunity for fraud and extortion, and it had grown into a disgraceful traffic, which was a source of revenue to the priests.

The dealers demanded exorbitant prices for the animals sold, and they shared their profits with the priests and rulers, who thus enriched themselves at the expense of the people. The worshipers had been taught to believe that if they did not offer sacrifice, the blessing of God would not rest on their children or their lands. Thus a high price for the animals could be secured; for after coming so far, the people would not return to their homes without performing the act of devotion for which they had come.

A great number of sacrifices were offered at the time of the Passover, and the sales at the temple were very large. The consequent confusion indicated a noisy cattle market, rather than the sacred temple of God. There could be heard sharp bargaining, the lowing of cattle, the bleating of sheep, the cooing of doves mingled with the chinking of coin and angry disputation. So great was the confusion that the worshipers were disturbed, and the words addressed to the Most High were drowned in the uproar that invaded the temple. The Jews were exceedingly proud of their piety. They rejoiced over their temple, and regarded a word spoken in its disfavor as blasphemy: they were very rigorous in the performance of ceremonies connected with it; but the love of money had overruled their scruples. They were scarcely aware how far they had wandered from the original purpose of the service instituted by God Himself.

When the Lord descended upon Mount Sinai, the place was consecrated by His presence. Moses was commanded to put bounds around the mount and sanctify it, and the word of the Lord was heard in warning: "Take heed to yourselves, that ye go not up into the mount, or touch the border of it; whosoever toucheth the mount shall be surely put to death; there shall not an hand touch it, but he shall surely be stoned, or shot through; whether it be beast or man, it shall not live." Exodus 19:12, 13. Thus was taught the lesson that wherever God manifests His presence, the place is holy. The precincts of God's temple should have been regarded as sacred. But in the strife for gain, all this was lost sight of.

The priests and rulers were called to be the representatives of God to the nation; they should have corrected the abuses of the temple court. They should have given to the people an example of integrity and compassion. Instead of studying their own profit, they should have considered the situation and needs of the worshipers, and should have been ready to assist those who were not able to buy the required sacrifices. But this they did not do. Avarice had hardened their hearts.

There came to this feast those who were suffering, those who were in want and distress. The blind, the lame, the deaf, were there. Some were brought on beds. Many came who were too poor to purchase the humblest offering for the Lord, too poor even to buy food with which to satisfy their own hunger. These were greatly distressed by the statements of the priests. The priests boasted of their piety; they claimed to be the guardians of the people; but they were without sympathy or compassion. The poor, the sick, the dying, made their vain plea for favor. Their suffering awakened no pity in the hearts of the priests.

As Jesus came into the temple, He took in the whole scene. He saw the unfair transactions. He saw the distress of the poor, who thought that without shedding of blood, there would be no forgiveness for their sins. He saw the outer court of His temple converted into a place of unholy traffic. The sacred inclosure had become one vast exchange.

Christ saw that something must be done. Numerous ceremonies were enjoined upon the people without the proper instruction as to their import. The worshipers offered their sacrifices without understanding that they were typical of the only perfect Sacrifice. And among them, unrecognized and unhonored, stood the One symbolized by all their service. He had given directions in regard to the offerings. He understood their symbolical value, and He saw that they were now perverted and misunderstood. Spiritual worship was fast disappearing. No link bound the priests and rulers to their God. Christ's work was to establish an altogether different worship.

With searching glance, Christ takes in the scene before Him, as He stands upon the steps of the temple court. With prophetic eye He looks into futurity, and sees not only years, but centuries and ages. He sees how priests and rulers will turn the needy from their right, and forbid that the gospel shall be preached to the poor. He sees how the love of God will be concealed from sinners, and men will make merchandise of His grace. As He beholds the scene, indignation, authority, and power are expressed in His countenance. The attention of the people is attracted to Him. The eyes of those engaged in their unholy traffic are riveted upon His face. They cannot withdraw their gaze. They feel that this man reads their inmost thoughts, and discovers their hidden motives. Some attempt to conceal their faces, as if their evil deeds were written upon their countenances, to be scanned by those searching eyes.

The confusion is hushed. The sound of traffic and bargaining has ceased. The silence becomes painful. A sense of awe overpowers the assembly. It is as if they were arraigned before the tribunal of God to answer for their deeds. Looking upon Christ, they behold divinity flash through the garb of humanity. The Majesty of heaven stands as the Judge will stand at the last day, — not now encircled with the glory that will then attend Him, but with the same power to read the soul. His eye sweeps over the multitude, taking in every individual. His form seems to rise above them in commanding dignity, and a divine light illuminates His countenance. He speaks, and His clear, ringing voice — the same that upon Mount Sinai proclaimed the law that priests and rulers are transgressing — is heard echoing through the arches of the temple: "Take these things hence; make not My Father's house an house of merchandise."

Slowly descending the steps, and raising the scourge of cords gathered up on entering the inclosure, He bids the bargaining company depart from the precincts of the temple. With a zeal and severity He has never before manifested, He overthrows the tables of the money-changers. The coin falls, ringing sharply upon the marble pavement. None presume to question His authority. None dare stop to gather up their ill-gotten gain. Jesus does not smite them with the whip of cords, but in His hand that simple scourge seems terrible as a flaming sword. Officers of the temple, speculating priests, brokers and cattle traders, with their sheep and oxen, rush from the place, with the one thought of escaping from the condemnation of His presence.

A panic sweeps over the multitude, who feel the overshadowing of His divinity. Cries of terror escape from hundreds of blanched lips. Even the disciples tremble. They are awestruck by the words and manner of Jesus, so unlike His usual demeanor. They remember that it is written of Him, "The zeal of Thine house hath eaten Me up." Psalms 69:9. Soon the tumultuous throng with their merchandise are far removed from the temple of the Lord. The courts are free from unholy traffic, and a deep silence and solemnity settles upon the scene of confusion. The presence of the Lord, that of old sanctified the mount, has now made sacred the temple reared in His honor.

In the cleansing of the temple, Jesus was announcing His mission as the Messiah, and entering upon His work. That temple, erected for the abode of the divine presence, was designed to be an object lesson for Israel and for the world.

From eternal ages it was God's purpose that every created being, from the bright and holy seraph to man, should be a temple for the indwelling of the Creator. Because of sin, humanity ceased to be a temple for God. Darkened and defiled by evil, the heart of man no longer revealed the glory of the divine One. But by the incarnation of the Son of God, the purpose of Heaven is fulfilled. God dwells in humanity, and through saving grace the heart of man becomes again His temple. God designed that the temple at Jerusalem should be a continual witness to the high destiny open to every soul. But the Jews had not understood the significance of the building they regarded with so much pride. They did not yield themselves as holy temples for the divine Spirit. The courts of the temple at Jerusalem, filled with the tumult of unholy traffic, represented all too truly the temple of the heart, defiled by the presence of sensual passion and unholy thoughts. In cleansing the temple from the world's buyers and sellers, Jesus announced His mission to cleanse the heart from the defilement of sin, — from the earthly desires, the selfish lusts, the evil habits, that corrupt the soul. "The Lord, whom ye seek, shall suddenly come to His temple, even the messenger of the covenant, whom ye delight in: behold, He shall come, saith the Lord of hosts. But who may abide the day of His coming? and who shall stand when He appeareth? for He is like a refiner's fire, and like fuller's soap; and He shall sit as a refiner and purifier of silver: and He shall purify the sons of Levi, and purge them as gold and silver." Malachi 3:1-3.

"Know ye not that ye are the temple of God, and that the Spirit of God dwelleth in you? If any man defile the temple of God, him shall God destroy; for the temple of God is holy, which temple ye are." 1 Corinthians 3:16,17. No man can of himself cast out the evil throng that have taken possession of the heart. Only Christ can cleanse the soul temple. But He will not force an entrance. He comes not into the heart as to the temple of old; but He says, "Behold, I stand at the door, and knock; if any man hear My voice, and open the door, I will come in to him." Revelation 3:20. He will come, not for one day merely; for He says, "I will dwell in them, and walk in them; . . . and they shall be My people." "He will subdue our iniquities; and Thou wilt cast all their sins into the depths of the sea." 2 Corinthians 6:16; Micah 7:19. His presence will cleanse and sanctify the soul, so that it may be a holy temple unto the Lord, and "an habitation of God through the Spirit." Ephesians 2:21, 22.

Overpowered with terror, the priests and rulers had fled from the temple court, and from the searching glance that read their hearts. In their flight they met others on their way to the temple, and bade them turn back, telling them what they had seen and heard. Christ looked upon the fleeing men with yearning pity for their fear, and their ignorance of what constituted true worship. In this scene He saw symbolized the dispersion of the whole Jewish nation for their wickedness and impenitence.

And why did the priests flee from the temple? Why did they not stand their ground? He who commanded them to go was a carpenter's son, a poor Galilean, without earthly rank or power. Why did they not resist Him? Why did they leave the gain so ill acquired, and flee at the command of one whose outward appearance was so humble?

Christ spoke with the authority of a king, and in His appearance, and in the tones of His voice, there was that which they had no power to resist. At the word of command they realized, as they had never realized before, their true position as hypocrites and robbers. When divinity flashed through humanity, not only did they see indignation on Christ's countenance; they realized the import of His words. They felt as if before the throne of the eternal Judge, with their sentence passed on them for time and for eternity. For a time they were convinced that Christ was a prophet; and many believed Him to be the Messiah. The Holy Spirit flashed into their minds the utterances of the prophets concerning Christ. Would they yield to this conviction?

Repent they would not. They knew that Christ's sympathy for the poor had been aroused. They knew that they had been guilty of extortion in their dealings with the people. Because Christ discerned their thoughts they hated Him. His public rebuke was humiliating to their pride, and they were jealous of His growing influence with the people. They determined to challenge Him as to the power by which He had driven them forth, and who gave Him this power.

Slowly and thoughtfully, but with hate in their hearts, they returned to the temple. But what a change had taken place during their absence. When they fled, the poor remained behind; and these were now looking to Jesus, whose countenance expressed His love and sympathy. With tears in His eyes, He said to the trembling ones around Him, Fear not; I will deliver thee, and thou shalt glorify Me. For this cause came I into the world.

The people pressed into Christ's presence with urgent, pitiful appeals, Master, bless me. His ear heard every cry. With pity exceeding that of a tender mother, He bent over the suffering little ones. All received attention. Every one was healed of whatever disease he had. The dumb opened their lips in praise; the blind beheld the face of their Restorer. The hearts of the sufferers were made glad.

As the priests and temple officials witnessed this great work, what a revelation to them were the sounds that fell on their ears. The people were relating the story of the pain they had suffered, of their disappointed hopes, of painful days and sleepless nights. When the last spark of hope seemed to be dead, Christ had healed them. The burden was so heavy, one said; but I have found a Helper. He is the Christ of God, and I will devote my life to His service. Parents said to their children, He has saved your life; lift up your voice and praise Him. The voices of children and youth, fathers and mothers, friends and spectators, blended in thanksgiving and praise. Hope and gladness filled their hearts. Peace came to their minds. They were restored soul and body, and they returned home, proclaiming everywhere the matchless love of Jesus.

At the crucifixion of Christ, those who had thus been healed did not join with the rabble throng in crying, "Crucify Him, crucify Him." Their sympathies were with Jesus; for they had felt His great sympathy and wonderful power. They knew Him to be their Saviour; for He had given them health of body and soul. They listened to the preaching of the apostles, and the entrance of God's word

---

> **"**Because of sin, humanity ceased to be a temple for God. . . . The heart of man no longer revealed the glory of the Divine One. But by the incarnation of the Son of God, the purpose of Heaven is fulfilled. God dwells in humanity, and through saving grace the heart of man becomes again His temple.**"**

---

into their hearts gave them understanding. They became agents of God's mercy, and instruments of His salvation.

The crowd that had fled from the temple court, after a time slowly drifted back. They had partially recovered from the panic that had seized them, but their faces expressed irresolution and timidity. They looked with amazement on the works of Jesus, and were convicted that in Him the prophecies concerning the Messiah were fulfilled. The sin of the desecration of the temple rested, in a great degree, upon the priests. It was by their arrangement that the court had been turned into a market place. The people were comparatively innocent. They were impressed by the divine authority of Jesus; but with them the influence of the priests and rulers was paramount. They regarded Christ's mission as an innovation, and questioned His right to interfere with what was permitted by the authorities of the temple. They were offended because the traffic had been interrupted, and they stifled the convictions of the Holy Spirit.

Above all others the priests and rulers should have seen in Jesus the anointed of the Lord; for in their hands were the sacred scrolls that described His mission, and they knew that the cleansing of the temple was a manifestation of more than human power. Much as they hated Jesus, they could not free themselves from the thought that He might be a prophet sent by God to restore the sanctity of the temple. With a deference born of this fear, they went to Him with the inquiry, "What sign showest Thou unto us, seeing that Thou doest these things?"

Jesus had shown them a sign. In flashing light into their hearts, and in doing before them the works which the Messiah was to do, He had given convincing evidence of His character. Now when they asked for a sign, He answered them by a parable, showing that He read their malice, and saw to what lengths it would lead them. "Destroy this temple," He said, "and in three days I will raise it up."

In these words His meaning was twofold. He referred not only to the destruction of the Jewish temple and worship, but to His own death, — the destruction of the temple of His body. This the Jews were already plotting. As the priests and rulers returned to the temple, they had proposed to kill Jesus, and thus rid themselves of the troubler. Yet when He set before them their purpose, they did not understand Him. They took His words as applying only to the temple at Jerusalem, and with indignation exclaimed, "Forty and six years was this temple in building, and wilt Thou rear it up in three days?" Now they felt that Jesus had justified their unbelief, and they were confirmed in their rejection of Him.

Christ did not design that His words should be understood by the unbelieving Jews, nor even by His disciples at this time. He knew that they would be misconstrued by His enemies, and would be turned against Him. At His trial they would be brought as an accusation, and on Calvary they would be flung at Him as a taunt. But to explain them now would give His disciples a knowledge of His sufferings, and bring upon them sorrow which as yet they were not able to bear. And an explanation would prematurely disclose to the Jews the result of their prejudice and unbelief. Already they had entered upon a path which they would steadily pursue until He should be led as a lamb to the slaughter.

It was for the sake of those who should believe on Him that these words of Christ were spoken. He knew that they would be repeated. Being spoken at the Passover, they would come to the ears of thousands, and be carried to all parts of the world. After He had risen from the dead, their meaning would be made plain. To many they would be conclusive evidence of His divinity.

Because of their spiritual darkness, even the disciples of Jesus often failed of comprehending His lessons. But many of these lessons were made plain to them by subsequent events. When He walked no more with them, His words were a stay to their hearts.

As referring to the temple at Jerusalem, the Saviour's words, "Destroy this temple, and in three days I will raise it up," had a deeper meaning than the hearers perceived. Christ was the foundation and life of the temple. Its services were typical of the sacrifice of the Son of God. The priesthood was established to represent the mediatorial character and work of Christ. The entire plan of sacrificial worship was a foreshadowing of the Saviour's death to redeem the world. There would be no efficacy in these offerings when the great event toward which they had pointed for ages was consummated.

Since the whole ritual economy was symbolical of Christ, it had no value apart from Him. When the Jews sealed their rejection of Christ by delivering Him to death, they rejected all that gave significance to the temple and its services. Its sacredness had departed. It was doomed to destruction. From that day sacrificial offerings and the service connected with them were meaningless. Like the offering of Cain, they did not express faith in the Saviour. In putting Christ to death, the Jews virtually destroyed their temple. When Christ was crucified, the inner veil of the temple was rent in twain from top to bottom, signifying that the great final sacrifice had been made, and that the system of sacrificial offerings was forever at an end.

"In three days I will raise it up." In the Saviour's death the powers of darkness seemed to prevail, and they exulted in their victory. But from the rent sepulcher of Joseph, Jesus came forth a conqueror. "Having spoiled principalities and powers, He made a show of them openly, triumphing over them." Colossians 2:15. By virtue of His death and resurrection He became the minister of the "true tabernacle, which the Lord pitched, and not man." Hebrews 8:2. Men reared the Jewish tabernacle; men builded the Jewish temple; but the sanctuary above, of which the earthly was a type, was built by no human architect. "Behold the Man whose name is The Branch; . . . He shall build the temple of the Lord; and He shall bear the glory, and shall sit and rule upon His throne; and He shall be a priest upon His throne." Zechariah 6:12, 13.

The sacrificial service that had pointed to Christ passed away; but the eyes of men were turned to the true sacrifice for the sins of the world. The earthly priesthood ceased; but we look to Jesus, the minister of the new covenant, and "to the blood of sprinkling, that speaketh better things than that of Abel." "The way into the holiest of all was not yet made manifest, while as the first tabernacle was yet standing; . . . but Christ being come an high priest of good things to come, by a greater and more perfect tabernacle, not made with hands, . . . by His own blood He entered in once into the holy place, having obtained eternal redemption for us." Hebrews 12:24; 9:8-12.

"Wherefore He is able also to save them to the uttermost that come unto God by Him, seeing He ever liveth to make intercession for them." Hebrews 7:25. Though the ministration was to be removed from the earthly to the heavenly temple; though the sanctuary and our great high priest would be invisible to human sight, yet the disciples were to suffer no loss thereby. They would realize no break in their communion, and no diminution of power because of the Saviour's absence. While Jesus ministers in the sanctuary above, He is still by His Spirit the minister of the church on earth. He is withdrawn from the eye of sense, but His parting promise is fulfilled, "Lo, I am with you alway, even unto the end of the world." Matthew 28:20. While He delegates His power to inferior ministers, His energizing presence is still with His church.

"Seeing then that we have a great high priest, . . . Jesus, the Son of God, let us hold fast our profession. For we have not an high priest which cannot be touched with the feeling of our infirmities; but was in all points tempted like as we are, yet without sin. Let us therefore come boldly unto the throne of grace, that we may obtain mercy, and find grace to help in time of need." Hebrews 4:14-16.

Nicodemus

Nicodemus held a high position of trust in the Jewish nation. He was highly educated, and possessed talents of no ordinary character, and he was an honored member of the national council. With others, he had been stirred by the teaching of Jesus. Though rich, learned, and honored, he had been strangely attracted by the humble Nazarene. The lessons that had fallen from the Saviour's lips had greatly impressed him, and he desired to learn more of these wonderful truths.

Christ's exercise of authority in the cleansing of the temple had roused the determined hatred of the priests and rulers. They feared the power of this stranger. Such boldness on the part of an obscure Galilean was not to be tolerated. They were bent on putting an end to His work. But not all were agreed in this purpose. There were some that feared to oppose one who was so evidently moved upon by the Spirit of God. They remembered how prophets had been slain for rebuking the sins of the leaders in Israel. They knew that the bondage of the Jews to a heathen nation was the result of their stubbornness in rejecting reproofs from God. They feared that in plotting against Jesus, the priests and rulers were following in the steps of their fathers, and would bring fresh calamities upon the nation. Nicodemus shared these feelings. In a council of the Sanhedrim, when the course to be pursued toward Jesus was considered, Nicodemus advised caution and moderation. He urged that if Jesus was really invested with authority from God, it would be perilous to reject His warnings. The priests dared not disregard this counsel, and for the time they took no open measures against the Saviour.

Since hearing Jesus, Nicodemus had anxiously studied the prophecies relating to the Messiah; and the more he searched, the stronger was his conviction that this was the One who was to come. With many others in Israel he had been greatly distressed by the profanation of the temple. He was a witness of the scene when Jesus drove out the buyers and the sellers; he beheld the wonderful manifestation of divine power; he saw the Saviour receiving the poor and healing the sick; he saw their looks of joy, and heard their words of praise; and he could not doubt that Jesus of Nazareth was the Sent of God.

He greatly desired an interview with Jesus, but shrank from seeking Him openly. It would be too humiliating for a ruler of the Jews to acknowledge himself in sympathy with a teacher as yet so little known. And should his visit come to the knowledge of the Sanhedrim, it would draw upon him their scorn and denunciation. He resolved upon a secret interview, excusing this on the ground that if he were to go openly, others might follow his example. Learning by special inquiry the Saviour's place of retirement in the Mount of Olives, he waited until the city was hushed in slumber, and then sought Him.

In the presence of Christ, Nicodemus felt a strange timidity, which he endeavored to conceal under an air of composure and dignity. "Rabbi," he said, "we know that Thou art a teacher come from God; for no man can do these miracles that Thou doest, except God be with him." By speaking of Christ's rare gifts as a teacher, and also of His wonderful power to perform miracles, he hoped to pave the way for his interview. His words were designed to express and to invite confidence; but they really expressed unbelief. He did not acknowledge Jesus to be the Messiah, but only a teacher sent from God.

Instead of recognizing this salutation, Jesus bent His eyes upon the speaker, as if reading his very soul. In His infinite wisdom He saw before Him a seeker after truth. He knew the object of this visit, and with a desire to deepen the conviction already resting upon His listener's mind, He came directly to the point, saying solemnly, yet kindly, "Verily, verily, I say unto thee, Except a man be born from above, he cannot see the kingdom of God." John 3:3, margin.

Nicodemus had come to the Lord thinking to enter into a discussion with Him, but Jesus laid bare the foundation principles of truth. He said to Nicodemus, It is not theoretical knowledge you need, so much as spiritual regeneration. You need not to have your curiosity satisfied, but to have a new heart. You must receive a new life from above, before you can appreciate heavenly things. Until this change takes place, making all things new, it will result in no saving good for you to discuss with Me My authority or My mission.

Nicodemus had heard the preaching of John the Baptist concerning repentance and baptism, and pointing the people to One who should baptize with the Holy Spirit. He himself had felt that there was a lack of spirituality among the Jews; that, to a great degree, they were controlled by bigotry and worldly ambition. He had hoped for a better state of things at the Messiah's coming. Yet the heart-searching message of the Baptist had failed to work in him conviction of sin. He was a strict Pharisee, and prided himself on his good works. He was widely esteemed for his benevolence and his liberality in sustaining the temple service, and he felt secure of the favor of God. He was startled at the thought of a kingdom too pure for him to see in his present state.

The figure of the new birth, which Jesus had used, was not wholly unfamiliar to Nicodemus. Converts from heathenism to the faith of Israel were often compared to children just born. Therefore he must have perceived that the words of Christ were not to be taken in a literal sense. But by virtue of his birth as an Israelite he regarded himself as sure of a place in the kingdom of God. He felt that he needed no change. Hence his surprise at the Saviour's words. He was irritated by their close application to himself. The pride of the Pharisee was struggling against the honest desire of the seeker after truth. He wondered that Christ should speak to him as He did, not respecting his position as ruler in Israel.

Surprised out of his self-possession, he answered Christ in words full of irony, "How can a man be born when he is old?" Like many others when cutting truth is brought home to the conscience, he revealed the fact that the natural man receiveth not the things of the Spirit of God. There is in him nothing that responds to spiritual things; for spiritual things are spiritually discerned.

But the Saviour did not meet argument with argument. Raising His hand with solemn, quiet dignity, He pressed the truth home with greater assurance, "Verily, verily, I say unto thee, Except a man be born of water and of the Spirit, he cannot enter into the kingdom of God."

Nicodemus knew that Christ here referred to water baptism, and the renewing of the heart by the Spirit of God. He was convinced that he was in the presence of the One whom John the Baptist had foretold.

Jesus continued: "That which is born of the flesh is flesh; and that which is born of the Spirit is spirit." By nature the heart is evil, and "who can bring a clean thing out of an unclean? not one." Job 14:4. No human invention can find a remedy for the sinning soul. "The carnal mind is enmity against God; for it is not subject to the law of God, neither indeed can be." "Out of the heart proceed evil thoughts, murders, adulteries, fornications, thefts, false witness, blasphemies." Romans 8:7; Matthew 15:19. The fountain of the heart must be purified before the streams can become pure. He who is trying to reach heaven by his own works in keeping the law, is attempting an impossibility. There is no safety for one who has merely a legal religion, a form of godliness. The Christian's life is not a modification or improvement of the old, but a transformation of nature. There is a death to self and sin, and a new life altogether. This change can be brought about only by the effectual working of the Holy Spirit.

Nicodemus was still perplexed, and Jesus used the wind to illustrate His meaning: "The wind bloweth where it listeth, and thou hearest the sound thereof, but canst not tell whence it cometh and whither it goeth: so is every one that is born of the Spirit."

The wind is heard among the branches of the trees, rustling the leaves and flowers; yet it is invisible, and no man knows whence it comes, or whither it goes. So with the work of the Holy Spirit upon the heart. It can no more be explained than can the movements of the wind. A person may not be able to tell the exact time or place, or to trace all the circumstances in the process of conversion; but this does not prove him to be unconverted. By an agency as unseen as the wind, Christ is constantly working upon the heart. Little by little, perhaps unconsciously to the receiver, impressions are made that tend to draw the soul to Christ. These may be received through meditating upon Him, through reading the Scriptures, or through hearing the word from the living preacher. Suddenly, as the Spirit comes with more direct appeal, the soul gladly surrenders itself to Jesus. By many this is called sudden conversion; but it is the result of long wooing by the Spirit of God, — a patient, protracted process.

While the wind is itself invisible, it produces effects that are seen and felt. So the work of the Spirit upon the soul will reveal itself in every act of him who has felt its saving power. When the Spirit of God takes possession of the heart, it transforms the life. Sinful thoughts are put away, evil deeds are renounced; love, humility, and peace take the place of anger, envy, and strife. Joy takes the place of sadness, and the countenance reflects the light of heaven. No one sees the hand that lifts the burden, or beholds the light descend from the courts above. The blessing comes when by faith the soul surrenders itself to God. Then that power which no human eye can see, creates a new being in the image of God.

It is impossible for finite minds to comprehend the work of redemption. Its mystery exceeds human knowledge; yet he who passes from death to life realizes that it is a divine reality. The beginning of redemption we may know here through a personal experience. Its results reach through the eternal ages.

While Jesus was speaking, some gleams of truth penetrated the ruler's mind. The softening, subduing influence of the Holy Spirit impressed his heart. Yet he did not fully understand the Saviour's words. He was not so much impressed by the necessity of the new birth as by the manner of its accomplishment. He said wonderingly, "How can these things be?"

"Art thou a master of Israel, and knowest not these things?" Jesus asked. Surely one entrusted with the religious instruction of the people should not be ignorant of truths so important. His words conveyed the lesson that instead of feeling irritated over the plain words of truth, Nicodemus should have had a very humble opinion of himself, because of his spiritual ignorance. Yet Christ spoke with such solemn dignity, and both look and tone expressed such earnest love, that Nicodemus was not offended as he realized his humiliating condition.

But as Jesus explained that His mission on earth was to establish a spiritual instead of a temporal kingdom, His hearer was troubled. Seeing this, Jesus added, "If I have told you earthly things, and ye believe not, how shall ye believe, if I tell you of heavenly things?" If Nicodemus could not receive Christ's teaching, illustrating the work of grace upon the heart, how could he comprehend the nature of His glorious heavenly kingdom? Not discerning the nature of Christ's work on earth, he could not understand His work in heaven.

The Jews whom Jesus had driven from the temple, claimed to be children of Abraham, but they fled from the Saviour's presence because they could not endure the glory of God which was manifested in Him. Thus they gave evidence that they were not fitted by the grace of God to participate in the sacred services of the temple. They were zealous to maintain an appearance of holiness, but they neglected holiness of heart. While they were sticklers for the letter of the law, they were constantly violating its spirit. Their great need was that very change which Christ had been explaining to Nicodemus, — a new moral birth, a cleansing from sin, and a renewing of knowledge and holiness.

There was no excuse for the blindness of Israel in regard to the work of regeneration. Under the inspiration of the Holy Spirit, Isaiah had written, "We are all as an unclean thing, and all our righteousness are as filthy rags." David had prayed, "Create in me a clean heart, O God; and renew a right spirit within me." And through Ezekiel the promise had been given, "A new heart also will I give you, and a new spirit will I put within you; and I will take away the stony heart out of your flesh, and I will give you an heart of flesh. And I will put My Spirit within you, and cause you to walk in My statutes." Isaiah 64:6; Psalms 51:10; Ezekiel 36:26, 27.

Nicodemus had read these scriptures with a clouded mind; but he now began to comprehend their meaning. He saw that the most rigid obedience to the mere letter of the law as applied to the outward life, could entitle no man to enter the kingdom of heaven. In the estimation of men, his

---

"While the wind is itself invisible, it produces effects that are seen and felt. So the work of the Spirit upon the soul will reveal itself in every act of him who has felt its saving power. . . . Joy takes the place of sadness, and the countenance reflects the light of heaven."

---

life had been just and honorable; but in the presence of Christ he felt that his heart was unclean, and his life unholy.

Nicodemus was being drawn to Christ. As the Saviour explained to him concerning the new birth, he longed to have this change wrought in himself. By what means could it be accomplished? Jesus answered the unspoken question: "As Moses lifted up the serpent in the wilderness, even so must the Son of man be lifted up; that whosoever believeth in Him should not perish, but have eternal life."

Here was ground with which Nicodemus was familiar. The symbol of the uplifted serpent made plain to him the Saviour's mission. When the people of Israel were dying from the sting of the fiery serpents, God directed Moses to make a serpent of brass, and place it on high in the midst of the congregation. Then the word was sounded throughout the encampment that all who would look upon the serpent should live. The people well knew that in itself the serpent had no power to help them. It was a symbol of Christ. As the image made in the likeness of the destroying serpents was lifted up for their healing, so One made "in the likeness of sinful flesh" (Romans 8:3.) was to be their Redeemer. Many of the Israelites regarded the sacrificial service as having in itself virtue to set them free from sin. God desired to teach them that it had no more value than that serpent of brass. It was to lead their minds to the Saviour. Whether for the healing of their wounds or the pardon of their sins, they could do nothing for themselves but show their faith in the Gift of God. They were to look and live.

Those who had been bitten by the serpents might have delayed to look. They might have questioned how there could be efficacy in that brazen symbol. They might have demanded a scientific explanation. But no explanation was given. They must accept the word of God to them through Moses. To refuse to look, was to perish.

Not through controversy and discussion is the soul enlightened. We must look and live. Nicodemus received the lesson, and carried it with him. He searched the Scriptures in a new way, not for the discussion of a theory, but in order to receive life for the soul. He began to see the kingdom of heaven as he submitted himself to the leading of the Holy Spirit.

There are thousands today who need to learn the same truth that was taught to Nicodemus by the uplifted serpent. They depend on their obedience to the law of God to commend them to His favor. When they are bidden to look to Jesus, and believe that He saves them solely through His grace, they exclaim, "How can these things be?"

Like Nicodemus, we must be willing to enter into life in the same way as the chief of sinners. Than Christ, "there is none other name under heaven given among men, whereby we must be saved." Acts 4:12. Through faith we receive the grace of God; but faith is not our Saviour. It earns nothing. It is the hand by which we lay hold upon Christ, and appropriate He merits, the remedy for sin. And we cannot even repent without the aid of the Spirit of God. The Scripture says of Christ, "Him hath God exalted with His right hand, to be a Prince and a Saviour for to give repentance to Israel, and forgiveness of sins." Acts 5:31. Repentance comes from Christ as truly as does pardon.

How, then, are we to be saved? — "As Moses lifted up the serpent in the wilderness," so the Son of man has been lifted up, and every one who has been deceived and bitten by the serpent, may look and live. "Behold the Lamb of God, which taketh away the sin of the world." John 1:29. The light shining from the cross reveals the love of God. His love is drawing us to Himself. If we do not resist this drawing, we shall be led to the foot of the cross in repentance for the sins that have crucified the Saviour. Then the Spirit of God through faith produces a new life in the soul. The thoughts and desires are brought into obedience to the will of Christ. The heart, the mind, are created anew in the image of Him who works in us to subdue all things to Himself. Then the law of God is written in the mind and heart, and we can say with Christ, "I delight to do Thy will, O my God." Psalms 40:8.

In the interview with Nicodemus, Jesus unfolded the plan of salvation, and His mission to the world. In none of His subsequent discourses did He explain so fully, step by step, the work necessary to be done in the hearts of all who would inherit the kingdom of heaven. At the very beginning of His ministry He opened the truth to a member of the Sanhedrim, to the mind that was most receptive, and to an appointed teacher of the people. But the leaders of Israel did not welcome the light. Nicodemus hid the truth in his heart, and for three years there was little apparent fruit.

But Jesus was acquainted with the soil into which He cast the seed. The words spoken at night to one listener in the lonely mountain were not lost. For a time Nicodemus did not publicly acknowledge Christ, but he watched His life, and pondered His teachings. In the Sanhedrim council he repeatedly thwarted the schemes of the priests to destroy Him. When at last Jesus was lifted up on the cross, Nicodemus remembered the teaching upon Olivet: "As Moses lifted up the serpent in the wilderness, even so must the Son of man be lifted up; that whosoever believeth in Him should not perish, but have eternal life." The light from that secret interview illumined the cross upon Calvary, and Nicodemus saw in Jesus the world's Redeemer.

After the Lord's ascension, when the disciples were scattered by persecution, Nicodemus came boldly to the front. He employed his wealth in sustaining the infant church that the Jews had expected to be blotted out at the death of Christ. In the time of peril he who had been so cautious and questioning, was firm as a rock, encouraging the faith of the disciples, and furnishing means to carry forward the work of the gospel. He was scorned and persecuted by those who had paid him reverence in other days. He became poor in this world's goods; yet he faltered not in the faith which had its beginning in that night conference with Jesus.

Nicodemus related to John the story of that interview, and by his pen it was recorded for the instruction of millions. The truths there taught are as important today as they were on that solemn night in the shadowy mountain, when the Jewish ruler came to learn the way of life from the lowly Teacher of Galilee.

"He Must Increase"

For a time the Baptist's influence over the nation had been greater than that of its rulers, priests, or princes. If he had announced himself as the Messiah, and raised a revolt against Rome, priests and people would have flocked to his standard. Every consideration that appeals to the ambition of the world's conquerors, Satan had stood ready to urge upon John the Baptist. But with the evidence before him of his power, he had steadfastly refused the splendid bribe. The attention which was fixed upon him, he had directed to Another.

Now he saw the tide of popularity turning away from himself to the Saviour. Day by day the crowds about him lessened. When Jesus came from Jerusalem to the region about Jordan, the people flocked to hear Him. The number of His disciples increased daily. Many came for baptism, and while Christ Himself did not baptize, He sanctioned the administration of the ordinance by His disciples. Thus He set His seal upon the mission of His forerunner. But the disciples of John looked with jealousy upon the growing popularity of Jesus. They stood ready to criticize His work, and it was not long before they found occasion. A question arose between them and the Jews as to whether baptism availed to cleanse the soul from sin; they maintained that the baptism of Jesus differed essentially from that of John. Soon they were in dispute with Christ's disciples in regard to the form of words proper to use at baptism, and finally as to the right of the latter to baptize at all.

The disciples of John came to him with their grievances, saying, "Rabbi, He that was with thee beyond Jordan, to whom thou bearest witness, behold, the same baptizeth, and all men come to Him." Through these words, Satan brought temptation upon John. Though John's mission seemed about to close, it was still possible for him to hinder the work of Christ. If he had sympathized with himself, and expressed grief or disappointment at being superseded, he would have sown the seeds of dissension, would have encouraged envy and jealousy, and would seriously have impeded the progress of the gospel.

John had by nature the faults and weaknesses common to humanity, but the touch of divine love had transformed him. He dwelt in an atmosphere uncontaminated with selfishness and ambition, and far above the miasma of jealousy. He manifested no sympathy with the dissatisfaction of his disciples, but showed how clearly he understood his relation to the Messiah, and how gladly he welcomed the One for whom he had prepared the way.

He said, "A man can receive nothing, except it be given him from heaven. Ye yourselves bear me witness, that I said, I am not the Christ, but that I am sent before Him. He that hath the bride is the bridegroom. But the friend of the bridegroom, which standeth and heareth him, rejoiceth greatly because of the bridegroom's voice." John represented himself as the friend who acted as a messenger between the betrothed parties, preparing the way for the marriage. When the bridegroom had received his bride, the mission of the friend was fulfilled. He rejoiced in the happiness of those whose union he had promoted. So John had been called to direct the people to Jesus, and it was his joy to witness the success of the Saviour's work. He said, "This my joy therefore is fulfilled. He must increase, but I must decrease."

Looking in faith to the Redeemer, John had risen to the height of self-abnegation. He sought not to attract men to himself, but to lift their thoughts higher and still higher, until they should rest upon the Lamb of God. He himself

72

This chapter is based on John 3:22-36.

had been only a voice, a cry in the wilderness. Now with joy he accepted silence and obscurity, that the eyes of all might be turned to the Light of life.

Those who are true to their calling as messengers for God, will not seek honor for themselves. Love for self will be swallowed up in love for Christ. No rivalry will mar the precious cause of the gospel. They will recognize that it is their work to proclaim, as did John the Baptist, "Behold the Lamb of God, which taketh away the sin of the world." John 1:29. They will lift up Jesus, and with Him humanity will be lifted up. "Thus saith the high and lofty One that inhabiteth eternity, whose name is Holy: I dwell in the high and holy place, with him also that is of a contrite and humble spirit, to revive the spirit of the humble, and to revive the heart of the contrite ones." Isaiah 57:15.

The soul of the prophet, emptied of self, was filled with the light of the divine. As he witnessed to the Saviour's glory, his words were almost a counterpart of those that Christ himself had spoken in His interview with Nicodemus. John said, "He that cometh from above is above all: he that is of the earth is earthly, and speaketh of the earth: He that cometh from heaven is above all. . . . For He whom God hath sent speaketh the words of God: for God giveth not the Spirit by measure unto Him." Christ could say, "I seek not Mine own will, but the will of the Father which hath sent Me." To Him it is declared, "Thou hast loved righteousness, and hated iniquity; therefore God, even Thy God, hath anointed Thee with the oil of gladness above Thy fellows." John 5:30; Hebrews 1:9. The Father "giveth not the Spirit by measure unto Him."

So with the followers of Christ. We can receive of heaven's light only as we are willing to be emptied of self. We cannot discern the character of God, or accept Christ by faith, unless we consent to the bringing into captivity of every thought to the obedience of Christ. To all who do this, the Holy Spirit is given without measure. In Christ "dwelleth all the fulness of the Godhead bodily, and in Him ye are made full." Colossians 2:9, 10, R. V.

The disciples of John had declared that all men were coming to Christ; but with clearer insight, John said, "No man receiveth His witness;" so few were ready to accept Him as the Saviour from sin. But "he that hath received His witness hath set his seal to this, that God is true." John 3:33, R.V. "He that believeth on the Son hath everlasting life." No need of disputation as to whether Christ's baptism or John's purified from sin. It is the grace of Christ that gives life to the soul. Apart from Christ, baptism, like any other service, is a worthless form. "He that believeth not the Son shall not see life."

The success of Christ's work, which the Baptist had received with such joy, was reported also to the authorities at Jerusalem. The priests and rabbis had been jealous of John's influence as they saw the people leaving the synagogues and flocking to the wilderness; but here was One who had still greater power to attract the multitudes. Those leaders in Israel were not willing to say with John, "He must increase, but I must decrease." They arose with a new determination to put an end to the work that was drawing the people away from them.

Jesus knew that they would spare no effort to create a division between His own disciples and those of John. He knew that the storm was gathering which would sweep away one of the greatest prophets ever given to the world. Wishing to avoid all occasion for misunderstanding or dissension, He quietly ceased His labors, and withdrew to Galilee. We also, while loyal to truth, should try to avoid all that may lead to discord and misapprehension. For whenever these arise, they result in the loss of souls. Whenever circumstances occur that threaten to cause division, we should follow the example of Jesus and of John the Baptist.

John had been called to lead out as a reformer. Because of this, his disciples were in danger of fixing their attention upon him, feeling that the success of the work depended upon his labors, and losing sight of the fact that he was only an instrument through which God had wrought. But the work of John was not sufficient to lay the foundation of the Christian church. When he had fulfilled his mission, another work was to be done, which his testimony could not accomplish. His disciples did not understand this. When they saw Christ coming in to take the work, they were jealous and dissatisfied.

The same dangers still exist. God calls a man to do a certain work; and when he has carried it as far as he is qualified to take it, the Lord brings in others, to carry it still farther. But, like John's disciples, many feel that the success of the work depends on the first laborer. Attention is fixed upon the human instead of the divine, jealousy comes in, and the work of God is marred. The one thus unduly honored is tempted to cherish self-confidence. He does not realize his dependence on God. The people are taught to rely on man for guidance, and thus they fall into error, and are led away from God.

The work of God is not to bear the image and superscription of man. From time to time the Lord will bring in different agencies, through whom His purpose can best be accomplished. Happy are they who are willing for self to be humbled, saying with John the Baptist, "He must increase, but I must decrease."

At Jacob's Well

On the way to Galilee Jesus passed through Samaria. It was noon when He reached the beautiful vale of Shechem. At the opening of this valley was Jacob's well. Wearied with His journey, He sat down here to rest while His disciples went to buy food.

The Jews and the Samaritans were bitter enemies, and as far as possible avoided all dealing with each other. To trade with the Samaritans in case of necessity was indeed counted lawful by the rabbis; but all social intercourse with them was condemned. A Jew would not borrow from a Samaritan, nor receive a kindness, not even a morsel of bread or a cup of water. The disciples, in buying food, were acting in harmony with the custom of their nation. But beyond this they did not go. To ask a favor of the Samaritans, or in any way seek to benefit them, did not enter into the thought of even Christ's disciples.

As Jesus sat by the well side, He was faint from hunger and thirst. The journey since morning had been long, and now the sun of noontide beat upon Him. His thirst was increased by the thought of the cool, refreshing water so near, yet inaccessible to Him; for He had no rope nor water jar, and the well was deep. The lot of humanity was His, and He waited for some one to come to draw.

A woman of Samaria approached, and seeming unconscious of His presence, filled her pitcher with water. As she turned to go away, Jesus asked her for a drink. Such a favor no oriental would withhold. In the East, water was called "the gift of God." To offer a drink to the thirsty traveler was held to be a duty so sacred that the Arabs of the desert would go out of their way in order to perform it. The hatred between Jews and Samaritans prevented the woman from offering a kindness to Jesus; but the Saviour was seeking to find the key to this heart, and with the tact born of divine love, He asked, not offered, a favor. The offer of a kindness might have been rejected; but trust awakens trust. The King of heaven came to this outcast soul, asking a service at her hands. He who made the ocean, who controls the waters of the great deep, who opened the springs and channels of the earth, rested from His weariness at Jacob's well, and was dependent upon a stranger's kindness for even the gift of a drink of water.

The woman saw that Jesus was a Jew. In her surprise she forgot to grant His request, but tried to learn the reason for it. "How is it," she said, "that Thou, being a Jew, askest drink of me, which am a woman of Samaria?"

Jesus answered, "If thou knewest the gift of God, and who it is that saith to thee, Give Me to drink, thou wouldst have asked of Him, and He would have given thee living water." You wonder that I should ask of you even so small a favor as a draught of water from the well at our feet. Had you asked of Me, I would have given you to drink of the water of everlasting life.

The woman had not comprehended the words of Christ, but she felt their solemn import. Her light, bantering manner began to change. Supposing that Jesus spoke of the well before them, she said, "Sir, Thou hast nothing to draw with, and the well is deep; from whence then hast Thou that living water? Art Thou greater than our father Jacob, which gave us the well, and drank thereof himself?" She saw before her only a thirsty traveler, wayworn and dusty. In her mind she compared Him with the honored patriarch Jacob. She cherished the feeling which is so natural, that no other well could be equal to that provided by the fathers. She was looking backward to the fathers, forward to the Messiah's coming, while the Hope of the fathers, the Messiah Himself, was beside her, and she

74   This chapter is based on John 4:1-42.   (183-184)

knew Him not. How many thirsting souls are today close by the living fountain, yet looking far away for the well-springs of life! "Say not in thine heart, Who shall ascend into heaven? (that is, to bring Christ down from above); or, Who shall descend into the deep? (that is, to bring up Christ again from the dead.) . . . The word is nigh thee, even in thy mouth, and in thy heart. . . . If thou shalt confess with thy mouth the Lord Jesus, and shalt believe in thine heart that God hath raised Him from the dead, thou shalt be saved." Romans 10: 6-9.

Jesus did not immediately answer the question in regard to Himself, but with solemn earnestness He said, "Whosoever drinketh of this water shall thirst again; but whosoever drinketh of the water that I shall give him shall never thirst; but the water that I shall give him shall be in him a well of water springing up into everlasting life."

He who seeks to quench his thirst at the fountains of this world, will drink only to thirst again. Everywhere men are unsatisfied. They long for something to supply the need of the soul. Only One can meet that want. The need of the world, "the desire of all nations," is Christ. The divine grace which He alone can impart, is as living water, purifying, refreshing, and invigorating the soul.

Jesus did not convey the idea that merely one draught of the water of life would suffice the receiver. He who tastes of the love of Christ will continually long for more; but he seeks for nothing else. The riches, honors, and pleasures of the world do not attract him. The constant cry of his heart is, "More of Thee." And He who reveals to the soul its necessity, is waiting to satisfy its hunger and thirst. Every human resource and dependence will fail. The cisterns will be emptied, the pools become dry; but our Redeemer is an inexhaustible fountain. We may drink, and drink again, and ever find a fresh supply. He in whom Christ dwells, has within himself the fountain of blessing, — "a well of water springing up into everlasting life." From this source he may draw strength and grace sufficient for all his needs.

As Jesus spoke of the living water, the woman looked upon Him with wondering attention. He had aroused her interest, and awakened a desire for the gift of which He spoke. She perceived that it was not the water of Jacob's well to which He referred; for of this she used continually, drinking, and thirsting again. "Sir," she said, "give me this water, that I thirst not, neither come hither to draw."

Jesus now abruptly turned the conversation. Before this soul could receive the gift He longed to bestow, she must be brought to recognize her sin and her Saviour. He "saith unto her, Go, call thy husband, and come hither." She answered, "I have no husband." Thus she hoped to prevent all questioning in that direction. But the Saviour continued, "Thou hast well said, I have no husband; for thou hast had five husbands; and he whom thou now hast is not thy husband: in that saidst thou truly."

The listener trembled. A mysterious hand was turning the pages of her life history, bringing to view that which she had hoped to keep forever hidden. Who was He that could read the secrets of her life? There came to her thoughts of eternity, of the future Judgment, when all that is now hidden shall be revealed. In its light, conscience was awakened.

She could deny nothing; but she tried to evade all mention of a subject so unwelcome. With deep reverence, she said, "Sir, I perceive that Thou art a prophet." Then, hoping to silence conviction, she turned to points of religious controversy. If this was a prophet, surely He could give her instruction concerning these matters that had been so long disputed.

Patiently Jesus permitted her to lead the conversation whither she would. Meanwhile He watched for the opportunity of again bringing the truth home to her heart. "Our fathers worshiped in this mountain," she said, "and ye say that in Jerusalem is the place where men ought to worship." Just in sight was Mount Gerizim. Its temple was demolished, and only the altar remained. The place of worship had been a subject of contention between the Jews and the Samaritans. Some of the ancestors of the latter people had once belonged to Israel; but because of their sins, the Lord suffered them to be overcome by an idolatrous nation. For many generations they were intermingled with idolaters, whose religion gradually contaminated their own. It is true they held that their idols were only to remind them of the living God, the Ruler of the universe; nevertheless the people were led to reverence their graven images.

When the temple at Jerusalem was rebuilt in the days of Ezra, the Samaritans wished to join the Jews in its erection. This privilege was refused them, and a bitter animosity sprung up between the two peoples. The Samaritans built a rival temple on Mount Gerizim. Here they worshiped in accordance with the Mosaic ritual, though they did not wholly renounce idolatry. But disasters attended them, their temple was destroyed by their enemies, and they seemed to be under a curse; yet they still clung to their traditions and their forms of worship. They would not acknowledge the temple at Jerusalem as the house of God, nor admit that the religion of the Jews was superior to their own.

In answer to the woman, Jesus said, "Believe Me, the hour cometh, when ye shall neither in this mountain, nor yet at Jerusalem, worship the Father. Ye worship ye know not what: we know what we worship; for salvation is of the Jews." Jesus had shown that He was free from Jewish prejudice against the Samaritans. Now He sought to break down the prejudice of this Samaritan against the Jews. While referring to the fact that the faith of the Samaritans was corrupted with idolatry, He declared that the great truths of redemption had been committed to the Jews, and that from among them the Messiah was to appear. In the Sacred Writings they had a clear presentation of the character of God and the principles of His government. Jesus classed Himself with the Jews as those to whom God had given a knowledge of Himself.

He desired to lift the thoughts of His hearer above matters of form and ceremony, and questions of controversy. "The hour cometh," He said, "and now is, when the true worshipers shall worship the Father in spirit and in truth; for the Father seeketh such to worship Him. God is a Spirit; and they that worship Him must worship Him in spirit and in truth."

Here is declared the same truth that Jesus had revealed to Nicodemus when He said, "Except a man be born from above, he cannot see the kingdom of God." John 3:3, margin. Not by seeking a holy mountain or a sacred temple are men brought into communion with heaven. Religion is not to be confined to external forms and ceremonies. The religion that comes from God is the only religion that will lead to God. In order to serve Him aright, we must be born of the divine Spirit. This will purify the heart and renew the mind, giving us a new capacity for knowing and loving God. It will give us a willing obedience to all His requirements. This is true worship. It is the fruit of the working of the Holy Spirit. By the Spirit every sincere prayer is indited, and such prayer is acceptable to God. Wherever a soul reaches out after God, there the Spirit's working is manifest, and God will reveal Himself to that soul. For such worshipers He is seeking. He waits to receive them, and to make them His sons and daughters.

As the woman talked with Jesus, she was impressed with His words. Never had she heard such sentiments from the priests of her own people or from the Jews. As the past of her life had been spread out before her, she had been made sensible of her great want. She realized her soul thirst, which the waters of the well of Sychar could never satisfy. Nothing that had hitherto come in contact with her had so awakened her to a higher need. Jesus had convinced her that He read the secrets of her life; yet she felt that He was her friend, pitying and loving her. While the very purity of His presence condemned her sin, He had spoken no word of denunciation, but had told her of His grace, that could renew the soul. She began to have some conviction of His character. The question arose in her mind, "Might not this be the long-looked-for Messiah?" She said to Him, "I know that Messiah cometh, which is called Christ; when He is come, He will tell us all things." Jesus answered, "I that speak unto thee am He."

As the woman heard these words, faith sprung up in her heart. She accepted the wonderful announcement from the lips of the divine Teacher.

This woman was in an appreciative state of mind. She was ready to receive the noblest revelation; for she was interested in the Scriptures, and the Holy Spirit had been preparing her mind to receive more light. She had studied the Old Testament promise, "The Lord thy God will raise up unto thee a Prophet from the midst of thee, of thy brethren, like unto me; unto Him ye shall hearken." Deuteronomy 18:15. She longed to understand this prophecy. Light was already flashing into her mind. The water of life, the spiritual life which Christ gives to every thirsty soul, had begun to spring up in her heart. The Spirit of the Lord was working with her.

The plain statement made by Christ to this woman could not have been made to the self-righteous Jews. Christ was far more reserved when He spoke to them. That which had been withheld from the Jews, and which the disciples were afterward enjoined to keep secret, was revealed to her. Jesus saw that she would make use of her knowledge in bringing others to share His grace.

When the disciples returned from their errand, they were surprised to find their Master speaking with the woman. He had not taken the refreshing draught that He desired, and He did not stop to eat the food His disciples had brought. When the woman had gone, the disciples entreated Him to eat. They saw Him silent, absorbed, as in rapt meditation. His face was beaming with light, and they feared to interrupt His communion with heaven. But they knew that He was faint and weary, and thought it their duty to remind Him of His physical necessities. Jesus recognized their loving interest, and He said, "I have meat to eat that ye know not of."

The disciples wondered who could have brought Him food; but He explained, "My meat is to do the will of Him that sent Me, and to accomplish His work." John 4:34, R. V. As His words to the woman had aroused her conscience, Jesus rejoiced. He saw her drinking of the water of life, and His own hunger and thirst were satisfied. The accomplishment of the mission which He had left heaven to perform, strengthened the Saviour for His labor, and lifted Him above the necessities of humanity. To minister to a soul hungering and thirsting for the truth was more grateful to Him than eating or drinking. It was a comfort, a refreshment to Him. Benevolence was the life of His soul.

Our Redeemer thirsts for recognition. He hungers for the sympathy and love of those whom He has purchased with His own blood. He longs with inexpressible desire that they should come to Him and have life. As the mother watches for the smile of recognition from her little child, which tells of the dawning of intelligence, so does Christ watch for the expression of grateful love which shows that spiritual life is begun in the soul.

The woman had been filled with joy as she listened to Christ's words. The wonderful revelation was almost overpowering. Leaving her waterpot, she returned to the city, to carry the message to others. Jesus knew why she had gone. Leaving her waterpot spoke unmistakably as to the effect of His words. It was the earnest desire of her soul to obtain the living water; and she forgot her errand to the well, she forgot the Saviour's thirst, which she had purposed to supply. With heart overflowing with gladness, she hastened on her way, to impart to others the precious light she had received.

"Come, see a man which told me all things that ever I did," she said to the men of the city. "Is not this the Christ?"

Behold God is my salvation; I will trust, and not be afraid: for the Lord Jehovah is my strength and my song; he also is become my salvation. Therefore with joy shall ye draw water out of the wells of Salvation.

Isaiah 12:2, 3

And whosoever shall give to drink unto one of these little ones a cup of cold water only in the name of a disciple, verily I say unto you, he shall in no wise lose his reward.

Matthew 10:42

Give, and it shall be given unto you; good measure, pressed down, and shaken together; and running over; shall men give into your bosom. For with the same measure that ye mete withal it shall be measured to you again.

Luke 6:38

Gena Cowen

Her words touched their hearts. There was a new expression on her face, a change in her whole appearance. They were interested to see Jesus. "Then they went out of the city, and came unto Him."

As Jesus still sat at the well side, He looked over the fields of grain that were spread out before Him, their tender green touched by the golden sunlight. Pointing His disciples to the scene, He employed it as a symbol: "Say not ye, There are yet four months, and then cometh harvest? Behold, I say unto you, Lift up your eyes, and look on the fields; for they are white already to harvest." And as He spoke, He looked on the groups that were coming to the well. It was four months to the time for harvesting the grain, but here was a harvest ready for the reaper.

"He that reapeth," He said, "receiveth wages, and gathereth fruit unto life eternal; that both he that soweth and he that reapeth may rejoice together. And herein is that saying true, One soweth, and another reapeth." Here Christ points out the sacred service owed to God by those who receive the gospel. They are to be His living agencies. He requires their individual service. And whether we sow or reap, we are working for God. One scatters the seed; another gathers in the harvest; and both the sower and the reaper receive wages. They rejoice together in the reward of their labor.

Jesus said to the disciples, "I sent you to reap that whereon ye bestowed no labor. Other men labored, and ye are entered into their labors." The Saviour was here looking forward to the great ingathering on the day of Pentecost. The disciples were not to regard this as the result of their own efforts. They were entering into other men's labors. Ever since the fall of Adam, Christ had been committing the seed of the word to His chosen servants, to be sown in human hearts. And an unseen agency, even as omnipotent power, had worked silently but effectually to produce the harvest. The dew and rain and sunshine of God's grace had been given, to refresh and nourish the seed of truth. Christ was about to water the seed with His own blood. His disciples were privileged to be laborers together with God. They were co-workers with Christ and with the holy men of old. By the outpouring of the Holy Spirit at Pentecost, thousands were to be converted in a day. This was the result of Christ's sowing, the harvest of His work.

In the words spoken to the woman at the well, good seed had been sown, and how quickly the harvest was received. The Samaritans came and heard Jesus, and believed on Him. Crowding about Him at the well, they plied Him with questions, and eagerly received His explanations of many things that had been obscure to them. As they listened, their perplexity began to clear away. They were like a people in great darkness tracing up a sudden ray of light till they had found the day. But they were not satisfied with this short conference. They were anxious to hear more, and to have their friends also listen to this wonderful teacher. They invited Him to their city, and begged Him to remain with them. For two days He tarried in Samaria, and many more believed on Him.

The Pharisees despised the simplicity of Jesus. They ignored His miracles, and demanded a sign that He was the Son of God. But the Samaritans asked no sign, and Jesus performed no miracles among them, save in revealing the secrets of her life to the woman at the well. Yet many received Him. In their new joy they said to the woman, "Now we believe, not because of thy saying; for

---

"Our Redeemer thirsts for recognition. He hungers for the sympathy and love of those whom He has purchased with His own blood. He longs with inexpressible desire that they should come to Him and have life."

---

we have heard Him ourselves, and know that this is indeed the Christ, the Saviour of the world."

The Samaritans believed that the Messiah was to come as the Redeemer, not only of the Jews, but of the world. The Holy Spirit through Moses had foretold Him as a prophet sent from God. Through Jacob it had been declared that unto Him should the gathering of the people be; and through Abraham, that in Him all the nations of the earth should be blessed. On these scriptures the people of Samaria based their faith in the Messiah. The fact that the Jews had misinterpreted the later prophets, attributing to the first advent the glory of Christ's second coming, had led the Samaritans to discard all the sacred writings except those given through Moses. But as the Saviour swept away these false interpretations, many accepted the later prophecies and the words of Christ Himself in regard to the kingdom of God.

Jesus had begun to break down the partition wall between Jew and Gentile, and to preach salvation to the world. Though He was a Jew, He mingled freely with the Samaritans, setting at naught the Pharisaic customs of His nation. In face of their prejudices He accepted the hospitality of this despised people. He slept under their roofs,

ate with them at their tables, — partaking of the food prepared and served by their hands, — taught in their streets,
and treated them with the utmost kindness and courtesy.

In the temple at Jerusalem a low wall separated the outer
court from all other portions of the sacred building. Upon
this wall were inscriptions in different languages, stating
that none but Jews were allowed to pass this boundary.
Had a Gentile presumed to enter the inner inclosure, he
would have desecrated the temple, and would have paid
the penalty with his life. But Jesus, the originator of the
temple and its service, drew the Gentiles to Him by the tie
of human sympathy, while His divine grace brought to
them the salvation which the Jews rejected.

The stay of Jesus in Samaria was designed to be a
blessing to His disciples, who were still under the influence of Jewish bigotry. They felt that loyalty to their own
nation required them to cherish enmity toward the Samaritans. They wondered at the conduct of Jesus. They could
not refuse to follow His example, and during the two days
in Samaria, fidelity to Him kept their prejudices under
control; yet in heart they were unreconciled. They were
slow to learn that their contempt and hatred must give
place to pity and sympathy. But after the Lord's ascension,
His lessons came back to them with a new meaning. After
the outpouring of the Holy Spirit, they recalled the
Saviour's look, His words, the respect and tenderness of
His bearing toward these despised strangers. When Peter
went to preach in Samaria, he brought the same spirit into
his own work. When John was called to Ephesus and
Smyrna, he remembered the experience at Shechem, and
was filled with gratitude to the divine Teacher, who,
foreseeing the difficulties they must meet, had given them
help in His own example.

The Saviour is still carrying forward the same work as
when He proffered the water of life to the woman of
Samaria. Those who call themselves His followers, may
despise and shun the outcast ones; but no circumstance of
birth or nationality, no condition of life, can turn away His
love from the children of men. To every soul, however
sinful, Jesus says, If thou hadst asked of Me, I would have
given thee living water.

The gospel invitation is not to be narrowed down, and
presented only to a select few, who, we suppose, will do
us honor if they accept it. The message is to be given to
all. Wherever hearts are open to receive the truth, Christ
is ready to instruct them. He reveals to them the Father,
and the worship acceptable to Him who reads the heart.
For such He uses no parables. To them, as to the woman
at the well, He says, "I that speak unto thee am He."

When Jesus sat down to rest at Jacob's well, He had
come from Judea, where His ministry had produced little
fruit. He had been rejected by the priests and rabbis, and
even the people who professed to be His disciples had
failed of perceiving His divine character. He was faint and
weary; yet He did not neglect the opportunity of speaking
to one woman, though she was a stranger, an alien from
Israel, and living in open sin.

The Saviour did not wait for congregations to assemble.
Often He began His lessons with only a few gathered about
Him, but one by one the passers-by paused to listen, until
a multitude heard with wonder and awe the words of God
through the Heaven-sent Teacher. The worker for Christ
should not feel that he cannot speak with the same earnestness to a few hearers as to a larger company. There may
be only one to hear the message; but who can tell how
far-reaching will be its influence? It seemed a small matter, even to His disciples, for the Saviour to spend His time
upon a woman of Samaria. But He reasoned more earnestly and eloquently with her than with kings, council-
lors, or high priests. The lessons He gave to that woman
have been repeated to the earth's remotest bounds.

As soon as she had found the Saviour, the Samaritan
woman brought others to Him. She proved herself a more
effective missionary than His own disciples. The disciples
saw nothing in Samaria to indicate that it was an encouraging field. Their thoughts were fixed upon a great work
to be done in the future. They did not see that right around
them was a harvest to be gathered. But through the woman
whom they despised, a whole cityful were brought to hear
the Saviour. She carried the light at once to her countrymen.

This woman represents the working of a practical faith
in Christ. Every true disciple is born into the kingdom of
God as a missionary. He who drinks of the living water
becomes a fountain of life. The receiver becomes a giver.
The grace of Christ in the soul is like a spring in the desert,
welling up to refresh all, and making those who are ready
to perish eager to drink of the water of life.

"Except Ye See Signs & Wonders"

The Galileans who returned from the Passover brought back the report of the wonderful works of Jesus. The judgment passed upon His acts by the dignitaries at Jerusalem opened His way in Galilee. Many of the people lamented the abuse of the temple and the greed and arrogance of the priests. They hoped that this man, who had put the rulers to flight, might be the looked-for Deliverer. Now tidings had come that seemed to confirm their brightest anticipations. It was reported that the prophet had declared Himself to be the Messiah.

But the people of Nazareth did not believe on Him. For this reason, Jesus did not visit Nazareth on His way to Cana. The Saviour declared to His disciples that a prophet has no honor in his own country. Men estimate character by that which they themselves are capable of appreciating. The narrow and worldly-minded judged of Christ by His humble birth, His lowly garb, and daily toil. They could not appreciate the purity of that spirit upon which was no stain of sin.

The news of Christ's return to Cana soon spread throughout Galilee, bringing hope to the suffering and distressed. In Capernaum the tidings attracted the attention of a Jewish nobleman who was an officer in the king's service. A son of the officer was suffering from what seemed to be an incurable disease. Physicians had given him up to die; but when the father heard of Jesus, he determined to seek help from Him. The child was very low, and, it was feared, might not live till his return; yet the nobleman felt that he must present the case in person. He hoped that a father's prayers might awaken the sympathy of the great Physician.

On reaching Cana he found a throng surrounding Jesus. With an anxious heart he pressed through to the Saviour's presence. His faith faltered when he saw only a plainly dressed man, dusty and worn with travel. He doubted that this person could do what he had come to ask of him; yet he secured an interview with Jesus, told his errand, and besought the Saviour to accompany him to his home. But already his sorrow was known to Jesus. Before the officer had left his home, the Saviour had beheld his affliction.

But He knew also that the father had, in his own mind, made conditions concerning his belief in Jesus. Unless his petition should be granted, he would not receive Him as the Messiah. While the officer waited in an agony of suspense, Jesus said, "Except ye see signs and wonders, ye will not believe."

Notwithstanding all the evidence that Jesus was the Christ, the petitioner had determined to make his belief in Him conditional on the granting of his own request. The Saviour contrasted this questioning unbelief with the simple faith of the Samaritans, who asked for no miracle or sign. His word, the ever-present evidence of His divinity, had a convincing power that reached their hearts. Christ was pained that His own people, to whom the sacred oracles had been committed, should fail to hear the voice of God speaking to them in His Son.

Yet the nobleman had a degree of faith; for he had come to ask what seemed to him the most precious of all blessings. Jesus had a greater gift to bestow. He desired, not only to heal the child, but to make the officer and his household sharers in the blessings of salvation, and to kindle a light in Capernaum, which was so soon to be the field of His own labors. But the nobleman must realize his need before he would desire the grace of Christ. This courtier represented many of his nation. They were interested in Jesus from selfish motives. They hoped to receive some special benefit through His power, and they staked

This chapter is based on John 4:43-54.

their faith on the granting of this temporal favor; but they were ignorant as to their spiritual disease, and saw not their need of divine grace.

Like a flash of light, the Saviour's words to the nobleman laid bare his heart. He saw that his motives in seeking Jesus were selfish. His vacillating faith appeared to him in its true character. In deep distress he realized that his doubt might cost the life of his son. He knew that he was in the presence of One who could read the thoughts, and to whom all things were possible. In an agony of supplication he cried, "Sir, come down ere my child die!" His faith took hold upon Christ as did Jacob, when, wrestling with the angel, he cried, "I will not let thee go, except thou bless me." Genesis 32:26.

Like Jacob he prevailed. The Saviour cannot withdraw from the soul that clings to Him, pleading its great need. "Go thy way," He said; "thy son liveth." The nobleman left the Saviour's presence with a peace and joy he had never known before. Not only did he believe that his son would be restored, but with strong confidence he trusted in Christ as the Redeemer.

At the same hour the watchers beside the dying child in the home at Capernaum beheld a sudden and mysterious change. The shadow of death was lifted from the sufferer's face. The flush of fever gave place to the soft glow of returning health. The dim eyes brightened with intelligence, and strength returned to the feeble, emaciated frame. No signs of his malady lingered about the child. His burning flesh had become soft and moist, and he sank into a quiet sleep. The fever had left him in the very heat of the day. The family were amazed, and great was the rejoicing.

Cana was not so far from Capernaum but that the officer might have reached his home on the evening after his interview with Jesus; but he did not hasten on the homeward journey. It was not until the next morning that he reached Capernaum. What a homecoming was that! When he went to find Jesus, his heart was heavy with sorrow. The sunshine seemed cruel to him, the songs of the birds a mockery. How different his feelings now! All nature wears a new aspect. He sees with new eyes. As he journeys in the quiet of the early morning, all nature seems to be praising God with him. While he is still some distance from his own dwelling, servants come out to meet him, anxious to relieve the suspense they are sure he must feel. He shows no surprise at the news they bring, but with a depth of interest they cannot know, he asks at what hour the child began to mend. They answer, "Yesterday at the seventh hour the fever left him." At the very moment when the father's faith grasped the assurance, "Thy son liveth," divine love touched the dying child.

The father hurries on to greet his son. He clasps him to his heart as one restored from the dead, and thanks God again and again for this wonderful restoration.

The nobleman longed to know more of Christ. As he afterward heard His teaching, he and all his household became disciples. Their affliction was sanctified to the conversion of the entire family. Tidings of the miracle spread; and in Capernaum, where so many of His mighty works were performed, the way was prepared for Christ's personal ministry.

He who blessed the nobleman at Capernaum is just as desirous of blessing us. But like the afflicted father, we are often led to seek Jesus by the desire for some earthly good; and upon the granting of our request we rest our confidence in His love. The Saviour longs to give us a greater blessing than we ask; and He delays the answer to our request that He may show us the evil of our own hearts, and our deep need of His grace. He desires us to renounce the selfishness that leads us to seek Him. Confessing our helplessness and bitter need, we are to trust ourselves wholly to His love.

The nobleman wanted to *see* the fulfilment of his prayer before he should believe; but he had to accept the word of Jesus, that his request was heard, and the blessing granted. This lesson we also have to learn. Not because we see or feel that God hears us, are we to believe. We are to trust in His promises. When we come to Him in faith, every petition enters the heart of God. When we have asked for His blessing, we should believe that we receive it, and thank Him that we *have* received it. Then we are to go about our duties, assured that the blessing will be realized when we need it most. When we have learned to do this, we shall know that our prayers are answered. God will do for us "exceeding abundantly," "according to the riches of His glory," and "the working of His mighty power." Ephesians 3:20, 16; 1:19.

Bethesda and the Sanhedrin

"Now there is at Jerusalem by the sheep market a pool, which is called in the Hebrew tongue Bethesda, having five porches. In these lay a great multitude of impotent folk, of blind, halt, withered, waiting for the moving of the water."

At certain seasons the waters of this pool were agitated, and it was commonly believed that this was the result of supernatural power, and that whoever first after the troubling of the pool stepped into the waters, would be healed of whatever disease he had. Hundreds of sufferers visited the place; but so great was the crowd when the water was troubled that they rushed forward, trampling under foot men, women, and children, weaker than themselves. Many could not get near the pool. Many who had succeeded in reaching it, died upon its brink. Shelters had been erected about the place, that the sick might be protected from the heat by day and the chilliness of the night. There were some who spent the night in these porches, creeping to the edge of the pool day after day, in the vain hope of relief.

Jesus was again at Jerusalem. Walking alone, in apparent meditation and prayer, He came to the pool. He saw the wretched sufferers watching for that which they supposed to be their only chance of cure. He longed to exercise His healing power, and make every sufferer whole. But it was the Sabbath day. Multitudes were going to the temple for worship, and He knew that such an act of healing would so excite the prejudice of the Jews as to cut short His work.

But the Saviour saw one case of supreme wretchedness. It was that of a man who had been a helpless cripple for thirty-eight years. His disease was in a great degree the result of his own sin, and was looked upon as a judgment from God. Alone and friendless, feeling that he was shut out from God's mercy, the sufferer had passed long years of misery. At the time when it was expected that the waters would be troubled, those who pitied his helplessness would bear him to the porches. But at the favored moment he had no one to help him in. He had seen the rippling of the water, but had never been able to get farther than the edge of the pool. Others stronger than he would plunge in before him. He could not contend successfully with the selfish, scrambling crowd. His persistent efforts toward the one object, and his anxiety and continual disappointment, were fast wearing away the remnant of his strength.

The sick man was lying on his mat, and occasionally lifting his head to gaze at the pool, when a tender, compassionate face bent over him, and the words, "Wilt thou be made whole?" arrested his attention. Hope came to his heart. He felt that in some way he was to have help. But the glow of encouragement soon faded. He remembered how often he had tried to reach the pool, and now he had little prospect of living till it should again be troubled. He turned away wearily, saying, "Sir, I have no man, when the water is troubled, to put me into the pool; but while I am coming, another steppeth down before me."

Jesus does not ask this sufferer to exercise faith in Him. He simply says, "Rise, take up thy bed, and walk." But the man's faith takes hold upon that word. Every nerve and muscle thrills with new life, and healthful action comes to his crippled limbs. Without question he sets his will to obey the command of Christ, and all his muscles respond to his will. Springing to his feet, he finds himself an active man.

Jesus had given him no assurance of divine help. The man might have stopped to doubt, and lost his one chance of healing. But he believed Christ's word, and in acting upon it he received strength.

This chapter is based on John 5.

Through the same faith we may receive spiritual healing. By sin we have been severed from the life of God. Our souls are palsied. Of ourselves we are no more capable of living a holy life than was the impotent man capable of walking. There are many who realize their helplessness, and who long for that spiritual life which will bring them into harmony with God; they are vainly striving to obtain it. In despair they cry, "O wretched man that I am! who shall deliver me from this body of death?" Romans 7:24, margin. Let these desponding, struggling ones look up. The Saviour is bending over the purchase of His blood, saying with inexpressible tenderness and pity, "Wilt thou be made whole?" He bids you arise in health and peace. Do not wait to feel that you are made whole. Believe His word, and it will be fulfilled. Put your will on the side of Christ. Will to serve Him, and in acting upon His word you will receive strength. Whatever may be the evil practice, the master passion which through long indulgence binds both soul and body, Christ is able and longs to deliver. He will impart life to the soul that is "dead in trespasses." Ephesians 2:1. He will set free the captive that is held by weakness and misfortune and the chains of sin.

The restored paralytic stooped to take up his bed, which was only a rug and a blanket, and as he straightened himself again with a sense of delight, he looked around for his deliverer; but Jesus was lost in the crowd. The man feared that he would not know Him if he should see Him again. As he hurried on his way with firm, free step, praising God and rejoicing in his new-found strength, he met several of the Pharisees, and immediately told them of his cure. He was surprised at the coldness with which they listened to his story.

With lowering brows they interrupted him, asking why he was carrying his bed on the Sabbath day. They sternly reminded him that it was not lawful to bear burdens on the Lord's day. In his joy the man had forgotten that it was the Sabbath; yet he felt no condemnation for obeying the command of one who had such power from God. He answered boldly, "He that made me whole, the same said unto me, Take up thy bed, and walk." They asked who it was that had done this, but he could not tell. These rulers knew well that only One had shown Himself able to perform this miracle; but they wished for direct proof that it was Jesus, that they might condemn Him as a Sabbath-breaker. In their judgment He had not only broken the law in healing the sick man on the Sabbath, but had committed sacrilege in bidding him bear away his bed.

The Jews had so perverted the law that they made it a yoke of bondage. Their meaningless requirements had become a byword among other nations. Especially was the Sabbath hedged in by all manner of senseless restrictions. It was not to them a delight, the holy of the Lord, and honorable. The scribes and Pharisees had made its observance an intolerable burden. A Jew was not allowed to kindle a fire nor even to light a candle on the Sabbath. As a consequence the people were dependent upon the Gentiles for many services which their rules forbade them to do for themselves. They did not reflect that if these acts were sinful, those who employed others to perform them were as guilty as if they had done the work themselves. They thought that salvation was restricted to the Jews, and that the condition of all others, being already hopeless, could be made no worse. But God has given no commandments which cannot be obeyed by all. His laws sanction no unreasonable or selfish restrictions.

In the temple Jesus met the man who had been healed. He had come to bring a sin offering and also a thank offering for the great mercy he had received. Finding him among the worshipers, Jesus made Himself known, with the warning words, "Behold, thou art made whole; sin no more, lest a worse thing come unto thee."

> **"Do not wait to feel that you are made whole. Believe His word, and it will be fulfilled. Put your will on the side of Christ. . . . and in acting upon His word you will receive strength. . . . He will set free the captive that is held by weakness and misfortune and the chains of sin."**

The healed man was overjoyed at meeting his deliverer. Ignorant of the enmity toward Jesus, he told the Pharisees who had questioned him, that this was He who had performed the cure. "Therefore did the Jews persecute Jesus, and sought to slay Him, because He had done these things on the Sabbath day."

Jesus was brought before the Sanhedrim to answer the charge of Sabbathbreaking. Had the Jews at this time been an independent nation, such a charge would have served their purpose for putting Him to death. This their subjection to the Romans prevented. The Jews had not the power to inflict capital punishment, and the accusations brought against Christ would have no weight in a Roman court. There were other objects, however, which they hoped to secure. Notwithstanding their efforts to counteract His work, Christ was gaining, even in Jerusalem, an influence

BETHESDA AND THE SANHEDRIN

over the people greater than their own. Multitudes who were not interested in the harangues of the rabbis, were attracted by His teaching. They could understand His words, and their hearts were warmed and comforted. He spoke of God, not as an avenging judge, but as a tender father, and He revealed the image of God as mirrored in Himself. His words were like balm to the wounded spirit. Both by His words and by His works of mercy He was breaking the oppressive power of the old traditions and man-made commandments, and presenting the love of God in its exhaustless fullness.

In one of the earliest prophecies of Christ it is written, "The scepter shall not depart from Judah, nor a lawgiver from between his feet, until Shiloh come; and unto Him shall the gathering of the people be." Genesis 49:10. The people were gathering to Christ. The sympathetic hearts of the multitude accepted lessons of love and benevolence in preference to the rigid ceremonies required by the priests. If the priests and rabbis had not interposed, His teaching would have wrought such a reformation as this world has never witnessed. But in order to maintain their own power, these leaders determined to break down the influence of Jesus. His arraignment before the Sanhedrim, and an open condemnation of His teachings, would aid in effecting this; for the people still had great reverence for their religious leaders. Whoever dared to condemn the rabbinical requirements, or attempt to lighten the burdens they had brought upon the people, was regarded as guilty, not only of blasphemy, but of treason. On this ground the rabbis hoped to excite suspicion of Christ. They represented Him as trying to overthrow the established customs, thus causing division among the people, and preparing the way for complete subjugation by the Romans.

But the plans which these rabbis were working so zealously to fulfill originated in another council than that of the Sanhedrin. After Satan had failed to overcome Christ in the wilderness, he combined his forces to oppose Him in His ministry, and if possible to thwart His work. What he could not accomplish by direct, personal effort, he determined to effect by strategy. No sooner had he withdrawn from the conflict in the wilderness than in council with his confederate angels he matured his plans for still further blinding the minds of the Jewish people, that they might not recognize their Redeemer. He planned to work through his human agencies in the religious world, by imbuing them with his own enmity against the champion of truth. He would lead them to reject Christ and to make His life as bitter as possible, hoping to discourage Him in His mission. And the leaders in Israel became instruments of Satan in warring against the Saviour.

Jesus had come to "magnify the law, and make it honorable." He was not to lessen its dignity, but to exalt it. The Scripture says, "He shall not fail nor be discouraged, till He have set judgment in the earth." Isaiah 42:21, 4. He had come to free the Sabbath from those burdensome requirements that had made it a curse instead of a blessing.

For this reason He had chosen the Sabbath upon which to perform the act of healing at Bethesda. He could have healed the sick man as well on any other day of the week; or He might simply have cured him, without bidding him bear away his bed. But this would not have given Him the opportunity He desired. A wise purpose underlay every act of Christ's life on earth. Everything He did was important in itself and in its teaching. Among the afflicted ones at the pool He selected the worst case upon whom to exercise His healing power, and bade the man carry his bed through the city in order to publish the great work that had been wrought upon him. This would raise the question of what it was lawful to do on the Sabbath, and would open the way for Him to denounce the restrictions of the Jews in regard to the Lord's day, and to declare their traditions void.

Jesus stated to them that the work of relieving the afflicted was in harmony with the Sabbath law. It was in harmony with the work of God's angels, who are ever descending and ascending between heaven and earth to minister to suffering humanity. Jesus declared, "My Father worketh hitherto, and I work." All days are God's, in which to carry out His plans for the human race. If the Jews' interpretation of the law was correct, then Jehovah was at fault, whose work has quickened and upheld every living thing since first He laid the foundations of the earth; then He who pronounced His work good, and instituted the Sabbath to commemorate its completion, must put a period to His labor, and stop the never-ending routing of the universe.

Should God forbid the sun to perform its office upon the Sabbath, cut off its genial rays from warming the earth and nourishing vegetation? Must the system of worlds stand still through that holy day? Should He command the brooks to stay from watering the fields and forests, and bid the waves of the sea still their ceaseless ebbing and flowing? Must the wheat and corn stop growing, and the ripening cluster defer its purple bloom? Must the trees and flowers put forth no bud nor blossom on the Sabbath?

In such a case, men would miss the fruits of the earth, and the blessings that make life desirable. Nature must continue her unvarying course. God could not for a moment stay His hand, or man would faint and die. And man also has a work to perform on this day. The necessities of life must be attended to, the sick must be cared for, the wants of the needy must be supplied. He will not be held guiltless who neglects to relieve suffering on the Sabbath. God's holy rest day was made for man, and acts of mercy are in perfect harmony with its intent. God does not desire His creatures to suffer an hour's pain that may be relieved upon the Sabbath or any other day.

The demands upon God are even greater upon the Sabbath than upon other days. His people then leave their usual employment, and spend the time in meditation and worship. They ask more favors of Him on the Sabbath than upon other days. They demand His special attention. They crave His choicest blessings. God does not wait for the Sabbath to pass before He grants these requests. Heaven's work never ceases, and men should never rest from doing good. The Sabbath is not intended to be a period of useless inactivity. The law forbids secular labor on the rest day of the Lord; the toil that gains a livelihood must cease; no labor for worldly pleasure or profit is lawful upon that day; but as God ceased His labor of creating, and rested upon the Sabbath and blessed it, so man is to leave the occupations of his daily life, and devote those sacred hours to healthful rest, to worship, and to holy deeds. The work of Christ in healing the sick was in perfect accord with the law. It honored the Sabbath.

Jesus claimed equal rights with God in doing a work equally sacred, and of the same character with that which engaged the Father in heaven. But the Pharisees were still more incensed. He had not only broken the law, according to their understanding, but in calling God "His own Father" (John 5:18, R. V.) had declared Himself equal with God.

The whole nation of the Jews called God their Father, therefore they would not have been so enraged if Christ had represented Himself as standing in the same relation to God. But they accused Him of blasphemy, showing that they understood Him as making this claim in the highest sense.

These adversaries of Christ had no arguments with which to meet the truths He brought home to their consciences. They could only cite their customs and traditions, and these seemed weak and vapid when compared with the arguments Jesus had drawn from the word of God and the unceasing round of nature. Had the rabbis felt any desire to receive light, they would have been convinced that Jesus spoke the truth. But they evaded the points He made concerning the Sabbath, and sought to stir up anger against Him because He claimed to be equal with God. The fury of the rulers knew no bounds. Had they not feared the people, the priests and rabbis would have slain Jesus on the spot. But the popular sentiment in His favor was strong. Many recognized in Jesus the friend who had healed their diseases and comforted their sorrows, and they justified His healing of the sufferer at Bethesda. So for the time the leaders were obliged to restrain their hatred.

Jesus repelled the charge of blasphemy. My authority, He said, for doing the work of which you accuse Me, is that I am the Son of God, one with Him in nature, in will, and in purpose. In all His works of creation and providence, I co-operate with God. "The Son can do nothing of Himself, but what He seeth the Father do." The priests and rabbis were taking the Son of God to task for the very work He had been sent into the world to do. By their sins they had separated themselves from God, and in their pride were moving independently of Him. They felt sufficient in themselves for all things, and realized no need of a higher wisdom to direct their acts. But the Son of God was surrendered to the Father's will, and dependent upon His power. So utterly was Christ emptied of self that He made no plans for Himself. He accepted God's plans for Him, and day by day the Father unfolded His plans. So should we depend upon God, that our lives may be the simple outworking of His will.

When Moses was about to build the sanctuary as a dwelling place for God, he was directed to make all things according to the pattern shown him in the mount. Moses was full of zeal to do God's work; the most talented, skillful men were at hand to carry out his suggestions. Yet he was not to make a bell, a pomegranate, a tassel, a fringe, a curtain, or any vessel of the sanctuary, except according to the pattern shown him. God called him into the mount, and revealed to him the heavenly things. The Lord covered him with His own glory, that he might see the pattern, and according to it all things were made. So to Israel, whom He desired to make His dwelling place, He had revealed His glorious ideal of character. The pattern was shown them in the mount when the law was given from Sinai, and when the Lord passed by before Moses and proclaimed, "The Lord, the Lord God, merciful and gracious, longsuffering, and abundant in goodness and truth, keeping mercy for thousands, forgiving iniquity and transgression and sin." Exodus 34:6, 7.

Israel had chosen their own ways. They had not builded according to the pattern; but Christ, the true temple for God's indwelling, molded every detail of His earthly life in harmony with God's ideal. He said, "I delight to do Thy will, O My God; yea, Thy law is within My heart." Psalms 40:8. So our characters are to be builded "for an habitation of God through the Spirit." And we are to "make all things according to the pattern," even Him who "suffered for us, leaving us an example that ye should follow His steps." Ephesians 2:22; Hebrews 8:5; 1 Peter 2:21.

The words of Christ teach that we should regard ourselves as inseparably bound to our Father in heaven. Whatever our position, we are dependent upon God, who holds all destinies in His hands. He has appointed us our work, and has endowed us with faculties and means for that work. So long as we surrender the will to God, and trust in His strength and wisdom, we shall be guided in safe paths, to fulfill our appointed part in His great plan. But the one who depends upon his own wisdom and power, is separating himself from God. Instead of working in unison with Christ, he is fulfilling the purpose of the enemy of God and man.

The Saviour continued: "What things soever He [the Father] doeth, these also doeth the Son likewise. . . . As the Father raiseth up the dead, and quickeneth them, even so the Son quickeneth whom He will." The Sadducees held that there would be no resurrection of the body; but Jesus tells them that one of the greatest works of His Father is raising the dead, and that He Himself has power to do the same work. "The hour is coming, and now is, when the dead shall hear the voice of the Son of God; and they that hear shall live." The Pharisees believed in the resurrection of the dead. Christ declares that even now the power which gives life to the dead is among them, and they are to behold its manifestation. This same resurrection power is that which gives life to the soul "dead in trespasses and sins." Ephesians 2:1. That spirit of life in Christ Jesus, "the power of His resurrection," sets men "free from the law of sin and death." Philippians 3:10; Romans 8:2. The dominion of evil is broken, and through faith the soul is kept from sin. He who opens his heart to the Spirit of Christ becomes a partaker of that mighty power which shall bring forth his body from the grave.

The humble Nazarene asserts His real nobility. He rises above humanity, throws off the guise of sin and shame, and stands revealed, the Honored of the angels, the Son of God, One with the Creator of the universe. His hearers are spellbound. No man has ever spoken words like His, or borne himself with such a kingly majesty. His utterances are clear and plain, fully declaring His mission, and the duty of the world. "For the Father judgeth no man, but hath committed all judgment unto the Son; that all men should honor the Son, even as they honor the Father. He that honoreth not the Son honoreth not the Father which hath sent Him. . . . For as the Father hath life in Himself; so hath He given to the Son to have life in Himself; and hath given Him authority to execute judgment also, because He is the Son of man."

The priests and rulers had set themselves up as judges, to condemn Christ's work, but He declared Himself their judge, and the judge of all the earth. The world has been committed to Christ, and through Him has come every blessing from God to the fallen race. He was the Redeemer before as after His incarnation. As soon as there was sin, there was a Saviour. He has given light and life to all, and according to the measure of light given, each is to be judged. And He who has given the light, He who has followed the soul with tenderest entreaty, seeking to win it from sin to holiness, is in one its Advocate and Judge. From the opening of the great controversy in heaven, Satan has maintained his cause through deception; and Christ has been working to unveil his schemes and to break his power. It is He who has encountered the deceiver, and who through all the ages has been seeking to wrest the captives from his grasp, who will pass judgment upon every soul.

And God "hath given Him authority to execute judgment also, because He is the Son of man." Because He has tasted the very dregs of human affliction and temptation, and understands the frailties and sins of men; because in our behalf He has victoriously withstood the temptations of Satan, and will deal justly and tenderly with the souls that His own blood has been poured out to save, — because of this, the Son of man is appointed to execute the judgment.

But Christ's mission was not for judgment, but for salvation. "God sent not His Son into the world to condemn the world; but that the world through Him might be saved." John 3:17. And before the Sanhedrim Jesus declared, "He that heareth My word, and believeth Him that sent Me, hath eternal life, and cometh not into judgment, but hath passed out of death into life." John 5:24, R. V.

Bidding His hearers marvel not, Christ opened before them, in still wider view, the mystery of the future. "The hour cometh," He said, "in which all that are in the tombs shall hear His voice, and shall come forth; they that have done good, unto the resurrection of life; and they that have done ill, unto the resurrection of judgment." John 5:28-29, R. V.

This assurance of the future life was that for which Israel had so long waited, and which they had hoped to receive at the Messiah's advent. The only light that can lighten the gloom of the grave, was shining upon them. But self-will is blind. Jesus had violated the traditions of the rabbis, and disregarded their authority, and they would not believe.

The time, the place, the occasion, the intensity of feeling that pervaded the assembly, all combined to make the words of Jesus before the Sanhedrim the more impressive. The highest religious authorities of the nation were seeking the life of Him who declared Himself the restorer of Israel. The Lord of the Sabbath was arraigned before an earthly tribunal to answer the charge of breaking the Sabbath law. When He so fearlessly declared His mission, His judges looked upon Him with astonishment and rage; but His words were unanswerable. They could not condemn Him. He denied the right of the priests and rabbis to question Him, or to interfere with His work. They were invested with no such authority. Their claims were based upon their own pride and arrogance. He refused to plead guilty of their charges, or to be catechized by them.

Instead of apologizing for the act of which they complained, or explaining His purpose in doing it, Jesus turned upon the rulers, and the accused became the accuser. He rebuked them for the hardness of their hearts, and their ignorance of the Scriptures. He declared that they had rejected the word of God, inasmuch as they had rejected Him whom God had sent. "Ye search the Scriptures, because ye think that in them ye have eternal life; and these are they which bear witness of Me." John 5:39, R. V.

In every page, whether history, or precept, or prophecy, the Old Testament Scriptures are irradiated with the glory of the Son of God. So far as it was of divine institution, the entire system of Judaism was a compacted prophecy of the gospel. To Christ "give all the prophets witness." Acts 10:43. From the promise given to Adam, down through the patriarchal line and the legal economy, heaven's glorious light made plain the footsteps of the Redeemer. Seers beheld the Star of Bethlehem, the Shiloh to come, as future things swept before them in mysterious procession. In every sacrifice, Christ's death was shown. In every cloud of incense His righteousness ascended. By every jubilee trumpet His name was sounded. In the awful mystery of the holy of holies His glory dwelt.

The Jews had the Scriptures in their possession, and supposed that in their mere outward knowledge of the word, they had eternal life. But Jesus said, "Ye have not His word abiding in you." Having rejected Christ in His word, they rejected Him in person. "Ye will not come to Me," He said, "that ye might have life."

The Jewish leaders had studied the teachings of the prophets concerning the kingdom of the Messiah; but they had done this, not with a sincere desire to know the truth, but with the purpose of finding evidence to sustain their ambitious hopes. When Christ came in a manner contrary to their expectations, they would not receive Him; and in order to justify themselves, they tried to prove Him a deceiver. When once they had set their feet in this path, it was easy for Satan to strengthen their opposition to Christ. The very words that should have been received as evidence of His divinity, were interpreted against Him. Thus they turned the truth of God into a lie, and the more directly the Saviour spoke to them in His works of mercy, the more determined they were in resisting the light.

Jesus said, "I receive not honor from men." It was not the influence of the Sanhedrim, it was not their sanction He desired. He could receive no honor from their approbation. He was invested with the honor and authority of Heaven. Had He desired it, angels would have come to do Him homage; the Father would again have testified to His divinity. But for their own sake, for the sake of the nation whose leaders they were, He desired the Jewish rulers to discern His character, and receive the blessings He came to bring them.

"I am come in My Father's name, and ye receive Me not; if another shall come in his own name, him ye will receive." Jesus came by the authority of God, bearing His image, fulfilling His word, and seeking His glory; yet He was not accepted by the leaders in Israel; but when others should come, assuming the character of Christ, but actuated by their own will and seeking their own glory, they would be received. And why? — Because he who is seeking his own glory, appeals to the desire for self-exaltation in others. To such appeals the Jews could respond. They would receive the false teacher because he flattered their pride by sanctioning their cherished opinions and traditions. But the teaching of Christ did not coincide with their ideas. It was spiritual, and demanded the sacrifice of self; therefore they would not receive it. They were not acquainted with God, and to them His voice through Christ was the voice of a stranger.

Is not the same thing repeated in our day? Are there not many, even religious leaders, who are hardening their hearts against the Holy Spirit, making it impossible for them to recognize the voice of God? Are they not rejecting the word of God, that they may keep their own traditions?

"Had ye believed Moses," said Jesus, "ye would have believed Me; for he wrote of Me. But if ye believe not his writings, how shall ye believe My words?" It was Christ who had spoken to Israel through Moses. If they had listened to the divine voice that spoke through their great leader, they would have recognized it in the teachings of Christ. Had they believed Moses, they would have believed Him of whom Moses wrote.

Jesus knew that the priests and rabbis were determined to take His life; yet He clearly explained to them His unity with the Father, and His relation to the world. They saw that their opposition to Him was without excuse, yet their murderous hatred was not quenched. Fear seized them as they witnessed the convincing power that attended His ministry; but they resisted His appeals, and locked themselves in darkness.

They had signally failed to subvert the authority of Jesus or to alienate the respect and attention of the people, many of whom were convicted by His words. The rulers themselves had felt deep condemnation as He had pressed their guilt home upon their consciences; yet this only made them the more bitter against Him. They were determined to take His life. They sent messengers all over the country to warn the people against Jesus as an impostor. Spies were sent to watch Him, and report what He said and did. The precious Saviour was now most surely standing under the shadow of the cross.

Imprisonment and Death of John

John the Baptist had been first in heralding Christ's kingdom, and he was first also in suffering. From the free air of the wilderness and the vast throngs that had hung upon his words. he was now shut in by the walls of a dungeon cell. He had become a prisoner in the fortress of Herod Antipas. In the territory east of Jordan, which was under the dominion of Antipas, much of John's ministry had been spent. Herod himself had listened to the preaching of the Baptist. The dissolute king had trembled under the call to repentance. "Herod feared John, knowing that he was a just man and an holy; . . . and when he heard him, he did many things, and heard him gladly." John dealt with him faithfully, denouncing his iniquitous alliance with Herodias, his brother's wife. For a time Herod feebly sought to break the chain of lust that bound him; but Herodias fastened him the more firmly in her toils, and found revenge upon the Baptist by inducing Herod to cast him into prison.

The life of John had been one of active labor, and the gloom and inaction of his prison life weighed heavily upon him. As week after week passed, bringing no change, despondency and doubt crept over him. His disciples did not forsake him. They were allowed access to the prison, and they brought him tidings of the works of Jesus, and told how the people were flocking to Him. But they questioned why, if this new teacher was the Messiah, He did nothing to effect John's release. How could He permit His faithful herald to be deprived of liberty and perhaps of life?

These questions were not without effect. Doubts which otherwise would never have arisen were suggested to John. Satan rejoiced to hear the words of these disciples, and to see how they bruised the soul of the Lord's messenger. O how often those who think themselves the friends of a good man, and who are eager to show their fidelity to him, prove to be his most dangerous enemies. How often, instead of strengthening his faith, their words depress and dishearten.

Like the Saviour's disciples, John the Baptist did not understand the nature of Christ's kingdom. He expected Jesus to take the throne of David; and as time passed, and the Saviour made no claim to kingly authority, John became perplexed and troubled. He had declared to the people that in order for the way to be prepared before the Lord, the prophecy of Isaiah must be fulfilled; the mountains and hills must be brought low, the crooked made straight and the rough places plain. He had looked for the high places of human pride and power to be cast down. He had pointed to the Messiah as the One whose fan was in His hand, and who would thoroughly purge His floor, who would gather the wheat into His garner, and burn up the chaff with unquenchable fire. Like the prophet Elijah, in whose spirit and power he had come to Israel, he looked for the Lord to reveal Himself as a God that answereth by fire.

In his mission the Baptist had stood as a fearless reprover of iniquity, both in high places and in low. He had dared to face King Herod with the plain rebuke of sin. He had not counted his life dear unto himself that he might fulfill his appointed work. And now from his dungeon he watched for the Lion of the tribe of Judah to cast down the pride of the oppressor, and to deliver the poor and him that cried. But Jesus seemed to content Himself with gathering disciples about Him, and healing and teaching the people. He was eating at the tables of the publicans, while every day the Roman yoke rested more heavily upon Israel, while King Herod and his vile paramour worked their will, and the cries of the poor and suffering went up to heaven.

To the desert prophet all this seemed a mystery beyond his fathoming. There were hours when the whisperings of demons tortured his spirit, and the shadow of a terrible fear crept over him. Could it be that the long-hoped-for Deliverer had not yet appeared? Then what meant the message that he himself had been impelled to bear? John had been bitterly disappointed in the result of his mission. He had expected that the message from God would have the same effect as when the law was read in the days of Josiah and of Ezra; (2 Chronicles 34: Nehemiah 8, 9.) that there would follow a deep-seated work of repentance and returning unto the Lord. For the success of this mission his whole life had been sacrificed. Had it been in vain?

John was troubled to see that through love for him, his own disciples were cherishing unbelief in regard to Jesus. Had his work for them been fruitless? Had he been unfaithful in his mission, that he was now cut off from labor? If the promised Deliverer had appeared, and John had been found true to his calling, would not Jesus now overthrow the oppressor's power, and set free His herald?

But the Baptist did not surrender his faith in Christ. The memory of the voice from heaven and the descending dove, the spotless purity of Jesus, the power of the Holy Spirit that had rested upon John as he came into the Saviour's presence, and the testimony of the prophetic scriptures,—all witnessed that Jesus of Nazareth was the Promised One.

John would not discuss his doubts and anxieties with his companions. He determined to send a message of inquiry to Jesus. This he intrusted to two of his disciples, hoping that an interview with the Saviour would confirm their faith, and bring assurance to their brethren. And he longed for some word from Christ spoken directly for himself.

The disciples came to Jesus with their message, "Art Thou He that should come, or do we look for another?"

How short the time since the Baptist had pointed to Jesus, and proclaimed, "Behold the Lamb of God, which taketh away the sin of the world." "He it is, who coming after me is preferred before me." John 1:29, 27. And now the question, "Art Thou He that should come?" It was keenly bitter and disappointing to human nature. If John, the faithful forerunner, failed to discern Christ's mission, what could be expected from the self-seeking multitude?

The Saviour did not at once answer the disciples' question. As they stood wondering at His silence, the sick and afflicted were coming to Him to be healed. The blind were groping their way through the crowd; diseased ones of all classes, some urging their own way, some borne by their friends, were eagerly pressing into the presence of Jesus. The voice of the mighty Healer penetrated the deaf ear. A word, a touch of His hand, opened the blind eyes to behold the light of day, the scenes of nature, the faces of friends, and the face of the Deliverer. Jesus rebuked disease and banished fever. His voice reached the ears of the dying,

and they arose in health and vigor. Paralyzed demoniacs obeyed His word, their madness left them, and they worshiped Him. While He healed their diseases, He taught the people. The poor peasants and laborers, who were shunned by the rabbis as unclean, gathered close about Him, and He spoke to them the words of eternal life.

Thus the day wore away, the disciples of John seeing and hearing all. At last Jesus called them to Him, and bade them go and tell John what they had witnessed, adding, "Blessed is he, whosoever shall find none occasion of stumbling in Me." Luke 7:23, R. V. The evidence of His divinity was seen in its adaptation to the needs of suffering humanity. His glory was shown in His condescension to our low estate.

The disciples bore the message, and it was enough. John recalled the prophecy concerning the Messiah, "The Lord hath anointed Me to preach good tidings unto the meek; He hath sent Me to bind up the brokenhearted, to proclaim liberty to the captives, and the opening of the prison to them that are bound; to proclaim the acceptable year of the Lord." Isaiah 61:1,2. The works of Christ not only declared Him to be the Messiah, but showed in what manner His kingdom was to be established. To John was opened the same truth that had come to Elijah in the desert, when "a great and strong wind rent the mountains, and brake in pieces the rocks before the Lord; but the Lord was not in the wind: and after the wind an earthquake; but the Lord was not in the earthquake: and after the earthquake a fire; but the Lord was not in the fire:" (1 Kings 19:11, 12.) and after the fire, God spoke to the prophet by a still, small voice. So Jesus was to do His work, not with the clash of arms and the overturning of thrones and kingdoms, but through speaking to the hearts of men by a life of mercy and self-sacrifice.

The principle of the Baptist's own life of self-abnegation was the principle of the Messiah's kingdom. John well knew how foreign all this was to the principles and hopes of the leaders in Israel. That which was to him convincing evidence of Christ's divinity, would be no evidence to them. They were looking for a Messiah who had not been promised. John saw that the Saviour's mission could win from them only hatred and condemnation. He, the forerunner, was but drinking of the cup which Christ Himself must drain to its dregs.

The Saviour's words, "Blessed is he, whosoever shall find none occasion of stumbling in Me," were a gentle reproof to John. It was not lost upon him. Understanding more clearly now the nature of Christ's mission, he yielded himself to God for life or for death, as should best serve the interests of the cause he loved.

After the messengers had departed, Jesus spoke to the people concerning John. The Saviour's heart went out in sympathy to the faithful witness now buried in Herod's dungeon. He would not leave the people to conclude that God had forsaken John, or that his faith had failed in the day of trial. "What went ye out into the wilderness to see?" He said. "A reed shaken with the wind?"

The tall reeds that grew beside the Jordan, bending before every breeze, were fitting representatives of the rabbis who had stood as critics and judges of the Baptist's mission. They were swayed this way and that, by the winds of popular opinion. They would not humble themselves to receive the heart-searching message of the Baptist, yet for fear of the people they dared not openly oppose his work. But God's messenger was of no such craven spirit. The multitudes who were gathered about Christ had been witnesses to the work of John. They had heard his fearless rebuke of sin. To the self-righteous Pharisees, the priestly Sadducees, King Herod and his court, princes and soldiers, publicans and peasants, John had spoken with equal plainness. He was no trembling reed, swayed by the winds of human praise or prejudice. In the prison he was the same in his loyalty to God and his zeal for righteousness as when he preached God's message in the wilderness. In his faithfulness to principle he was as firm as a rock.

Jesus continued, "But what went ye out for to see? A man clothed in soft raiment? Behold, they which are gorgeously appareled and live delicately, are in kings' courts." John had been called to reprove the sins and excesses of his time, and his plain dress and self-denying life were in harmony with the character of his mission. Rich apparel and the luxuries of this life are not the portion of God's servants, but of those who live "in kings' courts," the rulers of this world, to whom pertain its power and its riches. Jesus wished to direct attention to the contrast between the clothing of John, and that worn by the priests and rulers. These officials arrayed themselves in rich robes and costly ornaments. They loved display, and hoped to dazzle the people, and thus command greater consideration. They were more anxious to gain the admiration of men than to obtain the purity of heart which would win the approval of God. Thus they revealed that their allegiance was not given to God, but to the kingdom of this world.

"But what," said Jesus, "went ye out for to see? A prophet? Yea, I say unto you, and more than a prophet. For this is he, of whom it is written, —

"Behold, I send My messenger before Thy face,
Which shall prepare Thy way before Thee.

"Verily I say unto you, Among them that are born of women there hath not risen a greater than John the Baptist." In the announcement to Zacharias before the birth of John, the angel had declared, "He shall be great in the sight of the Lord." Luke 1:15. In the estimation of Heaven, what is it that constitutes greatness? — Not that which the world accounts greatness; not wealth, or rank, or noble descent, or intellectual gifts, in themselves considered. If intellectual greatness, apart from any higher consideration, is worthy of honor, then our homage is due to Satan, whose intellectual power no man has ever equaled. But when perverted to self-serving, the greater the gift, the greater curse it becomes. It is moral worth that God values. Love and purity are the attributes He prizes most. John was great in the sight of the Lord, when, before the messengers from the Sanhedrim, before the people, and before his own disciples, he refrained from seeking honor for himself, but pointed all to Jesus as the Promised One. His unselfish joy in the ministry of Christ, presents the highest type of nobility ever revealed in man.

The witness borne of him after his death, by those who had heard his testimony to Jesus, was, "John did no miracle; but all things that John spake of this man were true." John 10:41. It was not given to John to call down fire from heaven, or to raise the dead, as Elijah did, nor to wield Moses' rod of power in the name of God. He was sent to herald the Saviour's advent, and to call upon the people to prepare for His coming. So faithfully did he fulfill his mission, that as the people recalled what he had taught them of Jesus, they could say, "All things that John spake of this man were true." Such witness to Christ every disciple of the Master is called upon to bear.

As the Messiah's herald, John was "much more than a prophet." For while prophets had seen from afar Christ's advent, to John it was given to behold Him, to hear the testimony from heaven to His Messiahship, and to present Him to Israel as the Sent of God. Yet Jesus said. "He that is least in the kingdom of heaven is greater than he."

The prophet John was the connecting link between the two dispensations. As God's representative he stood forth to show the relation of the law and the prophets to the Christian dispensation. He was the lesser light, which was to be followed by a greater. The mind of John was illuminated by the Holy Spirit, that he might shed light upon his people; but no other ever has shone or ever will shine so clearly upon fallen man as that which emanated from the teaching and example of Jesus. Christ and His mission had been but dimly understood as typified in the shadowy sacrifices. Even John had not fully comprehended the future, immortal life through the Saviour.

Aside from the joy that John found in his mission, his life had been one of sorrow. His voice had been seldom heard except in the wilderness. His was a lonely lot. And he was not permitted to see the result of his own labors. It was not his privilege to be with Christ, and witness the manifestation of divine power attending the greater light. It was not for him to see the blind restored to sight, the sick healed, and the dead raised to life. He did not behold the light that shone through every word of Christ, shedding glory upon the promises of prophecy. The least disciple who saw Christ's mighty works and heard His words was in this sense more highly privileged than John the Baptist, and therefore is said to have been greater than he.

Through the vast throngs that had listened to John's preaching, his fame had spread throughout the land. A deep interest was felt as to the result of his imprisonment. Yet his blameless life, and the strong public sentiment in his favor, led to the belief that no violent measures would be taken against him.

Herod believed John to be a prophet of God, and he fully intended to set him at liberty. But he delayed his purpose from fear of Herodias.

Herodias knew that by direct measures she could never win Herod's consent to the death of John, and she resolved to accomplish her purpose by stratagem. On the king's birthday an entertainment was to be given to the officers of state, and the nobles of the court. There would be feasting and drunkenness. Herod would thus be thrown off his guard, and might then be influenced according to her will.

When the great day arrived, and the king with his lords was feasting and drinking, Herodias sent her daughter into the banqueting hall to dance for the entertainment of the guests. Salome was in the first flush of womanhood, and her voluptuous beauty captivated the senses of the lordly revelers. It was not customary for the ladies of the court to appear at these festivities, and a flattering compliment was paid to Herod when this daughter of Israel's priests and princes, danced for the amusement of his guests.

The king was dazed with wine. Passion held sway, and reason was dethroned. He saw only the hall of pleasure, with its reveling guests, the banquet table, the sparkling wine and the flashing lights, and the young girl dancing before him. In the recklessness of the moment, he desired to make some display that would exalt him before the great men of his realm. With an oath he promised to give the daughter of Herodias whatever she might ask, even to the half of his kingdom.

Salome hastened to her mother, to know what she should ask. The answer was ready, — the head of John the Baptist. Salome knew not of the thirst for revenge in her mother's heart, and she shrank from presenting the request; but the determination of Herodias prevailed. The girl returned with the terrible petition, "I will that thou forthwith give me in a charger the head of John the Baptist." Mark 6:25, R. V.

Herod was astonished and confounded. The riotous mirth ceased, and an ominous silence settled down upon the scene of revelry. The king was horror-stricken at the thought of taking the life of John. Yet his word was pledged, and he was unwilling to appear fickle or rash. The oath had been made in honor of his guests, and if one of them had offered a word against the fulfillment of his promise, he would gladly have spared the prophet. He gave them opportunity to speak in the prisoner's behalf. They had traveled long distances in order to hear the preaching of John, and they knew him to be a man without crime, and a servant of God. But though shocked at the girl's demand, they were too besotted to interpose a remonstrance. No voice was raised to save the life of Heaven's messenger. These men occupied high positions of trust in the nation, and upon them rested grave responsibilities; yet they had given themselves up to feasting and drunkenness until the senses were benumbed. Their heads were turned with the giddy scene of music and dancing, and conscience lay dormant. By their silence they pronounced the sentence of death upon the prophet of God to satisfy the revenge of an abandoned woman.

Herod waited in vain to be released from his oath; then he reluctantly commanded the execution of the prophet. Soon the head of John was brought in before the king and his guests. Forever sealed were those lips that had faithfully warned Herod to turn from his life of sin. Never more would that voice be heard calling men to repentance. The revels of one night had cost the life of one of the greatest of the prophets.

O how often has the life of the innocent been sacrificed through the intemperance of those who should have been guardians of justice. He who puts the intoxicating cup to his lips makes himself responsible for all the injustice he may commit under its besotting power. By benumbing his senses he makes it impossible for him to judge calmly or to have a clear perception of right and wrong. He opens the way for Satan to work through him in oppressing and destroying the innocent. "Wine is a mocker, strong drink is raging; and whosoever is deceived thereby is not wise." Thus it is that "judgment is turned away backward, ... and he that departeth from evil maketh himself a prey." Proverbs 20:1; Isaiah 59;14,15. Those who have jurisdiction over the lives of their fellow men, should be held guilty of a crime when they yield to intemperance. All who execute the laws should be lawkeepers. They should be men of self-control. They need to have full command of their physical, mental, and moral powers, that they may possess vigor of intellect, and a high sense of justice.

The head of John the Baptist was carried to Herodias, who received it with fiendish satisfaction. She exulted in her revenge, and flattered herself that Herod's conscience would no longer be troubled. But no happiness resulted to her from her sin. Her name became notorious and abhorred, while Herod was more tormented by remorse than he had been by the warnings of the prophet. The influence of John's teachings was not silenced; it was to extend to every generation till the close of time.

Herod's sin was ever before him. He was constantly seeking to find relief from the accusings of a guilty conscience. His confidence in John was unshaken. As he recalled his life of self-denial, his solemn, earnest appeals, his sound judgment in counsel, and then remembered how he had come to his death, Herod could find no rest. Engaged in the affairs of the state, receiving honors from men, he bore a smiling face and dignified mien, while he concealed an anxious heart, ever oppressed with the fear that a curse was upon him.

Herod had been deeply impressed by the words of John, that nothing can be hidden from God. He was convinced that God was present in every place, that He had witnessed the revelry of the banqueting room, that He had heard the command to behead John, and had seen the exultation of Herodias, and the insult she offered to the severed head of her reprover. And many things that Herod had heard from the lips of the prophet now spoke to his conscience more distinctly than had the preaching in the wilderness.

When Herod heard of the works of Christ, he was exceedingly troubled. He thought that God had raised John from the dead, and sent him forth with still greater power to condemn sin. He was in constant fear that John would avenge his death by passing condemnation upon him and his house. Herod was reaping that which God had declared to be the result of a course of sin, — "a trembling heart, and failing of eyes, and sorrow of mind; and thy life shall hang in doubt before thee; and thou shalt fear day and night, and shalt have none assurance of thy life: in the morning thou shalt say, Would God it were even! and at even thou shalt say, Would God it were morning! for the fear of thine heart wherewith thou shalt fear, and for the sight of thine eyes, which thou shalt see." Deuteronomy 28:65-67. The sinner's own thoughts are his accusers; and there can be no torture keener than the stings of a guilty conscience, which give him no rest day nor night.

To many minds a deep mystery surrounds the fate of John the Baptist. They question why he should have been left to languish and die in prison. The mystery of this dark providence our human vision cannot penetrate; but it can never shake our confidence in God when we remember that John was but a sharer in the sufferings of Christ. All who follow Christ will wear the crown of sacrifice. They will surely be misunderstood by selfish men, and will be made a mark for the fierce assaults of Satan. It is this principle of self-sacrifice that his kingdom is established to destroy, and he will war against it wherever manifested.

The childhood, youth, and manhood of John had been characterized by firmness and moral power. When his voice was heard in the wilderness saying. "Prepare ye the way of the Lord; make His paths straight," Matthew 3:3. Satan feared for the safety of his kingdom. The sinfulness of sin was revealed in such a manner that men trembled. Satan's power over many who had been under his control was broken. He had been unwearied in his efforts to draw away the Baptist from a life of unreserved surrender to God; but he had failed. And he had failed to overcome Jesus. In the temptation in the wilderness, Satan had been defeated, and his rage was great. Now he determined to bring sorrow upon Christ by striking John. The One whom he could not entice to sin, he would cause to suffer.

Jesus did not interpose to deliver His servant. He knew that John would bear the test. Gladly would the Saviour have come to John, to brighten the dungeon gloom with His own presence. But He was not to place Himself in the hands of enemies and imperil His own mission. Gladly would He have delivered His faithful servant. But for the sake of thousands who in after years must pass from prison to death, John was to drink the cup of martyrdom. As the followers of Jesus should languish in lonely cells, or perish by the sword, the rack, or the fagot, apparently forsaken by God and man, what a stay to their hearts would be the thought that John the Baptist, to whose faithfulness Christ Himself had borne witness, had passed through a similar experience.

Satan was permitted to cut short the earthly life of God's messenger; but that life which "is hid with Christ in God," (Colossians 3:3.) the destroyer could not reach. He exulted that he had brought sorrow upon Christ, but he had failed of conquering John. Death itself only placed him forever beyond the power of temptation. In this warfare, Satan was revealing his own character. Before the witnessing universe he made manifest his enmity toward God and man.

Though no miraculous deliverance was granted John, he was not forsaken. He had always the companionship of heavenly angels, who opened to him the prophecies concerning Christ, and the precious promises of Scripture. These were his stay, as they were to be the stay of God's people through the coming ages. To John the Baptist, as to those that came after him, was given the assurance, "Lo, I am with you all the days even unto the end." Matthew 28:20, margin, R. V.

God never leads His children otherwise than they would choose to be led, if they could see the end from the beginning, and discern the glory of the purpose which they are fulfilling as co-workers with Him. Not Enoch, who was translated to heaven, not Elijah, who ascended in a chariot of fire, was greater or more honored than John the Baptist, who perished alone in the dungeon. "Unto you it is given in the behalf of Christ, not only to believe on Him, but also to suffer for His sake." Philippians 1:29. And of all the gifts that Heaven can bestow upon men, fellowship with Christ in His sufferings is the most weighty trust and the highest honor.

"The Kingdom of God Is at Hand"

"Jesus came into Galilee, preaching the gospel of the kingdom of God, and saying, The time is fulfilled, and the kingdom of God is at hand; repent ye, and believe the gospel." Mark 1:14, 15.

The Messiah's coming had been first announced in Judea. In the temple at Jerusalem the birth of the forerunner had been foretold to Zacharias as he ministered before the altar. On the hills of Bethlehem the angels had proclaimed the birth of Jesus. To Jerusalem the magi had come in search of Him. In the temple Simeon and Anna had testified to His divinity. "Jerusalem and all Judea" had listened to the preaching of John the Baptist; and the deputation from the Sanhedrim, with the multitude, had heard his testimony concerning Jesus. In Judea, Christ had received His first disciples. Here much of His early ministry had been spent. The flashing forth of His divinity in the cleansing of the temple, His miracles of healing, and the lessons of divine truth that fell from His lips, all proclaimed that which after the healing at Bethesda He had declared before the Sanhedrim, — His Sonship to the Eternal.

If the leaders in Israel had received Christ, He would have honored them as His messengers to carry the gospel to the world. To them first was given the opportunity to become heralds of the kingdom and grace of God. But Israel knew not the time of her visitation. The jealousy and distrust of the Jewish leaders had ripened into open hatred, and the hearts of the people were turned away from Jesus.

The Sanhedrin had rejected Christ's message and was bent upon His death; therefore Jesus departed from Jerusalem, from the priests, the temple, the religious leaders, the people who had been instructed in the law, and turned to another class to proclaim His message, and to gather out those who should carry the gospel to all nations.

As the light and life of men was rejected by the ecclesiastical authorities in the days of Christ, so it has been rejected in every succeeding generation. Again and again the history of Christ's withdrawal from Judea has been repeated. When the Reformers preached the word of God, they had no thought of separating themselves from the established church; but the religious leaders would not tolerate the light, and those that bore it were forced to seek another class, who were longing for the truth. In our day few of the professed followers of the Reformers are actuated by their spirit. Few are listening for the voice of God, and ready to accept truth in whatever guise it may be presented. Often those who follow in the steps of the Reformers are forced to turn away from the churches they love, in order to declare the plain teaching of the word of God. And many times those who are seeking for light are by the same teaching obliged to leave the church of their fathers, that they may render obedience.

The people of Galilee were despised by the rabbis of Jerusalem as rude and unlearned, yet they presented a more favorable field for the Saviour's work. They were more earnest and sincere; less under the control of bigotry; their minds were more open for the reception of truth. In going to Galilee, Jesus was not seeking seclusion or isolation. The province was at this time the home of a crowded population, with a much larger admixture of people of other nations than was found in Judea.

As Jesus traveled through Galilee, teaching and healing, multitudes flocked to Him from the cities and villages. Many came even from Judea and the adjoining provinces. Often He was obliged to hide Himself from the people.

94

THE KINGDOM OF GOD IS AT HAND

The enthusiasm ran so high that it was necessary to take precautions lest the Roman authorities should be aroused to fear an insurrection. Never before had there been such a period as this for the world. Heaven was brought down to men. Hungering and thirsting souls that had waited long for the redemption of Israel now feasted upon the grace of a merciful Saviour.

The burden of Christ's preaching was, "The time is fulfilled, and the kingdom of God is at hand; repent ye, and believe the gospel." Thus the gospel message, as given by the Saviour Himself, was based on the prophecies. The "time" which He declared to be fulfilled was the period made known by the angel Gabriel to Daniel. "Seventy weeks," said the angel, "are determined upon thy people and upon thy holy city, to finish the transgression, and to make an end of sins, and to make reconciliation for iniquity, and to bring in everlasting righteousness, and to seal up the vision and prophecy, and to anoint the most holy." Daniel 9:24. A day in prophecy stands for a year. (See Numbers 14:34; Ezekiel 4:6.) The seventy weeks, or four hundred and ninety days, represent four hundred and ninety years. A starting point for this period is given: "Know therefore and understand, that from the going forth of the commandment to restore and to build Jerusalem unto the Messiah the Prince shall be seven weeks, and threescore and two weeks," (Daniel 9:25.) sixty-nine weeks, or four hundred and eighty-three years. The commandment to restore and build Jerusalem, as completed by the decree of Artaxerxes Longimanus, (See Ezra 6:14; 7:1, 9, margin.) went into effect in the autumn of 457 B.C. From this time four hundred and eighty-three years extend to the autumn of A.D. 27. According to the prophecy, this period was to reach to the Messiah, the Anointed One. In A.D. 27, Jesus at His baptism received the anointing of the Holy Spirit, and soon afterward began His ministry. Then the message was proclaimed. "The time is fulfilled."

Then, said the angel, "He shall confirm the covenant with many for one week [seven years]." For seven years after the Saviour entered on His ministry, the gospel was to be preached especially to the Jews; for three and a half years by Christ Himself, and afterward by the apostles. "In the midst of the week He shall cause the sacrifice and the oblation to cease." Daniel 9:27. In the spring of A.D. 31, Christ the true sacrifice was offered on Calvary. Then the veil of the temple was rent in twain, showing that the sacredness and significance of the sacrificial service had departed. The time had come for the earthly sacrifice and oblation to cease.

The one week—seven years—ended in A.D. 34. Then by the stoning of Stephen the Jews finally sealed their rejection of the gospel; the disciples who were scattered abroad by persecution "went everywhere preaching the word;" (Acts 8:4.) and shortly after, Saul the persecutor was converted and became Paul, the apostle to the Gentiles.

The time of Christ's coming, His anointing by the Holy Spirit, His death, and the giving of the gospel to the Gentiles, were definitely pointed out. It was the privilege of the Jewish people to understand these prophecies, and to recognize their fulfillment in the mission of Jesus. Christ urged upon His disciples the importance of prophetic study Referring to the prophecy given to Daniel in regard to their time, He said, "Whoso readeth, let him understand." Matthew 24:15. After His resurrection He

---

"As the message of Christ's first advent announced the kingdom of His grace, so the message of His second advent announces the kingdom of His glory. And the second message, like the first, is based on the prophecies. The words of the angel to Daniel relating to the last days were to be understood in the time of the end."

---

explained to the disciples in "all the prophets" "the things concerning Himself." Luke 24:27. The Saviour had spoken through all the prophets. "The Spirit of Christ which was in them" "testified beforehand the sufferings of Christ, and the glory that should follow." 1 Peter 1:11.

It was Gabriel, the angel next in rank to the Son of God, who came with the divine message to Daniel. It was Gabriel, "His angel," whom Christ sent to open the future to the beloved John; and a blessing is pronounced on those who read and hear the words of the prophecy, and keep the things written therein. Revelation 1:3.

"The Lord God will do nothing, but He revealeth His secret unto His servants and prophets." While "the secret things belong unto the Lord our God," "those things which are revealed belong unto us and to our children forever." Amos 3:7; Deuteronomy 29:29. God has given these things to us, and His blessing will attend the reverent, prayerful study of the prophetic scriptures.

As the message of Christ's first advent announced the kingdom of His grace, so the message of His second advent announces the kingdom of His glory. And the second message, like the first, is based on the prophecies. The words of the angel to Daniel relating to the last days were to be understood in the time of the end. At that time, "many shall run to and fro, and knowledge shall be increased." "The wicked shall do wickedly; and none of the wicked shall understand; but the wise shall understand." Daniel 12:4, 10. The Saviour Himself has given signs of His coming, and He says, "When ye see these things come to pass, know ye that the kingdom of God is nigh at hand." "And take heed to yourselves, lest at any time your hearts be overcharged with surfeiting, and drunkenness, and cares of this life, and so that day come upon you unawares." "Watch ye therefore, and pray always, that ye may be accounted worthy to escape all these things that shall come to pass, and to stand before the Son of man." Luke 21:31, 34, 36.

We have reached the period foretold in these scriptures. The time of the end is come, the visions of the prophets are unsealed, and their solemn warnings point us to our Lord's coming in glory as near at hand.

The Jews misinterpreted and misapplied the word of God, and they knew not the time of their visitation. The years of the ministry of Christ and His apostles, — the precious last years of grace to the chosen people, — they spent in plotting the destruction of the Lord's messengers. Earthly ambitions absorbed them, and the offer of the spiritual kingdom came to them in vain. So today the kingdom of this world absorbs men's thoughts, and they take no note of the rapidly fulfilling prophecies, and the tokens of the swift-coming kingdom of God.

"But ye, brethren, are not in darkness, that that day should overtake you as a thief. Ye are all the children of light, and the children of the day; we are not of the night, nor of darkness." While we are not to know the hour of our Lord's return, we may know when it is near. "Therefore let us not sleep, as do others; but let us watch and be sober." 1 Thessalonians 5:4-6.

"Is Not This the Carpenter's Son?"

A cross the bright days of Christ's ministry in Galilee, one shadow lay. The people of Nazareth rejected Him. "Is not this the carpenter's son?" they said.

During His childhood and youth, Jesus had worshiped among His brethren in the synagogue at Nazareth. Since the opening of His ministry He had been absent from them, but they had not been ignorant of what had befallen him. As He again appeared among them, their interest and expectation were excited to the highest pitch. Here were the familiar forms and faces of those whom He had known from infancy. Here were His mother, His brothers and sisters, and all eyes were turned upon Him as He entered the synagogue upon the Sabbath day, and took His place among the worshipers.

In the regular service for the day, the elder read from the prophets, and exhorted the people still to hope for the Coming One, who would bring in a glorious reign, and banish all oppression. He sought to encourage his hearers by rehearsing the evidence that the Messiah's coming was near. He described the glory of His advent, keeping prominent the thought that He would appear at the head of armies to deliver Israel.

When a rabbi was present at the synagogue, he was expected to deliver the sermon, and any Israelite might give the reading from the prophets. Upon this Sabbath Jesus was requested to take part in the service. He "stood up to read, and there was delivered unto Him a roll of the prophet Isaiah." Luke 4:16, 17, R. V., margin. The scripture which He read, was one that was understood as referring to the Messiah: —

"The Spirit of the Lord is upon Me,
Because He hath anointed Me to preach the gospel to the poor;

He hath sent Me to heal the brokenhearted,
To preach deliverance to the captives,
And recovering of sight to the blind,
To set at liberty them that are bruised,
To preach the acceptable year of the Lord."

"And He closed the roll, and gave it back to the attendant; . . . and the eyes of all in the synagogue were fastened on Him. . . . And all bare Him witness, and wondered at the words of grace which proceeded out of His mouth." Luke 4:20-22, R. V., margin.

Jesus stood before the people as a living expositor of the prophecies concerning Himself. Explaining the words He had read, He spoke of the Messiah as a reliever of the oppressed, a liberator of captives, a healer of the afflicted, restoring sight to the blind, and revealing to the world the light of truth. His impressive manner and the wonderful import of His words thrilled the hearers with a power they had never felt before. The tide of divine influence broke every barrier down; like Moses, they beheld the Invisible. As their hearts were moved upon by the Holy Spirit, they responded with fervent amens, and praises to the Lord.

But when Jesus announced, "This day is this scripture fulfilled in your ears," they were suddenly recalled to think of themselves, and of the claims of Him who had been addressing them. They, Israelites, children of Abraham, had been represented as in bondage. They had been addressed as prisoners to be delivered from the power of evil; as in darkness, and needing the light of truth. Their pride was offended, and their fears were roused. The words of Jesus indicated that His work for them was to be altogether different from what they desired. Their deeds might be investigated too closely. Notwithstanding their exactness

This chapter is based on Luke 4:16-30.

in outward ceremonies, they shrank from inspection by those clear, searching eyes.

Who is this Jesus? they questioned. He who had claimed for Himself the glory of the Messiah, was the son of a carpenter, and had worked at His trade with His father Joseph. They had seen Him toiling up and down the hills, they were acquainted with His brothers and sisters, and knew His life and labors. They had seen Him develop from childhood to youth, and from youth to manhood. Although His life had been spotless, they would not believe that He was the Promised One.

What a contrast between His teaching in regard to the new kingdom and that which they had heard from their elder! Jesus had said nothing of delivering them from the Romans. They had heard of His miracles, and had hoped that His power would be exercised for their advantage, but they had seen no indication of such purpose.

As they opened the door to doubt, their hearts became so much the harder for having been momentarily softened. Satan was determined that blind eyes should not that day be opened, nor souls bound in slavery be set at liberty. With intense energy he worked to fasten them in unbelief. They made no account of the sign already given, when they had been stirred by the conviction that it was their Redeemer who addressed them.

But Jesus now gave them an evidence of His divinity by revealing their secret thoughts. "He said to them, Doubtless ye will say unto Me this parable, Physician, heal thyself; whatsoever we have heard done at Capernaum, do also here in Thine own country. And He said, Verily I say unto you, No prophet is acceptable in his own country. But of a truth I say unto you, There was many widows in Israel in the days of Elijah, when the heaven was shut up three years and six months, when there came a great famine over all the land; and unto none of them was Elijah sent, but only to Zarephath, in the land of Sidon, unto a woman that was a widow. And there were many lepers in Israel in the time of Elisha the prophet; and none of them was cleansed, but only Naaman, the Syrian." Luke 4:23-27, R. V.

By this relation of events in the lives of the prophets, Jesus met the questionings of His hearers. The servants whom God had chosen for a special work, were not allowed to labor for a hardhearted and unbelieving people. But those who had hearts to feel and faith to believe were especially favored with evidences of His power through the prophets. In the days of Elijah, Israel had departed from God. They clung to their sins, and rejected the warnings of the Spirit through the Lord's messengers. Thus they cut themselves off from the channel by which God's blessing could come to them. The Lord passed by the homes of Israel, and found a refuge for His servant in a heathen land, with a woman who did not belong to the chosen people. But this woman was favored because she had followed the light she had received, and her heart was open to the greater light that God sent her through His prophet.

It was for the same reason that in Elisha's time the lepers of Israel were passed by. But Naaman, a heathen nobleman, had been faithful to his convictions of right, and had felt his great need of help. He was in a condition to receive the gifts of God's grace. He was not only cleansed from his leprosy, but blessed with a knowledge of the true God.

Our standing before God depends, not upon the amount of light we have received, but upon the use we make of what we have. Thus even the heathen who choose the right as far as they can distinguish it, are in a more favorable condition than are those who have had a great light, and profess to serve God, but who disregard the light, and by their daily life contradict their profession.

The words of Jesus to His hearers in the synagogue struck at the root of their self-righteousness, pressing home upon them the bitter truth that they had departed from God, and forfeited their claim to be His people. Every word cut like a knife as their real condition was set before them. They now scorned the faith with which Jesus had at first inspired them. They would not admit that He who had sprung from poverty and lowliness was other than a common man.

Their unbelief bred malice. Satan controlled them, and in wrath they cried out against the Saviour. They had turned from Him whose mission it was to heal and restore; now they manifested the attributes of the destroyer.

When Jesus referred to the blessings given to the Gentiles, the fierce national pride of His hearers was aroused, and His words were drowned in a tumult of voices. These people had prided themselves on keeping the law; but now that their prejudices were offended, they were ready to commit murder. The assembly broke up, and laying hands upon Jesus, they thrust Him from the synagogue, and out of the city. All seemed eager for His destruction. They hurried Him to the brow of a precipice, intending to cast Him down headlong. Shouts and maledictions filled the air. Some were casting stones at Him, when suddenly He disappeared from among them. The heavenly messengers who had been by His side in the synagogue were with Him in the midst of that maddened throng. They shut Him in from His enemies, and conducted Him to a place of safety.

So angels protected Lot, and led him out safely from the midst of Sodom. So they protected Elisha in the little mountain city. When the encircling hills were filled with the horses and chariots of the king of Syria, and the great host of his armed men, Elisha beheld the nearer hill slopes covered with the armies of God, — horses and chariots of fire round about the servant of the Lord.

So, in all ages, angels have been near to Christ's faithful followers. The vast confederacy of evil is arrayed against all who would overcome; but Christ would have us look to the things which are not seen, to the armies of heaven encamped about all who love God, to deliver them. From what dangers, seen and unseen, we have been preserved through the interposition of the angels, we shall never know, until in the light of eternity we see the providences of God. Then we shall know that the whole family of heaven was interested in the family here below, and that messengers from the throne of God attended our steps from day to day.

When Jesus in the synagogue read from the prophecy, He stopped short of the final specification concerning the Messiah's work. Having read the words, "To proclaim the acceptable year of the Lord," He omitted the phrase, "and the day of vengeance of our God." Isaiah 61:2. This was just as much truth as was the first of the prophecy, and by His silence Jesus did not deny the truth. But this last

> **"Truth was unpopular in Christ's day. It is unpopular in our day. It has been unpopular ever since Satan first gave man a disrelish for it by presenting fables that lead to self-exaltation. Do we not today meet theories and doctrines that have no foundation in the word of God?"**

expression was that upon which His hearers delighted to dwell, and which they were desirous of fulfilling. They denounced judgments against the heathen, not discerning that their own guilt was even greater than that of others. They themselves were in deepest need of the mercy they were so ready to deny to the heathen. That day in the synagogue, when Jesus stood among them, was their opportunity to accept the call of Heaven. He who "delighteth in mercy" (Micah 7:18.) would fain have saved them from the ruin which their sins were inviting.

Not without one more call to repentance could He give them up. Toward the close of His ministry in Galilee, He again visited the home of His childhood. Since His rejection there, the fame of His preaching and His miracles had filled the land. None now could deny that He possessed more than human power. The people of Nazareth knew that He went about doing good, and healing all that were oppressed by Satan. About them were whole villages where there was not a moan of sickness in any house; for He had passed through them, and healed all their sick. The

mercy revealed in every act of His life, testified to His divine anointing.

Again as they listened to His words the Nazarenes were moved by the divine Spirit. But even now they would not admit that this man, who had been brought up among them, was other or greater than themselves. Still there rankled the bitter memory that while He had claimed for Himself to be the Promised One, He had really denied them a place with Israel; for He had shown them to be less worthy of God's favor than a heathen man and woman. Hence though they questioned, "Whence hath this man this wisdom, and these mighty works?" they would not receive Him as the Christ of God. Because of their unbelief, the Saviour could not work many miracles among them. Only a few hearts were open to His blessing, and reluctantly He departed, never to return.

Unbelief, having once been cherished, continued to control the men of Nazareth. So it controlled the Sanhedrim and the nation. With priests and people, the first rejection of the demonstration of the Holy Spirit's power was the beginning of the end. In order to prove that their first resistance was right, they continued ever after to cavil at the words of Christ. Their rejection of the Spirit culminated in the cross of Calvary, in the destruction of their city, in the scattering of the nation to the winds of heaven.

O, how Christ longed to open to Israel the precious treasures of the truth! But such was their spiritual blindness that it was impossible to reveal to them the truths relating to His kingdom. They clung to their creed and their useless ceremonies, when the truth of Heaven awaited their acceptance. They spent their money for chaff and husks, when the bread of life was within their reach. Why did they not go to the word of God, and search diligently to know whether they were in error? The Old Testament Scriptures stated plainly every detail of Christ's ministry, and again and again He quoted from the prophets, and declared, "Today is this scripture fulfilled in your ears." If they had honestly searched the Scriptures, bringing their theories to the test of God's word, Jesus need not have wept over their impenitence. He need not have declared, "Behold, your house is left unto you desolate." Luke 13:35. They might have been acquainted with the evidence of His Messiahship, and the calamity that laid their proud city in ruins might have been averted. But the minds of the Jews had become narrowed by their unreasoning bigotry. The lessons of Christ revealed their deficiencies of character, and demanded repentance. If they accepted His teachings, their practises must be changed, and their cherished hopes relinquished. In order to be honored by Heaven, they must sacrifice the honor of men. If they obeyed the words of this new rabbi, they must go contrary to the opinions of the great thinkers and teachers of the time.

Truth was unpopular in Christ's day. It is unpopular in our day. It has been unpopular ever since Satan first gave man a disrelish for it by presenting fables that lead to self-exaltation. Do we not today meet theories and doctrines that have no foundation in the word of God? Men cling as tenaciously to them as did the Jews to their traditions.

The Jewish leaders were filled with spiritual pride. Their desire for the glorification of self manifested itself even in the service of the sanctuary. They loved the highest seats in the synagogue. They loved greetings in the marketplaces, and were gratified with the sound of their titles on the lips of men. As real piety declined, they became more jealous for their traditions and ceremonies.

Because their understanding was darkened by selfish prejudice, they could not harmonize the power of Christ's convicting words with the humility of His life. They did not appreciate the fact that real greatness can dispense with outward show. This man's poverty seemed wholly inconsistent with His claim to be the Messiah. They questioned, If He was what He claimed to be, why was He so unpretending? If He was satisfied to be without the force of arms, what would become of their nation? How could the power and glory so long anticipated, bring the nations as subjects to the city of the Jews? Had not the priests taught that Israel was to bear rule over all the earth? and could it be possible that the great religious teachers were in error?

But it was not simply the absence of outward glory in His life that led the Jews to reject Jesus. He was the embodiment of purity, and they were impure. He dwelt among men an example of spotless integrity. His blameless life flashed light upon their hearts. His sincerity revealed their insincerity. It made manifest the hollowness of their pretentious piety, and discovered iniquity to them in its odious character. Such a light was unwelcome.

If Christ had called attention to the Pharisees, and had extolled their learning and piety, they would have hailed Him with joy. But when He spoke of the kingdom of heaven as a dispensation of mercy for all mankind, He was presenting a phase of religion they would not tolerate. Their own example and teaching had never been such as to make the service of God seem desirable. When they saw Jesus giving attention to the very ones they hated and repulsed, it stirred up the worst passions of their proud hearts. Notwithstanding their boast that under the "Lion of the tribe of Judah," Revelation 5:5. Israel should be exalted to pre-eminence over all nations, they could have borne the disappointment of their ambitious hopes better than they could bear Christ's reproof of their sins, and the reproach they felt even from the presence of His purity.

The Call by the Sea

Day was breaking over the Sea of Galilee. The disciples, weary with a night of fruitless toil, were still in their fishing boats on the lake. Jesus had come to spend a quiet hour by the waterside. In the early morning He hoped for a little season of rest from the multitude that followed Him day after day. But soon the people began to gather about Him. Their numbers rapidly increased, so that He was pressed upon all sides. Meanwhile the disciples had come to land. In order to escape the pressure of the multitude, Jesus stepped into Peter's boat, and bade him pull out a little from the shore. Here Jesus could be better seen and heard by all, and from the boat He taught the multitude on the beach.

What a scene was this for angels to contemplate; — their glorious Commander, sitting in a fisherman's boat, swayed to and fro by the restless waves, and proclaiming the good news of salvation to the listening throng that were pressing down to the water's edge! He who was the Honored of heaven was declaring the great things of His kingdom in the open air, to the common people. Yet He could have had no more fitting scene for His labors. The lake, the mountains, the spreading fields, the sunlight flooding the earth, all furnished objects to illustrate His lessons and impress them upon the mind. And no lesson of Christ's fell fruitless. Every message from His lips came to some soul as the word of eternal life.

Every moment added to the multitude upon the shore. Aged men leaning upon their staffs, hardy peasants from the hills, fishermen from their toil on the lake, merchants and rabbis, the rich and learned, old and young, bringing their sick and suffering ones, pressed to hear the words of the divine Teacher. To such scenes as this the prophets had looked forward, and they wrote, —

"The land of Zebulun and the land of Naphtali,
  Toward the sea, beyond Jordan,
  Galilee of the Gentiles,
  The people which sat in darkness
  Saw a great light,
  And to them which sat in the region
  and shadow of death,
  To them did light spring up." Isaiah 9:1-2, R. V.

Besides the throng on the shores of Gennesaret, Jesus in His sermon by the sea had other audiences before His mind. Looking down the ages, He saw His faithful ones in prison and judgment hall, in temptation and loneliness and affliction. Every scene of joy and conflict and perplexity was open before Him. In the words spoken to those gathered about Him, He was speaking also to these other souls, the very words that would come to them as a message of hope in trial, of comfort in sorrow, and heavenly light in darkness. Through the Holy Spirit, that voice which was speaking from the fisherman's boat on the Sea of Galilee, would be heard speaking peace to human hearts to the close of time.

The discourse ended, Jesus turned to Peter, and bade him launch out into the sea, and let down his net for a draught. But Peter was disheartened. All night he had taken nothing. During the lonely hours he had thought of the fate of John the Baptist, who was languishing alone in his dungeon. He had thought of the prospect before Jesus and His followers, of the ill success of the mission to Judea, and the malice of the priests and rabbis. Even his own occupation had failed him; and as he watched by the empty nets, the future had seemed dark with discouragement. "Master," he said, "we have toiled all the night, and have taken nothing; nevertheless at Thy word I will let down the net."

This chapter is based on Matt. 4:18-22; Mark 1:16-20; Luke 5:1-11.   (244-246)

Night was the only favorable time for fishing with nets in the clear waters of the lake. After toiling all night without success, it seemed hopeless to cast the net by day; but Jesus had given the command, and love for their Master moved the disciples to obey. Simon and his brother together let down the net. As they attempted to draw it in, so great was the quantity of fish enclosed that it began to break. They were obliged to summon James and John to their aid. When the catch was secured, both the boats were so heavily laden that they were in danger of sinking.

But Peter was unmindful now of boats or lading. This miracle, above any other he had ever witnessed, was to him a manifestation of divine power. In Jesus he saw One who held all nature under His control. The presence of divinity revealed his own unholiness. Love for his Master, shame for his own unbelief, gratitude for the condescension of Christ, above all, the sense of his uncleanness in the presence of infinite purity, overwhelmed him. While his companions were securing the contents of the net, Peter fell at the Saviour's feet, exclaiming, "Depart from me; for I am a sinful man, O Lord."

It was the same presence of divine holiness that had caused the prophet Daniel to fall as one dead before the angel of God. He said, "My comeliness was turned in me into corruption, and I retained no strength." So when Isaiah beheld the glory of the Lord, he exclaimed, "Woe is me! for I am undone; because I am a man of unclean lips, and I dwell in the midst of a people of unclean lips; for mine eyes have seen the King, the Lord of hosts." Daniel 10:8; Isaiah 6:5. Humanity, with its weakness and sin, was brought in contrast with the perfection of divinity, and he felt altogether deficient and unholy. Thus it has been with all who have been granted a view of God's greatness and majesty.

Peter exclaimed, "Depart from me; for I am a sinful man;" yet he clung to the feet of Jesus, feeling that he could not be parted from Him. The Saviour answered, "Fear not; from henceforth thou shalt catch men." It was after Isaiah has beheld the holiness of God and his own unworthiness, that he was intrusted with the divine message. It was after Peter had been led to self-renunciation and dependence upon divine power, that he received the call to his work for Christ.

Until this time none of the disciples had fully united as co-laborers with Jesus. They had witnessed many of His miracles, and had listened to His teaching; but they had not entirely forsaken their former employment. The imprisonment of John the Baptist had been to them all a bitter disappointment. If such were to be the outcome of John's mission, they could have little hope for their Master, with all the religious leaders combined against Him. Under the circumstances it was a relief to them to return for a short time to their fishing. But now Jesus called them to forsake their former life, and unite their interests with His. Peter had accepted the call. Upon reaching the shore, Jesus bade the three other disciples, "Follow Me, and I will make you fishers of men." Immediately they left all, and followed Him.

Before asking them to leave their nets and fishing boats, Jesus had given them the assurance that God would supply their needs. The use of Peter's boat for the work of the gospel had been richly repaid. He who is "rich unto all that call upon Him," has said, "Give, and it shall be given unto you; good measure, pressed down, and shaken together, and running over." Romans 10:12; Luke 6:38. In this measure He had rewarded the disciple's service. And every sacrifice that is made in His ministry will be recom-

---

"He who loves Christ the most will do the greatest amount of good. There is no limit to the usefulness of one who, by putting self aside, makes room for the working of the Holy Spirit upon his heart, and lives a life wholly consecrated to God."

---

pensed according to "the exceeding riches of His grace." Ephesians 3:20; 2:7.

During that sad night on the lake, when they were separated from Christ, the disciples were pressed hard by unbelief, and weary with fruitless toil. But His presence kindled their faith, and brought them joy and success. So it is with us; apart from Christ, our work is fruitless, and it is easy to distrust and murmur. But when He is near, and we labor under His direction, we rejoice in the evidence of His power. It is Satan's work to discourage the soul; it is Christ's work to inspire with faith and hope.

The deeper lesson which the miracle conveyed for the disciples, is a lesson for us also, — that He whose word could gather the fishes from the sea, could also impress human hearts, and draw them by the cords of His love, so that his servants might become "fishers of men."

They were humble and unlearned men, those fishers of Galilee; but Christ, the light of the world, was abundantly able to qualify them for the position for which He had chosen them. The Saviour did not despise education; for when controlled by the love of God, and devoted to His service, intellectual culture is a blessing. But he passed by the wise men of His time, because they were so self-confident that they could not sympathize with suffering humanity, and become co-laborers with the Man of Nazareth. In their bigotry they scorned to be taught by Christ. The Lord Jesus seeks the co-operation of those who will become unobstructed channels for the communication of His grace. The first thing to be learned by all who would become workers together with God, is the lesson of self-distrust; then they are prepared to have imparted to them the character of Christ. This is not to be gained through education in the most scientific schools. It is the fruit of wisdom that is obtained from the divine Teacher alone.

Jesus chose unlearned fishermen because they had not been schooled in the traditions and erroneous customs of their time. They were men of native ability, and they were humble and teachable, — men whom He could educate for His work. In the common walks of life there is many a man patiently treading the round of daily toil, unconscious that he possesses powers which, if called into action, would raise him to an equality with the world's most honorable men. The touch of a skillful hand is needed to arouse those dormant faculties. It was such men that Jesus called to be His co-laborers; and He gave them the advantage of association with Himself. Never had the world's great men such a teacher. When the disciples came forth from the Saviour's training, they were no longer ignorant and uncultured. They had become like Him in mind and character, and men took knowledge of them that they had been with Jesus.

It is not the highest work of education to communicate knowledge merely, but to impart that vitalizing energy which is received through the contact of mind with mind, and soul with soul. It is only life that can beget life. What privilege, then, was theirs who for three years were in daily contact with that divine life from which flowed every life-giving impulse that has blessed the world. Above all his companions, John the beloved disciple yielded himself to the power of that wondrous life. He says, "The life was manifested, and we have seen it, and bear witness, and show unto you that eternal life, which was with the Father, and was manifested unto us." "Of His fullness have all we received, and grace for grace." 1 John 1:2; John 1:16.

In the apostles of our Lord there was nothing to bring glory to themselves. It was evident that the success of their labors was due only to God. The lives of these men, the characters they developed, and the mighty work that God wrought through them, are a testimony to what He will do for all who are teachable and obedient.

He who loves Christ the most, will do the greatest amount of good. There is no limit to the usefulness of one who, by putting self aside, makes room for the working of the Holy Spirit upon his heart, and lives a life wholly consecrated to God. If men will endure the necessary discipline, without complaining, or fainting by the way, God will teach them hour by hour, and day by day. He longs to reveal His grace. If His people will remove the obstructions, He will pour forth the waters of salvation in abundant streams through the human channels. If men in humble life were encouraged to do all the good they could do, if restraining hands were not laid upon them to repress their zeal, there would be a hundred workers for Christ where now there is one.

God takes men as they are, and educates them for His service, if they will yield themselves to Him. The Spirit of God, received into the soul, will quicken all its faculties. Under the guidance of the Holy Spirit, the mind that is devoted unreservedly to God, develops harmoniously, and is strengthened to comprehend and fulfill the requirements of God. The weak, vacillating character becomes changed to one of strength and steadfastness. Continual devotion establishes so close a relation between Jesus and His disciple that the Christian becomes like Him in mind and character. Through a connection with Christ he will have clearer and broader views. His discernment will be more penetrative, his judgment better balanced. He who longs to be of service to Christ is so quickened by the life-giving power of the Sun of Righteousness, that he is enabled to bear much fruit to the glory of God.

Men of the highest education in the arts and sciences have learned precious lessons from Christians in humble life who were designated by the world as unlearned. But these obscure disciples had obtained an education in the highest of all schools. They had sat at the feet of Him who spoke as "never man spake."

At Capernaum

At Capernaum Jesus dwelt in the intervals of His journeys to and fro, and it came to be known as "His own city." It was on the shores of the Sea of Galilee, and near the borders of the beautiful plain of Gennesaret, if not actually upon it.

The deep depression of the lake gives to the plain that skirts its shores the genial climate of the south. Here in the days of Christ flourished the palm tree and the olive, here were orchards and vineyards, green fields, and brightly blooming flowers in rich luxuriance, all watered by living streams bursting from the cliffs. The shores of the lake, and the hills that at a little distance encircle it, were dotted with towns and villages. The lake was covered with fishing boats. Everywhere was the stir of busy, active life.

Capernaum itself was well adapted to be the center of the Saviour's work. Being on the highway from Damascus to Jerusalem and Egypt, and to the Mediterranean Sea, it was a great thoroughfare of travel. People from many lands passed through the city, or tarried for rest in their journeyings to and fro. Here Jesus could meet all nations and all ranks, the rich and great as well as the poor and lowly, and His lessons would be carried to other countries and into many households. Investigation of the prophecies would thus be excited, attention would be directed to the Saviour, and His mission would be brought before the world.

Notwithstanding the action of the Sanhedrim against Jesus, the people eagerly awaited the development of His mission. All heaven was astir with interest. Angels were preparing the way for His ministry, moving upon men's hearts, and drawing them to the Saviour.

In Capernaum the nobleman's son whom Christ had healed, was a witness to His power. And the court official and his household joyfully testified of their faith. When it was known that the Teacher Himself was among them, the whole city was aroused. Multitudes flocked to His presence. On the Sabbath the people crowded the synagogue until great numbers had to turn away, unable to find entrance.

All who heard the Saviour "were astonished at His doctrine; for His word was with power." "He taught them as one having authority, and not as the scribes." Luke 4:32; Matthew 7:29. The teaching of the scribes and elders was cold and formal, like a lesson learned by rote. To them the word of God possessed no vital power. Their own ideas and traditions were substituted for its teaching. In the accustomed round of service they professed to explain the law, but no inspiration from God stirred their own hearts or the hearts of their hearers.

Jesus had nothing to do with the various subjects of dissension among the Jews. It was His work to present the truth. His words shed a flood of light upon the teachings of patriarchs and prophets, and the Scriptures came to men as a new revelation. Never before had His hearers perceived such a depth of meaning in the word of God.

Jesus met the people on their own ground, as one who was acquainted with their perplexities. He made truth beautiful by presenting it in the most direct and simple way. His language was pure, refined, and clear as a running stream. His voice was as music to those who had listened to the monotonous tones of the rabbis. But while His teaching was simple, He spoke as one having authority. This characteristic set His teaching in contrast with that of all others. The rabbis spoke with doubt and hesitancy, as if the Scriptures might be interpreted to mean one thing or exactly the opposite. The hearers were daily involved in greater uncertainty. But Jesus taught the Scriptures as of unquestionable authority. Whatever His subject, it was presented with power, as if His words could not be controverted.

Yet He was earnest, rather than vehement. He spoke as one who had a definite purpose to fulfill. He was bringing to view the realities of the eternal world. In every theme, God was revealed. Jesus sought to break the spell of infatuation which keeps men absorbed in earthly things. He placed the things of this life in their true relation, as subordinate to those of eternal interest; but He did not ignore their importance. He taught that heaven and earth are linked together, and that a knowledge of divine truth prepares men better to perform the duties of everyday life. He spoke as one familiar with heaven, conscious of His relationship to God, yet recognizing His unity with every member of the human family.

His messages of mercy were varied to suit His audience. He knew "how to speak a word in season to him that is weary;" (Isaiah 50:4.) for grace was poured upon His lips, that He might convey to men in the most attractive way the treasures of truth. He had tact to meet the prejudiced minds, and surprise them with illustrations that won their attention. Through the imagination He reached the heart. His illustrations were taken from the things of daily life, and although they were simple, they had in them a wonderful depth of meaning. The birds of the air, the lilies of the field, the seed, the shepherd and the sheep, — with these objects Christ illustrated immortal truth; and ever afterward, when His hearers chanced to see these things of nature, they recalled His words. Christ's illustrations constantly repeated His lessons.

Christ never flattered men. He never spoke that which would exalt their fancies and imaginations, nor did He praise them for their clever inventions; but deep, unprejudiced thinkers received His teaching, and found that it tested their wisdom. They marveled at the spiritual truth expressed in the simplest language. The most highly educated were charmed with His words, and the uneducated were always profited. He had a message for the illiterate; and He made even the heathen to understand that He had a message for them.

His tender compassion fell with a touch of healing upon weary and troubled hearts. Even amid the turbulence of angry enemies He was surrounded with an atmosphere of peace. The beauty of His countenance, the loveliness of His character, above all, the love expressed in look and tone, drew to Him all who were not hardened in unbelief. Had it not been for the sweet, sympathetic spirit that shone out in every look and word, He would not have attracted the large congregations that He did. The afflicted ones who came to Him, felt that He linked His interest with theirs as a faithful and tender friend, and they desired to know more of the truths He taught. Heaven was brought near. They longed to abide in His presence, that the comfort of His love might be with them continually.

Jesus watched with deep earnestness the changing countenances of His hearers. The faces that expressed interest and pleasure, gave Him great satisfaction. As the arrows of truth pierced to the soul, breaking through the barriers of selfishness, and working contrition, and finally gratitude, the Saviour was made glad. When His eye swept over the throng of listeners, and He recognized among them the faces He had before seen, His countenance lighted up with joy. He saw in them hopeful subjects for His kingdom. When the truth, plainly spoken, touched some cherished

> **"History is repeating. With the open Bible before them, . . . many of the religious leaders of our time are destroying faith in it as the word of God. They busy themselves with dissecting the word, and set their own opinions above its plainest statements. In their hands God's word loses its regenerating power."**

idol, He marked the change of countenance, the cold, forbidding look, which told that the light was unwelcome. When He saw men refuse the message of peace, His heart was pierced to the very depths.

Jesus in the synagogue spoke of the kingdom He had come to establish, and of His mission to set free the captives of Satan. He was interrupted by a shriek of terror. A madman rushed forward from among the people, crying out, "Let us alone; what have we to do with Thee, Thou Jesus of Nazareth? art Thou come to destroy us? I know Thee who Thou art, the Holy One of God."

All was now confusion and alarm. The attention of the people was diverted from Christ, and His words were unheeded. This was Satan's purpose in leading his victim to the synagogue. But Jesus rebuked the demon, saying, "Hold thy peace, and come out of him. And when the devil had thrown him in the midst, he came out of him, and hurt him not."

The mind of this wretched sufferer had been darkened by Satan, but in the Saviour's presence a ray of light had pierced the gloom. He was roused to long for freedom from Satan's control; but the demon resisted the power of Christ. When the man tried to appeal to Jesus for help, the evil spirit put words into his mouth, and he cried out in an agony of fear. The demoniac partially comprehended that he was in the presence of One who could set him free: but when he tried to come within reach of that mighty hand, another's will held him; another's words found utterance through him. The conflict between the power of Satan and his own desire for freedom was terrible.

He who had conquered Satan in the wilderness of temptation was again brought face to face with His enemy. The demon exerted all his power to retain control of his victim. To lose ground here, would be to give Jesus a victory. It seemed that the tortured man must lose his life in the struggle with the foe that had been the ruin of his manhood. But the Saviour spoke with authority, and set the captive free. The man who had been possessed stood before the wondering people happy in the freedom of self-possession. Even the demon had testified to the divine power of the Saviour.

The man praised God for his deliverance. The eye that had so lately glared with the fire of insanity, now beamed with intelligence, and overflowed with grateful tears. The people were dumb with amazement. As soon as they recovered speech they exclaimed, one to another, "What is this? A new teaching! with authority He commandeth even the unclean spirits, and they obey Him." Mark 1:27, R. V.

The secret cause of the affliction that had made this man a fearful spectacle to his friends and a burden to himself, was in his own life. He had been fascinated by the pleasures of sin, and had thought to make life a grand carnival. He did not dream of becoming a terror to the world and the reproach of his family. He thought his time could be spent in innocent folly. But once in the downward path, his feet rapidly descended. Intemperance and frivolity perverted the noble attributes of his nature, and Satan took absolute control of him.

Remorse came too late. When he would have sacrificed wealth and pleasure to regain his lost manhood, he had become helpless in the grasp of the evil one. He had placed himself on the enemy's ground, and Satan had taken possession of all his faculties. The tempter had allured him with many charming presentations; but when once the wretched man was in his power, the fiend became relentless in his cruelty, and terrible in his angry visitations. So it will be with all who yield to evil; the fascinating pleasure of their early career ends in the darkness of despair or the madness of a ruined soul.

The same evil spirit that tempted Christ in the wilderness, and that possessed the maniac of Capernaum, controlled the unbelieving Jews. But with them he assumed an air of piety, seeking to deceive them as to their motives in rejecting the Saviour. Their condition was more hopeless than that of the demoniac; for they felt no need of Christ, and were therefore held fast under the power of Satan.

The period of Christ's personal ministry among men was the time of greatest activity for the forces of the kingdom of darkness. For ages Satan with his evil angels had been seeking to control the bodies and the souls of men, to bring upon them sin and suffering; then he had charged all this misery upon God. Jesus was revealing to men the character of God. He was breaking Satan's power, and setting his captives free. New life and love and power from heaven were moving upon the hearts of men, and the prince of evil was aroused to contend for the supremacy of his kingdom. Satan summoned all his forces, and at every step contested the work of Christ.

So it will be in the great final conflict of the controversy between righteousness and sin. While new life and light and power are descending from on high upon the disciples of Christ, a new life is springing up from beneath, and energizing the agencies of Satan. Intensity is taking possession of every earthly element. With a subtlety gained through centuries of conflict, the prince of evil works under a disguise. He appears clothed as an angel of light, and multitudes are "giving heed to seducing spirits, and doctrines of devils." 1 Timothy 4:1.

In the days of Christ the leaders and teachers of Israel were powerless to resist the work of Satan. They were neglecting the only means by which they could have withstood evil spirits. It was by the word of God that Christ overcame the wicked one. The leaders of Israel professed to be the expositors of God's word, but they had studied it only to sustain their traditions, and enforce their man-made observances. By their interpretation they made it express sentiments that God had never given. Their mystical construction made indistinct that which He had made plain. They disputed over insignificant technicalities, and practically denied the most essential truths. Thus infidelity was sown broadcast. God's word was robbed of its power, and evil spirits worked their will.

History is repeating. With the open Bible before them, and professing to reverence its teachings, many of the religious leaders of our time are destroying faith in it as the word of God. They busy themselves with dissecting the word, and set their own opinions above its plainest statements. In their hands God's word loses its regenerating power. This is why infidelity runs riot, and iniquity is rife.

When Satan has undermined faith in the Bible, he directs men to other sources for light and power. Thus he insinuates himself. Those who turn from the plain teaching of Scripture and the convicting power of God's Holy Spirit, are inviting the control of demons. Criticism and speculation concerning the Scriptures have opened the way for Spiritualism and Theosophy — those modernized forms of ancient heathenism — to gain a foothold even in the professed churches of our Lord Jesus Christ.

Side by side with the preaching of the gospel, agencies are at work which are but the medium of lying spirits. Many a man tampers with these merely from curiosity, but seeing evidence of the working of a more than human power, he is lured on and on, until he is controlled by a will stronger than his own. He cannot escape from its mysterious power.

> **"Every man is free to choose what power he will have to rule over him. None have fallen so low, none are so vile, but that they can find deliverance in Christ. The demoniac, in place of prayer, could utter only the words of Satan; yet the heart's unspoken appeal was heard."**

The defenses of the soul are broken down. He has no barrier against sin. When once the restraints of God's word and His Spirit are rejected, no man knows to what depths of degradation he may sink. Secret sin or master passion may hold him a captive as helpless as was the demoniac of Capernaum. Yet his condition is not hopeless.

The means by which we can overcome the wicked one is that by which Christ overcame, — the power of the word. God does not control our minds without our consent; but if we desire to know and to do His will, His promises are ours: "Ye shall know the truth, and the truth shall make you free." "If any man willeth to do His will, he shall know of the teaching." John 8:32; 7:17, R. V. Through faith in these promises, every man may be delivered from the snares of error and the control of sin.

Every man is free to choose what power he will have to rule over him. None have fallen so low, none are so vile, but that they can find deliverance in Christ. The demoniac, in place of prayer, could utter only the words of Satan; yet the heart's unspoken appeal was heard. No cry from a soul in need, though it fail of utterance in words, will be unheeded. Those who will consent to enter into covenant

relation with the God of heaven are not left to the power of Satan or to the infirmity of their own nature. They are invited by the Saviour, "Let him take hold of My strength, that he may make peace with Me; and he shall make peace with Me." Isaiah 27:5. The spirits of darkness will battle for the soul once under their dominion, but angels of God will contend for that soul with prevailing power. The Lord says, "Shall the prey be taken from the mighty, or the lawful captive delivered? . . . Thus saith the Lord, Even the captives of the mighty shall be taken away, and the prey of the terrible shall be delivered; for I will contend with him that contendeth with thee, and I will save thy children." Isaiah 49:24, 25.

While the congregation in the synagogue were still spellbound with awe, Jesus withdrew to the home of Peter for a little rest. But here also a shadow had fallen. The mother of Peter's wife lay sick, stricken with a "great fever." Jesus rebuked the disease, and the sufferer arose, and ministered to the wants of the Master and His disciples.

Tidings of the work of Christ spread rapidly throughout Capernaum. For fear of the rabbis, the people dared not come for healing upon the Sabbath; but no sooner had the sun disappeared below the horizon than there was a great commotion. From the homes, the shops, the marketplaces, the inhabitants of the city pressed toward the humble dwelling that sheltered Jesus. The sick were brought upon couches, they came leaning upon staffs, or supported by friends, they tottered feebly into the Saviour's presence.

Hour after hour they came and went; for none could know whether tomorrow would find the Healer still among them. Never before had Capernaum witnessed a day like this. The air was filled with the voice of triumph and shouts of deliverance. The Saviour was joyful in the joy He had awakened. As He witnessed the sufferings of those who had come to Him, His heart was stirred with sympathy, and He rejoiced in His power to restore them to health and happiness.

Not until the last sufferer had been relieved, did Jesus cease His work. It was far into the night when the multitude departed, and silence settled down upon the home of Simon. The long, exciting day was past, and Jesus sought rest. But while the city was still wrapped in slumber, the Saviour, "rising up a great while before day, went out, and departed into a solitary place, and there prayed."

Thus were spent the days in the earthly life of Jesus. He often dismissed His disciples to visit their homes and rest; but He gently resisted their efforts to draw Him away from His labors. All day He toiled, teaching the ignorant, healing the sick, giving sight to the blind, feeding the multitude; and at the eventide or in the early morning, He went away to the sanctuary of the mountains for communication with His Father. Often He passed the entire night in prayer and meditation, returning at daybreak to His work among the people.

Early in the morning, Peter and his companions came to Jesus, saying that already the people of Capernaum were seeking Him. The disciples had been bitterly disappointed at the reception which Christ had met hitherto. The authorities at Jerusalem were seeking to murder Him; even His own townsmen had tried to take His life; but at Capernaum He was welcomed with joyful enthusiasm, and the hopes of the disciples kindled anew. It might be that among the liberty-loving Galileans were to be found the supporters of the new kingdom. But with surprise they heard Christ's words, "I must preach the kingdom of God to other cities also; for therefore am I sent."

In the excitement which then pervaded Capernaum, there was danger that the object of His mission would be lost sight of. Jesus was not satisfied to attract attention to Himself merely as a wonder worker or a healer of physical diseases. He was seeking to draw men to Him as their Saviour. While the people were eager to believe that He had come as a king, to establish an earthly reign, He desired to turn their minds away from the earthly to the spiritual. Mere worldly success would interfere with His work.

And the wonder of the careless crowd jarred upon His spirit. In His life no self-assertion mingled. The homage which the world gives to position, or wealth, or talent, was foreign to the Son of man. None of the means that men employ to win allegiance or command homage did Jesus use. Centuries before His birth, it had been prophesied of Him, "He shall not cry, nor lift up, nor cause His voice to be heard in the street. A bruised reed shall He not break, and the dimly burning flax shall He not quench; He shall bring forth judgment unto truth. He shall not fail nor be discouraged, till He have set judgment in the earth." Isaiah 42:2-4, margin.

The Pharisees sought distinction by their scrupulous ceremonialism, and the ostentation of their worship and charities. They proved their zeal for religion by making it the theme of discussion. Disputes between opposing sects were loud and long, and it was not unusual to hear on the streets the voice of angry controversy from learned doctors of the law.

In marked contrast to all this was the life of Jesus. In that life no noisy disputation, no ostentatious worship, no act to gain applause, was ever witnessed. Christ was hid in God, and God was revealed in the character of His Son. To this revelation Jesus desired the minds of the people to be directed, and their homage to be given.

The Sun of Righteousness did not burst upon the world in splendor, to dazzle the senses with His glory. It is written of Christ, "His going forth is prepared as the morning." Hosea 6:3. Quietly and gently the daylight breaks upon the earth, dispelling the shadow of darkness, and waking the world to life. So did the Sun of Righteousness arise, "with healing in His wings." Malachi 4:2.

"Thou Canst Make Me Clean"

Of all diseases known in the East the leprosy was most dreaded. Its incurable and contagious character, and its horrible effect upon its victims, filled the bravest with fear. Among the Jews it was regarded as a judgment on account of sin, and hence was called, "The stroke," "the finger of God." Deep-rooted, ineradicable, deadly, it was looked upon as a symbol of sin. By the ritual law, the leper was pronounced unclean. Like one already dead, he was shut out from the habitations of men. Whatever he touched was unclean. The air was polluted by his breath. One who was suspected of having the disease must present himself to the priests, who were to examine and decide his case. If pronounced a leper, he was isolated from his family, cut off from the congregation of Israel, and was doomed to associate with those only who were similarly afflicted. The law was inflexible in its requirement. Even kings and rulers were not exempt. A monarch who was attacked by this terrible disease must yield up the scepter, and flee from society.

Away from his friends and his kindred, the leper must bear the curse of his malady. He was obliged to publish his own calamity, to rend his garments, and sound the alarm, warning all to flee from his contaminating presence. The cry, "Unclean! unclean!" coming in mournful tones from the lonely exile, was a signal heard with fear and abhorrence.

In the region of Christ's ministry, there were many of these sufferers, and the news of His work reached them, kindling a gleam of hope. But since the days of Elisha the prophet, such a thing had never been known as the cleansing of one upon whom this disease had fastened. They dared not expect Jesus to do for them what He had never done for any man. There was one, however, in whose heart faith began to spring up. Yet the man knew not how to reach Jesus. Debarred as he was from contact with his fellow men, how could he present himself to the Healer? And he questioned if Christ would heal *him*. Would He stoop to notice one believed to be suffering under the judgment of God? Would He not, like the Pharisees, and even the physicians, pronounce a curse upon him, and warn him to flee from the haunts of men? He thought of all that had been told him of Jesus. Not one who had sought His help had been turned away. The wretched man determined to find the Saviour. Though shut out from the cities, it might be that he could cross His path in some byway along the mountain roads, or find Him as He was teaching outside the towns. The difficulties were great, but this was his only hope.

The leper is guided to the Saviour. Jesus is teaching beside the lake, and the people are gathered about Him. Standing afar off, the leper catches a few words from the Saviour's lips. He sees Him laying His hands upon the sick. He sees the lame, the blind, the paralytic, and those dying of various maladies, rise up in health, praising God for their deliverance. Faith strengthens in his heart. He draws nearer and yet nearer to the gathered throng. The restrictions laid upon him, the safety of the people, and the fear with which all men regard him, are forgotten. He thinks only of the blessed hope of healing.

He is a loathsome spectacle. The disease has made frightful inroads, and his decaying body is horrible to look upon. At sight of him the people fall back in terror. They crowd upon one another in their eagerness to escape from contact with him. Some try to prevent him from approaching Jesus, but in vain. He neither sees nor hears them. Their expressions of loathing are lost upon him. He sees only the

110 This chapter is based on Matt. 8:2-4; 9:1-8, 32-34; Mark 1:40-45; 2:1-12; Luke 5:12-28. (262-263)

Son of God. He hears only the voice that speaks life to the dying. Pressing to Jesus, he casts himself at His feet with the cry, "Lord, if Thou wilt, Thou canst make *me* clean."

Jesus replied, "I will; be thou made clean," (Matthew 8:3, R. V.) and laid His hand upon him.

Immediately a change passed over the leper. His flesh became healthy, the nerves sensitive, the muscles firm. The rough, scaly surface peculiar to leprosy disappeared, and a soft glow, like that upon the skin of a healthy child, took its place.

Jesus charged the man not to make known the work that had been wrought, but straightway to present himself with an offering at the temple. Such an offering could not be accepted until the priests had made examination and pronounced the man wholly free from the disease. However unwilling they might be to perform this service, they could not evade an examination and decision of the case.

The words of Scripture show with what urgency Christ enjoined upon the man the necessity of silence and prompt action. "He straitly charged him, and forthwith sent him away; and saith unto him, See thou say nothing to any man; but go thy way, show thyself to the priest, and offer for thy cleansing those things which Moses commanded, for a testimony unto them." Had the priests known the facts concerning the healing of the leper, their hatred of Christ might have led them to render a dishonest sentence. Jesus desired the man to present himself at the temple before any rumors concerning the miracle had reached them. Thus an impartial decision could be secured, and the restored leper would be permitted to unite once more with his family and friends.

There were other objects which Christ had in view in enjoining silence on the man. The Saviour knew that His enemies were ever seeking to limit His work, and to turn the people from Him. He knew that if the healing of the leper were noised abroad, other sufferers from this terrible disease would crowd about Him, and the cry would be raised that the people would be contaminated by contact with them. Many of the lepers would not so use the gift of health as to make it a blessing to themselves or to others. And by drawing the lepers about Him, He would give occasion for the charge that He was breaking down the restrictions of the ritual law. Thus His work in preaching the gospel would be hindered.

The event justified Christ's warning. A multitude of people had witnessed the healing of the leper, and they were eager to learn of the priests' decision. When the man returned to his friends, there was great excitement. Notwithstanding the caution of Jesus, the man made no further effort to conceal the fact of his cure. It would indeed have been impossible to conceal it, but the leper published the matter abroad. Conceiving that it was only the modesty of Jesus which laid this restriction upon him, he went about proclaiming the power of this great Healer. He did not understand that every such manifestation made the priests and elders more determined to destroy Jesus. The restored man felt that the boon of health was very precious. He rejoiced in the vigor of manhood, and in his restoration to his family and society, and felt it impossible to refrain from giving glory to the Physician who had made him whole. But his act in blazing abroad the matter resulted in hindering the Saviour's work. It caused the people to flock to Him in such multitudes that He was forced for a time to cease His labors.

> **"When we pray for earthly blessings, the answer to our prayer may be delayed, or God may give us something other than we ask, but not so when we ask for deliverance from sin. It is His will to cleanse us from sin, to make us His children, and to enable us to live a holy life."**

Every act of Christ's ministry was far-reaching in its purpose. It comprehended more than appeared in the act itself. So in the case of the leper. While Jesus ministered to all who came unto Him, He yearned to bless those who came not. While He drew the publicans, the heathen, and the Samaritans, He longed to reach the priests and teachers who were shut in by prejudice and tradition. He left untried no means by which they might be reached. In sending the healed leper to the priests, He gave them a testimony calculated to disarm their prejudices.

The Pharisees had asserted that Christ's teaching was opposed to the law which God had given through Moses; but His direction to the cleansed leper to present an offering according to the law, disproved this charge. It was sufficient testimony for all who were willing to be convinced.

The leaders at Jerusalem had sent out spies to find some pretext for putting Christ to death. He responded by giving them an evidence of His love for humanity, His respect for the law, and His power to deliver from sin and death. Thus He bore witness of them: "They have rewarded Me evil for good, and hatred for My love." Psalms 109:5. He who on the mount gave the precept, "Love your enemies,"

Himself exemplified the principle, not rendering "evil for evil, or railing for railing; but contrariwise blessing." Matthew 5:44; 1 Peter 3:9.

The same priests who condemned the leper to banishment, certified his cure. This sentence, publicly pronounced and registered, was a standing testimony for Christ. And as the healed man was reinstated in the congregation of Israel, upon the priests' own assurance that there was not a taint of the disease upon him, he himself was a living witness for his Benefactor. Joyfully he presented his offering, and magnified the name of Jesus. The priests were convinced of the divine power of the Saviour. Opportunity was granted them to know the truth and to be profited by the light. Rejected, it would pass away, never to return. By many the light was rejected; yet it was not given in vain. Many hearts were moved that for a time made no sign. During the Saviour's life, His mission seemed to call forth little response of love from the priests and teachers; but after His ascension "a great company of the priests were obedient to the faith." Acts 6:7.

The work of Christ in cleansing the leper from his terrible disease is an illustration of His work in cleansing the soul from sin. The man who came to Jesus was "full of leprosy." Its deadly poison permeated his whole body. The disciples sought to prevent their Master from touching him; for he who touched a leper became himself unclean. But in laying His hand upon the leper, Jesus received no defilement. His touch imparted life-giving power. The leprosy was cleansed. Thus it is with the leprosy of sin,— deep-rooted, deadly, and impossible to be cleansed by human power. "The whole head is sick, and the whole heart faint. From the sole of the foot even unto the head there is no soundness in it, but wounds, and bruises, and putrefying sores." Isaiah 1:5, 6. But Jesus, coming to dwell in humanity, receives no pollution. His presence has healing virtue for the sinner. Whoever will fall at His feet, saying in faith, "Lord, if Thou wilt, Thou canst make me clean," shall hear the answer, "I will, be thou made clean." Matthew 8:2, 3, R. V.

In some instances of healing, Jesus did not at once grant the blessing sought. But in the case of leprosy, no sooner was the appeal made than it was granted. When we pray for earthly blessings, the answer to our prayer may be delayed, or God may give us something other than we ask, but not so when we ask for deliverance from sin. It is His will to cleanse us from sin, to make us His children, and to enable us to live a holy life. Christ "gave Himself for our sins, that He might deliver us from this present evil world, according to the will of God and our Father." And "this is the confidence that we have in Him, that, if we ask anything according to His will, He heareth us; and if we know that He hear us, whatsoever we ask, we know that we have the petitions that we desire of Him." Galatians 1:4; 1 John 5:14, 15. "If we confess our sins, He is faithful and just to forgive us our sins, and to cleanse us from all unrighteousness." 1 John 1:9.

In the healing of the paralytic at Capernaum, Christ again taught the same truth. It was to manifest His power to forgive sins, that the miracle was performed. And the healing of the paralytic also illustrates other precious truths. It is full of hope and encouragement, and from its connection with the caviling Pharisees, it has a lesson of warning as well.

Like the leper, this paralytic had lost all hope of recovery. His disease was the result of a life of sin, and his sufferings were embittered by remorse. He had long before appealed to the Pharisees and doctors, hoping for relief from mental suffering and physical pain. But they coldly pronounced him incurable, and abandoned him to the wrath of God. The Pharisees regarded affliction as an evidence of divine displeasure, and they held themselves aloof from the sick and the needy. Yet often these very ones who exalted themselves as holy, were more guilty than the sufferers they condemned.

The palsied man was entirely helpless, and seeing no prospect of aid from any quarter, he had sunk into despair. Then he heard of the wonderful works of Jesus. He was told that others as sinful and helpless as he had been healed; even lepers had been cleansed. And the friends who reported these things encouraged him to believe that he too might be cured if he could be carried to Jesus. But his hope fell when he remembered how the disease had been brought upon him. He feared that the pure physician would not tolerate him in His presence.

Yet it was not physical restoration he desired so much as relief from the burden of sin. If he could see Jesus, and receive the assurance of forgiveness, and peace with Heaven, he would be content to live or die, according to God's will. The cry of the dying man was, O that I might come into His presence! There was no time to lose; already his wasted flesh was showing signs of decay. He besought his friends to carry him on his bed to Jesus, and this they gladly undertook to do. But so dense was the crowd that had assembled in and about the house where the Saviour was, that it was impossible for the sick man and his friends to reach Him, or even to come within hearing of His voice.

Jesus was teaching in the house of Peter. According to their custom, His disciples sat close about Him, and "there were Pharisees and doctors of the law sitting by, which were come out of every town of Galilee, and Judea, and Jerusalem." These had come as spies, seeking an accusation against Jesus. Outside of these officials thronged the promiscuous multitude, the eager, the reverent, the curious, and the unbelieving. Different nationalities and all grades of society were represented. "And the power of the Lord was present to heal." The Spirit of life brooded over the assembly, but Pharisees and doctors did not discern its presence. They felt no sense of need, and the healing was not for them. "He hath filled the hungry with good things; and the rich He hath sent empty away." Luke 1:53.

Again and again the bearers of the paralytic tried to push their way through the crowd, but in vain. The sick man

looked about him in unutterable anguish. When the longed-for help was so near, how could he relinquish hope? At his suggestion his friends bore him to the top of the house, and, breaking up the roof, let him down at the feet of Jesus. The discourse was interrupted. The Saviour looked upon the mournful countenance, and saw the pleading eyes fixed upon Him. He understood the case; He had drawn to Himself that perplexed and doubting spirit. While the paralytic was yet at home, the Saviour had

---

"Oh, wondrous love of Christ, stooping to heal the guilty and the afflicted! Divinity sorrowing over and soothing the ills of suffering humanity! . . . Who can doubt the message of salvation? Who can slight the mercies of a compassionate Redeemer?"

---

brought conviction to his conscience. When he repented of his sins, and believed in the power of Jesus to make him whole, the life-giving mercies of the Saviour had first blessed his longing heart. Jesus had watched the first glimmer of faith grow into a belief that He was the sinner's only helper, and had seen it grow stronger with every effort to come into His presence.

Now, in words that fell like music on the sufferer's ear, the Saviour said, "Son, be of good cheer; thy sins be forgiven thee."

The burden of despair rolls from the sick man's soul; the peace of forgiveness rests upon his spirit, and shines out upon his countenance. His physical pain is gone, and his whole being is transformed. The helpless paralytic is healed! The guilty sinner is pardoned!

In simple faith he accepted the words of Jesus as the boon of new life. He urged no further request, but lay in blissful silence, too happy for words. The light of heaven irradiated his countenance, and the people looked with awe upon the scene.

The rabbis had waited anxiously to see what disposition Christ would make of this case. They recollected how the man had appealed to them for help, and they had refused him hope or sympathy. Not satisfied with this, they had

declared that he was suffering the curse of God for his sins. These things came fresh to their minds when they saw the sick man before them. They marked the interest with which all were watching the scene, and they felt a terrible fear of losing their own influence over the people.

These dignitaries did not exchange words together, but looking into one another's faces they read the same thought in each, that something must be done to arrest the tide of feeling. Jesus had declared that the sins of the paralytic were forgiven. The Pharisees caught at these words as blasphemy, and conceived that they could present this as a sin worthy of death. They said in their hearts, "He blasphemeth; who can forgive sins but one, even God?" Mark 2:7, R. V.

Fixing His glance upon them, beneath which they cowered, and drew back, Jesus said, "Wherefore think ye evil in your hearts? For whether is it easier to say, Thy sins be forgiven thee; or to say, Arise, and walk? But that ye may know that the Son of man hath power on earth to forgive sins," he said, turning to the paralytic, "Arise, take up thy bed, and go unto thine house."

Then he who had been borne on a litter to Jesus, rises to his feet with the elasticity and strength of youth. The life-giving blood bounds through his veins. Every organ of his body springs into sudden activity. The glow of health succeeds the pallor of approaching death. "And immediately he arose, took up the bed, and went forth before them all; insomuch that they were all amazed, and glorified God, saying, We never saw it on this fashion."

O, wondrous love of Christ, stooping to heal the guilty and the afflicted! divinity sorrowing over and soothing the ills of suffering humanity! O, marvelous power thus displayed to the children of men! Who can doubt the message of salvation? Who can slight the mercies of a compassionate Redeemer?

It required nothing less than creative power to restore health to that decaying body. The same voice that spoke life to man created from the dust of the earth, had spoken life to the dying paralytic. And the same power that gave life to the body, had renewed the heart. He who at the creation "spake, and it was," who "commanded, and it stood fast," (Psalms 33:9.) had spoken life to the soul dead in trespasses and sins. The healing of the body was an evidence of the power that had renewed the heart. Christ bade the paralytic arise and walk, "that ye may know," He said, "that the Son of man hath power on earth to forgive sins."

The paralytic found in Christ healing for both the soul and the body. The spiritual healing was followed by physical restoration. This lesson should not be overlooked. There are today thousands suffering from physical disease, who, like the paralytic, are longing for the message, "Thy sins are forgiven." The burden of sin, with its unrest and unsatisfied desires, is the foundation of their maladies. They can find no relief until they come to the Healer of the

114

soul. The peace which He alone can give, would impart vigor to the mind, and health to the body.

Jesus came to "destroy the works of the devil." "In Him was life," and He says, "I am come that they might have life, and that they might have it more abundantly." He is "a quickening spirit." 1 John 3:8; John 1:4; 10:10; 1 Corinthians 15:45. And He still has the same life-giving power as when on earth He healed the sick, and spoke forgiveness to the sinner. He "forgiveth all thine iniquities," He "healeth all thy diseases." Psalms 103:3.

The effect produced upon the people by the healing of the paralytic was as if heaven had opened, and revealed the glories of the better world. As the man who had been cured, passed through the multitude, blessing God at every step, and bearing his burden as if it were a feather's weight, the people fell back to give him room, and with awe-stricken faces gazed upon him, whispering softly among themselves, "We have seen strange things today."

The Pharisees were dumb with amazement and overwhelmed with defeat. They saw that here was no opportunity for their jealousy to inflame the multitude. The wonderful work wrought upon the man whom they had given over to the wrath of God, had so impressed the people that the rabbis were for the time forgotten. They saw that Christ possessed a power which they had ascribed to God alone; yet the gentle dignity of His manner was in marked contrast to their own haughty bearing. They were disconcerted and abashed, recognizing, but not confessing, the presence of a superior being. The stronger the evidence that Jesus had power on earth to forgive sins, the more firmly they entrenched themselves in unbelief. From the home of Peter, where they had seen the paralytic restored by His word, they went away to invent new schemes for silencing the Son of God.

Physical disease, however malignant and deep-seated, was healed by the power of Christ; but the disease of the soul took a firmer hold upon those who closed their eyes against the light. Leprosy and palsy were not so terrible as bigotry and unbelief.

In the home of the healed paralytic there was great rejoicing when he returned to his family, carrying with ease the couch upon which he had been slowly borne from their presence but a short time before. They gathered round with tears of joy, scarcely daring to believe their eyes. He stood before them in the full vigor of manhood. Those arms that they had seen lifeless were quick to obey his will. The flesh that had been shrunken and leaden-hued was now fresh and ruddy. He walked with a firm, free step. Joy and hope were written in every lineament of his countenance; and an expression of purity and peace had taken the place of the marks of sin and suffering. Glad thanksgiving went up from that home, and God was glorified through His Son, who had restored hope to the hopeless, and strength to the stricken one. This man and his family were ready to lay down their lives for Jesus. No doubt dimmed their faith, no unbelief marred their fealty to Him who had brought light into their darkened home.

Levi-Matthew

Of the Roman officials in Palestine, none were more hated than the publicans. The fact that the taxes were imposed by a foreign power was a continual irritation to the Jews, being a reminder that their independence had departed. And the taxgatherers were not merely the instruments of Roman oppression; they were extortioners on their own account, enriching themselves at the expense of the people. A Jew who accepted this office at the hands of the Romans was looked upon as betraying the honor of his nation. He was despised as an apostate, and was classed with the vilest of society.

To this class belonged Levi-Matthew, who, after the four disciples at Gennesaret, was the next to be called to Christ's service. The Pharisees had judged Matthew according to his employment, but Jesus saw in this man a heart open for the reception of truth. Matthew had listened to the Saviour's teaching. As the convicting Spirit of God revealed his sinfulness, he longed to seek help from Christ; but he was accustomed to the exclusiveness of the rabbis, and had no thought that this great teacher would notice him.

Sitting at his toll booth one day, the publican saw Jesus approaching. Great was his astonishment to hear the words addressed to himself, "Follow Me."

Matthew "left all, rose up, and followed Him." There was no hesitation, no questioning, no thought of the lucrative business to be exchanged for poverty and hardship. It was enough for him that he was to be with Jesus, that he might listen to His words, and unite with Him in His work.

So it was with the disciples previously called. When Jesus bade Peter and his companions follow Him, immediately they left their boats and nets. Some of these disciples had friends dependent on them for support; but when they received the Saviour's invitation, they did not hesitate, and inquire, "How shall I live, and sustain my family?" They were obedient to the call; and when afterward Jesus asked them, "When I sent you without purse, and scrip, and shoes, lacked ye anything?" they could answer, "Nothing." Luke 22:35.

To Matthew in his wealth, and to Andrew and Peter in their poverty, the same test was brought; the same consecration was made by each. At the moment of success, when the nets were filled with fish, and the impulses of the old life were strongest, Jesus asked the disciples at the sea to leave all for the work of the gospel. So every soul is tested as to whether the desire for temporal good or for fellowship with Christ is strongest.

Principle is always exacting. No man can succeed in the service of God unless his whole heart is in the work, and he counts all things but loss for the excellency of the knowledge of Christ. No man who makes any reserve can be the disciple of Christ, much less can he be His colaborer. When men appreciate the great salvation, the self-sacrifice seen in Christ's life will be seen in theirs. Wherever He leads the way, they will rejoice to follow.

The calling of Matthew to be one of Christ's disciples, excited great indignation. For a religious teacher to choose a publican as one of his immediate attendants was an offense against the religious, social, and national customs. By appealing to the prejudices of the people the Pharisees hoped to turn the current of popular feeling against Jesus.

Among the publicans a widespread interest was created. Their hearts were drawn toward the divine Teacher. In the joy of his new discipleship, Matthew longed to bring his former associates to Jesus. Accordingly he made a feast at his own house, and called together his relatives and

This chapter is based on Matt. 9:9-17; Mark 2:14-22; Luke 5:27-39.

friends. Not only were publicans included, but many others who were of doubtful reputation, and were proscribed by their more scrupulous neighbors.

The entertainment was given in honor of Jesus, and He did not hesitate to accept the courtesy. He well knew that this would give offense to the Pharisaic party, and would also compromise Him in the eyes of the people. But no question of policy could influence His movements. With Him external distinctions weighed nothing. That which appealed to His heart was a soul thirsting for the water of life.

Jesus sat as an honored guest at the table of the publicans, by His sympathy and social kindliness showing that He recognized the dignity of humanity; and men longed to become worthy of His confidence. Upon their thirsty hearts His words fell with blessed, life-giving power. New impulses were awakened, and the possibility of a new life opened to these outcasts of society.

At such gatherings as this, not a few were impressed by the Saviour's teaching, who did not acknowledge Him until after His ascension. When the Holy Spirit was poured out, and three thousand were converted in a day, there were among them many who first heard the truth at the table of the publicans, and some of these became messengers of the gospel. To Matthew himself the example of Jesus at the feast was a constant lesson. The despised publican became one of the most devoted evangelists, in his own ministry following closely in his Master's steps.

When the rabbis learned of the presence of Jesus at Matthew's feast, they seized the opportunity of accusing Him. But they chose to work through the disciples. By arousing their prejudices they hoped to alienate them from their Master. It was their policy to accuse Christ to the disciples, and the disciples to Christ, aiming their arrows where they would be most likely to wound. This is the way in which Satan has worked ever since the disaffection in heaven; and all who try to cause discord and alienation are actuated by his spirit.

"Why eateth your Master with publicans and sinners?" questioned the envious rabbis.

Jesus did not wait for His disciples to answer the charge, but Himself replied: "They that be whole need not a physician, but they that are sick. But go ye and learn what that meaneth, I will have mercy, and not sacrifice; for I am not come to call the righteous, but sinners to repentance." The Pharisees claimed to be spiritually whole, and therefore in no need of a physician, while they regarded the publicans and Gentiles as perishing from diseases of the soul. Then was it not His work, as a physician, to go to the very class that needed His help?

But although the Pharisees thought so highly of themselves, they were really in a worse condition than the ones they despised. The publicans were less bigoted and self-sufficient, and thus were more open to the influence of truth. Jesus said to the rabbis, "Go ye and learn what that meaneth, I will have mercy, and not sacrifice." Thus He

showed that while they claimed to expound the word of God, they were wholly ignorant of its spirit.

The Pharisees were silenced for the time, but only became more determined in their enmity. They next sought out the disciples of John the Baptist, and tried to set them against the Saviour. These Pharisees had not accepted the mission of the Baptist. They had pointed in scorn to his abstemious life, his simple habits, his coarse garments, and had declared him a fanatic. Because he denounced their hypocrisy, they had resisted his words, and had tried to stir up the people against him. The Spirit of God had moved upon the hearts of these scorners, convicting them of sin; but they had rejected the counsel of God, and had declared that John was possessed of a devil.

Now when Jesus came mingling with the people, eating and drinking at their tables, they accused Him of being a glutton and a winebibber. The very ones who made this charge were themselves guilty. As God is misrepresented, and clothed by Satan with his own attributes, so the Lord's messengers were falsified by these wicked men.

The Pharisees would not consider that Jesus was eating with publicans and sinners in order to bring the light of heaven to those who sat in darkness. They would not see that every word dropped by the divine Teacher was a living seed that would germinate and bear fruit to the glory of God. They had determined not to accept the light; and although they had opposed the mission of the Baptist, they were now ready to court the friendship of his disciples, hoping to secure their co-operation against Jesus. They represented that Jesus was setting at naught the ancient traditions; and they contrasted the austere piety of the Baptist with the course of Jesus in feasting with publicans and sinners.

The disciples of John were at this time in great sorrow. It was before their visit to Jesus with John's message. Their beloved teacher was in prison, and they passed their days in mourning. And Jesus was making no effort to release John, and even appeared to cast discredit on his teaching. If John had been sent by God, why did Jesus and His disciples pursue a course so widely different?

The disciples of John had not a clear understanding of Christ's work; they thought there might be some foundation for the charges of the Pharisees. They observed many of the rules prescribed by the rabbis, and even hoped to be justified by the works of the law. Fasting was practiced by the Jews as an act of merit, and the most rigid among them fasted two days in every week. The Pharisees and John's disciples were fasting when the latter came to Jesus with the inquiry, "Why do we and the Pharisees fast oft, but Thy disciples fast not?"

Very tenderly Jesus answered them. He did not try to correct their erroneous conception of fasting, but only to set them right in regard to His own mission. And He did this by employing the same figure that the Baptist himself had used in his testimony to Jesus. John had said, "He that hath the bride is the bridegroom; but the friend of the bridegroom, which standeth and heareth him, rejoiceth greatly because of the bridegroom's voice: this my joy therefore is fulfilled." John 3:29. The disciples of John could not fail to recall these words of their teacher, as, taking up the illustration, Jesus said, "Can ye make the children of the bridechamber fast, while the bridegroom is with them?"

The Prince of heaven was among His people. The greatest gift of God had been given to the world. Joy to the poor; for Christ had come to make them heirs of His kingdom. Joy to the rich; for He would teach them how to secure eternal riches. Joy to the ignorant; He would make them wise unto salvation. Joy to the learned; He would open to them deeper mysteries than they had ever fathomed; truths that had been hidden from the foundation of the world would be opened to men by the Saviour's mission.

John the Baptist had rejoiced to behold the Saviour. What occasion for rejoicing had the disciples who were privileged to walk and talk with the Majesty of heaven. This was not a time for them to mourn and fast. They must open their hearts to receive the light of His glory, that they might shed light upon those who sat in darkness and in the shadow of death.

It was a bright picture which the words of Christ had called up, but across it lay a heavy shadow, which His eye alone discerned. "The days will come," He said, "when the bridegroom shall be taken away from them, and then shall they fast in those days." When they should see their Lord betrayed and crucified, the disciples would mourn and fast. In His last words to them in the upper chamber, He said, "A little while, and ye shall not see Me; and again, a little while, and ye shall see Me. Verily, verily, I say unto you, That ye shall weep and lament, but the world shall rejoice; and ye shall be sorrowful, but your sorrow shall be turned into joy." John 16:19, 20.

When He should come forth from the tomb, their sorrow would be turned to joy. After His ascension He was to be absent in person; but through the Comforter He would still be with them, and they were not to spend their time in mourning. This was what Satan wanted. He desired them to give the world the impression that they had been deceived and disappointed; but by faith they were to look to the sanctuary above, where Jesus was ministering for them; they were to open their hearts to the Holy Spirit, His representative, and to rejoice in the light of His presence. Yet days of temptation and trial would come, when they would be brought into conflict with the rulers of this world, and the leaders of the kingdom of darkness; when Christ was not personally with them, and they failed to discern the Comforter, then it would be more fitting for them to fast.

The Pharisees sought to exalt themselves by their rigorous observance of forms, while their hearts were filled with envy and strife. "Behold," says the Scripture, "ye fast for strife and debate, and to smite with the fist of wickedness; ye shall not fast as ye do this day, to make your voice to be heard on high. Is it such a fast that I have chosen? a day for a man to afflict his soul? is it to bow down his head as a bulrush, and to spread sackcloth and ashes under him? wilt thou call this a fast, and an acceptable day to the Lord?" Isaiah 58:4, 5.

The true fast is no mere formal service. The Scripture describes the fast that God has chosen,—"to loose the bands of wickedness, to undo the heavy burdens, and to let the oppressed go free, and that ye break every yoke;" to "draw out thy soul to the hungry, and satisfy the afflicted soul." Isaiah 58:6, 10. Here is set forth the very spirit and character of the work of Christ. His whole life was a sacrifice of Himself for the saving of the world. Whether fasting in the wilderness of temptation or eating with the publicans at Matthew's feast, He was giving His life for the redemption of the lost. Not in idle mourning, in mere bodily humiliation and multitudinous sacrifices, is the true spirit of devotion manifested, but it is shown in the surrender of self in willing service to God and man.

Continuing His answer to the disciples of John, Jesus spoke a parable, saying, "No man putteth a piece of a new garment upon an old; if otherwise, then both the new maketh a rent, and the piece that was taken out of the new agreeth not with the old." The message of John the Baptist was not to be interwoven with tradition and superstition. An attempt to blend the pretense of the Pharisees with the devotion of John would only make more evident the breach between them.

Nor could the principles of Christ's teaching be united with the forms of Pharisaism. Christ was not to close up the breach that had been made by the teachings of John. He would make more distinct the separation between the old and the new. Jesus further illustrated this fact, saying, "No man putteth new wine into old bottles; else the new wine will burst the bottles, and be spilled, and the bottles shall perish." The skin bottles which were used as vessels to contain the new wine, after a time became dry and brittle, and were then worthless to serve the same purpose again. In this familiar illustration Jesus presented the condition of the Jewish leaders. Priests and scribes and rulers were fixed in a rut of ceremonies and traditions. Their hearts had become contracted, like the dried-up wine skins to which he had compared them. While they remained satisfied with a legal religion, it was impossible for them to become the depositaries of the living truth of heaven. They thought their own righteousness all-sufficient, and did not desire that a new element should be brought into their religion. The good will of God to men they did not accept as something apart from themselves. They connected it with their own merit because of their good works. The faith that works by love and purifies the soul, could find no place for union with the religion of the Pharisees, made up of ceremonies and the injunctions of men. The effort to unite the teachings of Jesus with the established religion would be vain. The vital truth of God, like fermenting wine, would burst the old, decaying bottles of the Pharisaical tradition.

The Pharisees thought themselves too wise to need instruction, too righteous to need salvation, too highly honored to need the honor that comes from Christ. The Saviour turned away from them to find others who would receive the message of heaven. In the untutored fishermen, in the publican at the market place, in the woman of Samaria, in the common people who heard Him gladly, He found His new bottles for the new wine. The instrumentalities to be used in the gospel work are those souls who gladly receive the light which God sends them. These are His agencies for imparting the knowledge of truth to the world. If through the grace of Christ His people will become new bottles, He will fill them with new wine.

The teaching of Christ, though it was represented by the new wine, was not a new doctrine, but the revelation of that which had been taught from the beginning. But to the Pharisees the truth of God had lost its original significance and beauty. To them Christ's teaching was new in almost every respect, and it was unrecognized and unacknowledged.

Jesus pointed out the power of false teaching to destroy the appreciation and desire for truth. "No man," He said, "having drunk old wine, straightway desireth new; for he saith, The old is better." All the truth that has been given to the world through patriarchs and prophets shone out in new beauty in the words of Christ. But the scribes and Pharisees had no desire for the precious new wine. Until emptied of the old traditions, customs, and practices, they had no place in mind or heart for the teachings of Christ. They clung to the dead forms, and turned away from the living truth and the power of God.

It was this that proved the ruin of the Jews, and it will prove the ruin of many souls in our own day. Thousands are making the same mistake as did the Pharisees whom Christ reproved at Matthew's feast. Rather than give up some cherished idea, or discard some idol of opinion, many refuse the truth which comes down from the Father of light. They trust in self, and depend upon their own wisdom, and do not realize their spiritual poverty. They insist on being saved in some way by which they may perform some important work. When they see that there is no way of weaving self into the work, they reject the salvation provided.

A legal religion can never lead souls to Christ; for it is a loveless, Christless religion. Fasting or prayer that is actuated by a self-justifying spirit, is an abomination in the sight of God. The solemn assembly for worship, the round of religious ceremonies, the external humiliation, the imposing sacrifice, proclaim that the doer of these things regards himself as righteous, and as entitled to heaven, but it is all a deception. Our own works can never purchase salvation.

As it was in the days of Christ, so it is now; the Pharisees do not know their spiritual destitution. To them comes the message, "Because thou sayest, I am rich, and increased with goods, and have need of nothing; and knowest not that thou art wretched, and miserable, and poor, and blind, and naked: I counsel thee to buy of Me gold tried in the fire, that thou mayest be rich; and white raiment, that thou mayest be clothed, and that the shame of thy nakedness do not appear." Revelation 3:17, 18. Faith and love are the gold tried in the fire. But with many the gold has become dim, and the rich treasure has been lost. The righteousness of Christ is to them as a robe unworn, a fountain untouched. To them it is said, "I have somewhat against thee, because thou hast left thy first love. Remember therefore from whence thou art fallen, and repent, and do the first works; or less I will come unto thee quickly, and will remove thy candlestick out of his place, except thou repent." Revelation 2:4, 5.

"The sacrifices of God are a broken spirit; a broken and a contrite heart, O God, Thou wilt not despise." Psalms 51:17. Man must be emptied of self before he can be, in the fullest sense, a believer in Jesus. When self is renounced, then the Lord can make man a new creature. New bottles can contain the new wine. The love of Christ will animate the believer with new life. In him who looks unto the author and finisher of our faith, the character of Christ will be manifest.

The Sabbath

The Sabbath was hallowed at the creation. As ordained for man, it had its origin when "the morning stars sang together, and all the sons of God shouted for joy." Peace brooded over the world; for earth was in harmony with heaven. "God saw everything that He had made, and behold, it was very good;" (Job 38:7; Genesis 1:31) and He rested in the joy of His completed work.

Because He had rested upon the Sabbath, "God blessed the seventh day, and sanctified it," — set it apart to a holy use. He gave it to Adam as a day of rest. It was a memorial of the work of creation, and thus a sign of God's power and His love. The Scripture says, "He hath made His wonderful works to be remembered." "The things that are made," declare "the invisible things of Him since the creation of the world," "even His everlasting power and divinity." Genesis 2:3; Psalms 3:4; Romans 1:20, R. V.

All things were created by the Son of God. "In the beginning was the Word, and the Word was with God. . . . All things were made by Him; and without Him was not anything made that was made." John 1:1-3. And since the Sabbath is a memorial of the work of creation, it is a token of the love and power of Christ.

The Sabbath calls our thoughts to nature, and brings us into communion with the Creator. In the song of the bird, the sighing of the trees, and the music of the sea, we still may hear His voice who talked with Adam in Eden in the cool of the day. And as we behold His power in nature we find comfort, for the word that created all things is that which speaks life to the soul. He "who commanded the light to shine out of darkness, hath shined in our hearts, to give the light of the knowledge of the glory of God in the face of Jesus Christ." 2 Corinthians 4:6.

It was this thought that awoke the song, —

"Thou, Lord, hast made me glad through Thy work;
I will triumph in the works of Thy hands.
O Lord, how great are Thy works!
And Thy thoughts are very deep." Psalms 92:4, 5.

And the Holy Spirit through the prophet Isaiah declares: "To whom then will ye liken God? or what likeness will ye compare unto Him? . . . Have ye not known? have ye not heard? hath it not been told you from the beginning? have ye not understood from the foundations of the earth? It is He that sitteth upon the circle of the earth, and the inhabitants thereof are as grasshoppers; that stretcheth out the heavens as a curtain, and spreadeth them out as a tent to dwell in. . . . To whom then will ye liken Me, or shall I be equal? saith the Holy One. Lift up your eyes on high, and behold who hath created these things, that bringeth out their host by number; He calleth them all by names, by the greatness of His might, for that He is strong in power; not one faileth. Why sayest thou, O Jacob, and speakest, O Israel, My way is hid from the Lord, and my judgment is passed over from my God? Hast thou not known? hast thou not heard, that the everlasting God, the Lord, the Creator of the ends of the earth, fainteth not, neither is weary? . . . He giveth power to the faint; and to them that have no might He increaseth strength." "Fear thou not; for I am with thee: be not dismayed; for I am thy God: I will strengthen thee; yea, I will help thee; yea, I will uphold thee with the right hand of My righteousness." "Look unto Me, and be ye saved, all the ends of the earth; for I am God, and there is none else." This is the message written in nature, which the Sabbath is appointed to keep in memory. When the Lord bade Israel hallow His Sabbaths, He said, "They shall be a sign between Me and you, that

120

ye may know that I am Jehovah your God." Isaiah 40:18-29; 41:10; 45:22; Ezekiel 20:20.

The Sabbath was embodied in the law given from Sinai; but it was not then first made known as a day of rest. The people of Israel had a knowledge of it before they came to Sinai. On the way thither the Sabbath was kept. When some profaned it, the Lord reproved them, saying, "How long refuse ye to keep My commandments and My laws?" Exodus 16:28.

The Sabbath was not for Israel merely, but for the world. It had been made known to man in Eden, and, like the other precepts of the decalogue, it is of imperishable obligation. Of that law of which the fourth commandment forms a part, Christ declares, "Till heaven and earth pass, one jot or one tittle shall in no wise pass from the law." So long as the heavens and the earth endure, the Sabbath will continue as a sign of the Creator's power. And when Eden shall bloom on earth again, God's holy rest day will be honored by all beneath the sun. "From one Sabbath to another" the inhabitants of the glorified new earth shall go up "to worship before Me, saith the Lord." Matthew 5:18; Isaiah 66:23.

No other institution which was committed to the Jews tended so fully to distinguish them from surrounding nations as did the Sabbath. God designed that its observance should designate them as his worshipers. It was to be a token of their separation from idolatry, and their connection with the true God. But in order to keep the Sabbath holy, men must themselves be holy. Through faith they must become partakers of the righteousness of Christ. When the command was given to Israel, "Remember the Sabbath day, to keep it holy," the Lord said also to them, "Ye shall be holy men unto Me." Exodus 20:8; 22:31. Only thus could the Sabbath distinguish Israel as the worshipers of God.

As the Jews departed from God, and failed to make the righteousness of Christ their own by faith, the Sabbath lost its significance to them. Satan was seeking to exalt himself and to draw men away from Christ, and he worked to pervert the Sabbath, because it is the sign of the power of Christ. The Jewish leaders accomplished the will of Satan by surrounding God's rest day with burdensome requirements. In the days of Christ the Sabbath had become so perverted that its observance reflected the character of selfish and arbitrary men, rather than the character of the loving Heavenly Father. The rabbis virtually represented God as giving laws which it was impossible for men to obey. They led the people to look upon God as a tyrant, and to think that the observance of the Sabbath, as He required it, made men hardhearted and cruel. It was the work of Christ to clear away these misconceptions. Although the rabbis followed Him with merciless hostility, He did not even appear to conform to their requirements, but went straight forward, keeping the Sabbath according to the law of God.

Upon one Sabbath day, as the Saviour and His disciples returned from the place of worship, they passed through a field of ripening grain. Jesus had continued His work to a late hour, and while passing through the fields, the disciples began to gather the heads of grain, and to eat the kernels after rubbing them in their hands. On any other day this act would have excited no comment, for one passing through a field of grain, an orchard, or a vineyard, was at liberty to gather what he desired to eat. (See Deuteronomy 23:24, 25.) But to do this on the Sabbath was held to be an act of desecration. Not only was the gathering of the grain a kind of reaping, but the rubbing of it in hands was a kind of threshing. Thus, in the opinion of the rabbis, there was a double offense.

The spies at once complained to Jesus, saying, "Behold, thy disciples do that which is not lawful to do upon the Sabbath day."

When accused of Sabbathbreaking at Bethesda, Jesus defended Himself by affirming His Sonship to God, and declaring that He worked in harmony with the Father. Now that the disciples are attacked, He cites His accusers to examples from the Old Testament, acts performed on the Sabbath by those who were in the service of God.

The Jewish teachers prided themselves on their knowledge of the Scriptures, and in the Saviour's answer there was an implied rebuke for their ignorance of the sacred writings. "Have ye not read so much as this," He said, "what David did, when himself was an hungered, and they which were with him; how he went into the house of God, and did take and eat the showbread, . . . which it is not lawful to eat but for the priests alone?" "And He said unto them, The Sabbath was made for man, and not man for the Sabbath." "Have ye not read in the law, how that on the Sabbath days the priests in the temple profane the Sabbath, and are blameless? But I say unto you, That in this place is one greater than the temple." "The Son of man is Lord also of the Sabbath." Luke 6:3, 4; Mark 2:27, 28; Matthew 12:5, 6.

If it was right for David to satisfy his hunger by eating of the bread that had been set apart to a holy use, then it was right for the disciples to supply their need by plucking the grain upon the sacred hours of the Sabbath. Again, the priests in the temple performed greater labor on the Sabbath than upon other days. The same labor in secular business would be sinful; but the work of the priests was in the service of God. They were performing those rites that pointed to the redeeming power of Christ, and their labor was in harmony with the object of the Sabbath. But now Christ Himself had come. The disciples, in doing the work of Christ, were engaged in God's service, and that which was necessary for the accomplishment of this work, it was right to do on the Sabbath day.

Christ would teach His disciples and His enemies, that the service of God is first of all. The object of God's work in this world is the redemption of man; therefore that which is necessary to be done on the Sabbath in the accomplishment of this work, is in accord with the Sabbath law. Jesus then crowned His argument by declaring Himself the "Lord of the Sabbath,"—One above all question and above all law. This infinite Judge acquits the disciples of blame, appealing to the very statutes they are accused of violating.

Jesus did not let the matter pass with administering a rebuke to His enemies. He declared that in their blindness they had mistaken the object of the Sabbath. He said, "If ye had known what this meaneth, I will have mercy, and not sacrifice, ye would not have condemned the guiltless."

❝As the Jews departed from God, and failed to make the righteousness of Christ their own by faith, the Sabbath lost its significance to them. Satan was seeking to exalt himself . . . and he worked to pervert the Sabbath, because it is the sign of the power of Christ.❞

Matthew 12:7. Their many heartless rites could not supply the lack of that truthful integrity and tender love which will ever characterize the true worshiper of God.

Again Christ reiterated the truth that the sacrifices were in themselves of no value. They were a means, and not an end. Their object was to direct men to the Saviour, and thus to bring them into harmony with God. It is the service of love that God values. When this is lacking, the mere round of ceremony is an offense to Him. So with the Sabbath. It was designed to bring men into communion with God; but when the mind was absorbed with wearisome rites, the object of the Sabbath was thwarted. Its mere outward observance was a mockery.

Upon another Sabbath, as Jesus entered a synagogue. He saw there a man who had a withered hand. The Pharisees watched Him, eager to see what He would do. The Saviour well knew that in healing on the Sabbath He would be regarded as a transgressor, but He did not hesitate to break down the wall of traditional requirements that barricaded the Sabbath. Jesus bade the afflicted man stand forth, and

then asked, "It is lawful to do good on the Sabbath days, or to do evil? to save life, or to kill?" It was a maxim among the Jews that a failure to do good, when one had opportunity, was to do evil; to neglect to save life, was to kill. Thus Jesus met the rabbis on their own ground. "But they held their peace. And when He had looked round about on them with anger, being grieved for the hardness of their hearts, He saith unto the man, Stretch forth thine hand. And he stretched it out; and his hand was restored whole as the other." Mark 3:4, 5.

When questioned, "Is it lawful to heal on the Sabbath days?" Jesus answered, "What man shall there be among *you*, that shall have one sheep, and if it fall into a pit on the Sabbath day, will he not lay hold on it, and lift it out? How much then is a man better than a sheep? Wherefore it is lawful to do well on the Sabbath days." Matthew 12:10-12.

The spies dared not answer Christ in the presence of the multitude, for fear of involving themselves in difficulty. They knew that He had spoken the truth. Rather than violate their traditions, they would leave a man to suffer, while they would relieve a brute because of the loss to the owner if it were neglected. Thus greater care was shown for a dumb animal than for man, who is made in the image of God. This illustrates the working of all false religions. They originate in man's desire to exalt himself above God, but they result in degrading man below the brute. Every religion that was against the sovereignty of God defrauds man of the glory which was his at the creation, and which is to be restored to him in Christ. Every false religion teaches its adherents to be careless of human needs, sufferings, and rights. The gospel places a high value upon humanity as the purchase of the blood of Christ, and it teaches a tender regard for the wants and woes of man. The Lord says, "I will make a man more precious than fine gold; even a man than the golden wedge of Ophir." Isaiah 13:12.

When Jesus turned upon the Pharisees with the question whether it was lawful on the Sabbath day to do good or to do evil, to save life or to kill, He confronted them with their own wicked purposes. They were hunting His life with bitter hatred, while He was saving life, and bringing happiness to multitudes. Was it better to slay upon the Sabbath, as they were planning to do, than to heal the afflicted, as He had done? Was it more righteous to have murder in the heart upon God's holy day, than love to all men, which finds expression in deeds of mercy?

In the healing of the withered hand, Jesus condemned the custom of the Jews, and left the fourth commandment standing as God had given it. "It is lawful to do well on the Sabbath days," He declared. By sweeping away the senseless restrictions of the Jews, Christ honored the Sabbath, while those who complained of Him were dishonoring God's holy day.

Those who hold that Christ abolished the law, teach that He broke the Sabbath, and justified His disciples in doing the same. Thus they are really taking the same ground as did the caviling Jews. In this they contradict the testimony of Christ Himself, who declared, "I have kept My Father's commandments, and abide in His love." John 15:10. Neither the Saviour nor His followers broke the law of the Sabbath. Christ was a living representative of the law. No violation of its holy precepts was found in His life. Looking upon a nation of witnesses who were seeking occasion to condemn Him, He could say unchallenged, "Which of you convicteth Me of sin?" John 8:46, R. V.

The Saviour had not come to set aside what patriarchs and prophets had spoken; for He Himself had spoken through these representative men. All the truths of God's word came from Him. But these priceless gems had been placed in false settings. Their precious light had been made to minister to error. God desired them to be removed from their settings of error and replaced in the framework of truth. This work only a divine hand could accomplish. By its connection with error, the truth had been serving the cause of the enemy of God and man. Christ had come to place it where it would glorify God, and work the salvation of humanity.

"The Sabbath was made for man, and not man for the Sabbath," Jesus said. The institutions that God has established are for the benefit of mankind. "All things are for your sakes." "Whether Paul, or Apollos, or Cephas, or the world, or life, or death, or things present, or things to come; all are yours; and ye are Christ's; and Christ is God's." 2 Corinthians 4:15; 1 Corinthians 3:22, 23. The law of ten commandments, of which the Sabbath forms a part, God gave to His people as a blessing. "The Lord commanded us," said Moses, "to do all these statutes, to fear the Lord our God, for our good always, that He might preserve us alive." Deuteronomy 6:24. And through the psalmist the message was given to Israel, "Serve the Lord with gladness; come before His presence with singing. Know ye that the Lord He is God; it is He that hath made us, and not we ourselves; we are His people, and the sheep of His pasture.

Enter into His gates with thanksgiving, and into His courts with praise." Psalms 100:2-4. And of all who "keep the Sabbath from polluting it," the Lord declares, "Even them will I bring to My holy mountain, and make them joyful in My house of prayer." Isaiah 56:6, 7.

"Wherefore the Son of man is Lord also of the Sabbath." These words are full of instruction and comfort. Because the Sabbath was made for man, it is the Lord's day. It belongs to Christ. For "all things were made by Him; and without Him was not anything made that was made." John 1:3. Since He made all things, He made the Sabbath. By Him it was set apart as a memorial of the work of creation. It points to Him as both the Creator and the Sanctifier. It declares that He who created all things in heaven and in earth, and by whom all things hold together, is the head of the church, and that by His power we are reconciled to God. For, speaking of Israel, He said, "I gave them My Sabbaths, to be a sign between Me and them, that they might know that I am the Lord that sanctify them," — make them holy. Ezekiel 20:12. Then the Sabbath is a sign of Christ's power to make us holy. And it is given to all whom Christ makes holy. As a sign of His sanctifying power, the Sabbath is given to all who through Christ become a part of the Israel of God.

And the Lord says, "If thou turn away thy foot from the Sabbath, from doing thy pleasure on My holy day, and call the Sabbath a delight, the holy of the Lord, honorable; . . . then shalt thou delight thyself in the Lord." Isaiah 58:13, 14. To all who receive the Sabbath as a sign of Christ's creative and redeeming power, it will be a delight. Seeing Christ in it, they delight themselves in Him. The Sabbath points them to the works of creation as an evidence of His mighty power in redemption. While it calls to mind the lost peace of Eden, it tells of peace restored through the Saviour. And every object in nature repeats His invitation, "Come unto Me, all ye that labor and are heavy laden, and I will give you rest." Matthew 11:28.

"He Ordained Twelve"

"And He goeth up into a mountain, and calleth unto Him whom He would; and they came unto Him. And He ordained twelve, that they should be with Him, and that He might send them forth to preach."

It was beneath the sheltering trees of the mountainside, but a little distance from the Sea of Galilee, that the Twelve were called to the apostolate, and the sermon on the mount was given. The fields and hills were the favorite resorts of Jesus, and much of His teaching was given under the open sky, rather than in the temple or the synagogues. No synagogue could have received the throngs that followed Him; but not for this reason only did He choose to teach in the fields and groves. Jesus loved the scenes of nature. To Him each quiet retreat was a sacred temple.

It was under the trees of Eden that the first dwellers on earth had chosen their sanctuary. There Christ had communed with the father of mankind. When banished from Paradise, our first parents still worshipped in the fields and groves, and there Christ met them with the gospel of His grace. It was Christ who spoke with Abraham under the oaks at Mamre; with Isaac as he went out to pray in the fields at the eventide; with Jacob on the hillside at Bethel, with Moses among the mountains of Midian; and with the boy David as he watched his flocks. It was at Christ's direction that for fifteen centuries the Hebrew people had left their homes for one week every year, and had dwelt in booths formed from the green branches "of goodly trees, branches of palm trees, and the boughs of thick trees, and willows of the brook." Leviticus 23:40.

In training His disciples, Jesus chose to withdraw from the confusion of the city to the quiet of the fields and hills, as more in harmony with the lessons of self-abnegation He desired to teach them. And during His ministry He loved to gather the people about Him under the blue heavens, on some grassy hillside, or on the beach beside the lake. Here, surrounded by the works of His own creation, He could turn the thoughts of His hearers from the artificial to the natural. In the growth and development of nature were revealed the principles of His kingdom. As men should lift up their eyes to the hills of God, and behold the wonderful works of His hands, they could learn precious lessons of divine truth. Christ's teaching would be repeated to them in the things of nature. So it is with all who go into the fields with Christ in their hearts. They will feel themselves surrounded with a holy influence. The things of nature take up the parables of our Lord, and repeat His counsels. By communion with God in nature, the mind is uplifted, and the heart finds rest.

The first step was now to be taken in the organization of the church that after Christ's departure was to be His representative on earth. No costly sanctuary was at their command, but the Saviour led His disciples to the retreat He loved, and in their minds the sacred experiences of that day were forever linked with the beauty of mountain and vale and sea.

Jesus had called His disciples that He might send them forth as His witnesses, to declare to the world what they had seen and heard of Him. Their office was the most important to which human beings had ever been called, and was second only to that of Christ Himself. They were to be workers together with God for the saving of the world. As in the Old Testament the twelve patriarchs stand as representatives of Israel, so the twelve apostles were to stand as representatives of the gospel church.

The Saviour knew the character of the men whom He had chosen; all their weakness and errors were open before

This chapter is based on Mark 3:13-19; Luke 6:12-16.

Him; He knew the perils through which they must pass, the responsibility that would rest upon them; and His heart yearned over these chosen ones. Alone upon a mountain near the Sea of Galilee He spent the entire night in prayer for them, while they were sleeping at the foot of the mountain. With the first light of dawn He summoned them to meet Him; for He had something of importance to communicate to them.

These disciples had been for some time associated with Jesus in active labor. John and James, Andrew and Peter, with Philip, Nathanael, and Matthew, had been more closely connected with Him than the others, and had witnessed more of His miracles. Peter, James, and John stood in still nearer relationship to Him. They were almost constantly with Him, witnessing His miracles, and hearing His words. John pressed into still closer intimacy with Jesus, so that he is distinguished as the one whom Jesus loved. The Saviour loved them all, but John's was the most receptive spirit. He was younger than the others, and with more of the child's confiding trust he opened his heart to Jesus. Thus he came more into sympathy with Christ, and through him the Saviour's deepest spiritual teaching was communicated to His people.

At the head of one of the groups into which the apostles are divided, stands the name of Philip. He was the first disciple to whom Jesus addressed the distinct command, "Follow Me." Philip was of Bethsaida, the city of Andrew and Peter. He had listened to the teaching of John the Baptist, and had heard his announcement of Christ as the Lamb of God. Philip was a sincere seeker for truth, but he was slow of heart to believe. Although he had joined himself to Christ, yet his announcement of Him to Nathanael shows that he was not fully convinced of the divinity of Jesus. Though Christ had been proclaimed by the voice from heaven as the Son of God, to Philip He was "Jesus of Nazareth, the son of Joseph." John 1:45. Again, when the five thousand were fed, Philip's lack of faith was shown. It was to test him that Jesus questioned, "Whence shall we buy bread, that these may eat?" Philip's answer was on the side of unbelief: "Two hundred pennyworth of bread is not sufficient for them, that every one of them may take a little." John 6:5, 7. Jesus was grieved. Although Philip had seen His works and felt His power, yet he had not faith. When the Greeks inquired of Philip concerning Jesus, he did not seize upon the opportunity of introducing them to the Saviour, but he went to tell Andrew. Again, in those last hours before the crucifixion, the words of Philip were such as to discourage faith When Thomas said to Jesus, "Lord, we know not whither Thou goest; and how can we know the way?" the Saviour answered, "I am the Way, the Truth, and the Life. . . . If ye had known Me, ye should have known My Father also." From Philip came the response of unbelief: "Lord, show us the Father, and it sufficeth us." John 14:5-8. So slow of heart, so weak in faith, was that disciple who for three years had been with Jesus.

In happy contrast to Philip's unbelief was the childlike trust of Nathanael. He was a man of intensely earnest nature, one whose faith took hold upon unseen realities. Yet Philip was a student in the school of Christ, and the divine Teacher bore patiently with his unbelief and dullness. When the Holy Spirit was poured out upon the disciples, Philip became a teacher after the divine order. He knew whereof he spoke, and he taught with an assurance that carried conviction to the hearers.

While Jesus was preparing the disciples for their ordination, one who had not been summoned, urged his presence among them. It was Judas Iscariot, a man who professed to be a follower of Christ. He now came forward, soliciting a place in this inner circle of disciples With great earnestness and apparent sincerity he declared, "Master, I will follow Thee whithersoever Thou goest." Jesus neither repulsed nor welcomed him, but uttered only the mournful words: "The foxes have holes, and the birds of the air have nests; but the Son of man hath not where to lay His head." Matthew 8:19, 20. Judas believed Jesus to be the Messiah; and by joining the apostles, he hoped to secure a high position in the new kingdom. This hope Jesus designed to cut off by the statement of His poverty.

The disciples were anxious that Judas should become one of their number. He was of commanding appearance, a man of keen discernment and executive ability, and they commended him to Jesus as one who would greatly assist Him in His work. They were surprised that Jesus received him so coolly.

The disciples had been much disappointed that Jesus had not tried to secure the co-operation of the leaders in Israel. They felt that it was a mistake not to strengthen His cause by securing the support of these influential men. If He had repulsed Judas, they would, in their own minds, have questioned the wisdom of their Master. The after history of Judas would show them the danger of allowing any worldly consideration to have weight in deciding the fitness of men for the work of God. The co-operation of such men as the disciples were anxious to secure, would have betrayed the work into the hands of its worst enemies.

Yet when Judas joined the disciples, he was not insensible to the beauty of the character of Christ. He felt the influence of that divine power which was drawing souls to the Saviour. He who came not to break the bruised reed nor quench the smoking flax, would not repulse this soul while even one desire was reaching toward the light. The Saviour read the heart of Judas; He knew the depths of iniquity to which, unless delivered by the grace of God, Judas would sink. In connecting this man with Himself, He placed him where he might, day by day, be brought in contact with the outflowing of His own unselfish love. If he would open his heart to Christ, divine grace would banish the demon of selfishness, and even Judas might become a subject of the kingdom of God.

God takes men as they are, with the human elements in their character and trains them for His service, if they will be disciplined and learn of Him. They are not chosen because they are perfect, but notwithstanding their imperfections, that through the knowledge and practice of the truth, through the grace of Christ, they may become transformed into His image.

Judas had the same opportunities as had the other disciples. He listened to the same precious lessons. But the practice of the truth, which Christ required, was at variance with the desires and purposes of Judas, and he would not yield his ideas in order to receive wisdom from Heaven.

How tenderly the Saviour dealt with him who was to be His betrayer. In His teaching, Jesus dwelt upon principles of benevolence that struck at the very root of covetousness.

"However imperfect and sinful we may be, the Lord holds out to us the offer of partnership with Himself, of apprenticeship to Christ. He invites us to come under the divine instruction, that, uniting with Christ, we may work the works of God."

He presented before Judas the heinous character of greed, and many a time the disciple realized that his character had been portrayed, and his sin pointed out; but he would not confess and forsake his unrighteousness. He was self-sufficient, and instead of resisting temptation, he continued to follow his fraudulent practices. Christ was before him, a living example of what he must become if he reaped the benefit of the divine mediation and ministry; but lesson after lesson fell unheeded on the ears of Judas.

Jesus dealt him no sharp rebuke for his covetousness, but with divine patience bore with this erring man, even while giving him evidence that He read his heart as an open book. He presented before him the highest incentives for rightdoing; and in rejecting the light of Heaven, Judas would be without excuse.

Instead of walking in the light, Judas chose to retain his defects. Evil desires, revengeful passions, dark and sullen thoughts, were cherished, until Satan had full control of the man. Judas became a representative of the enemy of Christ.

When he came into association with Jesus, he had some precious traits of character, that might have been made a blessing to the church. If he had been willing to wear the yoke of Christ, he might have been among the chief of the apostles; but he hardened his heart when his defects were pointed out, and in pride and rebellion chose his own selfish ambitions, and thus unfitted himself for the work that God would have given him to do.

All the disciples had serious faults when Jesus called them to His service. Even John, who came into closest association with the meek and lowly One, was not himself naturally meek and yielding. He and his brother were called "the sons of thunder." While they were with Jesus, any slight shown to Him aroused their indignation and combativeness. Evil temper, revenge, the spirit of criticism, were in all in the beloved disciple. He was proud, and ambitious to be first in the kingdom of God. But day by day, in contrast with his own violent spirit, he beheld the tenderness and forbearance of Jesus, and heard His lessons of humility and patience. He opened his heart to the divine influence, and became not only a hearer but a doer of the Saviour's words. Self was hid in Christ. He learned to wear the yoke of Christ and to bear His burden.

Jesus reproved His disciples, He warned and cautioned them; but John and his brethren did not leave him; they chose Jesus, notwithstanding the reproofs. The Saviour did not withdraw from them because of their weakness and errors. They continued to the end to share His trials and to learn the lessons of His life. By beholding Christ, they became transformed in character.

The apostles differed widely in habits and disposition. There were the publican, Levi-Matthew, and the fiery zealot Simon, the uncompromising hater of the authority of Rome; the generous, impulsive Peter, and the mean-spirited Judas; Thomas, truehearted, yet timid and fearful, Philip, slow of heart, and inclined to doubt, and the ambitious, outspoken sons of Zebedee, with their brethren. These were brought together, with their different faults, all with inherited and cultivated tendencies to evil but in and through Christ they were to dwell in the family of God, learning to become one in faith, in doctrine, in spirit. They would have their tests, their grievances, their differences of opinion; but while Christ was abiding in the heart, there could be no dissension. His love would lead to love for one another; the lessons of the Master would lead to the harmonizing of all differences, bringing the disciples into unity, till they would be of one mind and one judgment. Christ is the great center, and they would approach one another just in proportion as they approached the center.

When Jesus had ended His instruction to the disciples, He gathered the little band close about Him, and kneeling in the midst of them, and laying His hands upon their heads, He offered a prayer dedicating them to His sacred work. Thus the Lord's disciples were ordained to the gospel ministry.

As His representatives among men, Christ does not choose angels who have never fallen, but human beings, men of like passions with those they seek to save. Christ took upon Himself humanity, that He might reach humanity. Divinity needed humanity; for it required both the divine and the human to bring salvation to the world. Divinity needed humanity, that humanity might afford a channel of communication between God and man. So with the servants and messengers of Christ. Man needs a power outside of and beyond himself, to restore him to the likeness of God, and enable him to do the work of God; but this does not make the human agency unessential. Humanity lays hold upon divine power, Christ dwells in the heart by faith; and through co-operation with the divine, the power of man becomes efficient for good.

He who called the fisherman of Galilee is still calling men to His service. And He is just as willing to manifest His power through us as through the first disciples. However imperfect and sinful we may be, the Lord holds out to us the offer of partnership with Himself, of apprenticeship to Christ. He invites us to come under the divine instruction, that, uniting with Christ, we may work the works of God.

"We have this treasure in earthen vessels, that the exceeding greatness of the power may be of God, and not from ourselves." 2 Corinthians 4:7, R. V. This is why the preaching of the gospel was committed to erring men rather than to the angels. It is manifest that the power which works through the weakness of humanity, is the power of God; and thus we are encouraged to believe that the power which can help others as weak as ourselves, can help us. And those who are themselves "compassed with infirmity," should be able to "have compassion on the ignorant, and on them that are out of the way." Hebrews 5:2. Having been in peril themselves, they are acquainted with the dangers and difficulties of the way, and for this reason are called to reach out for others in like peril. There are souls perplexed with doubt, burdened with infirmities, weak in faith, and unable to grasp the Unseen; but a friend whom they can see, coming to them in Christ's stead, can be a connecting link to fasten their trembling faith upon Christ.

We are to be laborers together with the heavenly angels in presenting Jesus to the world. With almost impatient eagerness the angels wait for our co-operation; for man must be the channel to communicate with man. And when we give ourselves to Christ in wholehearted devotion, angels rejoice that they may speak through our voices to reveal God's love.

The Sermon on the Mount

Christ seldom gathered His disciples alone to receive His words. He did not choose for His audience those only who knew the way of life. It was His work to reach the multitudes who were in ignorance and error. He gave His lessons of truth where they could reach the darkened understanding. He Himself was the Truth, standing with girded loins and hands ever outstretched to bless, and in words of warning, entreaty, and encouragement, seeking to uplift all who would come unto Him.

The Sermon on the Mount, though given especially to the disciples, was spoken in the hearing of the multitude. After the ordination of the apostles, Jesus went with them to the seaside. Here in the early morning the people had begun to assemble. Besides the usual crowds from the Galilean towns, there were people from Judea, and even from Jerusalem itself; from Perea, from Decapolis, from Idumea, away to the south of Judea; and from Tyre and Sidon, the Phenician cities on the shore of the Mediterranean. "When they had heard what great things He did," they "came to hear Him and to be healed of their diseases: . . . there went virtue out of Him, and healed them all." Mark 3:8; Luke 6:17-19.

The narrow beach did not afford even standing room within reach of His voice for all who desired to hear Him, and Jesus led the way back to the mountainside. Reaching a level space that offered a pleasant gathering place for the vast assembly, He seated Himself on the grass, and the disciples and the multitude followed His example.

The disciples' place was always next to Jesus. The people constantly pressed upon Him, yet the disciples understood that they were not to be crowded away from His presence. They sat close beside Him, that they might not lose a word of His instruction. They were attentive listeners, eager to understand the truths they were to make known to all lands and all ages.

With a feeling that something more than usual might be expected, they now pressed about their Master. They believed that the kingdom was soon to be established, and from the events of the morning they gathered assurance that some announcement concerning it was about to be made. A feeling of expectancy pervaded the multitude also, and eager faces gave evidence of the deep interest. As the people sat upon the green hillside, awaiting the words of the divine Teacher, their hearts were filled with thoughts of future glory. There were scribes and Pharisees who looked forward to the day when they should have dominion over the hated Romans, and possess the riches and splendor of the world's great empire. The poor peasants and fishermen hoped to hear the assurance that their wretched hovels, the scanty food, the life of toil, and fear of want, were to be exchanged for mansions of plenty and days of ease. In place of the one coarse garment which was their covering by day, and their blanket at night, they hoped that Christ would give them the rich and costly robes of their conquerors. All hearts thrilled with the proud hope that Israel was soon to be honored before the nations as the chosen of the Lord, and Jerusalem exalted as the head of a universal kingdom.

Christ disappointed the hope of worldly greatness. In the Sermon on the Mount, He sought to undo the work that had been wrought by false education, and to give His hearers a right conception of His kingdom and of His own character. Yet He did not make a direct attack on the errors of the people. He saw the misery of the world on account of sin, yet He did not present before them a vivid delineation of their wretchedness. He taught them of something infinitely better than they had known. Without combating their ideas of the kingdom of God, He told them the conditions of entrance therein, leaving them to draw their own conclusions as to its nature. The truths He taught are no less important to us than to the multitude that followed Him. We no less than they need to learn the foundation principles of the kingdom of God.

Christ's first words to the people on the mount were words of blessing. Happy are they, He said, who recognize their spiritual poverty, and feel their need of redemption. The gospel is to be preached to the poor. Not to the spiritually proud, those who claim to be rich and in need of nothing, is it revealed, but to those who are humble and contrite. One fountain only has been opened for sin, a fountain for the poor in spirit.

The proud heart strives to earn salvation; but both our title to heaven and our fitness for it are found in the righteousness of Christ. The Lord can do nothing toward the recovery of man until, convinced of his own weakness, and stripped of all self-sufficiency, he yields himself to the control of God. Then he can receive the gift that God is waiting to bestow. From the soul that feels his need, nothing is withheld. He has unrestricted access to Him in whom all fulness dwells. "For thus saith the high and lofty One that inhabiteth eternity, whose name is Holy; I dwell in the high and holy place; with him also that is of a contrite and humble spirit, to revive the spirit of the humble, and to revive the heart of the contrite ones." Isaiah 57:15.

"Blessed are they that mourn; for they shall be comforted." By these words, Christ does not teach that mourning in itself has power to remove the guilt of sin. He gives no sanction to pretense or to voluntary humility. The mourning of which He speaks, does not consist in melancholy and lamentation. While we sorrow on account of sin, we are to rejoice in the precious privilege of being children of God.

We often sorrow because our evil deeds bring unpleasant consequences to ourselves; but this is not repentance. Real sorrow for sin is the result of the working of the Holy Spirit. The Spirit reveals the ingratitude of the heart that has slighted and grieved the Saviour, and brings us in contrition to the foot of the cross. By every sin, Jesus is wounded afresh; and as we look upon Him whom we have pierced, we mourn for the sins that have brought anguish upon Him. Such mourning will lead to the renunciation of sin.

The worldling may pronounce this sorrow a weakness; but it is the strength which binds the penitent to the Infinite One with links that cannot be broken. It shows that the angels of God are bringing back to the soul the graces that were lost through hardness of heart and transgression. The tears of the penitent are only the raindrops that precede the sunshine of holiness. This sorrow heralds a joy which will be a living fountain in the soul. "Only acknowledge thine iniquity, that thou hast transgressed against the Lord thy God;" "and I will not cause mine anger to fall upon you;

for I am merciful, saith the Lord." Jeremiah 3:13, 12. "Unto them that mourn in Zion," He has appointed to give "beauty for ashes, the oil of joy for mourning, the garment of praise for the spirit of heaviness." Isaiah 61:3.

And for those also who mourn in trial and sorrow, there is comfort. The bitterness of grief and humiliation is better than the indulgences of sin. Through affliction God reveals to us the plague spots in our characters, that by His grace we may overcome our faults. Unknown chapters in regard

---

"By every sin Jesus is wounded afresh; and as we look upon Him whom we have pierced, we mourn for the sins that have brought anguish upon Him. Such mourning will lead to the renunciation of sin."

---

to ourselves are opened to us, and the test comes, whether we will accept the reproof and the counsel of God. When brought into trial, we are not to fret and complain. We should not rebel, or worry ourselves out of the hand of Christ. We are to humble the soul before God. The ways of the Lord are obscure to him who desires to see things in a light pleasing to himself. They appear dark and joyless to our human nature. But God's ways are ways of mercy, and the end is salvation. Elijah knew not what he was doing when in the desert he said that he had had enough of life, and prayed that he might die. The Lord in His mercy did not take him at his word. There was yet a great work for Elijah to do; and when his work was done, he was not to perish in discouragement and solitude in the wilderness. Not for him the descent into the dust of death, but the ascent in glory, with the convoy of celestial chariots, to the throne on high.

God's word for the sorrowing is, "I have seen his ways, and will heal him; I will lead him also, and restore comforts unto him and to his mourners." "I will turn their mourning into joy, and will comfort them, and make them rejoice from their sorrow." Isaiah 57:18; Jeremiah 31:13.

"Blessed are the meek." The difficulties we have to encounter may be very much lessened by that meekness which hides itself in Christ. If we possess the humility of our Master, we shall rise above the slights, the rebuffs, the annoyances to which we are daily exposed, and they will cease to cast a gloom over the spirit. The highest evidence of nobility in a Christian is self-control. He who under abuse or cruelty fails to maintain a calm and trustful spirit, robs God of His right to reveal in him His own perfection of character. Lowliness of heart is the strength that gives victory to the followers of Christ; it is the token of their connection with the courts above.

"Though the Lord be high, yet hath He respect unto the lowly." Psalms 138:6. Those who reveal the meek and lowly spirit of Christ are tenderly regarded by God. They may be looked upon with scorn by the world, but they are of great value in His sight. Not only the wise, the great, the beneficent, will gain a passport to the heavenly courts; not only the busy worker, full of zeal and restless activity. No; the poor in spirit, who crave the presence of an abiding Christ, the humble in heart, whose highest ambition is to do God's will, — these will gain an abundant entrance. They will be among that number who have washed their robes and made them white in the blood of the Lamb. "Therefore are they before the throne of God, and serve Him day and night in His temple; and He that sitteth on the throne shall dwell among them." Revelation 7:15.

"Blessed are they which do hunger and thirst after righteousness." The sense of unworthiness will lead the heart to hunger and thirst for righteousness, and this desire will not be disappointed. Those who make room in their hearts for Jesus will realize His love. All who long to bear the likeness of the character of God shall be satisfied. The Holy Spirit never leaves unassisted the soul who is looking unto Jesus. He takes of the things of Christ and shows them unto him. If the eye is kept fixed on Christ, the work of the Spirit ceases not until the soul is conformed to His image. The pure element of love will expand the soul, giving it a capacity for higher attainments, for increased knowledge of heavenly things, so that it will not rest short of the fullness. "Blessed are they which do hunger and thirst after righteousness; for they shall be filled."

The merciful shall find mercy, and the pure in heart shall see God. Every impure thought defiles the soul, impairs the moral sense, and tends to obliterate the impressions of the Holy Spirit. It dims the spiritual vision, so that men cannot behold God. The Lord may and does forgive the repenting sinner; but though forgiven, the soul is marred. All impurity of speech or of thought must be shunned by him who would have clear discernment of spiritual truth.

But the words of Christ cover more than freedom from sensual impurity, more than freedom from that ceremonial defilement which the Jews so rigorously shunned. Selfishness prevents us from beholding God. The self-seeking spirit judges of God as altogether such a one as itself. Until we have renounced this, we cannot understand Him who is love. Only the unselfish heart, the humble and trustful spirit, shall see God as "merciful and gracious, longsuffering and abundant in goodness and truth." Exodus 34:6.

"Blessed are the peacemakers." The peace of Christ is born of truth. It is harmony with God. The world is at enmity with the law of God; sinners are at enmity with their Maker; and as a result they are at enmity with one another. But the psalmist declares, "Great peace have they which love Thy law; and nothing shall offend them." Psalms 119:165. Men cannot manufacture peace. Human plans for the purification and uplifting of individuals or of society will fail of producing peace, because they do not reach the heart. The only power that can create or perpetuate true peace is the grace of Christ. When this is implanted in the heart, it will cast out the evil passions that cause strife and dissension. "Instead of the thorn shall come up the fir tree, and instead of the brier shall come up the myrtle tree;" and life's desert "shall rejoice, and blossom as the rose." Isaiah 55:13; 35:1.

The multitudes were amazed at this teaching, which was so at variance with the precepts and example of the Pharisees. The people had come to think that happiness consisted in the possession of the things of this world, and that fame and the honor of men were much to be coveted. It was very pleasing to be called "Rabbi," and to be extolled as wise and religious, having their virtues paraded before the public. This was regarded as the crown of happiness. But in the presence of that vast throng, Jesus declared that earthly gain and honor were all the reward such persons would ever receive. He spoke with certainty, and a convincing power attended His words. The people were silenced, and a feeling of fear crept over them. They looked at one another doubtfully. Who of them would be saved if this man's teachings were true? Many were convicted that this remarkable teacher was actuated by the Spirit of God, and that the sentiments He uttered were divine.

After explaining what constitutes true happiness, and how it may be obtained, Jesus more definitely pointed out the duty of His disciples, as teachers chosen of God to lead others into the path of righteousness and eternal life. He knew that they would often suffer from disappointment and discouragement, that they would meet with decided opposition, that they would be insulted, and their testimony rejected. Well He knew that in the fulfillment of their mission, the humble men who listened so attentively to His words were to bear calumny, torture, imprisonment, and death, and He continued: —

"Blessed are they which are persecuted for righteousness' sake; for theirs is the kingdom of heaven. Blessed are ye when men shall revile you, and persecute you, and shall say all manner of evil against you falsely, for My sake. Rejoice, and be exceeding glad; for great is your reward in heaven; for so persecuted they the prophets which were before you."

The world loves sin, and hates righteousness, and this was the cause of its hostility to Jesus. All who refuse His infinite love, will find Christianity a disturbing element. The light of Christ sweeps away the darkness that covers their sins, and the need of reform is made manifest. While those who yield to the influence of the Holy Spirit begin war with themselves, those who cling to sin war against the truth and its representatives.

Thus strife is created, and Christ's followers are accused as troublers of the people. But it is fellowship with God that brings them the world's enmity. They are bearing the reproach of Christ. They are treading the path that has been trodden by the noblest of the earth. Not with sorrow, but with rejoicing, should they meet persecution. Each fiery trial is God's agent for their refining. Each is fitting them for their work as colaborers with Him. Each conflict has its place in the great battle for righteousness, and each will add to the joy of their final triumph. Having this in view, the test of their faith and patience will be cheerfully accepted rather than dreaded and avoided. Anxious to fulfill their obligation to the world, fixing their desire upon the approval of God, His servants are to fulfill every duty, irrespective of the fear or the favor of men.

"Ye are the salt of the earth," Jesus said. Do not withdraw yourselves from the world in order to escape persecution. You are to abide among men, that the savor of the divine love may be as salt to preserve the world from corruption.

Hearts that respond to the influence of the Holy Spirit are the channels through which God's blessing flows. Were those who serve God removed from the earth, and His Spirit withdrawn from among men, this world would be left to desolation and destruction, the fruit of Satan's dominion. Though the wicked know it not, they owe even the blessings of this life to the presence, in the world, of God's people whom they despise and oppress. But if Christians are such in name only, they are like the salt that has lost its savor. They have no influence for good in the world. Through their misrepresentation of God they are worse than unbelievers.

"Ye are the light of the world." The Jews thought to confine the benefits of salvation to their own nation; but Christ showed them that salvation is like the sunshine. It belongs to the whole world. The religion of the Bible is not to be confined between the covers of a book, nor within the walls of a church. It is not to be brought out occasionally for our own benefit, and then to be carefully laid aside again. It is to sanctify the daily life, to manifest itself in every business transaction and in all our social relations.

True character is not shaped from without, and put on; it radiates from within. If we wish to direct others in the path of righteousness, the principles of righteousness must be enshrined in our own hearts. Our profession of faith may proclaim the theory of religion, but it is our practical piety that holds forth the word of truth. The consistent life, the holy conversation, the unswerving integrity, the active, benevolent spirit, the godly example, — these are the mediums through which light is conveyed to the world.

Jesus had not dwelt on the specifications of the law, but He did not leave His hearers to conclude that He had come to set aside its requirements. He knew that spies stood ready to seize upon every word that might be wrested to serve their purpose. He knew the prejudice that existed in the minds of many of His hearers, and He said nothing to unsettle their faith in the religion and institutions that had been committed to them through Moses. Christ Himself had given both the moral and the ceremonial law. He did not come to destroy confidence in His own instruction. It was because of His great reverence for the law and the prophets, that He sought to break through the wall of traditional requirements which hemmed in the Jews. While He set aside their false interpretations of the law, He carefully guarded His disciples against yielding up the vital truths committed to the Hebrews.

The Pharisees prided themselves on their obedience to the law; yet they knew so little of its principles through everyday practice that to them the Saviour's words sounded like heresy. As He swept away the rubbish under which the truth had been buried, they thought He was sweeping away the truth itself. They whispered to one another that He was making light of the law. He read their thoughts, and answered them, saying, —

"Think not that I am come to destroy the law, or the prophets; I am not come to destroy, but to fulfill." Here Jesus refutes the charge of the Pharisees. His mission to the world is to vindicate the sacred claims of that law which they charge Him with breaking. If the law of God could have been changed or abrogated, then Christ need not have suffered the consequences of our transgression. He came to explain the relation of the law to man, and to illustrate its precepts by His own life of obedience.

God has given us His holy precepts, because He loves mankind. To shield us from the results of transgression, He reveals the principles of righteousness. The law is an expression of the thought of God; when received in Christ, it becomes our thought. It lifts us above the power of natural desires and tendencies, above temptations that lead to sin. God desires us to be happy, and He gave us the precepts of the law that in obeying them we might have joy. When at Jesus' birth the angels sang, —

"Glory to God in the highest,
And on earth peace, good will toward men," Luke 2:14. — they were declaring the principles of the law which He had come to magnify and make honorable.

When the law was proclaimed from Sinai, God made known to men the holiness of His character, that by contrast they might see the sinfulness of their own. The law was given to convict them of sin, and reveal their need of a Saviour. It would do this as its principles were applied to the heart by the Holy Spirit. This work it is still to do. In the life of Christ the principles of the law are made plain; and as the Holy Spirit of God touches the heart; as the light of Christ reveals to men their need of His cleansing blood and His justifying righteousness, the law is still an agent in bringing us to Christ, that we may be justified by faith. "The law of the Lord is perfect, converting the soul." Psalms 19:7.

"Till heaven and earth pass," said Jesus, "one jot or one tittle shall in no wise pass from the law, till all be fulfilled." The sun shining in the heavens, the solid earth upon which you dwell, are God's witnesses that His law is changeless and eternal. Though they may pass away, the divine precepts shall endure. "It is easier for heaven and earth to pass, than one tittle of the law to fail." Luke 16:17. The system of types that pointed to Jesus as the Lamb of God was to be abolished at His death; but the precepts of the decalogue are as immutable as the throne of God.

"The plan of redemption contemplates our complete recovery from the power of Satan. . . . Christ came to destroy the works of the devil, and He has made provision that the Holy Spirit shall be imparted to every repentant soul, to keep him from sinning."

Since "the law of the Lord is perfect," every variation from it must be evil. Those who disobey the commandments of God, and teach others to do so, are condemned by Christ. The Saviour's life of obedience maintained the claims of the law; it proved that the law could be kept in humanity, and showed the excellence of character that obedience would develop. All who obey as He did, are likewise declaring that the law is "holy, and just, and good." Romans 7:12. On the other hand, all who break God's commandments are sustaining Satan's claim that the law is unjust, and cannot be obeyed. Thus they second the deceptions of the great adversary, and cast dishonor upon God. They are the children of the wicked one, who was the first rebel against God's law. To admit them into heaven would again bring in the elements of discord and rebellion, and imperil the well-being of the universe. No man who wilfully disregards one principle of the law shall enter the kingdom of heaven.

The rabbis counted their righteousness a passport to heaven; but Jesus declared it to be insufficient and unworthy. External ceremonies and a theoretical knowledge of truth constituted Pharisaical righteousness. The rabbis claimed to be holy through their own efforts in keeping the law; but their works had divorced righteousness from religion. While they were punctilious in ritual observances, their lives were immoral and debased. Their so-called righteousness could never enter the kingdom of heaven.

The greatest deception of the human mind in Christ's day was, that a mere assent to the truth constitutes righteousness. In all human experience a theoretical knowledge of the truth has been proved to be insufficient for the saving of the soul. It does not bring forth the fruits of righteousness. A jealous regard for what is termed theological truth, often accompanies a hatred of genuine truth as made manifest in life. The darkest chapters of history are burdened with the record of crimes committed by bigoted religionists. The Pharisees claimed to be children of Abraham, and boasted of their possession of the oracles of God; yet these advantages did not preserve them from selfishness, malignity, greed for gain, and the basest hypocrisy. They thought themselves the greatest religionists of the world, but their so-called orthodoxy led them to crucify the Lord of glory.

The same danger still exists. Many take it for granted that they are Christians, simply because they subscribe to certain theological tenets. But they have not brought the truth into practical life. They have not believed and loved it, therefore they have not received the power and grace that come through sanctification of the truth. Men may profess faith in the truth; but if it does not make them sincere, kind, patient, forbearing, heavenly minded, it is a curse to its possessors, and through their influence it is a curse to the world.

The righteousness which Christ taught is conformity of heart and life to the revealed will of God. Sinful men can become righteous only as they have faith in God, and maintain a vital connection with Him. Then true godliness will elevate the thoughts and ennoble the life. Then the external forms of religion accord with the Christian's internal purity. Then the ceremonies required in the service of God are not meaningless rites, like those of the hypocritical Pharisees.

Jesus takes up the commandments separately, and explains the depth and breadth of their requirement. Instead of removing one jot of their force, He shows how far-reaching their principles are, and exposes the fatal mistake of the Jews in their outward show of obedience. He declares that by the evil thought or the lustful look the law of God is transgressed. One who becomes a party to the least injustice is breaking the law, and degrading his own moral nature. Murder first exists in the mind. He who gives hatred a place in his heart is setting his feet in the path of the murderer, and his offerings are abhorrent to God.

The Jews cultivated a spirit of retaliation. In their hatred of the Romans they gave utterance to hard denunciations, and pleased the wicked one by manifesting his attributes.

Thus they were training themselves to do the terrible deeds to which he led them on. In the religious life of the Pharisees there was nothing to recommend piety to the Gentiles. Jesus bade them not to deceive themselves with the thought that they could in heart rise up against their oppressors, and cherish the longing to avenge their wrongs.

It is true there is an indignation that is justifiable, even in the followers of Christ. When they see that God is dishonored, and His service brought into disrepute; when they see the innocent oppressed, a righteous indignation stirs the soul. Such anger, born of sensitive morals, is not a sin. But those who at any supposed provocation feel at liberty to indulge anger or resentment, are opening the heart to Satan. Bitterness and animosity must be banished from the soul if we would be in harmony with heaven.

The Saviour goes farther than this. He says, "If thou bring thy gift to the altar, and there rememberest that thy brother hath aught against thee, leave there thy gift before the altar, and go thy way; first be reconciled to thy brother, and then come and offer thy gift." Many are zealous in religious services, while between them and their brethren are unhappy differences which they might reconcile. God requires them to do all in their power to restore harmony. Until they do this, He cannot accept their services. The Christian's duty in this matter is clearly pointed out.

God pours His blessings upon all. "He maketh His sun to rise on the evil and on the good, and sendeth rain on the just and on the unjust." He is "kind unto the unthankful and to the evil." Luke 6:35. He bids us to be like Him. "Bless them that curse you," said Jesus; "do good to them that hate you, . . . that ye may be the children of your Father which is in heaven." These are the principles of the law, and they are the wellsprings of life.

God's ideal for His children is higher than the highest human thought can reach. "Be ye therefore perfect, even as your Father which is in heaven is perfect." This command is a promise. The plan of redemption contemplates our complete recovery from the power of Satan. Christ always separates the contrite soul from sin. He came to destroy the works of the devil, and He has made provision that the Holy Spirit shall be imparted to every repentant soul, to keep him from sinning.

The tempter's agency is not to be accounted an excuse for one wrong act. Satan is jubilant when he hears the professed followers of Christ making excuses for their deformity of character. It is these excuses that lead to sin. There is no excuse for sinning. A holy temper, a Christlike life, is accessible to every repenting, believing child of God.

The ideal of Christian character is Christlikeness. As the Son of man was perfect in His life, so His followers are to be perfect in their life. Jesus was in all things made like unto His brethren. He became flesh, even as we are. He was hungry and thirsty and weary. He was sustained by food and refreshed by sleep. He shared the lot of man; yet He was the blameless Son of God. He was God in the flesh. His character is to be ours. The Lord says of those who believe in Him, "I will dwell in them, and walk in them; and I will be their God, and they shall be My people." 2 Corinthians 6:16.

Christ is the ladder that Jacob saw, the base resting on the earth, and the topmost round reaching to the gate of heaven, to the very threshold of glory. If that ladder had failed by a single step of reaching the earth, we should have been lost. But Christ reaches us where we are. He took our nature and overcame, that we through taking His nature might overcome. Made "in the likeness of sinful flesh," Romans 8:3. He lived a sinless life. Now by His divinity He lays hold upon the throne of heaven, while by His humanity He reaches us. He bids us by faith in Him attain to the glory of the character of God. Therefore are we to be perfect, even as our "Father which is in heaven is perfect."

Jesus had shown in what righteousness consists, and had pointed to God as its source. Now He turned to practical duties. In almsgiving, in prayer, in fasting, He said, let nothing be done to attract attention or win praise to self. Give in sincerity, for the benefit of the suffering poor. In prayer, let the soul commune with God. In fasting, go not with the head bowed down, and heart filled with thoughts of self. The heart of the Pharisee is a barren and profitless soil, in which no seeds of divine life can flourish. It is he who yields himself most unreservedly to God that will render Him the most acceptable service. For through fellowship with God men become workers together with Him in presenting His character in humanity.

The service rendered in sincerity of heart has great recompense. "Thy Father, which seeth in secret, Himself shall reward thee openly." By the life we live through the grace of Christ, the character is formed. The original loveliness begins to be restored to the soul. The attributes of the character of Christ are imparted, and the image of the Divine begins to shine forth. The faces of men and women who walk and work with God, express the peace of heaven. They are surrounded with the atmosphere of heaven. For these souls the kingdom of God has begun. They have Christ's joy, the joy of being a blessing to humanity. They have the honor of being accepted for the Master's use; they are trusted to do His work in His name.

"No man can serve two masters." We cannot serve God with a divided heart. Bible religion is not one influence among many others; its influence is to be supreme, pervading and controlling every other. It is not to be like a dash of color brushed here and there upon the canvas, but it is to pervade the whole life, as if the canvas were dipped into the color, until every thread of the fabric were dyed a deep, unfading hue.

"If therefore thine eye be single, thy whole body shall be full of light. But if thine eye be evil, thy whole body shall be full of darkness." Purity and steadfastness of purpose are the conditions of receiving light from God. He who desires to know the truth, must be willing to accept all that it reveals. He can make no compromise with error. To be wavering and halfhearted in allegiance to truth, is to choose the darkness of error and Satanic delusion.

Worldly policy and the undeviating principles of righteousness, do not blend into each other imperceptibly, like the colors of the rainbow. Between the two a broad, clear line is drawn by the eternal God. The likeness of Christ stands out as distinct from that of Satan as midday in contrast with midnight. And only those who live the life of Christ, are His co-workers. If one sin is cherished in the soul, or one wrong practice retained in the life, the whole being is contaminated. The man becomes an instrument of unrighteousness.

All who have chosen God's service are to rest in His care. Christ pointed to the birds flying in the heavens, to the flowers of the field, and bade His hearers consider these objects of God's creation. "Are ye not of much more value than they?" Matthew 6:26, R. V. He said. The measure of divine attention bestowed on any object is proportionate to its rank in the scale of being. The little brown sparrow is watched over by Providence. The flowers of the field, the grass that carpets the earth, share the notice and care of our Heavenly Father. The great Master Artist had taken thought for the lilies, making them so beautiful that they outshine the glory of Solomon. How much more does He care for man, who is the image and glory of God. He longs to see His children reveal a character after His similitude. As the sunbeam imparts to the flowers their varied and delicate tints, so does God impart to the soul the beauty of His own character.

All who choose Christ's kingdom of love and righteousness and peace, making its interest paramount to all other, are linked to the world above, and every blessing needed for this life is theirs. In the book of God's providence, the volume of life, we are each given a page. That page contains every particular of our history; even the hairs of the head are numbered. God's children are never absent from His mind.

"Be not therefore anxious for the morrow." Matthew 6:34, R. V. We are to follow Christ day by day. God does not bestow help for tomorrow. He does not give His children all the directions for their life journey at once, lest they should become confused. He tells them just as much as they can remember and perform. The strength and wisdom imparted are for the present emergency. "If any of you lack wisdom,"—for today,—"let him ask of God, that giveth to all men liberally, and upbraideth not; and it shall be given him." James 1:5.

"Judge not, that ye be not judged." Do not think yourself better than other men, and set yourself up as their judge. Since you cannot discern motive, you are incapable of judging another. In criticizing him, you are passing sentence upon yourself; for you show that you are a participant with Satan, the accuser of the brethren. The Lord says, "Examine yourselves whether ye be in the faith; prove your own selves." This is our work. "If we would judge ourselves, we should not be judged." 2 Corinthians 13:5; 1 Corinthians 11:31.

The good tree will produce good fruit. If the fruit is unpalatable and worthless, the tree is evil. So the fruit borne in the life testifies as to the condition of the heart and the excellence of the character. Good works can never purchase salvation, but they are an evidence of the faith that acts by love and purifies the soul. And though the eternal reward is not bestowed because of our merit, yet it will be in proportion to the work that has been done through the grace of Christ.

Thus Christ set forth the principles of His kingdom, and showed them to be the great rule of life. To impress the lesson He adds an illustration. It is not enough, He says, for you to hear My words. By obedience you must make them the foundation of your character. Self is but shifting sand. If you build upon human theories and inventions, your house will fall. By the winds of temptation, the tempests of trial, it will be swept away. But these principles that I have given will endure. Receive Me; build on My words.

"Every one therefore which heareth these words of Mine, and doeth them, shall be likened unto a wise man, which built his house upon the rock: and the rain descended, and the floods came, and the winds blew, and beat upon that house; and it fell not; for it was founded upon the rock." Matthew 7:24, 25, R. V.

The Centurion

Christ had said to the nobleman whose son He healed, "Except ye see signs and wonders, ye will not believe." John 4:48. He was grieved that His own nation should require these outward signs of His Messiahship. Again and again He had marveled at their unbelief. But He marveled at the faith of the centurion who came to Him. The centurion did not question the Saviour's power. He did not even ask Him to come in person to perform the miracle. "Speak the word only," he said, "and my servant shall be healed."

The centurion's servant had been stricken with palsy, and lay at the point of death. Among the Romans the servants were slaves, bought and sold in the marketplaces, and treated with abuse and cruelty; but the centurion was tenderly attached to his servant, and greatly desired his recovery. He believed that Jesus could heal him. He had not seen the Saviour, but the reports he heard had inspired him with faith. Notwithstanding the formalism of the Jews, this Roman was convinced that their religion was superior to his own. Already he had broken through the barriers of national prejudice and hatred that separated the conquerors from the conquered people. He had manifested respect for the service of God, and had shown kindness to the Jews as His worshipers. In the teaching of Christ, as it had been reported to him, he found that which met the need of the soul. All that was spiritual within him responded to the Saviour's words. But he felt unworthy to come into the presence of Jesus, and he appealed to the Jewish elders to make request for the healing of his servant. They were acquainted with the great Teacher, and would, he thought, know how to approach Him so as to win His favor.

As Jesus entered Capernaum, He was met by a delegation of the elders, who told Him of the centurion's desire. They urged "that he was worthy for whom He should do this; for he loveth our nation, and he hath built us a synagogue."

Jesus immediately set out for the officer's home; but, pressed by the multitude, He advanced slowly. The news of His coming preceded Him, and the centurion, in his self-distrust, sent Him the message, "Lord, trouble not Thyself; for I am not worthy that Thou shouldst enter under my roof." But the Saviour kept on His way, and the centurion, venturing at last to approach Him, completed the message, saying, "Neither thought I myself worthy to come unto Thee;" "but speak the word only, and my servant shall be healed. For I am a man under authority, having soldiers under me: and I say to this man, Go, and he goeth; and to another, Come, and he cometh; and to my servant, Do this, and he doeth it." As I represent the power of Rome, and my soldiers recognize my authority as supreme, so dost Thou represent the power of the infinite God, and all created things obey Thy word. Thou canst command the disease to depart, and it shall obey Thee. Thou canst summon Thy heavenly messengers, and they shall impart healing virtue. Speak but the word, and my servant shall be healed.

"When Jesus heard these things, He marveled at him, and turned Him about, and said unto the people that followed Him, I say unto you, I have not found so great faith, no, not in Israel." And to the centurion He said, "As thou hast believed, so be it done unto thee. And his servant was healed in the selfsame hour."

The Jewish elders who recommended the centurion to Christ, had shown how far they were from possessing the

136   This chapter is based on Matt. 8:5-13; Luke 7:1-17.   (315-316)

spirit of the gospel. They did not recognize that our great need is our only claim on God's mercy. In their self-righteousness they commended the centurion because of the favor he had shown to "our nation." But the centurion said of himself, "I am not worthy." His heart had been touched by the grace of Christ. He saw his own unworthiness; yet he feared not to ask help. He trusted not to his own goodness; his argument was his great need. His faith took hold upon Christ in His true character. He did not believe in Him merely as a worker of miracles, but as the friend and Saviour of mankind.

It is thus that every sinner may come to Christ. "Not by works of righteousness which we have done, but according to His mercy He saved us." Titus 3:5. When Satan tells you that you are a sinner, and cannot hope to receive blessing from God, tell him that Christ came into the world to save sinners. We have nothing to recommend us to God; but the plea that we may urge now and ever is our utterly helpless condition, that makes His redeeming power a necessity. Renouncing all self-dependence, we may look to the cross of Calvary and say,—

"In my hand no price I bring;
Simply to Thy cross I cling."

The Jews had been instructed from childhood concerning the work of the Messiah. The inspired utterances of patriarchs and prophets, and the symbolic teaching of the sacrificial service, had been theirs. But they had disregarded the light; and now they saw in Jesus nothing to be desired. But the centurion, born in heathenism, educated in the idolatry of imperial Rome, trained as a soldier, seemingly cut off from spiritual life by his education and surroundings, and still further shut out by the bigotry of the Jews, and by the contempt of his own countrymen for the people of Israel,—this man perceived the truth to which the children of Abraham were blinded. He did not wait to see whether the Jews themselves would receive the One who claimed to be their Messiah. As the "light which lighteth every man that cometh into the world" John 1:9. had shone upon him, he had, though afar off, discerned the glory of the Son of God.

To Jesus this was an earnest of the work which the gospel was to accomplish among the Gentiles. With joy He looked forward to the gathering of souls from all nations to His kingdom. With deep sadness He pictured to the Jews the result of their rejection of His grace: "I say unto you, That many shall come from the east and west, and shall sit down with Abraham, and Isaac, and Jacob, in the kingdom of heaven. But the children of the kingdom shall be cast out into outer darkness; there shall be weeping and gnashing of teeth." Alas, how many are still preparing for the same fatal disappointment! While souls in heathen darkness accept His grace, how many there are in Christian lands upon whom the light shines only to be disregarded.

More than twenty miles from Capernaum, on a tableland overlooking the wide, beautiful plain of Esdraelon, lay the village of Nain, and thither Jesus next bent His steps. Many of His disciples and others were with Him, and all along the way the people came, longing for His words of love and pity, bringing their sick for His healing, and ever with the hope that He who wielded such wondrous power would make Himself known as the King of Israel. A multitude thronged His steps, and it was a glad, expectant company that followed Him up the rocky path toward the gate of the mountain village.

"He who stood beside the sorrowing mother at the gate of Nain . . . is touched with sympathy for our grief. His heart, that loved and pitied, is a heart of unchangeable tenderness. His word, that called the dead to life, is no less efficacious now . . . That power is not diminished by the lapse of years . . . To all who believe on Him He is still a living Saviour."

As they draw near, a funeral train is seen coming from the gates. With slow, sad steps it is proceeding to the place of burial. On an open bier carried in front is the body of the dead, and about it are the mourners, filling the air with their wailing cries. All the people of the town seem to have gathered to show their respect for the dead and their sympathy with the bereaved.

It was a sight to awaken sympathy. The deceased was the only son of his mother, and she a widow. The lonely mourner was following to the grave her sole earthly support and comfort. "When the Lord saw her, He had compassion on her." As she moved on blindly, weeping, noting not His presence, He came close beside her, and gently said, "Weep not." Jesus was about to change her grief to joy, yet He could not forbear this expression of tender sympathy.

"He came and touched the bier;" to Him even contact with death could impart no defilement. The bearers stood still, and the lamentations of the mourners ceased. The two companies gathered about the bier, hoping against hope. One was present who had banished disease and vanquished demons; was death also subject to His power?

In clear, authoritative voice the words are spoken, "Young man, I say unto thee, Arise." That voice pierces the ears of the dead. The young man opens his eyes. Jesus takes him by the hand, and lifts him up. His gaze falls upon her who has been weeping beside him, and mother and son unite in a long, clinging, joyous embrace. The multitude look on in silence, as if spellbound. "There came a fear on all." Hushed and reverent they stood for a little time, as if in the very presence of God. Then they "glorified God, saying, That a great prophet is risen up among us; and, That God hath visited His people." The funeral train returned to Nain as a triumphal procession. "And this rumor of Him went forth throughout all Judea, and throughout all the region round about."

He who stood beside the sorrowing mother at the gate of Nain, watches with every mourning one beside the bier. He is touched with sympathy for our grief. His heart, that loved and pitied, is a heart of unchangeable tenderness. His word, that called the dead to life, is no less efficacious now than when spoken to the young man of Nain. He says, "All power is given unto Me in heaven and in earth." Matthew 28:18. That power is not diminished by the lapse of years, nor exhausted by the ceaseless activity of His overflowing grace. To all who believe on Him He is still a living Saviour.

Jesus changed the mother's grief to joy when He gave back her son; yet the youth was but called forth to this earthly life, to endure its sorrows, its toils, and its perils, and to pass again under the power of death. But Jesus comforts our sorrow for the dead with a message of infinite hope: "I am He that liveth, and was dead; and, behold, I am alive forevermore, . . . and have the keys of hell and of death." "Forasmuch then as the children are partakers of flesh and blood, He also Himself likewise took part of the same; that through death He might destroy him that had the power of death, that is, the devil; and deliver them who through fear of death were all their lifetime subject to bondage." Revelation 1:18; Hebrews 2:14, 15.

Satan cannot hold the dead in his grasp when the Son of God bids them live. He cannot hold in spiritual death one soul who in faith receives Christ's word of power. God is saying to all who are dead in sin, "Awake, thou that sleepest, and arise from the dead." Ephesians 5:14. That word is eternal life. As the word of God which bade the first man live, still gives us life; as Christ's word, "Young man, I say unto thee, Arise," gave life to the youth of Nain, so that word, "Arise from the dead," is life to the soul that receives it. God "hath delivered us from the power of darkness, and hath translated us into the kingdom of His dear Son." Colossians 1:13. It is all offered us in His word. If we receive the word, we have the deliverance.

And "if the Spirit of Him that raised up Jesus from the dead dwell in you, He that raised up Christ from the dead shall also quicken your mortal bodies by His Spirit that dwelleth in you." "For the Lord Himself shall descend from heaven with a shout, with the voice of the archangel, and with the trump of God; and the dead in Christ shall rise first; then we which are alive and remain shall be caught up together with them in the clouds, to meet the Lord in the air: and so shall we ever be with the Lord." Romans 8:11; 1 Thessalonians 4:16: 17. This is the word of comfort wherewith He bids us comfort one another.

"Who are My Brethren?"

The sons of Joseph were far from being in sympathy with Jesus in His work. The reports that reached them in regard to His life and labors filled them with astonishment and dismay. They heard that He devoted entire nights to prayer, that through the day He was thronged by great companies of people, and did not give Himself time so much as to eat. His friends felt that He was wearing Himself out by His incessant labor; they were unable to account for His attitude toward the Pharisees, and there were some who feared that His reason was becoming unsettled.

His brothers heard of this, and also of the charge brought by the Pharisees that He cast out devils through the power of Satan. They felt keenly the reproach that came upon them through their relation to Jesus. They knew what a tumult His words and works created, and were not only alarmed at His bold statements, but indignant at His denunciation of the scribes and Pharisees. They decided that He must be persuaded or constrained to cease this manner of labor, and they induced Mary to unite with them, thinking that through His love for her they might prevail upon Him to be more prudent.

It was just before this that Jesus had a second time performed the miracle of healing a man possessed, blind and dumb, and the Pharisees had reiterated the charge, "He casteth out devils through the prince of the devils." Matthew 9:34. Christ told them plainly that in attributing the work of the Holy Spirit to Satan, they were cutting themselves off from the fountain of blessing. Those who had spoken against Jesus Himself, not discerning His divine character, might receive forgiveness; for through the Holy Spirit they might be brought to see their error and repent. Whatever the sin, if the soul repents and believes, the guilt is washed away in the blood of Christ; but he who rejects the work of the Holy Spirit is placing himself where repentance and faith cannot come to him. It is by the Spirit that God works upon the heart; when men wilfully reject the Spirit, and declare it to be from Satan, they cut off the channel by which God can communicate with them. When the Spirit is finally rejected, there is no more that God can do for the soul.

The Pharisees to whom Jesus spoke this warning did not themselves believe the charge they brought against Him. There was not one of those dignitaries but had felt drawn toward the Saviour. They had heard the Spirit's voice in their own hearts declaring Him to be the Anointed of Israel, and urging them to confess themselves His disciples. In the light of His presence they had realized their unholiness, and had longed for a righteousness which they could not create. But after their rejection of Him it would be too humiliating to receive Him as the Messiah. Having set their feet in the path of unbelief, they were too proud to confess their error. And in order to avoid acknowledging the truth, they tried with desperate violence to dispute the Saviour's teaching. The evidence of His power and mercy exasperated them. They could not prevent the Saviour from working miracles, they could not silence His teaching; but they did everything in their power to misrepresent Him and to falsify His words. Still the convicting Spirit of God followed them, and they had to build up many barriers in order to withstand its power. The mightiest agency that can be brought to bear upon the human heart was striving with them, but they would not yield.

It is not God that blinds the eyes of men or hardens their hearts. He sends them light to correct their errors, and to lead them in safe paths; it is by the rejection of this light that the eyes are blinded and the heart hardened. Often the process is gradual, and almost imperceptible. Light comes to the soul through God's word, through His servants, or by the direct agency of His Spirit; but when one ray of light is disregarded, there is a partial benumbing of the spiritual perceptions, and the second revealing of light is less clearly discerned. So the darkness increases, until it is night in the soul. Thus it had been with these Jewish leaders. They were convinced that a divine power attended Christ, but in order to resist the truth, they attributed the work of the Holy Spirit to Satan. In doing this they deliberately chose deception; they yielded themselves to Satan, and henceforth they were controlled by his power.

Closely connected with Christ's warning in regard to the sin against the Holy Spirit is a warning against idle and evil words. The words are an indication of that which is in the heart. "Out of the abundance of the heart the mouth speaketh." But the words are more than an indication of character; they have power to react on the character. Men are influenced by their own words. Often under a momentary impulse, prompted by Satan, they give utterance to jealousy or evil surmising, expressing that which they do not really believe; but the expression reacts on the thoughts. They are deceived by their words, and come to believe that true which was spoken at Satan's instigation. Having once expressed an opinion or decision, they are often too proud to retract it, and try to prove themselves in the right, until they come to believe that they are. It is dangerous to utter a word of doubt, dangerous to question and criticize divine light. The habit of careless and irrelevant criticism reacts upon the character, in fostering irreverence and unbelief. Many a man indulging this habit has gone on unconscious of danger, until he was ready to criticize and reject the work of the Holy Spirit. Jesus said, "Every idle word that men shall speak, they shall give account thereof in the day of Judgment. For by thy words thou shalt be justified, and by thy words thou shalt be condemned."

Then He added a warning to those who had been impressed by His words, who had heard Him gladly, but who had not surrendered themselves for the indwelling of the Holy Spirit. It is not only by resistance but by neglect that the soul is destroyed. "When the unclean spirit is gone out of a man," said Jesus, "he walketh through dry places, seeking rest, and findeth none. Then he saith, I will return into my house from whence I came out; and when he is come, he findeth it empty, swept, and garnished. Then goeth he, and taketh with himself seven other spirits more wicked than himself, and they enter in and dwell there."

There were many in Christ's day, as there are today, over whom the control of Satan for the time seemed broken; through the grace of God they were set free from the evil spirits that had held dominion over the soul. They rejoiced in the love of God; but, like the stony-ground hearers of the parable, they did not abide in His love. They did not surrender themselves to God daily, that Christ might dwell in the heart; and when the evil spirit returned, "with seven other spirits more wicked than himself," they were wholly dominated by the power of evil.

When the soul surrenders itself to Christ, a new power takes possession of the new heart. A change is wrought which can never accomplish for himself. It is a supernatural work, bringing a supernatural element into human nature. The soul that is yielded to Christ, becomes His own fortress, which He holds in a revolted world, and He intends that no authority shall be known in it but His own. A soul thus kept in possession by the heavenly agencies, is impregnable to the assaults of Satan. But unless we do yield ourselves to the control of Christ, we shall be dominated by the wicked one. We must inevitably be under the control of the one or the other of the two great powers that are contending for the supremacy of the world. It is not necessary for us deliberately to choose the service of the kingdom of darkness in order to come under its dominion. We have only to neglect to ally ourselves with the kingdom of light. If we do not co-operate with the heavenly agencies, Satan will take possession of the heart, and will make it his abiding place. The only defense against evil is the indwelling of Christ in the heart through faith in His righteousness. Unless we become vitally connected with God, we can never resist the unhallowed effects of self-love, self-indulgence, and temptation to sin. We may leave off many bad habits, for the time we may part company with Satan; but without a vital connection with God, through the surrender of ourselves to Him moment by moment, we shall be overcome. Without a personal acquaintance with Christ, and a continual communion, we are at the mercy of the enemy, and shall do his bidding in the end.

"The last state of that man is worse than the first. Even so," said Jesus, "shall it be also unto this wicked generation." There are none so hardened as those who have slighted the invitation of mercy, and done despite to the Spirit of grace. The most common manifestation of the sin against the Holy Spirit, is in persistently slighting Heaven's invitation to repent. Every step in the rejection of Christ is a step toward the rejection of salvation, and toward the sin against the Holy Spirit.

In rejecting Christ the Jewish people committed the unpardonable sin; and by refusing the invitation of mercy, we may commit the same error. We offer insult to the Prince of life, and put Him to shame before the synagogue of Satan, and before the heavenly universe, when we refuse to listen to His delegated messengers, and instead listen to the agents of Satan who would draw the soul away from Christ. So long as one does this, he can find no hope or pardon, and he will finally lose all desire to be reconciled to God.

While Jesus was still teaching the people, His disciples brought the message that His mother and His brothers were without, and desired to see Him. He knew what was in their hearts, and "He answered and said unto him that told Him,

Who is My mother? and who are My brethren? And He stretched forth His hand toward His disciples, and said, Behold My mother and My brethren! For whosoever shall do the will of My Father which is in heaven, the same is My brother, and sister, and mother."

All who would receive Christ by faith, were united to Him by a tie closer than that of human kinship. They would become one with Him, as He was one with the Father. As a believer and doer of His words, His mother was more nearly and savingly related to Him than through her natural relationship. His brothers would receive no benefit from their connection with Him unless they accepted Him as their personal Saviour.

What a support Christ would have found in His earthly relatives if they had believed in Him as one from heaven, and had co-operated with Him in doing the work of God! Their unbelief cast a shadow over the earthly life of Jesus. It was a part of the bitterness of that cup of woe which He drained for us.

The enmity kindled in the human heart against the gospel was keenly felt by the Son of God, and it was most painful to Him in His home; for His own heart was full of kindness and love, and He appreciated tender regard in the family relation. His brothers desired that He should concede to their ideas, when such a course would have been utterly out of harmony with His divine mission. They looked upon Him as in need of their counsel. They judged Him from their human point of view, and thought that if He would speak only such things as would be acceptable to the scribes and Pharisees, He would avoid the disagreeable controversy that His words aroused. They thought that He was beside Himself in claiming divine authority, and in placing Himself before the rabbis as a reprover of their sins. They knew that the Pharisees were seeking occasion to accuse Him, and they felt that He had given them sufficient occasion.

With their short measuring line they could not fathom the mission which He came to fulfill, and therefore could not sympathize with Him in His trials. Their coarse, unappreciative words showed that they had no true perception of His character, and did not discern that the divine blended with the human. They often saw Him full of grief; but instead of comforting Him, their spirit and words only wounded His heart. His sensitive nature was tortured, His motives were misunderstood, His work was uncomprehended.

His brothers often brought forward the philosophy of the Pharisees, which was threadbare and hoary with age, and presumed to think that they could teach Him who understood all truth, and comprehended all mysteries. They freely condemned that which they could not understand. Their reproaches probed Him to the quick, and His soul was wearied and distressed. They avowed faith in God, and thought they were vindicating God, when God was with them in the flesh, and they knew Him not.

These things made His path a thorny one to travel. So pained was Christ by the misapprehension in His own home, that it was a relief to Him to go where it did not exist. There was one home that He loved to visit, — the home of Lazarus, and Mary, and Martha; for in the atmosphere of faith and love His spirit had rest. Yet there were none on earth who could comprehend His divine mission, or know the burden which He bore in behalf of humanity. Often He could find relief only in being alone, and communing with His Heavenly Father.

Those who are called to suffer for Christ's sake, who have to endure misapprehension and distrust, even in their own home, may find comfort in the thought that Jesus has endured the same. He is moved with compassion for them. He bids them find companionship in Him, and relief where He found it, in communion with the Father.

Those who accept Christ as their personal Saviour are not left as orphans, to bear the trials of life alone. He receives them as members of the heavenly family; He bids them call His Father their Father. They are His "little ones," dear to the heart of God, bound to Him by the most tender and abiding ties. He has toward them an exceeding tenderness, as far surpassing what our father or mother has felt toward us in our helplessness, as the divine is above the human.

Of Christ's relation to His people, there is a beautiful illustration in the laws given to Israel. When through poverty a Hebrew had been forced to part with his patrimony, and to sell himself as a bondservant, the duty of redeeming him and his inheritance fell to the one who was nearest of kin. (See Leviticus 25:25, 47-49; Ruth 2:20.) So the work of redeeming us and our inheritance, lost through sin, fell upon Him who is "near of kin" unto us. It was to redeem us that He became our kinsman. Closer than father, mother, brother, friend, or lover, is the Lord our Saviour. "Fear not," He says, "for I have redeemed thee. I have called thee by thy name; thou art Mine." "Since thou wast precious in My sight, thou hast been honorable, and I have loved thee; therefore will I give men for thee, and people for thy life." Isaiah 43:1, 4.

Christ loves the heavenly beings that surround His throne; but what shall account for the great love wherewith He has loved us? We cannot understand it, but we can know it true in our own experience. And if we do hold the relation of kinship to Him, with what tenderness should we regard those who are brethren and sisters of our Lord. Should we not be quick to recognize the claims of our divine relationship? Adopted into the family of God, should we not honor our Father and our kindred?

The Invitation

Come unto Me, all ye that labor and are heavy laden, and I will give you rest."

These words of comfort were spoken to the multitude that followed Jesus. The Saviour had said that only through Himself could men receive a knowledge of God. He had spoken of His disciples as the ones to whom a knowledge of heavenly things had been given. But He left none to feel themselves shut out from His care and love. All who labor and are heavy laden may come unto Him.

Scribes and rabbis, with their punctilious attention to religious forms, had a sense of want that rites of penance could never satisfy. Publicans and sinners might pretend to be content with the sensual and earthly, but in their hearts were distrust and fear. Jesus looked upon the distressed and heart burdened, those whose hopes were blighted, and who with earthly joys were seeking to quiet the longing of the soul, and He invited all to find rest in Him.

Tenderly He bade the toiling people, "Take My yoke upon you, and learn of Me; for I am meek and lowly in heart: and ye shall find rest unto your souls."

In these words, Christ is speaking to every human being. Whether they know it or not, all are weary and heavy laden. All are weighed down with burdens that only Christ can remove. The heaviest burden that we bear is the burden of sin. If we were left to bear this burden, it would crush us. But the Sinless One has taken our place. "The Lord hath laid on Him the iniquity of us all." Isaiah 53:6. He has borne the burden of our guilt. He will take the load from our weary shoulders. He will give us rest. The burden of care and sorrow also He will bear. He invites us to cast all our care upon Him; for He carries us upon His heart.

The Elder Brother of our race is by the eternal throne. He looks upon every soul who is turning his face toward Him as the Saviour. He knows by experience what are the weaknesses of humanity, what are our wants, and where lies the strength of our temptations; for He was in all points tempted like as we are, yet without sin. He is watching over you, trembling child of God. Are you tempted? He will deliver. Are you weak? He will strengthen. Are you ignorant? He will enlighten. Are you wounded? He will heal. The Lord "telleth the number of the stars;" and yet "He healeth the broken in heart, and bindeth up their wounds." Psalms 147:4, 3. "Come unto Me," is His invitation. Whatever your anxieties and trials, spread out your case before the Lord. Your spirit will be braced for endurance. The way will be opened for you to disentangle yourself from embarrassment and difficulty. The weaker and more helpless you know yourself to be, the stronger will you become in His strength. The heavier your burdens, the more blessed the rest in casting them upon the Burden Bearer. The rest that Christ offers depends upon conditions, but these conditions are plainly specified. They are those with which all can comply. He tells us just how His rest is to be found.

"Take My yoke upon you," Jesus says. The yoke is an instrument of service. Cattle are yoked for labor, and the yoke is essential that they may labor effectually. By this illustration, Christ teaches us that we are called to service as long as life shall last. We are to take upon us His yoke, that we may be co-workers with Him.

The yoke that binds to service is the law of God. The great law of love revealed in Eden, proclaimed upon Sinai, and in the new covenant written in the heart, is that which binds the human worker to the will of God. If we were left to follow our own inclinations, to go just where our will would lead us, we should fall into Satan's ranks and become possessors of his attributes. Therefore God confines us to His will, which is high, and noble, and elevating. He desires that we shall patiently and wisely take up the duties of service. The yoke of service Christ Himself has borne in humanity. He said, "I delight to do Thy will, O My God; yea, Thy law is within My heart." Psalms 40:8. "I came down from heaven, not to do Mine own will, but the will of Him that sent Me." John 6:38. Love for God, zeal for His glory, and love for fallen humanity, brought Jesus to earth to suffer and to die. This was the controlling power of His life. This principle He bids us adopt.

There are many whose hearts are aching under a load of care because they seek to reach the world's standard. They have chosen its service, accepted its perplexities, adopted its customs. Thus their character is marred, and their life made a weariness. In order to gratify ambition and worldly desires, they wound the conscience, and bring upon themselves an additional burden of remorse. The continual worry is wearing out the life forces. Our Lord desires them to lay aside this yoke of bondage. He invites them to accept His yoke; He says, "My yoke is easy, and My burden is light." He bids them seek first the kingdom of God and His righteousness, and His promise is, that all things needful to them for this life shall be added. Worry is blind, and cannot discern the future; but Jesus sees the end from the beginning. In every difficulty He has His way prepared to bring relief. Our Heavenly Father has a thousand ways to provide for us, of which we know nothing. Those who accept the one principle of making the service and honor of God supreme, will find perplexities vanish, and a plain path before their feet.

"Learn of Me," says Jesus; "for I am meek and lowly in heart, and ye shall find rest." We are to enter the school of Christ, to learn from Him meekness and lowliness. Redemption is that process by which the soul is trained for heaven. This training means a knowledge of Christ. It means emancipation from ideas, habits, and practices that have been gained in the school of the prince of darkness. The soul must be delivered from all that is opposed to loyalty to God.

In the heart of Christ, where reigned perfect harmony with God, there was perfect peace. He was never elated by applause, nor dejected by censure or disappointment. Amid the greatest opposition and the most cruel treatment, He was still of good courage. But many who profess to be His followers have an anxious, troubled heart, because they are afraid to trust themselves with God. They do not make a complete surrender to Him; for they shrink from the consequences that such a surrender may involve. Unless they do make this surrender, they cannot find peace.

It is the love of self that brings unrest. When we are born from above, the same mind will be in us that was in Jesus, the mind that led Him to humble Himself that we might be saved. Then we shall not be seeking the highest place. We

shall desire to sit at the feet of Jesus, and learn of Him. We shall understand that the value of our work does not consist in making a show and noise in the world, and in being active and zealous in our own strength. The value of our work is in proportion to the impartation of the Holy Spirit. Trust in God brings holier qualities of mind, so that in patience we may possess our souls.

"There are many whose hearts are aching under a load of care because they seek to reach the world's standard. They have chosen its service, accepted its perplexities, adopted its customs. . . . Worry is blind, and cannot discern the future; but Jesus sees the end from the beginning. In every difficulty He has His way prepared to bring relief. Our Heavenly Father has a thousand ways to provide for us, of which we know nothing."

The yoke is placed upon the oxen to aid them in drawing the load, to lighten the burden. So with the yoke of Christ. When our will is swallowed up in the will of God, and we use His gifts to bless others, we shall find life's burden light. He who walks in the way of God's commandments is walking in company with Christ, and in His love the heart is at rest. When Moses prayed, "Show me now Thy way, that I may know Thee," the Lord answered him, "My presence shall go with thee, and I will give thee rest." And through the prophets the message was given, "Thus saith the Lord: Stand ye in the ways, and see, and ask for the old paths, where is the good way, and walk therein, and ye shall find rest for your souls." Exodus 33:13, 14; Jeremiah 6:16. And He says, "O that thou hadst hearkened to My

commandments! then had thy peace been as a river, and thy righteousness as the waves of the sea." Isaiah 48:18.

Those who take Christ at His word, and surrender their souls to His keeping, their lives to His ordering, will find peace and quietude. Nothing of the world can make them sad when Jesus makes them glad by His presence. In perfect acquiescence there is perfect rest. The Lord says, "Thou wilt keep him in perfect peace whose mind is stayed on Thee; because he trusteth in Thee." Isaiah 26:3. Our lives may seem a tangle; but as we commit ourselves to the wise Master Worker, He will bring out the pattern of life and character that will be to His own glory. And that character which expresses the glory — character — of Christ, will be received into the Paradise of God. A renovated race shall walk with Him in white, for they are worthy.

As through Jesus we enter into rest, heaven begins here. We respond to His invitation, Come, learn of Me, and in thus coming we begin the life eternal. Heaven is a ceaseless approaching to God through Christ. The longer we are in the heaven of bliss, the more and still more of glory will be opened to us; and the more we know of God, the more intense will be our happiness. As we walk with Jesus in this life, we may be filled with His love, satisfied with His presence. All that human nature can bear, we may receive here. But what is this compared with the hereafter? There "are they before the throne of God, and serve Him day and night in His temple; and He that sitteth on the throne shall dwell among them. They shall hunger no more, neither thirst any more; neither shall the sun light on them, nor any heat. For the Lamb which is in the midst of the throne shall feed them, and shall lead them unto living fountains of waters; and God shall wipe away all tears from their eyes." Revelation 7:15-17.

"Peace, Be Still"

It had been an eventful day in the life of Jesus. Beside the Sea of Galilee, He had spoken His first parables, by familiar illustrations again explaining to the people the nature of His kingdom and the manner in which it was to be established. He had likened His own work to that of the sower; the development of His kingdom to the growth of the mustard seed and the effect of leaven in the measure of meal. The great final separation of the righteous and the wicked He had pictured in the parables of the wheat and tares and the fishing net. The exceeding preciousness of the truths He taught had been illustrated by the hidden treasure and the pearl of great price, while in the parable of the householder He taught His disciples how they were to labor as His representatives.

All day He had been teaching and healing; and as evening came on, the crowds still pressed upon Him. Day after day He had ministered to them, scarcely pausing for food or rest. The malicious criticism and misrepresentation with which the Pharisees constantly pursued Him, made His labors much more severe and harassing; and now the close of the day found Him so utterly wearied that He determined to seek retirement in some solitary place across the lake.

The eastern shore of Gennesaret was not uninhabited, for there were towns here and there beside the lake; yet it was a desolate region when compared with the western side. It contained a population more heathen than Jewish, and had little communication with Galilee. Thus it offered Jesus the seclusion He sought, and He now bade His disciples accompany Him thither.

After He had dismissed the multitude, they took Him, even "as He was," into the boat, and hastily set off. But they were not to depart alone. There were other fishing boats lying near the shore, and these were quickly crowded with people who followed Jesus, eager still to see and hear Him.

The Saviour was at last relieved from the pressure of the multitude, and, overcome with weariness and hunger, He lay down in the stern of the boat, and soon fell asleep. The evening had been calm and pleasant, and quiet rested upon the lake; but suddenly darkness overspread the sky, the wind swept wildly down the mountain gorges along the eastern shore, and a fierce tempest burst upon the lake.

The sun had set, and the blackness of night settled down upon the stormy sea. The waves, lashed into fury by the howling winds, dashed fiercely over the disciples' boat, and threatened to engulf it. Those hardy fishermen had spent their lives upon the lake, and had guided their craft safely through many a storm; but now their strength and skill availed nothing. They were helpless in the grasp of the tempest, and hope failed them as they saw that their boat was filling.

Absorbed in their efforts to save themselves, they had forgotten that Jesus was on board. Now, seeing their labor vain, and only death before them, they remembered at whose command they had set out to cross the sea. In Jesus was their only hope. In their helplessness and despair they cried, "Master, Master!" But the dense darkness hid Him from their sight. Their voices were drowned by the roaring of the tempest, and there was no reply. Doubt and fear assailed them. Had Jesus forsaken them? Was He who had conquered disease and demons, and even death, powerless to help His disciples now? Was He unmindful of them in their distress?

Again they call, but there is no answer except the shrieking of the angry blast. Already their boat is sinking. A

This chapter is based on Matt. 8:23-34; Mark 4:35-41; 5:1-20; Luke 8:22-39.

moment, and apparently they will be swallowed up by the hungry waters.

Suddenly a flash of lightning pierces the darkness, and they see Jesus lying asleep, undisturbed by the tumult. In amazement and despair they exclaim, "Master, carest Thou not that we perish?" How can He rest so peacefully, while they are in danger, and battling with death?

Their cry arouses Jesus. As the lightning's glare reveals Him, they see the peace of heaven in His face; they read in His glance self-forgetful, tender love, and, their hearts turning to Him, cry, "Lord, save us; we perish."

Never did a soul utter that cry unheeded. As the disciples grasp their oars to make a last effort, Jesus rises. He stands in the midst of His disciples, while the tempest rages, the waves break over them, and the lightning illuminates His countenance. He lifts His hand, so often employed in deeds of mercy, and says to the angry sea, "Peace, be still."

The storm ceases. The billows sink to rest. The clouds roll away, and the stars shine forth. The boat rests upon a quiet sea. Then turning to His disciples, Jesus asks sorrowfully, "Why are ye fearful? Have ye not yet faith?" Mark 4:40, R. V.

A hush fell upon the disciples. Even Peter did not attempt to express the awe that filled his heart. The boats that had set out to accompany Jesus had been in the same peril with that of the disciples. Terror and despair had seized their occupants; but the command of Jesus brought quiet to the scene of tumult. The fury of the storm had driven the boats into close proximity, and all on board beheld the miracle. In the calm that followed, fear was forgotten. The people whispered among themselves, "What manner of man is this, that even the wind and the sea obey Him?"

When Jesus was awakened to meet the storm, He was in perfect peace. There was no trace of fear in word or look, for no fear was in His heart. But He rested not in the possession of almighty power. It was not as the "Master of earth and sea and sky" that He reposed in quiet. That power He had laid down, and He says, "I can of Mine own self do nothing." John 5:30. He trusted in the Father's might. It was in faith — faith in God's love and care — that Jesus rested, and the power of that word which stilled the storm was the power of God.

As Jesus rested by faith in the Father's care, so we are to rest in the care of our Saviour. If the disciples had trusted in Him, they would have been kept in peace. Their fear in the time of danger revealed their unbelief. In their efforts to save themselves, they forgot Jesus; and it was only when, in despair of self-dependence, they turned to Him, that He could give them help.

How often the disciple's experience is ours! When the tempests of temptation gather, and the fierce lightnings flash, and the waves sweep over us, we battle with the storm alone, forgetting that there is One who can help us. We trust to our own strength till our hope is lost, and we are ready to perish. Then we remember Jesus, and if we call upon Him to save us, we shall not cry in vain. Though

He sorrowfully reproves our unbelief and self-confidence, He never fails to give us the help we need. Whether on the land or on the sea, if we have the Saviour in our hearts, there is no need of fear. Living faith in the Redeemer will smooth the sea of life, and will deliver us from danger in the way that He knows to be best.

There is another spiritual lesson in this miracle of the stilling of the tempest. Every man's experience testifies to the truth of the words of Scripture, "The wicked are like the troubled sea, when it cannot rest.... There is no peace, saith my God, to the wicked." Isaiah 57:20, 21. Sin has destroyed our peace. While self is unsubdued, we can find no rest. The masterful passions of the heart no human power can control. We are as helpless here as were the disciples to quiet the raging storm. But He who spoke peace to the billows of Galilee, has spoken the word of peace for every soul. However fierce the tempest, those who turn to Jesus with the cry, "Lord, save us," will find deliverance. His grace, that reconciles the soul to God, quiets the strife of human passion, and in His love the heart is at rest. "He maketh the storm a calm, so that the waves thereof are still. Then are they glad because they be quiet; so He bringeth them unto their desired haven." Psalms 107:29, 30. "Being justified by faith, we have peace with God through our Lord Jesus Christ," "The work of righteousness shall be peace, and the effect of righteousness quietness and assurance forever." Romans 5:1; Isaiah 32:17.

In the early morning the Saviour and His companions came to shore, and the light of the rising sun touched sea and land as with the benediction of peace. But no sooner had they stepped upon the beach than their eyes were greeted by a sight more terrible than the fury of the tempest. From some hiding place among the tombs, two madmen rushed upon them, as if to tear them in pieces. Hanging about these men were parts of chains which they had broken in escaping from confinement. Their flesh was torn and bleeding where they had cut themselves with sharp stones. Their eyes glared out from their long and matted hair, the very likeness of humanity seemed to have been blotted out by the demons that possessed them, and they looked more like wild beasts than like men.

The disciples and their companions fled in terror; but presently they noticed that Jesus was not with them, and they turned to look for Him. He was standing where they had left Him. He who had stilled the tempest, who had before met Satan and conquered him, did not flee before these demons. When the men, gnashing their teeth, and foaming at the mouth, approached Him, Jesus raised that hand which had beckoned the waves to rest, and the men could come no nearer. They stood raging but helpless before Him.

With authority He bade the unclean spirits come out of them. His words penetrated the darkened minds of the unfortunate men. They realized dimly that One was near who could save them from the tormenting demons. They fell at the Saviour's feet to worship him; but when their lips were opened to entreat His mercy, the demons spoke through them, crying vehemently, "What have I to do with Thee, Jesus, Thou Son of God most high? I beseech Thee, torment me not."

Jesus asked, "What is thy name?" And the answer was, "My name is Legion; for we are many." Using the afflicted men as mediums of communication, they besought Jesus not to send them out of the country. Upon a mountainside not far distant a great herd of swine was feeding. Into these

---

"However fierce the tempest, those who turn to Jesus with the cry, 'Lord, save us,' will find deliverance. His grace, . . . quiets the strife of human passion, and in His love the heart is at rest. 'He maketh the storm a calm, so that the waves thereof are still.'"

---

the demons asked to be allowed to enter, and Jesus suffered them. Immediately a panic seized the herd. They rushed madly down the cliff, and, unable to check themselves upon the shore, plunged into the lake, and perished.

Meanwhile a marvelous change had come over the demoniacs. Light had shone into their minds. Their eyes beamed with intelligence. The coutenances so long deformed into the image of Satan, became suddenly mild, the bloodstained hands were quiet, and with glad voices the men praised God for their deliverance.

From the cliff the keepers of the swine had seen all that had occurred, and they hurried away to publish the news to their employers and to all the people. In fear and amazement the whole population flocked to meet Jesus. The two demoniacs had been the terror of the country. No one had been safe to pass the place where they were; for they would rush upon every traveler with the fury of demons. Now these men were clothed and in their right mind, sitting at the feet of Jesus, listening to His words, and glorifying the name of Him who had made them whole. But the people who beheld this wonderful scene did not rejoice. The loss of the swine seemed to them of greater moment than the deliverance of these captives of Satan.

It was in mercy to the owners of the swine that this loss had been permitted to come upon them. They were absorbed in earthly things, and cared not for the great interests of spiritual life. Jesus desired to break the spell of selfish indifference, that they might accept His grace. But regret and indignation for their temporal loss blinded their eyes to the Saviour's mercy.

The manifestation of supernatural power aroused the superstitions of the people, and excited their fears. Further calamities might follow from having this stranger among them. They apprehended financial ruin, and determined to be freed from His presence. Those who had crossed the lake with Jesus told of all that had happened on the preceding night; of their peril in the tempest, and how the wind and the sea had been stilled. But their words were without effect. In terror the people thronged about Jesus, beseeching Him to depart from them, and He complied, taking ship at once for the opposite shore.

The people of Gergesa had before them the living evidence of Christ's power and mercy. They saw the men who had been restored to reason; but they were so fearful of endangering their earthly interests, that He who had vanquished the prince of darkness before their eyes, was treated as an intruder, and the Gift of heaven was turned from their doors. We have not the opportunity of turning from the person of Christ as had the Gergesenes; but still there are many who refuse to obey His word, because obedience would involve the sacrifice of some worldly interest. Lest His presence shall cause them pecuniary loss, many reject His grace, and drive His Spirit from them.

But far different was the feeling of the restored demoniacs. They desired the company of their deliverer. In His presence they felt secure from the demons that had tormented their lives and wasted their manhood. As Jesus was about to enter the boat, they kept close to His side, knelt at His feet, and begged Him to keep them near Him, where they might ever listen to His words. But Jesus bade them go home and tell what great things the Lord had done for them.

Here was a work for them to do,—to go to a heathen home, and tell of the blessing they had received from Jesus. It was hard for them to be separated from the Saviour. Great difficulties were sure to beset them in association with their heathen countrymen. And their long isolation from society seemed to have disqualified them for the work He had indicated. But as soon as Jesus pointed out their duty, they were ready to obey. Not only did they tell their own households and neighbors about Jesus, but they went throughout Decapolis, everywhere declaring His power to save, and describing how He had freed them from the demons. In doing this work, they could receive a greater blessing than if, merely for benefit to themselves, they had remained in His presence. It is in working to spread the good news of salvation that we are brought near to the Saviour.

The two restored demoniacs were the first missionaries whom Christ sent to preach the gospel in the region of Decapolis. For a few moments only, these men had been privileged to hear the teachings of Christ. Not one sermon from His lips had ever fallen upon their ears. They could not instruct the people as the disciples who had been daily with Christ were able to do. But they bore in their own persons the evidence that Jesus was the Messiah. They could tell what they knew; what they themselves had seen, and heard, and felt of the power of Christ. This is what every one can do whose heart has been touched by the grace of God. John, the beloved disciple, wrote: "That which was from the beginning, which we have heard, which we have seen with our eyes, which we have looked upon, and our hands have handled, of the Word of life; . . . that which we have seen and heard declare we unto you." 1 John 1:1-3. As witnesses for Christ, we are to tell what we know, what we ourselves have seen and heard and felt. If we have been following Jesus step by step, we shall have something right to the point to tell concerning the way in which He has led us. We can tell how we have tested His promise, and found the promise true. We can bear witness to what we have known of the grace of Christ. This is the witness for which our Lord calls, and for want of which the world is perishing.

Though the people of Gergesa had not received Jesus, He did not leave them to the darkness they had chosen. When they bade Him depart from them, they had not heard His words. They were ignorant of that which they were rejecting. Therefore He again sent the light to them, and by those to whom they would not refuse to listen.

In causing the destruction of the swine, it was Satan's purpose to turn the people away from the Saviour, and prevent the preaching of the gospel in that region. But this very occurrence roused the whole country as nothing else could have done, and directed attention to Christ. Though the Saviour Himself departed, the men whom He had healed, remained as witnesses to His power. Those who had been mediums of the prince of darkness, became channels of light, messengers of the Son of God. Men marveled as they listened to the wondrous news. A door was opened to the gospel throughout that region. When Jesus returned to Decapolis, the people flocked about Him, and for three days, not merely the inhabitants of one town, but thousands from all the surrounding region, heard the message of salvation. Even the power of demons is under the control of our Saviour, and the working of evil is overruled for good.

The encounter with the demoniacs of Gergesa had a lesson for the disciples. It showed the depths of degradation to which Satan is seeking to drag the whole human race, and the mission of Christ to set men free from his power. Those wretched beings, dwelling in the place of graves, possessed by demons, in bondage to uncontrolled passions and loathsome lusts, represent what humanity would become if given up to Satanic jurisdiction. Satan's influence is constantly exerted upon men to distract the senses, control the mind for evil, and incite to violence and crime. He weakens the body, darkens the intellect, and debases the soul. Whenever men reject the Saviour's invitation, they are yielding themselves to Satan. Multitudes in every department in life, in the home, in business, and even in the church, are doing this today. It is because of this that violence and crime have overspread the earth; and moral darkness, like the pall of death, enshrouds the habitations of men. Through his specious temptations, Satan leads men to worse and worse evils, till utter depravity and ruin are the result. The only safeguard against his power is found in the presence of Jesus. Before men and angels, Satan has been revealed as man's enemy and destroyer; Christ, as man's friend and deliverer. His Spirit will develop in man all that will ennoble the character and dignify the nature. It will build man up for the glory of God in body and soul and spirit. "For God hath not given us the spirit of fear; but of power, and of love, and of a sound mind." 2 Timothy 1:7. He has called us "to the obtaining of the glory" — character — "of our Lord Jesus Christ;" has called us to be "conformed to the image of His Son." 2 Thessalonians 2:14; Romans 8:29.

And souls that have been degraded into instruments of Satan, are still through the power of Christ transformed into messengers of righteousness, and sent forth by the Son of God to tell what "great things the Lord hath done for thee, and hath had compassion on thee."

The Touch of Faith

Returning from Gergesa to the western shore, Jesus found a multitude gathered to receive Him, and they greeted Him with joy. He remained by the seaside for a time, teaching and healing, and then repaired to the house of Levi-Matthew to meet the publicans at the feast. Here Jairus, the ruler of the synagogue, found Him.

This elder of the Jews came to Jesus in great distress, and cast himself at His feet exclaiming, "My little daughter lieth at the point of death; I pray Thee, come and lay Thy hands on her, that she may be healed; and she shall live."

Jesus set out at once with the ruler for his home. Though the disciples had seen so many of His works of mercy, they were surprised at His compliance with the entreaty of the haughty rabbi; yet they accompanied their Master, and the people followed, eager and expectant. The ruler's house was not far distant, but Jesus and His companions advanced slowly, for the crowd pressed Him on every side. The anxious father was impatient of delay; but Jesus pitying the people, stopped now and then to relieve some suffering one, or to comfort a troubled heart.

While they were still on the way, a messenger pressed through the crowd, bearing to Jairus the news that his daughter was dead, and it was useless to trouble the Master further. The word caught the ear of Jesus. "Fear not," He said; "believe only, and she shall be made whole."

Jairus pressed closer to the Saviour, and together they hurried to the ruler's home. Already the hired mourners and flute players were there, filling the air with their clamor. The presence of the crowd, and the tumult, jarred upon the spirit of Jesus. He tried to silence them, saying, "Why make ye this ado, and weep? the damsel is not dead, but sleepeth." They were indignant at the words of the stranger. They had seen the child in the embrace of death, and they laughed Him to scorn. Requiring them all to leave the house, Jesus took with Him the father and mother of the maiden, and the three disciples, Peter, James, and John, and together they entered the chamber of death.

Jesus approached the bedside, and taking the child's hand in His own, He pronounced softly, in the familiar language of her home, the words, "Damsel, I say unto thee, Arise."

Instantly a tremor passed through the unconscious form. The pulses of life beat again. The lips unclosed with a smile. The eyes opened widely as if from sleep, and the maiden gazed with wonder on the group beside her. She arose, and her parents clasped her in their arms, and wept for joy.

On the way to the ruler's house, Jesus had met, in a crowd, a poor woman who for twelve years had suffered from a disease that made her life a burden. She had spent all her means upon physicians and remedies, only to be pronounced incurable. But her hopes revived when she heard of the cures that Christ performed. She felt assured that if she could only go to Him, she would be healed. In weakness and suffering she came to the seaside where He was teaching, and tried to press through the crowd, but in vain. Again she followed Him from the house of Levi-Matthew, but was still unable to reach Him. She had begun to despair, when, in making His way through the multitude, He came near where she was.

The golden opportunity had come. She was in the presence of the great Physician! But amid the confusion she could not speak to Him, nor catch more than a passing glimpse of His figure. Fearful of losing her one chance of relief, she pressed forward, saying to herself, "If I may but touch His garment, I shall be whole." As He was passing,

This chapter is based on Matthew 9:18-26; Mark 5:21-43; Luke 8:40-56.

she reached forward, and succeeded in barely touching the border of His garment. But in that moment she knew that she was healed. In that one touch was concentrated the faith of her life, and instantly her pain and feebleness gave place to the vigor of perfect health.

With a grateful heart she then tried to withdraw from the crowd; but suddenly Jesus stopped, and the people halted with Him. He turned, and looking about asked in a voice distinctly heard above the confusion of the multitude, "Who touched Me?" The people answered this query with a look of amazement. Jostled upon all sides, and rudely pressed hither and thither, as He was, it seemed a strange inquiry.

Peter, ever ready to speak, said, "Master, the multitude throng Thee and press Thee, and sayest Thou, Who touched Me?" Jesus answered, "Somebody hath touched Me; for I perceive that virtue is gone out of Me." The Saviour could distinguish the touch of faith from the casual contact of the careless throng. Such trust should not be passed without comment. He would speak to the humble woman words of comfort that would be to her a well-spring of joy,—words that would be a blessing to His followers to the close of time.

Looking toward the woman, Jesus insisted on knowing who had touched Him. Finding concealment vain, she came forward tremblingly, and cast herself at His feet. With grateful tears she told the story of her suffering, and how she had found relief. Jesus gently said, "Daughter, be of good comfort; thy faith hath made thee whole; go in peace." He gave no opportunity for superstition to claim healing virtue for the mere act of touching His garments. It was not through the outward contact with Him, but through the faith which took hold on His divine power, that the cure was wrought.

The wondering crowd that pressed close about Christ realized no accession of vital power. But when the suffering woman put forth her hand to touch Him, believing that she would be made whole, she felt the healing virtue. So in spiritual things. To talk of religion in a casual way, to pray without soul hunger and living faith, avails nothing. A nominal faith in Christ, which accepts Him merely as the Saviour of the world, can never bring healing to the soul. The faith that is unto salvation is not a mere intellectual assent to the truth. He who waits for entire knowledge before he will exercise faith, cannot receive blessing from God. It is not enough to believe *about* Christ; we must believe *in* Him. The only faith that will benefit us is that which embraces Him as a personal Saviour; which appropriates His merits to ourselves. Many hold faith as an opinion. Saving faith is a transaction, by which those who receive Christ join themselves in covenant relation with God. Genuine faith is life. A living faith means an increase of vigor, a confiding trust, by which the soul becomes a conquering power.

After healing the woman, Jesus desired her to acknowledge the blessing she had received. The gifts which the gospel offers, are not to be secured by stealth or enjoyed in secret. So the Lord calls upon us for confession of His goodness. "Ye are My witnesses, saith the Lord, that I am God." Isaiah 43:12.

Our confession of His faithfulness is Heaven's chosen agency for revealing Christ to the world. We are to acknowledge His grace as made known through the holy men of old; but that which will be most effectual is the testimony of our own experience. We are witnesses for God as we reveal in ourselves the working of a power that

"As He was passing, she reached forward, and succeeded in barely touching the border of His garment. But in that moment she knew that she was healed. In that one touch was concentrated the faith of her life, and instantly her pain and feebleness gave place to the vigor of perfect health."

is divine. Every individual has a life distinct from all others, and an experience differing essentially from theirs. God desires that our praise shall ascend to Him, marked by our own individuality. These precious acknowledgments to the praise of the glory of His grace, when supported by a Christlike life, have an irresistible power, that works for the salvation of souls.

When the ten lepers came to Jesus for healing, He bade them go and show themselves to the priest. On the way they were cleansed, but only one of them returned to give Him glory. The others went their way, forgetting Him who had made them whole. How many are still doing the same thing. The Lord works continually to benefit mankind. He is ever imparting His bounties. He raises up the sick from beds of languishing, He delivers men from peril which they do not see, He commissions heavenly angels to save them from calamity, to guard them from "the pestilence that walketh in darkness," and "the destruction that wasteth at noonday;" (Psalms 91:6.) but their hearts are unimpressed. He has given all the riches of heaven to redeem them, and yet they are unmindful of His great love.

By their ingratitude they close their hearts against the grace of God. Like the heath in the desert, they know not when good cometh, and their souls inhabit the parched places of the wilderness.

It is for our own benefit to keep every gift of God fresh in our memory. Thus faith is strengthened to claim and to receive more and more. There is greater encouragement for us in the least blessing we ourselves receive from God than in all the accounts we can read of the faith and experience of others. The soul that responds to the grace of God shall be like a watered garden. His health shall spring forth speedily; his light shall rise in obscurity, and the glory of the Lord shall be seen upon him. Let us then remember the loving-kindness of the Lord, and the multitude of His tender mercies. Like the people of Israel, let us set up our stones of witness, and inscribe upon them the precious story of what God has wrought for us. And as we review His dealings with us in our pilgrimage, let us, out of hearts melted with gratitude, declare, "What shall I render unto the Lord for all His benefits toward me? I will take the cup of salvation, and call upon the name of the Lord. I will pay my vows unto the Lord now in the presence of all His people." Psalms 116:12-14.

Let not your heart be troubled: ye believe in God, believe also in me. In my Father's house are many mansions: if it were not so, I would have told you. I go to prepare a place for you. And if I go and prepare a place for you, I will come again, and receive you unto myself; that where I am, there ye may be also.

John 14:1-3

For God so loved the world, that He gave His only begotten Son, that whosoever believeth in Him should not perish, but have everlasting life. For God sent not His Son into the world to condemn the world; but that the world through Him might be saved.

John 3:16, 17

Therefore being justified by faith, we have peace with God through our Lord Jesus Christ. By whom also we have access by faith into this grace wherein we stand, and rejoice in hope of the glory of God.

Romans 5:1, 2

If thou canst believe, all things are possible to him that believeth.

Mark 9:23

The First Evangelists

The apostles were members of the family of Jesus, and they had accompanied Him as He traveled on foot through Galilee. They had shared with Him the toils and hardships that overtook them. They had listened to His discourses, they had walked and talked with the Son of God, and from His daily instruction they had learned how to work for the elevation of humanity. As Jesus ministered to the vast multitudes that gathered about Him, His disciples were in attendance, eager to do His bidding and to lighten His labor. They assisted in arranging the people, bringing the afflicted ones to the Saviour, and promoting the comfort of all. They watched for interested hearers, explained the Scriptures to them, and in various ways worked for their spiritual benefit. They taught what they had learned of Jesus, and were every day obtaining a rich experience. But they needed also an experience in laboring alone. They were still in need of much instruction, great patience and tenderness. Now, while He was personally with them, to point out their errors, and counsel and correct them, the Saviour sent them forth as His representatives.

While they had been with Him, the disciples had often been perplexed by the teaching of the priests and Pharisees, but they had brought their perplexities to Jesus. He had set before them the truths of Scripture in contrast with tradition. Thus He had strengthened their confidence in God's word, and in a great measure had set them free from their fear of the rabbis, and their bondage to tradition. In the training of the disciples the example of the Saviour's life was far more effective than any mere doctrinal instruction. When they were separated from Him, every look and tone and word came back to them. Often when in conflict with the enemies of the gospel, they repeated His words, and as they saw their effect upon the people, they rejoiced greatly.

Calling the twelve about Him, Jesus bade them go out two and two through the towns and villages. None were sent forth alone, but brother was associated with brother, friend with friend. Thus they could help and encourage each other, counseling and praying together, each one's strength supplementing the other's weakness. In the same manner He afterward sent forth the seventy. It was the Saviour's purpose that the messengers of the gospel should be associated in this way. In our own time evangelistic work would be far more successful if this example were more closely followed.

The disciples' message was the same as that of John the Baptist and of Christ Himself: "The kingdom of heaven is at hand." They were to enter into no controversy with the people as to whether Jesus of Nazareth was the Messiah; but in His name they were to do the same works of mercy as He had done. He bade them, "Heal the sick, cleanse the lepers, raise the dead, cast out devils; freely ye have received, freely give."

During His ministry, Jesus devoted more time to healing the sick than to preaching. His miracles testified to the truth of His words, that He came not to destroy, but to save. His righteousness went before Him, and the glory of the Lord was His rereward. Wherever He went, the tidings of His mercy preceded Him. Where He had passed, the objects of His compassion were rejoicing in health, and making trial of their new-found powers. Crowds were collecting around them to hear from their lips the works that the Lord had wrought. His voice was the first sound that many had ever heard, His name the first word they had ever spoken, His face the first they had ever looked upon.

This chapter is based on Matthew 10; Mark 6:7-11; Luke 9:1-6.

Why should they not love Jesus, and sound His praise? As He passed through the towns and cities, He was like a vital current, diffusing life and joy wherever He went.

The followers of Christ are to labor as He did. We are to feed the hungry, clothe the naked, and comfort the suffering and afflicted. We are to minister to the despairing, and inspire hope in the hopeless. And to us also the promise will be fulfilled, "Thy righteousness shall go before thee; the glory of the Lord shall be thy rereward." Isaiah 58:8. The love of Christ, manifested in unselfish ministry, will be more effective in reforming the evildoer than will the sword or the court of justice. These are necessary to strike terror to the lawbreaker, but the loving missionary can do more than this. Often the heart will harden under reproof; but it will melt under the love of Christ. The missionary can not only relieve physical maladies, but he can lead the sinner to the great Physician, who can cleanse the soul from the leprosy of sin. Through His servants, God designs that the sick, the unfortunate, those possessed of evil spirits, shall hear His voice. Through His human agencies He desires to be a Comforter such as the world knows not.

The disciples on their first missionary tour were to go only to "the lost sheep of the house of Israel." If they had now preached the gospel to the Gentiles or the Samaritans, they would have lost their influence with the Jews. By exciting the prejudice of the Pharisees they would have involved themselves in controversy which would have discouraged them at the outset of their labors. Even the apostles were slow to understand that the gospel was to be carried to all nations. Until they themselves could grasp this truth, they were not prepared to labor for the Gentiles. If the Jews would receive the gospel, God purposed to make them His messengers to the Gentiles. Therefore they were first to hear the message.

All over the field of Christ's labor there were souls awakened to their need, and hungering and thirsting for the truth. The time had come to send the tidings of His love to these longing hearts. To all these the disciples were to go as His representatives. The believers would thus be led to look upon them as divinely appointed teachers, and when the Saviour should be taken from them, they would not be left without instructors.

On this first tour the disciples were to go only where Jesus had been before them, and had made friends. Their preparation for the journey was to be of the simplest kind. Nothing must be allowed to divert their minds from their great work, or in any way excite opposition and close the door for further labor. They were not to adopt the dress of the religious teachers, nor use any guise in apparel to distinguish them from the humble peasants. They were not to enter into the synagogues and call the people together for public service; their efforts were to be put forth in house-to-house labor. They were not to waste time in needless salutations, or in going from house to house for entertainment. But in every place they were to accept the hospitality of those who were worthy, those who would welcome them heartily as if entertaining Christ Himself. They were to enter the dwelling with the beautiful salutation, "Peace be to this house." Luke 10:5. That home would be blessed by their prayers, their songs of praise, and the opening of the Scriptures in the family circle.

These disciples were to be heralds of the truth, to prepare the way for the coming of their Master. The message they

---

"It is Satan's work to fill men's hearts with doubt. . . . He tempts them to sin . . . The Lord understands all this. Jesus assures His disciples of God's sympathy for them in their needs and weaknesses. Not a sigh is breathed, not a pain felt, not a grief pierces the soul, but the throb vibrates to the Father's heart."

---

had to bear was the word of eternal life, and the destiny of men depended upon their reception or rejection of it. To impress the people with its solemnity, Jesus bade His disciples, "Whosoever shall not receive you, nor hear your words, when ye depart out of that house or city, shake off the dust of your feet. Verily I say unto you, It shall be more tolerable for the land of Sodom and Gomorrah in the day of Judgment, than for that city."

Now the Saviour's eye penetrates the future; He beholds the broader fields in which, after His death, the disciples are to be witnesses for Him. His prophetic glance takes in the experience of His servants through all the ages till He shall come the second time. He shows His followers the conflicts they must meet; He reveals the character and plan of the battle. He lays open before them the perils they must encounter, the self-denial that will be required. He desires them to count the cost, that they may not be taken unawares by the enemy. Their warfare is not to be waged against flesh and blood, but "against the principalities, against the powers, against the world rulers of this darkness, against the spiritual hosts of wickedness in the heavenly places." Ephesians 6:12, R. V. They are to contend with supernatural forces, but they are assured of supernatural help. All the intelligences of heaven are in this army. And more than angels are in the ranks. The Holy Spirit, the representative of the Captain of the Lord's host, comes down to direct the battle. Our infirmities may be many, our sins and mistakes grievous; but the grace of God is for all who seek it with contrition. The power of Omnipotence is enlisted in behalf of those who trust in God.

"Behold," said Jesus, "I send you forth as sheep in the midst of wolves; be ye therefore wise as serpents, and harmless as doves." Christ Himself did not suppress one word of truth, but He spoke it always in love. He exercised the greatest tact, and thoughtful, kind attention in His intercourse with the people. He was never rude, never needlessly spoke a severe word, never gave needless pain to a sensitive soul. He did not censure human weakness. He fearlessly denounced hypocrisy, unbelief, and iniquity, but tears were in His voice as He uttered His scathing rebukes. He wept over Jerusalem, the city He loved, that refused to receive Him, the Way, the Truth, and the Life. They rejected Him, the Saviour, but He regarded them with pitying tenderness, and sorrow so deep that it broke His heart. Every soul was precious in His eyes. While He always bore Himself with divine dignity, He bowed with tenderest regard to every member of the family of God. In all men He saw fallen souls whom it was His mission to save.

The servants of Christ are not to act out the dictates of the natural heart. They need to have close communion with God, lest, under provocation, self rise up, and they pour forth a torrent of words that are unbefitting, that are not as dew, or the still showers that refresh the withering plants. This is what Satan wants them to do; for these are his methods. It is the dragon that is wroth; it is the spirit of Satan that is revealed in anger and accusing. But God's servants are to be representatives of Him. He desires them to deal only in the currency of heaven, the truth that bears His own image and superscription. The power by which they are to overcome evil is the power of Christ. The glory of Christ is their strength. They are to fix their eyes upon His loveliness. Then they can present the gospel with divine tact and gentleness. And the spirit that is kept gentle under provocation will speak more effectively in favor of the truth than will any argument, however forcible.

Those who are brought in controversy with the enemies of truth have to meet, not only men, but Satan and his agents. Let them remember the Saviour's words, "Behold, I send you forth as lambs among wolves." Luke 10:3. Let them rest in the love of God, and the spirit will be kept calm, even under personal abuse. The Lord will clothe them with a divine panoply. His Holy Spirit will influence the mind and heart, so that their voices shall not catch the notes of the baying of the wolves.

Continuing His instruction to His disciples, Jesus said, "Beware of men." They were not to put implicit confidence in those who knew not God, and open to them their counsels; for this would give Satan's agents an advantage. Man's inventions often counterwork God's plans. Those who build the temple of the Lord, are to build according to the pattern shown in the mount, — the divine similitude. God is dishonored and the gospel is betrayed when His servants depend on the counsel of men who are not under the guidance of the Holy Spirit. Worldly wisdom is foolishness with God. Those who rely upon it, will surely err.

"They will deliver you up to councils, ... yea, and before governors and kings shall ye be brought for My sake, for a testimony to them and to the Gentiles." Matthew 10:17, 18, R. V. Persecution will spread the light. The servants of Christ will be brought before the great men of the world, who, but for this, might never hear the gospel. The truth has been misrepresented to these men. They have listened to false charges concerning the faith of Christ's disciples. Often their only means of learning its real character is the testimony of those who are brought to trial for their faith. Under examination these are required to answer, and their judges to listen to the testimony borne. God's grace will be dispensed to His servants to meet the emergency. "It shall be given you," says Jesus, "in the same hour what ye shall speak. For it is not ye that speak, but the Spirit of your Father which speaketh in you." As the Spirit of God illuminates the minds of His servants, the truth will be presented in its divine power and preciousness. Those who reject the truth will stand to accuse and oppress the disciples. But under loss and suffering, even unto death, the Lord's children are to reveal the meekness of their divine Example. Thus will be seen the contrast between Satan's agents and the representatives of Christ. The Saviour will be lifted up before the rulers and the people.

The disciples were not endowed with the courage and fortitude of the martyrs until such grace was needed. Then the Saviour's promise was fulfilled. When Peter and John testified before the Sanhedrim council, men "marveled; and they took knowledge of them, that they had been with Jesus." Acts 4:13. Of Stephen it is written that "all that sat in the council, looking steadfastly on him, saw his face as it had been the face of an angel." Men "were not able to resist the wisdom and the spirit by which he spake." Acts 6:15, 10. And Paul, writing of his own trial at the court of the Caesars, says, "At my first defense no one took my part, but all forsook me. . . . But the Lord stood by me, and strengthened me; that through me the message might be fully proclaimed, and that all the Gentiles might hear; and I was delivered out of the mouth of the lion." 2 Timothy 4:16, 17, R. V.

The servants of Christ were to prepare no set speech to present when brought to trial. Their preparation was to be made day by day in treasuring up the precious truths of God's word, and through prayer strengthening their faith. When they were brought into trial, the Holy Spirit would bring to their remembrance the very truths that would be needed.

A daily, earnest striving to know God, and Jesus Christ whom He has sent, would bring power and efficiency to the soul. The knowledge obtained by diligent searching of the Scriptures, would be flashed into the memory at the right time. But if any had neglected to acquaint themselves with the words of Christ, if they had never tested the power of His grace in trial, they could not expect that the Holy

> "Christ Himself did not suppress one word of truth, but He spoke it always in love. . . . He was never rude . . . never gave needless pain to a sensitive soul. . . . He fearlessly denounced hypocrisy . . . but tears were in His voice as He uttered His scathing rebukes. . . . They rejected Him, but He regarded them with pitying tenderness, and sorrow so deep that it broke His heart. Every soul was precious in His eyes."

Spirit would bring His words to their remembrance. They were to serve God daily with undivided affection, and then trust Him.

So bitter would be the enmity to the gospel that even the tenderest earthly ties would be disregarded. The disciples of Christ would be betrayed to death by the members of their own households. "Ye shall be hated of all men for My name's sake," He added; "but he that shall endure unto the end, shall be saved." Mark 13:13. But He bade them not to expose themselves unnecessarily to persecution. He Himself often left one field of labor for another, in order to escape from those who were seeking His life. When He

was rejected at Nazareth, and His own townsmen tried to kill Him, He went down to Capernaum, and there the people were astonished at His teaching "for His word was with power." Luke 4:32. So His servants were not to be discouraged by persecution, but to seek a place where they could still labor for the salvation of souls.

The servant is not above his master. The Prince of heaven was called Beelzebub, and His disciples will be misrepresented in like manner. But whatever the danger, Christ's followers must avow their principles. They should scorn concealment. They cannot remain uncommitted until assured of safety in confessing the truth. They are set as watchmen, to warn men of their peril. The truth received from Christ must be imparted to all, freely and openly. Jesus said, "What I tell you in darkness, that speak ye in light; and what ye hear in the ear, that preach ye upon the housetops."

Jesus Himself never purchased peace by compromise. His heart overflowed with love for the whole human race, but He was never indulgent to their sins. He was too much their friend to remain silent while they were pursuing a course that would ruin their souls,—the souls He had purchased with His own blood. He labored that man should be true to himself, true to his higher and eternal interest. The servants of Christ are called to the same work, and they should beware lest, in seeking to prevent discord, they surrender the truth. They are to "follow after the things which make for peace" (Romans 14:19); but real peace can never be secured by compromising principle. And no man can be true to principle without exciting opposition. A Christianity that is spiritual will be opposed by the children of disobedience. But Jesus bade His disciples, "Fear not them which kill the body, but are not able to kill the soul." Those who are true to God need not fear the power of men nor the enmity of Satan. In Christ their eternal life is secure. Their only fear should be, lest they surrender the truth, and thus betray the trust with which God has honored them.

It is Satan's work to fill men's hearts with doubt. He leads them to look upon God as a stern judge. He tempts them to sin, and then to regard themselves as too vile to approach their Heavenly Father or to excite His pity. The Lord understands all this. Jesus assures His disciples of God's sympathy for them in their needs and weaknesses. Not a sigh is breathed, not a pain felt, not a grief pierces the soul, but the throb vibrates to the Father's heart.

The Bible shows us God in His high and holy place, not in a state of inactivity, not in silence and solitude, but surrounded by ten thousand times ten thousand and thousands of thousands of holy intelligences, all waiting to do His will. Through channels which we cannot discern, He is in active communication with every part of His dominion. But it is in this speck of a world, in the souls that He gave His only begotten Son to save, that His interest and the interest of all heaven is centered. God is bending from His throne to hear the cry of the oppressed. To every sincere prayer He answers, "Here am I." He uplifts the distressed and downtrodden. In all our afflictions He is afflicted. In every temptation and every trial the angel of His presence is near to deliver.

Not even a sparrow falls to the ground without the Father's notice. Satan's hatred against God leads him to hate every object of the Saviour's care. He seeks to mar the handiwork of God, and he delights in destroying even the dumb creatures. It is only through God's protecting care that the birds are preserved to gladden us with their songs of joy. But he does not forget even the sparrows. "Fear ye not therefore, ye are of more value than many sparrows."

Jesus continues: As you confess Me before men, so I will confess you before God and the holy angels. You are to be My witnesses upon earth, channels through which My grace can flow for the healing of the world. So I will be your representative in heaven. The Father beholds not your faulty character, but He sees you as clothed in My perfection. I am the medium through which Heaven's blessings shall come to you. And every one who confesses Me by sharing My sacrifice for the lost, shall be confessed as a sharer in the glory and joy of the redeemed.

He who would confess Christ, must have Christ abiding him. He cannot communicate that which he has not received. The disciples might speak fluently on doctrines, they might repeat the words of Christ Himself; but unless they possessed Christlike meekness and love, they were not confessing Him. A spirit contrary to the spirit of Christ would deny Him, whatever the profession. Men may deny Christ by evil-speaking, by foolish talking, by words that are untruthful or unkind. They may deny Him by shunning life's burdens, by the pursuit of sinful pleasure. They may deny Him by conforming to the world, by uncourteous behaviour, by the love of their own opinions, by justifying self, by cherishing doubt, borrowing trouble, and dwelling in dakrness. In all these ways they declare that Christ is not in them. And "whosoever shall deny Me before men," He says, "him will I also deny before My Father which is in heaven."

The Saviour bade His disciples not to hope that the world's enmity to the gospel would be overcome, and that after a time its opposition would cease. He said, "I came not to send peace, but a sword." This creating of strife is not the effect of the gospel, but the result of opposition to it. Of all persecution the hardest to bear is variance in the home, the estrangement of dearest earthly friends. But Jesus declares, "He that loveth father or mother more than Me is not worthy of Me; and he that loveth son or daughter more than Me is not worthy of Me. And he that taketh not his cross, and followeth after Me, is not worthy of Me."

The mission of Christ's servants is a high honor, and a sacred trust. "He that receiveth you," He says, "receiveth Me, and he that receiveth Me receiveth Him that sent Me." No act of kindness shown to them in His name will fail to be recognized and rewarded. And in the same tender recognition He includes the feeblest and lowliest of the family of God: "Whosoever shall give to drink unto one of these little ones" — those who are as children in their faith and their knowledge of Christ — "a cup of cold water only in the name of a disciple, verily I say unto you, he shall in no wise lose his reward."

Thus the Saviour ended His instruction. In the name of Christ the chosen twelve went out, as He had gone, "to preach the gospel to the poor, . . . to heal the broken-hearted, to preach deliverance to the captives, and recovering of sight to the blind, to set at liberty them that are bruised, to preach the acceptable year of the Lord." Luke 4:18, 19.

Come Rest Awhile

On returning from their missionary tour, "the apostles gathered themselves together unto Jesus, and told Him all things, both what they had done, and what they had taught. And He said unto them, Come ye yourselves apart into a desert place, and rest awhile: for there were many coming and going, and they had no leisure so much as to eat."

The disciples came to Jesus and told Him all things. Their intimate relationship with Him encouraged them to lay before Him their favorable and unfavorable experiences, their joy at seeing results from their labors, and their sorrow at their failures, their faults, and their weaknesses. They had committed errors in their first work as evangelists, and as they frankly told Christ of their experiences, He saw that they needed much instruction. He saw, that they had become weary in their labors, and that they needed to rest.

But where they then were, they could not obtain the needed privacy; "for there were many coming and going, and they had no leisure so much as to eat." The people were thronging after Christ, anxious to be healed, and eager to listen to His words. Many felt drawn to Him; for He seemed to them to be the fountain of all blessings. Many of those who then thronged about Chirst to receive the precious boon of health, accepted Him as their Saviour. Many others, afraid then to confess Him, because of the Pharisees, were converted at the descent of the Holy Spirit, and, before the angry priests and rulers, acknowledged Him as the Son of God.

But now Christ longed for retirement, that He might be with His disciples; for He had much to say to them. In their work they had passed through the test of conflict, and had encountered opposition in various forms. Hitherto they had consulted Christ in everything; but for some time they had been alone, and at times they had been much troubled to know what to do. They had found much encouragement in their work; for Chirst did not send them away without His Spirit, and by faith in Him they worked many miracles; but they needed now to feed on the Bread of Life. They needed to go to a place of retirement, where they could hold communion with Jesus, and receive instruction for future work.

"And He said unto them, Come ye yourselves apart into a desert place, and rest awhile." Christ is full of tenderness and compassion for all in His service. He would show His disciples that God does not require sacrifice, but mercy. They had been putting their whole souls into labor for the people, and this was exhausting their physical and mental strength. It was their duty to rest.

As the disciples had seen the success of their labors, they were in danger of taking credit to themselves, in danger of cherishing spiritual pride, and thus falling under Satan's temptations. A great work was before them, and first of all they must learn that their strength was not in self, but in God. Like Moses in the wilderness of Sinai, like David among the hills of Judea, or Elijah by the brook Cherith, the disciples needed to come apart from the scenes of their busy activity, to commune with Christ, with nature, and with their own hearts.

While the disciples had been absent on their missionary tour, Jesus had visited other towns and villages, preaching the gospel of the kingdom. It was about this time that He received tidings of the Baptist's death. This event brought vividly before Him the end to which His own steps were tending. The shadows were gathering thickly about His path. Priests and rabbis were watching to compass His

death, spies hung upon His steps, and on every hand plots for His ruin were multiplying. News of the preaching of the apostles throughout Galilee reached Herod, calling his attention to Jesus and His work. "This is John the Baptist," he said; "he is risen from the dead;" and he expressed a desire to see Jesus. Herod was in constant fear lest a revolution might be secretly carried forward, with the object of unseating him from the throne, and breaking the Roman yoke from the Jewish nation. Among the people the spirit of discontent and insurrection was rife. It was evident that Christ's public labors in Galilee could not be long continued. The scenes of His suffering were drawing near, and He longed to be apart for a season from the confusion of the multitude.

With saddened hearts the disciples of John had borne his mutilated body to its burial. Then they "went and told Jesus." These disciples had been envious of Christ when He seemed to be drawing the people away from John. They had sided with the Pharisees in accusing Him when He sat with the publicans at Matthew's feast. They had doubted His divine mission because He did not set the Baptist at liberty. But now that their teacher was dead, and they longed for consolation in their great sorrow, and for guidance as to their future work, they came to Jesus, and united their interest with His. They too needed a season of quiet for communion with the Saviour.

Near Bethsaida, at the northern end of the lake, was a lonely region, now beautiful with the fresh green of spring, that offered a welcome retreat to Jesus and His disciples. For this place they set out, going in their boat across the water. Here they would be away from the thoroughfares of travel, and the bustle and agitation of the city. The scenes of nature were in themselves a rest, a change grateful to the senses. Here they could listen to the words of Christ without hearing the angry interruptions, the retorts and accusations of the scribes and Pharisees. Here they could enjoy a short season of precious fellowship in the society of their Lord.

The rest which Christ and His disciples took was not self-indulgent rest. The time they spent in retirement was not devoted to pleasure seeking. They talked together regarding the work of God, and the possibility of bringing greater efficiency to the work. The disciples had been with Christ, and could understand Him; to them He need not talk in parables. He corrected their errors, and made plain to them the right way of approaching the people. He opened more fully to them the precious treasures of divine truth. They were vitalized by divine power, and inspired with hope and courage.

Though Jesus could work miracles, and had empowered His disciples to work miracles, He directed His worn servants to go apart into the country and rest. When He said that the harvest was great, and the laborers were few, He did not urge upon His disciples the necessity of ceaseless toil, but said, "Pray ye therefore the Lord of the harvest, that He will send forth laborers into His harvest."

Matthew 9:38. God has appointed to every man his work, according to his ability, (Ephesians 4:11-13.) and He would not have a few weighted with responsibilities, while others have no burden, no travail of soul.

Christ's words of compassion are spoken to His workers today just as surely as they were spoken to His disciples. "Come ye yourselves apart, . . . and rest awhile," He says to those who are worn and weary. It is not wise to be always under the strain of work and excitement, even in ministering to men's spiritual needs; for in this way personal piety is neglected, and the powers of mind and soul and body are overtaxed. Self-denial is required of the disciples of Christ, and sacrifices must be made; but care must also be exercised lest through their overzeal Satan take advantage of the weakness of humanity, and the work of God be marred.

In the estimation of the rabbis, it was the sum of religion to be always in a bustle of activity. They depended upon some outward performance to show their superior piety. Thus they separated their souls from God, and built themselves up in self-sufficiency. The same dangers still exist. As activity increases, and men become successful in doing any work for God, there is danger of trusting to human plans and methods. There is a tendency to pray less, and to have less faith. Like the disciples, we are in danger of losing sight of our dependence on God, and seeking to make a saviour of our activity. We need to look constantly to Jesus, realizing that it is His power which does the work. While we are to labor earnestly for the salvation of the lost, we must also take time for meditation, for prayer, and for the study of the word of God. Only the work accomplished with much prayer, and sanctified by the merit of Christ, will in the end prove to have been efficient for good.

No other life was ever so crowded with labor and responsibility as was that of Jesus; yet how often He was found in prayer. How constant was His communion with God. Again and again in the history of His earthly life are found records such as these: "Rising up a great while before day, He went out, and departed into a solitary place, and there prayed." "Great multitudes came together to hear, and to be healed by Him of their infirmities. And He withdrew Himself into the wilderness, and prayed." "And it came to pass in those days that He went out into a mountain to pray, and continued all night in prayer to God." Mark 1:35; Luke 5:15, 16; 6:12.

In a life wholly devoted to the good of others, the Saviour found it necessary to withdraw from the thoroughfares of travel and from the throng that followed Him day after day. He must turn aside from a life of ceaseless activity and contact with human needs, to seek retirement and unbroken communion with His Father. As one with us, a sharer in our needs and weaknesses, He was wholly dependent upon God, and in the secret place of prayer He sought divine strength, that He might go forth braced for duty and trial. In a world of sin, Jesus endured struggles and torture of soul. In communion with God He could unburden the sorrows that were crushing Him. Here He found comfort and joy.

In Christ the cry of humanity reached the Father of infinite pity. As a man He supplicated the throne of God, till His humanity was charged with a heavenly current that should connect humanity with divinity. Through continual communion He received life from God, that He might impart life to the world. His experience is to be ours.

"Come ye yourselves apart," He bids us. If we would give heed to His word, we should be stronger and more useful. The disciples sought Jesus, and told Him all things; and He encouraged and instructed them. If today we would take time to go to Jesus and tell Him our needs, we should not be disappointed; He would be at our right hand to help us. We need more simplicity, more trust and confidence in our Saviour. He whose name is called "the mighty God, the everlasting Father, the Prince of Peace;" He of whom it is written, "The government shall be upon His shoulder," is the Wonderful Counselor. We are invited to ask wisdom of Him. He "giveth to all men liberally, and upbraideth not," Isaiah 9:6; James 1:5.

In all who are under the training of God is to be revealed a life that is not in harmony with the world, its customs or its practices; and every one needs to have a personal experience in obtaining a knowledge of the will of God. We must individually hear Him speaking to the heart. When every other voice is hushed, and in quietness we wait before Him, the silence of the soul makes more distinct the voice of God. He bids us, "Be still, and know that I am God." Psalms 46:10. Here alone can true rest be found. And this is the effectual preparation for all labor for God. Amid the hurrying throng, and the strain of life's intense activities, the soul that is thus refreshed will be surrounded with an atmosphere of light and peace. The life will breathe out fragrance, and will reveal a divine power that will reach men's hearts.

"Give Ye Them to Eat"

Christ had retired to a secluded place with His disciples, but this rare season of peaceful quietude was soon broken. The disciples thought they had retired where they would not be disturbed; but as soon as the multitude missed the divine Teacher, they inquired, "Where is He?" Some among them had noticed the direction in which Christ and His disciples had gone. Many went by land to meet them, while others followed in their boats across the water. The Passover was at hand, and, from far and near, bands of pilgrims on their way to Jerusalem gathered to see Jesus. Additions were made to their number, until there were assembled five thousand men, besides women and children. Before Christ reached the shore, a multitude were waiting for Him. But He landed unobserved by them, and spent a little time apart with the disciples.

From the hillside He looked upon the moving multitude, and His heart was stirred with sympathy. Interrupted as He was, and robbed of His rest, He was not impatient. He saw a greater necessity demanding His attention as He watched the people coming and still coming. He was "moved with compassion toward them, because they were as sheep not having a shepherd." Leaving His retreat, He found a convenient place where He could minister to them. They received no help from the priests and rulers; but the healing waters of life flowed from Christ as He taught the multitude the way of salvation.

The people listened to the words of mercy flowing so freely from the lips of the Son of God. They heard the gracious words, so simple and so plain that they were as the balm of Gilead to their souls. The healing of His divine hand brought gladness and life to the dying, and ease and health to those suffering with disease. The day seemed to them like heaven upon earth, and they were utterly unconscious of how long it had been since they had eaten anything.

At length the day was far spent. The sun was sinking in the west, and yet the people lingered. Jesus had labored all day without food or rest. He was pale from weariness and hunger, and the disciples besought Him to cease from His toil. But He could not withdraw Himself from the multitude that pressed upon Him.

The disciples finally came to Him, urging that for their own sake the people should be sent away. Many had come from far, and had eaten nothing since morning. In the surrounding towns and villages they might be able to buy food. But Jesus said, "Give ye them to eat," and then, turning to Philip, questioned, "Whence shall we buy bread, that these may eat?" This He said to test the faith of the disciple. Philip looked over the sea of heads, and thought how impossible it would be to provide food to satisfy the wants of such a crowd. He answered that two hundred pennyworth of bread would not be nearly enough to divide among them, so that each might have a little. Jesus inquired how much food could be found among the company. "There is a lad here," said Andrew, "which hath five barley loaves, and two small fishes; but what are they among so many?" Jesus directed that these be brought to Him. Then He bade the disciples seat the people on the grass in parties of fifty or a hundred, to preserve order, and that all might witness what He was about to do. When this was accomplished, Jesus took the food, "and looking up to heaven, He blessed, and brake, and gave the loaves to His disciples, and the disciples to the multitude." "And they did all eat, and were filled. And they took up twelve baskets full of the fragments, and of the fishes."

He who taught the people the way to secure peace and happiness was just as thoughtful of their temporal necessities as of their spiritual need. The people were weary and faint. There were mothers with babes in their arms, and little children clinging to their skirts. Many had been standing for hours. They had been so intensely interested in Christ's words, that they had not once thought of sitting down, and the crowd was so great that there was danger of their trampling on one another. Jesus would give them a chance to rest, and He bade them sit down. There was much grass in the place, and all could rest in comfort.

Christ never worked a miracle except to supply a genuine necessity, and every miracle was of a character to lead the people to the tree of life, whose leaves are for the healing of the nations. The simple food passed round by the hands of the disciples contained a whole treasure of lessons. It was humble fare that had been provided; the fishes and barley loaves were the daily food of the fisher folk about the Sea of Galilee. Christ could have spread before the people a rich repast, but food prepared merely for the gratification of appetite would have conveyed no lesson for their good. Christ taught them in this lesson that the natural provisions of God for man had been perverted. And never did people enjoy the luxurious feasts prepared for the gratification of perverted taste as this people enjoyed the rest and the simple food which Christ provided so far from human habitations.

If men today were simple in their habits, living in harmony with nature's laws, as did Adam and Eve in the beginning, there would be an abundant supply for the needs of the human family. There would be fewer imaginary wants, and more opportunities to work in God's ways. But selfishness and the indulgence of unnatural taste, have brought sin and misery into the world, from excess on the one hand, and from want on the other.

Jesus did not seek to attract the people to Him by gratifying the desire for luxury. To that great throng, weary and hungry after the long, exciting day, the simple fare was an assurance not only of His power, but of His tender care for them in the common needs of life. The Saviour has not promised His followers the luxuries of the world; their fare may be plain, and even scanty; their lot may be shut in by poverty; but His word is pledged that their need shall be supplied, and He has promised that which is far better than worldly good, — the abiding comfort of His own presence.

In feeding the five thousand, Jesus lifts the veil from the world of nature, and reveals the power that is constantly exercised for our good. In the production of earth's harvests, God is working a miracle every day. Through natural agencies the same work is accomplished that was wrought in the feeding of the multitude. Men prepare the soil and sow the seed, but it is the life from God that causes the seed to germinate. It is God's rain and air and sunshine that cause it to put forth, "first the blade, then the ear, after that the full corn in the ear." Mark 4:28. It is God who is every day feeding millions from earth's harvest fields.

Men are called upon to co-operate with God in the care of the grain and the preparation of the loaf, and because of this they lose sight of the divine agency. They do not give God the glory due unto His holy name. The working of His power is ascribed to natural causes or to human instrumentality. Man is glorified in place of God, and His gracious gifts are perverted to selfish uses, and made a curse instead of a blessing. God is seeking to change all this. He desires that our dull senses shall be quickened to discern His merciful kindness and to glorify Him for the working of His power. He desires us to recognize Him in His gifts, that they may be, as He intended, a blessing to us. It was to accomplish this purpose that the miracles of Christ were performed.

> **"Christ never worked a miracle except to supply a genuine necessity, and every miracle was of a character to lead the people to the tree of life, whose leaves are for the healing of the nations."**

After the multitude had been fed, there was an abundance of food left. But He who had all the resources of infinite power at His command said, "Gather up the fragments that remain, that nothing be lost." These words meant more than putting the bread into the baskets. The lesson was twofold. Nothing is to be wasted. We are to let slip no temporal advantage. We should neglect nothing that will tend to benefit a human being. Let everything be gathered up that will relieve the necessity of earth's hungry ones. And there should be the same carefulness in spiritual things. When the baskets of fragments were collected, the people thought of their friends at home. They wanted them to share in the bread that Christ had blessed. The contents of the baskets were distributed among the eager throng, and were carried away into all the region round about. So those who were at the feast were to give to others the bread that comes down from heaven, to satisfy the hunger of the soul. They were to repeat what they had learned of the wonderful things of God. Nothing was to be lost. Not one word that concerned their eternal salvation was to fall useless to the ground.

The miracle of the loaves teaches a lesson of dependence upon God. When Christ fed the five thousand, the food was not nigh at hand. Apparently He had no means at His command. Here He was, with five thousand men, besides women and children, in the wilderness. He had not invited the large multitude to follow Him; they came without invitation or command; but He knew that after they had listened so long to His instruction, they would feel hungry and faint; for He was one with them in their need of food. They were far from home, and the night was close at hand. Many of them were without means to purchase food. He who for their sake had fasted forty days in the wilderness, would not suffer them to return fasting to their homes. The providence of God had placed Jesus where He was; and He depended on His Heavenly Father for the means to relieve the necessity.

And when we are brought into strait places, we are to depend on God. We are to exercise wisdom and judgment in every action of life, that we may not, by reckless movements, place ourselves in trial. We are not to plunge into difficulties, neglecting the means God has provided, and misusing the faculties He has given us. Christ's workers are to obey His instructions implicitly. The work is God's, and if we would bless others, His plans must be followed. Self cannot be made a center; self can receive no honor. If we plan according to our own ideas, the Lord will leave us to our own mistakes. But when, after following His directions, we are brought into strait places, He will deliver us. We are not to give up in discouragement, but in every emergency we are to seek help from Him who has infinite resources at His command. Often we shall be surrounded with trying circumstances, and then, in the fullest confidence, we must depend upon God. He will keep every soul that is brought into perplexity through trying to keep the way of the Lord.

Christ has bidden us, through the prophet, "Deal thy bread to the hungry," and "satisfy the afflicted soul;" "when thou seest the naked that thou cover him," and "bring the poor that are cast out to thy house." Isaiah 58:7-10. He has bidden us, "Go ye into all the world, and preach the gospel to every creature." Mark 16:15. But how often our hearts sink, and faith fails us, as we see how great is the need, and how small the means in our hands. Like Andrew looking upon the five barley loaves and the two little fishes, we exclaim, "What are they among so many?" Often we hesitate, unwilling to give all that we have, fearing to spend and to be spent for others. But Jesus has bidden us, "Give *ye* them to eat." His command is a promise; and behind it is the same power that fed the multitude beside the sea.

In Christ's act of supplying the temporal necessities of a hungry multitude, is wrapped up a deep spiritual lesson for all His workers. Christ received from the Father; He imparted to the disciples; they imparted to the multitude; and the people to one another. So all who are united to Christ will receive from Him the bread of life, the heavenly food, and impart it to others.

In full reliance upon God, Jesus took the small store of loaves; and although there was but a small portion for His own family of disciples, He did not invite them to eat, but began to distribute to them, bidding them serve the people. The food multiplied in His hands; and the hands of the disciples, reaching out to Christ, Himself the Bread of life, were never empty. The little store was sufficient for all. After the wants of the people had been supplied, the fragments were gathered up, and Christ and His disciples ate together of the precious, Heaven-supplied food.

The disciples were the channel of communication between Christ and the people. This should be a great encouragement to His disciples today. Christ is the great center, the source of all strength. His disciples are to receive their supplies from Him. The most intelligent, the most spiritually minded, can bestow only as they receive. Of themselves they can supply nothing for the needs of the soul. We can impart only that which we receive from Christ; and we can receive only as we impart to others. As we continue imparting, we continue to receive; and the more we impart, the more we shall receive. Thus we may be constantly believing, trusting, receiving, and imparting.

The work of building up the kingdom of Christ will go forward, though to all appearance it moves slowly, and impossibilities seem to testify against advance. The work is of God, and He will furnish means, and will send helpers, true, earnest disciples, whose hands also will be filled with food for the starving multitude. God is not unmindful of those who labor in love to give the word of life to perishing souls, who in their turn reach forth their hands for food for other hungry souls.

In our work for God there is danger of relying too largely upon what man with his talents and ability can do. Thus we lose sight of the one Master Worker. Too often the worker for Christ fails to realize his personal responsibility. He is in danger of shifting his burden upon organizations, instead of relying upon Him who is the source of all strength. It is a great mistake to trust in human wisdom or numbers in the work of God. Successful work for Christ depends not so much on numbers or talent as upon pureness of purpose, the true simplicity of earnest, dependent faith. Personal responsibilities must be borne, personal duties must be taken up, personal efforts must be made for those who do not know Christ. In the place of shifting your responsibility upon some one whom you think more richly endowed than you are, work according to your ability.

When the question comes home to your heart, "Whence shall we buy bread, that these may eat?" let not your answer be the response of unbelief. When the disciples heard the Saviour's direction, "Give ye them to eat," all the difficulties arose in their minds. They questioned, Shall we go away into the villages to buy food? So now, when the people are destitute of the bread of life, the Lord's children question, Shall we send for some one from afar, to come and feed them? But what said Christ? — "Bid the men sit down," and He fed them there. So when you are surrounded by souls in need, know that Christ is there. Commune with Him. Bring your barley loaves to Jesus.

The means in our possession may not seem to be sufficient for the work; but if we will move forward in faith, believing in the all-sufficient power of God, abundant resources will open before us. If the work be of God, He Himself will provide the means for its accomplishment. He will reward honest, simple reliance upon Him. The little that is wisely and economically used in the service of the Lord of heaven will increase in the very act of imparting. In the hand of Christ the small supply of food remained undiminished until the famished multitude were satisfied. If we go to the Source of all strength, with our hands of faith outstretched to receive, we shall be sustained in our work, even under the most forbidding circumstances, and shall be enabled to give to others the bread of life.

The Lord says, "Give, and it shall be given unto you," "He that soweth sparingly shall reap also sparingly; and he that soweth with blessings shall reap also with blessings. . . . And God is able to make all grace abound unto you; that ye, having always all sufficiency in everything, may abound unto every good work; as it is written, —

"He hath scattered abroad, he hath given to the poor;
His righteousness abideth forever.

"And He that supplieth seed to the sower and bread for food, shall supply and multiply your seed for sowing, and increase the fruits of your righteousness; ye being enriched in everything unto all liberality, which worketh through us thanksgiving to God." Luke 6:38; 2 Corinthians 9:6-11, R. V., margin.

A Night on the Lake

Seated upon the grassy plain, in the twilight of the spring evening, the people ate of the food that Christ had provided. The words they had heard that day had come to them as the voice of God. The works of healing they had witnessed, were such as only divine power could perform. But the miracle of the loaves appealed to every one in that vast multitude. All were sharers in its benefit. In the days of Moses, God had fed Israel with manna in the desert; and who was this that had fed them that day, but He whom Moses had foretold? No human power could create from five barley loaves and two small fishes, food sufficient to feed thousands of hungry people. And they said one to another, "This is of a truth that prophet that should come into the world."

All day the conviction has strengthened. That crowning act is assurance that the long-looked-for Deliverer is among them. The hopes of the people rise higher and higher. This is He who will make Judea an earthly paradise, a land flowing with milk and honey. He can satisfy every desire. He can break the power of the hated Romans. He can deliver Judah and Jerusalem. He can heal the soldiers who are wounded in battle. He can supply whole armies with food. He can conquer the nations, and give to Israel the long-sought dominion.

In their enthusiasm the people are ready at once to crown Him king. They see that He makes no effort to attract attention or secure honor to Himself. In this He is essentially different from the priests and rulers, and they fear that He will never urge His claim to David's throne. Consulting together, they agree to take Him by force, and proclaim Him the king of Israel. The disciples unite with the multitude in declaring the throne of David the rightful inheritance of their Master. It is the modesty of Christ, they say, that causes Him to refuse such honor. Let the people exalt their Deliverer. Let the arrogant priests and rulers be forced to honor Him who comes clothed with the authority of God.

They eagerly arrange to carry out their purpose; but Jesus sees what is on foot, and understands, as they cannot, what would be the result of such a movement. Even now the priests and rulers are hunting His life. They accuse Him of drawing the people away from them. Violence and insurrection would follow an effort to place Him on the throne, and the work of the spiritual kingdom would be hindered. Without delay the movement must be checked. Calling His disciples, Jesus bids them take the boat, and return at once to Capernaum, leaving Him to dismiss the people.

Never before had a command from Christ seemed so impossible of fulfillment. The disciples had long hoped for a popular movement to place Jesus on the throne; they could not endure the thought that all this enthusiasm should come to nothing. The multitudes that were assembling to keep the Passover were anxious to see the new prophet. To His followers this seemed the golden opportunity to establish their beloved Master on the throne of Israel. In the glow of this new ambition it was hard for them to go away by themselves, and leave Jesus alone upon that desolate shore. They protested against the arrangement; but Jesus now spoke with an authority He had never before assumed toward them. They knew that further opposition on their part would be useless, and in silence they turned toward the sea.

Jesus now commands the multitude to disperse; and His manner is so decisive that they dare not disobey. The words of praise and exaltation die on their lips. In the very act of advancing to seize Him, their steps are stayed, and

This chapter is based on Matthew 14:22-33; Mark 6:45-52; John 6:14-21.

the glad, eager look fades from their countenances. In that throng are men of strong mind and firm determination; but the kingly bearing of Jesus, and His few quiet words of command, quell the tumult, and frustrate their designs. They recognize in Him a power above all earthly authority, and without a question they submit.

When left alone, Jesus "went up into a mountain apart to pray." For hours He continued pleading with God. Not for Himself but for men were those prayers. He prayed for power to reveal to men the divine character of His mission, that Satan might not blind their understanding and pervert their judgment. The Saviour knew that His days of per-

---

"Day by day God instructs His children. . . . He is preparing them to act their part upon that wider stage to which His providence has appointed them. It is the issue of the daily test that determines their victory or defeat in life's great crisis."

---

sonal ministry on earth were nearly ended, and that few would receive Him as their Redeemer. In travail and conflict of soul He prayed for His disciples. They were to be grievously tried. Their long-cherished hopes, based on a popular delusion, were to be disappointed in a most painful and humiliating manner. In the place of His exaltation to the throne of David, they were to witness His crucifixion. This was to be indeed His true coronation. But they did not discern this, and in consequence strong temptations would come to them, which it would be difficult for them to recognize as temptations. Without the Holy Spirit to enlighten the mind and enlarge the comprehension, the faith of the disciples would fail. It was painful to Jesus that their conceptions of His kingdom were, to so great a degree, limited to worldly aggrandizement and honor. For them the burden was heavy upon His heart, and He poured out His supplications with bitter agony and tears.

The disciples had not put off immediately from the land, as Jesus directed them. They waited for a time, hoping that He would come to them. But as they saw that darkness was fast gathering, they "entered into a ship, and went over the sea toward Capernaum." They had left Jesus with dissatisfied hearts, more impatient with Him than ever before since acknowledging Him as their Lord. They murmured because they had not been permitted to proclaim Him king. They blamed themselves for yielding so readily to His command. They reasoned that if they had been more persistent, they might have accomplished their purpose.

Unbelief was taking possession of their minds and hearts. Love of honor had blinded them. They knew that Jesus was hated by the Pharisees, and they were eager to see Him exalted as they thought He should be. To be united with a teacher who could work mighty miracles, and yet to be reviled as deceivers, was a trial they could ill endure. Were they always to be accounted followers of a false prophet? Would Christ never assert His authority as king? Why did not He who possessed such power reveal Himself in His true character, and make their way less painful? Why had He not saved John the Baptist from a violent death? Thus the disciples reasoned, until they brought upon themselves great spiritual darkness. They questioned, Could Jesus be an impostor, as the Pharisees asserted?

The disciples had that day witnessed the wonderful works of Christ. It had seemed that heaven had come down to the earth. The memory of that precious, glorious day should have filled them with faith and hope. Had they, out of the abundance of their hearts, been conversing together in regard to these things, they would not have entered into temptation. But their disappointment had absorbed their thoughts. The words of Christ, "Gather up the fragments, that nothing be lost," were unheeded. Those were hours of large blessing to the disciples, but they had forgotten it all. They were in the midst of troubled waters. Their thoughts were stormy and unreasonable, and the Lord gave them something else to afflict their souls and occupy their minds. God often does this when men create burdens and troubles for themselves. The disciples had no need to make trouble. Already danger was fast approaching.

A violent tempest had been stealing upon them, and they were unprepared for it. It was a sudden contrast, for the day had been perfect; and when the gale struck them, they were afraid. They forgot their disaffection, their unbelief, their impatience. Every one worked to keep the boat from sinking. It was but a short distance by sea from Bethsaida to the point where they expected to meet Jesus, and in ordinary weather the journey required but a few hours; but now they were driven farther and farther from the point they sought. Until the fourth watch of the night they toiled at the oars. Then the weary men gave themselves up for lost. In storm and darkness the sea had taught them their own helplessness, and they longed for the presence of their Master.

Jesus had not forgotten them. The Watcher on the shore saw those fear-stricken men battling with the tempest. Not for a moment did He lose sight of His disciples. With deepest solicitude His eyes followed the storm-tossed boat with its precious burden; for these men were to be the light of the world. As a mother in tender love watches her child, so the compassionate Master watched His disciples. When their hearts were subdued, their unholy ambition quelled, and in humility they prayed for help, it was given them.

At the moment when they believe themselves lost, a gleam of light reveals a mysterious figure approaching them upon the water. But they know not that it is Jesus. The One who has come for their help, they count as an enemy. Terror overpowers them. The hands that have grasped the oars with muscles like iron, let go their hold. The boat rocks at the will of the waves; all eyes are riveted on this vision of a man walking upon the white-capped billows of the foaming sea.

They think it a phantom that omens their destruction, and they cry out for fear. Jesus advances as if He would pass them; but they recognize Him, and cry out, entreating His help. Their beloved Master turns, His voice silences their fear, "Be of good cheer; it is I; be not afraid."

As soon as they could credit the wondrous fact, Peter was almost beside himself with joy. As if he could scarcely yet believe, he cried out, "Lord, if it be Thou, bid me come unto Thee on the water. And He said, Come."

Looking unto Jesus, Peter walks securely; but as in self-satisfaction he glances back toward his companions in the boat, his eyes are turned from the Saviour. The wind is boisterous. The waves roll high, and come directly between him and the Master; and he is afraid. For a moment Christ is hidden from his view, and his faith gives way. He begins to sink. But while the billows talk with death, Peter lifts his eyes from the angry waters, and fixing them upon Jesus, cries, "Lord, save me." Immediately Jesus grasps the outstretched hand, saying, "O thou of little faith, wherefore didst thou doubt?"

Walking side by side, Peter's hand in that of his Master, they stepped into the boat together. But Peter was now subdued and silent. He had no reason to boast over his fellows, for through unbelief and self-exaltation he had very nearly lost his life. When he turned his eyes from Jesus, his footing was lost, and he sunk amid the waves.

When trouble comes upon us, how often we are like Peter. We look upon the waves, instead of keeping our eyes fixed upon the Saviour. Our footsteps slide, and the proud waters go over our souls. Jesus did not bid Peter come to Him that he should perish; He does not call us to follow Him, and then forsake us. "Fear not," He says; "for I have redeemed thee, I have called thee by thy name; thou art Mine. When thou passest through the waters, I will be with thee; and through the rivers, they shall not overflow thee; when thou walkest through the fire, thou shalt not be burned; neither shall the flame kindle upon thee. For I am the Lord thy God, the Holy One of Israel, thy Saviour." Isaiah 43:1-3.

Jesus read the character of His disciples. He knew how sorely their faith was to be tried. In this incident on the sea He desired to reveal to Peter his own weakness, — to show that his safety was in constant dependence upon divine power. Amid the storms of temptation he could walk safely only as in utter self-distrust he should rely upon the Saviour. It was on the point where he thought himself strong that Peter was weak; and not until he discerned his weakness could he realize his need of dependence upon Christ. Had he learned the lesson that Jesus sought to teach him in that experience on the sea, he would not have failed when the great test came upon him.

Day by day God instructs His children. By the circumstances of the daily life He is preparing them to act their part upon that wider stage to which His providence has appointed them. It is the issue of the daily test that determines their victory or defeat in life's great crisis.

Those who fail to realize their constant dependence upon God, will be overcome by temptation. We may now suppose that our feet stand secure, and that we shall never be moved. We may say with confidence, "I know in whom I have believed; nothing can shake my faith in God and in His word." But Satan is planning to take advantage of our hereditary and cultivated traits of character, and to blind our eyes to our own necessities and defects. Only through realizing our own weakness, and looking steadfastly unto Jesus, can we walk securely.

No sooner had Jesus taken His place in the boat than the wind ceased, "and immediately the ship was at the land whither they went." The night of horror was succeeded by the light of dawn. The disciples, and others who also were on board, bowed at the feet of Jesus with thankful hearts, saying, "Of a truth Thou art the Son of God!"

The Crisis in Galilee

When Christ forbade the people to declare Him king, He knew that a turning point in His history was reached. Multitudes who desired to exalt Him to the throne today, would turn from Him tomorrow. The disappointment of their selfish ambition would turn their love to hatred, and their praise to curses. Yet knowing this, He took no measures to avert the crisis. From the first He had held out to His followers no hope of earthly rewards. To one who came desiring to become His disciple He had said, "The foxes have holes, and the birds of the air have nests; but the Son of man hath not where to lay His head." Matthew 8:20. If men could have had the world with Christ, multitudes would have proffered Him their allegiance; but such service He could not accept. Of those now connected with Him, there were many who had been attracted by the hope of a worldly kingdom. These must be undeceived. The deep spiritual teaching in the miracle of the loaves had not been comprehended. This was to be made plain. And this new revelation would bring with it a closer test.

The miracle of the loaves was reported far and near, and very early next morning the people flocked to Bethsaida to see Jesus. They came in great numbers, by land and sea. Those who had left Him the preceding night returned, expecting to find Him still there; for there had been no boat by which He could pass to the other side. But their search was fruitless, and many repaired to Capernaum, still seeking Him.

Meanwhile He had arrived at Gennesaret, after an absence of but one day. As soon as it was known that He had landed, the people "ran through that whole region round about, and began to carry about in beds those that were sick, where they heard He was." Mark 6:55.

After a time He went to the synagogue, and there those who had come from Bethsaida found Him. They learned from His disciples how He had crossed the sea. The fury of the storm, and the many hours of fruitless rowing against adverse winds, the appearance of Christ walking upon the water, the fears thus aroused, His reassuring words, the adventure of Peter and its result, with the sudden stilling of the tempest and landing of the boat, were all faithfully recounted to the wondering crowd. Not content with this, however, many gathered about Jesus, questioning, "Rabbi, when camest Thou hither?" They hoped to receive from His own lips a further account of the miracle.

Jesus did not gratify their curiosity. He sadly said, "Ye seek Me, not because ye saw the miracles, but because ye did eat of the loaves, and were filled." They did not seek Him from any worthy motive; but as thèy had been fed with the loaves, they hoped still to receive temporal benefit by attaching themselves to Him. The Saviour bade them, "Labor not for the meat which perisheth, but for that meat which endureth unto everlasting life." Seek not merely for material benefit. Let it not be the chief effort to provide for the life that now is, but seek for spiritual food, even that wisdom which will endure unto everlasting life. This the Son of God alone can give; "for Him hath God the Father sealed."

For the moment the interest of the hearers was awakened. They exclaimed, "What shall we do, that we might work the works of God?" They had been performing many and burdensome works in order to recommend themselves to God; and they were ready to hear of any new observance by which they could secure greater merit. Their question meant, What shall we do that we may deserve heaven?

This chapter is based on John 6:22-71.

What is the price we are required to pay in order to obtain the life to come?

"Jesus answered and said unto them, This is the work of God, that ye believe on Him whom he hath sent." The price of heaven is Jesus. The way to heaven is through faith in "the Lamb of God, which taketh away the sin of the world." John 1:29.

But the people did not choose to receive this statement of divine truth. Jesus had done the very work which prophecy had foretold that the Messiah would do; but they had not witnessed what their selfish hopes had pictured as His work. Christ had indeed once fed the multitude with barley loaves; but in the days of Moses, Israel had been fed with manna forty years, and far greater blessings were expected from the Messiah. Their dissatisfied hearts queried why, if Jesus could perform so many wondrous works as they had witnessed, could He not give health, strength, and riches to all His people, free them from their oppressors, and exalt them to power and honor? The fact that He claimed to be the Sent of God, and yet refused to be Israel's king, was a mystery which they could not fathom. His refusal was misinterpreted. Many concluded that He dared not assert His claims because He Himself doubted as to the divine character of His mission. Thus they opened their hearts to unbelief, and the seed which Satan had sown bore fruit of its kind, in misunderstanding and defection.

Now, half mockingly, a rabbi questioned, "What sign showest Thou then, that we may see, and believe Thee? What dost Thou work? Our fathers did eat manna in the desert; as it is written, He gave them bread from heaven to eat."

The Jews honored Moses as the giver of the manna, ascribing praise to the instrument, and losing sight of Him by whom the work had been accomplished. Their fathers had murmured against Moses, and had doubted and denied his divine mission. Now in the same spirit the children rejected the One who bore the message of God to themselves. "Then said Jesus unto them, Verily, verily, I say unto you, Moses gave you not that bread from heaven." The giver of the manna was standing among them. It was Christ Himself who had led the Hebrews through the wilderness, and had daily fed them with the bread from heaven. That food was a type of the real bread from heaven. The life-giving Spirit, flowing from the infinite fullness of God, is the true manna. Jesus said, "The Bread of God is that which cometh down out of heaven, and giveth life unto the world." John 6:33, R. V.

Still thinking that it was temporal food to which Jesus referred, some of His hearers exclaimed, "Lord, evermore give us this bread." Jesus then spoke plainly: "I am the Bread of Life."

The figure which Christ used was a familiar one to the Jews. Moses, by the inspiration of the Holy Spirit, had said, "Man doth not live by bread only, but by every word that proceedeth out of the mouth of the Lord." And the prophet Jeremiah had written, "Thy words were found, and I did eat them; and Thy word was unto me the joy and rejoicing of mine heart." Deuteronomy 8:3; Jeremiah 15:16. The rabbis themselves had a saying, that the eating of bread, in its spiritual significance, was the study of the law and the practice of good works; and it was often said that at the Messiah's coming, all Israel would be fed. The teaching of the prophets made plain the deep spiritual lesson in the miracle of the loaves. This lesson Christ was seeking to open to His hearers in the synagogue. Had they understood the Scriptures, they would have understood His words when He said, "I am the Bread of Life." Only the day before, the great multitude, when faint and weary, had been fed by the bread which He had given. As from that bread they had received physical strength and refreshment, so from Christ they might receive spiritual strength unto eternal life. "He that cometh to Me," He said, "shall never hunger; and he that believeth on Me shall never thirst." But He added, "Ye also have seen me, and believe not."

They had seen Christ by the witness of the Holy Spirit, by the revelation of God to their souls. The living evidences of His power had been before them day after day, yet they asked for still another sign. Had this been given, they would have remained as unbelieving as before. If they were not convinced by what they had seen and heard, it was useless to show them more marvelous works. Unbelief will ever find excuse for doubt, and will reason away the most positive proof.

Again Christ appealed to those stubborn hearts. "Him that cometh to Me I will in no wise cast out." All who received Him in faith, He said, should have eternal life. Not one could be lost. No need for Pharisees and Sadducees to dispute concerning the future life. No longer need men mourn in hopeless grief over their dead. "This is the will of Him that sent Me, that every one which seeth the Son, and believeth on Him, may have everlasting life; and I will raise Him up at the last day."

But the leaders of the people were offended, "and they said, Is not this Jesus, the son of Joseph, whose father and mother we know? How is it then that He saith, I came down from heaven?" They tried to arouse prejudice by referring scornfully to the lowly origin of Jesus. They contemptuously alluded to His life as a Galilean laborer, and to His family as being poor and lowly. The claims of this uneducated carpenter, they said, were unworthy of their attention. And on account of His mysterious birth they insinuated that He was of doubtful parentage, thus representing the human circumstances of His birth as a blot upon His history.

Jesus did not attempt to explain the mystery of His birth. He made no answer to the questionings in regard to His having come down from heaven, as He had made none to the questions concerning His crossing the sea. He did not call attention to the miracles that marked His life. Voluntarily He had made Himself of no reputation, and taken upon Him the form of a servant. But His words and works revealed His character. All whose hearts were open to divine illumination would recognize in Him "the only begotten of the Father, full of grace and truth." John 1:14.

The prejudice of the Pharisees lay deeper than their questions would indicate; it had its root in the perversity of their hearts. Every word and act of Jesus aroused antagonism in them; for the spirit which they cherished could find in Him no answering chord.

"No man can come to Me, except the Father which hath sent Me draw him; and I will raise him up at the last day. It is written in the prophets, And they shall be all taught of God. Every man therefore that hath heard, and hath learned of the Father, cometh unto Me." None will ever come to Christ, save those who respond to the drawing of the Father's love. But God is drawing all hearts unto Him, and only those who resist His drawing will refuse to come to Christ.

In the words, "They shall be all taught of God," Jesus referred to the prophecy of Isaiah: "All thy children shall be taught of the Lord; and great shall be the peace of thy children." Isaiah 54:13. This scripture the Jews appropriated to themselves. It was their boast that God was their teacher. But Jesus showed how vain is this claim; for He said, "Every man therefore that hath heard, and hath learned of the Father, cometh unto Me." Only through Christ could they receive a knowledge of the Father. Humanity could not endure the vision of His glory. Those who had learned of God had been listening to the voice of His Son, and in Jesus of Nazareth they would recognize Him who through nature and revelation has declared the Father.

"Verily, verily, I say unto you, He that believeth on Me hath everlasting life." Through the beloved John, who listened to these words, the Holy Spirit declared to the churches, "This is the record, that God hath given unto us eternal life, and this life is in His Son. He that hath the Son hath life." 1 John 5:11, 12. And Jesus said, "I will raise him up at the last day." Christ became one flesh with us, in order that we might become one spirit with Him. It is by virtue of this union that we are to come forth from the grave,—not merely as a manifestation of the power of Christ, but because, through faith, His life has become ours. Those who see Christ in His true character, and receive Him into the heart, have everlasting life. It is through the Spirit that Christ dwells in us; and the Spirit of God, received into the heart by faith, is the beginning of the life eternal.

The people had referred Christ to the manna which their fathers ate in the wilderness, as if the furnishing of that food was a greater miracle than Jesus had performed; but He shows how meager was that gift when compared with the blessings He had come to bestow. The manna could sustain only this earthly existence; it did not prevent the approach of death, nor insure immortality; but the Bread of heaven would nourish the soul unto everlasting life. The Saviour said, "I am that Bread of Life. Your fathers did eat manna in the wilderness, and are dead. This is the Bread which cometh down from heaven, that a man may eat thereof, and not die. I am the living Bread which came down from heaven; if any man eat of this bread, he shall live forever." To this figure Christ now adds another. Only through dying could He impart life to men, and in the

> "To eat the flesh and drink the blood of Christ is to receive Him as a personal Saviour, believing that He forgives our sins, and that we are complete in Him. It is by beholding His love, by dwelling upon it, by drinking it in, that we are to become partakers of His nature. What food is to the body, Christ must be to the soul. . . . We must feed upon Him, receive Him into the heart, so that His life becomes our life."

words that follow He points to His death as the means of salvation. He says, "The bread that I will give is My flesh, which I will give for the life of the world."

The Jews were about to celebrate the Passover at Jerusalem, in commemoration of the night of Israel's deliverance, when the destroying angel smote the homes of Egypt. In the paschal lamb God desired them to behold the Lamb of God, and through the symbol receive Him who gave Himself for the life of the world. But the Jews had come to make the symbol all-important, while its significance was unnoticed. They discerned not the Lord's body. The same truth that was symbolized in the paschal service, was taught in the words of Christ. But it was still undiscerned.

Now the rabbis exclaimed angrily, "How can this man give us His flesh to eat?" They affected to understand His words in the same literal sense as did Nicodemus when he asked, "How can a man be born when he is old?" John 3:4. To some extent they comprehended the meaning of Jesus, but they were not willing to acknowledge it. By misconstruing His words, they hoped to prejudice the people against Him.

Christ did not soften down His symbolical representation. He reiterated the truth in yet stronger language: "Verily, verily, I say unto you, Except ye eat the flesh of the Son of man, and drink His blood, ye have no life in you. Whoso eateth My flesh, and drinketh My blood, hath eternal life; and I will raise him up at the last day. For My flesh is meat indeed, and My blood is drink indeed. He that eateth My flesh, and drinketh My blood, dwelleth in Me, and I in him."

To eat the flesh and drink the blood of Christ is to receive Him as a personal Saviour, believing that He forgives our sins, and that we are complete in Him. It is by beholding His love, by dwelling upon it, by drinking it in, that we are to become partakers of His nature. What food is to the body, Christ must be to the soul. Food cannot benefit us unless we eat it; unless it becomes a part of our being. So Christ is of no value to us if we do not know Him as a personal Saviour. A theoretical knowledge will do us no good. We must feed upon Him, receive Him into the heart, so that His life becomes our life. His love, His grace, must be assimilated.

But even these figures fail to present the privilege of the believer's relation to Christ. Jesus said, "As the living Father hath sent Me, and I live by the Father; so he that eateth Me, even he shall live by Me." As the Son of God lived by faith in the Father, so are we to live by faith in Christ. So fully was Jesus surrendered to the will of God that the Father alone appeared in His life. Although tempted in all points like as we are, He stood before the world untainted by the evil that surrounded Him. Thus we also are to overcome as Christ overcame.

Are you a follower of Christ? Then all that is written concerning the spiritual life is written for you, and may be attained through uniting yourself to Jesus. Is your zeal languishing? has your first love grown cold? Accept again of the proffered love of Christ. Eat of His flesh, drink of His blood, and you will become one with the Father and with the Son.

The unbelieving Jews refused to see any except the most literal meaning in the Saviour's words. By the ritual law they were forbidden to taste blood, and they now construed Christ's language into a sacrilegious speech, and disputed over it among themselves. Many even of the disciples said, "This is an hard saying; who can hear it?"

The Saviour answered them: "Doth *this* offend you? What and if ye shall see the Son of man ascend up where He was before? It is the spirit that quickeneth; the flesh profiteth nothing; the words that I speak unto you, they are Spirit, and they are life."

The life of Christ, that gives life to the world, is in His word. It was by His word that Jesus healed disease and cast out demons; by His word He stilled the sea, and raised the dead; and the people bore witness that His word was with power. He spoke the word of God, as He had spoken through all the prophets and teachers of the Old Testament. The whole Bible is a manifestation of Christ, and the Saviour desired to fix the faith of His followers on the word. When his visible presence should be withdrawn, the word must be their source of power. Like their Master, they were to live "by every word that proceedeth out of the mouth of God." Matthew 4:4.

As our physical life is sustained by food, so our spiritual life is sustained by the word of God. And every soul is to receive life from God's word for himself. As we must eat for ourselves in order to receive nourishment, so we must receive the word for ourselves. We are not to obtain it merely through the medium of another's mind. We should carefully study the Bible, asking God for the aid of the Holy Spirit, that we may understand His word. We should take one verse, and concentrate the mind on the task of ascertaining the thought which God has put in that verse for us. We should dwell upon the thought until it becomes our own, and we know "what saith the Lord."

In His promises and warnings, Jesus means me. God so loved the world, that He gave His only begotten Son, that *I* by believing in Him, might not perish, but have everlasting life. The experiences related in God's word are to be *my* experiences. Prayer and promise, precept and warning, are mine. "I am crucified with Christ: nevertheless I live; yet not I, but Christ liveth in me; and the life which I now live in the flesh I live by the faith of the Son of God, who loved *me*, and gave Himself for *me*." Galatians 2:20. As faith thus receives and assimilates the principles of truth, they become a part of the being, and the motive power of the life. The word of God, received into the soul, molds the thoughts, and enters into the development of character.

By looking constantly to Jesus with the eye of faith, we shall be strengthened. God will make the most precious revelations to His hungering, thirsting people. They will find that Christ is a personal Saviour. As they feed upon His word, they find that it is spirit and life. The word destroys the natural, earthly nature, and imparts a new life in Christ Jesus. The Holy Spirit comes to the soul as a Comforter. By the transforming agency of His grace, the image of God is reproduced in the disciple; he becomes a new creature. Love takes the place of hatred, and the heart receives the divine similitude. This is what it means to live "by every word that proceedeth out of the mouth of God." This is eating the Bread that comes down from heaven.

Christ had spoken a sacred, eternal truth regarding the relation between Himself and His followers. He knew the character of those who claimed to be His disciples, and His words tested their faith. He declared that they were to believe and act upon His teaching. All who received Him would partake of His nature, and be conformed to His character. This involved the relinquishment of their cherished ambitions. It required the complete surrender of themselves to Jesus. They were called to become self-sacrificing, meek and lowly in heart. They must walk in the narrow path traveled by the Man of Calvary, if they would share in the gift of life and the glory of heaven.

"Are you a follower of Christ? Then all that is written concerning the spiritual life is written for you, and may be attained through uniting yourself to Jesus. Is your zeal languishing? Has your first love grown cold? Accept again of the proffered love of Christ. Eat of His flesh, drink of His blood, and you will become one with the Father and with the Son."

The test was too great. The enthusiasm of those who had sought to take Him by force and make Him king grew cold. This discourse in the synagogue, they declared, had opened their eyes. Now they were undeceived. In their minds His words were a direct confession that He was not the Messiah, and that no earthly rewards were to be realized from connection with Him. They had welcomed His miracle-working power; they were eager to be freed from disease and suffering; but they would not come into sympathy with His self-sacrificing life. They cared not for the mysterious spiritual kingdom of which He spoke. The insincere, the selfish, who had sought Him, no longer desired Him. If He would not devote His power and influence to obtaining their freedom from the Romans, they would have nothing to do with Him.

Jesus told them plainly, "There are some of you that believe not;" adding, "Therefore said I unto you, that no man can come unto Me, except it were given unto him of My Father." He wished them to understand that if they were not drawn to Him, it was because their hearts were not open to the Holy Spirit. "The natural man receiveth not the things of the Spirit of God; for they are foolishness unto him: neither can he know them, because they are spiritually discerned." 1 Corinthians 2:14. It is by faith that the soul beholds the glory of Jesus. This glory is hidden, until, through the Holy Spirit, faith is kindled in the soul.

By the public rebuke of their unbelief these disciples were still further alienated from Jesus. They were greatly displeased, and wishing to wound the Saviour, and gratify the malice of the Pharisees, they turned their backs upon Him, and left Him with disdain. They had made their choice,—had taken the form without the spirit, the husk without the kernel. Their decision was never afterward reversed; for they walked no more with Jesus.

"Whose fan is in His hand, and He will thoroughly purge His floor, and gather His wheat into the garner." Matthew 3:12. This was one of the times of purging. By the words of truth, the chaff was being separated from the wheat. Because they were too vain and self-righteous to receive reproof, too world-loving to accept a life of humility, many turned away from Jesus. Many are still doing the same thing. Souls are tested today as were those disciples in the synagogue at Capernaum. When truth is brought home to the heart, they see that their lives are not in accordance with the will of God. They see the need of an entire change in themselves; but they are not willing to take up the self-denying work. Therefore they are angry when their sins are discovered. They go away offended, even as the disciples left Jesus, murmuring, "This is an hard saying; who can hear it?"

Praise and flattery would be pleasing to their ears; but the truth is unwelcome; they cannot hear it. When the crowds follow, and the multitudes are fed, and the shouts of triumph are heard, their voices are loud in praise; but when the searching of God's Spirit reveals their sin, and bids them leave it, they turn their backs upon the truth, and walk no more with Jesus.

As those disaffected disciples turned away from Christ, a different spirit took control of them. They could see nothing attractive in Him whom they had once found so interesting. They sought out His enemies, for they were in harmony with their spirit and work. They misinterpreted His words, falsified His statements, and impugned His motives. They sustained their course by gathering up every item that could be turned against Him; and such indignation was stirred up by these false reports that His life was in danger.

The news spread swiftly, that by His own confession, Jesus of Nazareth was not the Messiah. And thus in Galilee the current of popular feeling was turned against Him, as, the year before, it had been in Judea. Alas for Israel! They rejected their Saviour, because they longed for a conqueror who would give them temporal power. They wanted the

174

meat which perishes, and not that which endures unto everlasting life.

With a yearning heart, Jesus saw those who had been His disciples departing from Him, the Life and the Light of men. The consciousness that His compassion was unappreciated, His love unrequited, His mercy slighted, His salvation rejected, filled Him with sorrow that was inexpressible. It was such developments as these that made Him a man of sorrows, and acquainted with grief.

Without attempting to hinder those who were leaving Him, Jesus turned to the Twelve and said, "Will ye also go away?"

Peter replied by asking, "Lord, to whom shall we go?" "Thou hast the words of eternal life," he added. "And we believe and are sure that Thou art that Christ, the Son of the living God."

"To whom shall we go?" The teachers of Israel were slaves to formalism. The Pharisees and Sadducees were in constant contention. To leave Jesus was to fall among sticklers for rites and ceremonies, and ambitious men who sought their own glory. The disciples had found more peace and joy since they had accepted Christ than in all their previous lives. How could they go back to those who had scorned and persecuted the Friend of sinners? They had long been looking for the Messiah; now He had come, and they could not turn from His presence to those who were hunting His life, and had persecuted them for becoming His followers.

"To whom shall we go?" Not from the teaching of Christ, His lessons of love and mercy, to the darkness of unbelief, the wickedness of the world. While the Saviour was forsaken by many who had witnessed His wonderful works, Peter expressed the faith of the disciples,—"Thou art that Christ." The very thought of losing this anchor of their souls filled them with fear and pain. To be destitute of a Saviour, was to be adrift on a dark and stormy sea.

Many of the words and acts of Jesus appear mysterious to finite minds, but every word and act had its definite purpose in the work for our redemption; each was calculated to produce its own result. If we were capable of understanding His purposes, all would appear important, complete, and in harmony with His mission.

While we cannot now comprehend the works and ways of God, we can discern His great love, which underlies all His dealings with men. He who lives near to Jesus will understand much of the mystery of godliness. He will recognize the mercy that administers reproof, that tests the character, and brings to light the purpose of the heart.

When Jesus presented the testing truth that caused so many of His disciples to turn back, He knew what would be the result of His words; but He had a purpose of mercy to fulfill. He foresaw that in the hour of temptation every one of His beloved disciples would be severely tested. His agony in Gethsemane, His betrayal and crucifixion, would be to them a most trying ordeal. Had no previous test been given, many who were actuated by merely selfish motives would have been connected with them. When their Lord was condemned in the judgment hall; when the multitude who had hailed Him as their king hissed at Him and reviled Him; when the jeering crowd cried, "Crucify Him!"— when their worldly ambitions were disappointed, these self-seeking ones would, by renouncing their allegiance to Jesus, have brought upon the disciples a bitter, heart-burdening sorrow, in addition to their grief and disappointment in the ruin of their fondest hopes. In that hour of darkness, the example of those who turned from Him might have carried others with them. But Jesus brought about this crisis while by His personal presence He could still strengthen the faith of His true followers.

Compassionate Redeemer, who in the full knowledge of the doom that awaited Him, tenderly smoothed the way for the disciples, prepared them for their crowning trial, and strengthened them for the final test.

Tradition

The scribes and Pharisees, expecting to see Jesus at the Passover, had laid a trap for Him. But Jesus, knowing their purpose, had absented Himself from this gathering. "Then came together unto Him the Pharisees, and certain of the scribes." As He did not go to them, they came to Him. For a time it had seemed that the people of Galilee would receive Jesus as the Messiah, and that the power of the hierarchy in that region would be broken. The mission of the Twelve, indicating the extension of Christ's work, and bringing the disciples more directly into conflict with the rabbis, had excited anew the jealousy of the leaders at Jerusalem. The spies they sent to Capernaum in the early part of His ministry, who had tried to fix on Him the charge of Sabbathbreaking, had been put to confusion; but the rabbis were bent on carrying out their purpose. Now another deputation was sent to watch His movements, and find some accusation against Him.

As before, the ground of complaint was His disregard of the traditional precepts that encumbered the law of God. These were professedly designed to guard the observance of the law, but they were regarded as more sacred than the law itself. When they came in collision with the commandments given from Sinai, preference was given to the rabbinical precepts.

Among the observances most strenuously enforced, was that of ceremonial purification. A neglect of the forms to be observed before eating, was accounted a heinous sin, to be punished both in this world and in the next; and it was regarded as a virtue to destroy the transgressor.

The rules in regard to purification were numberless. The period of a lifetime was scarcely sufficient for one to learn them all. The life of those who tried to observe the rabbinical requirements was one long struggle against ceremonial defilement, an endless round of washings and purifications. While the people were occupied with trifling distinctions, and observances which God had not required, their attention was turned away from the great principles of His law.

Christ and His disciples did not observe these ceremonial washings, and the spies made this neglect the ground of their accusation. They did not, however, make a direct attack on Christ, but came to Him with criticism of His disciples. In the presence of the multitude they said, "Why do Thy disciples transgress the tradition of the elders? for they wash not their hands when they eat bread."

Whenever the message of truth comes home to souls with special power, Satan stirs up his agents to start a dispute over some minor question. Thus he seeks to attract attention from the real issue. Whenever a good work is begun, there are cavilers ready to enter into dispute over forms or technicalities, to draw minds away from the living realities. When it appears that God is about to work in a special manner for His people, let them not be enticed into a controversy that will work only ruin of souls. The questions that most concern us are, Do I believe with saving faith on the Son of God? Is my life in harmony with the divine law? "He that believeth on the Son hath everlasting life, and he that believeth not the Son shall not see life." "And hereby we do know that we know Him, if we keep His commandments." John 3:36; 1 John 2:3.

Jesus made no attempt to defend Himself or His disciples. He made no reference to the charges against Him, but proceeded to show the spirit that actuated these sticklers for human rites. He gave them an example of what they were repeatedly doing, and had done just before coming in search of Him. "Full well ye reject the commandment of God," He said, "that ye may keep your own tradition. For Moses said, Honor thy father and thy mother; and, Whoso curseth father or mother, let him die the death. But ye say, If a man shall say to his father or mother, It is Corban, that is to say, a gift, by whatsoever thou mightest be profited by me; he shall be free. And ye suffer him no more to do aught for his father or his mother." They set aside the fifth commandment as of no consequence, but were very exact in carrying out the traditions of the elders. They taught the people that the devotion of their property to the temple was a duty more sacred than even the support of their parents; and that, however great the necessity, it was sacrilege to impart to father or mother any part of what had been thus consecrated. An undutiful child had only to pronounce the word "Corban" over his property, thus devoting it to God, and he could retain it for his own use during his lifetime, and after his death it was to be appropriated to the temple service. Thus he was at liberty, both in life and in death, to dishonor and defraud his parents, under cover of a pretended devotion to God.

Never, by word or deed, did Jesus lessen man's obligation to present gifts and offerings to God. It was Christ who gave all the directions of the law in regard to tithes and offerings. When on earth He commended the poor woman who gave her all to the temple treasury. But the apparent zeal for God on the part of the priests and rabbis was a pretense to cover their desire for self-aggrandizement. The people were deceived by them. They were bearing heavy burdens which God had not imposed. Even the disciples of Christ were not wholly free from the yoke that had been bound upon them by inherited prejudice and rabbinical authority. Now, by revealing the true spirit of the rabbis, Jesus sought to free from the bondage of tradition all who were really desirous of serving God.

"Ye hypocrites," He said, addressing the wily spies, "well did Esaias prophesy of you, saying, This people draweth nigh unto Me with their mouth, and honoreth Me with their lips; but their heart is far from Me. But in vain they do worship Me, teaching for doctrines the commandments of men." The words of Christ were an arraignment of the whole system of Pharisaism. He declared that by placing their requirements above the divine precepts, the rabbis were setting themselves above God.

The deputies from Jerusalem were filled with rage. They could not accuse Christ as a violator of the law given from Sinai, for He spoke as its defender against their traditions. The great precepts of the law, which He had presented, appeared in striking contrast to the petty rules that men had devised.

To the multitude, and afterward more fully to His disciples, Jesus explained that defilement comes not from without, but from within. Purity and impurity pertain to the soul. It is the evil deed, the evil word, the evil thought, the transgression of the law of God, not the neglect of external, man-made ceremonies, that defiles a man.

The disciples noted the rage of the spies as their false teaching was exposed. They saw the angry looks, and heard the half-muttered words of dissatisfaction and revenge. Forgetting how often Christ had given evidence that He read the heart as an open book, they told Him of the effect of His words. Hoping that He might conciliate the enraged officials, they said to Jesus, "Knowest Thou that the Pharisees were offended, after they heard this saying?"

He answered, "Every plant, which My Heavenly Father hath not planted, shall be rooted up." The customs and traditions so highly valued by the rabbis, were of this world, not from heaven. However great their authority with the people, they could not endure the testing of God. Every human invention that has been substituted for the commandments of God, will be found worthless in that day when "God shall bring every work into judgment, with every secret thing, whether it be good, or whether it be evil." Ecclesiastes 12:14.

The substitution of the precepts of men for the commandments of God has not ceased. Even among Christians are found institutions and usages that have no better foundation than the traditions of the fathers. Such institutions, resting upon mere human authority, have supplanted those of divine appointment. Men cling to their traditions, and revere their customs, and cherish hatred against those who seek to show them their error. In this day, when we are bidden to call attention to the commandments of God and the faith of Jesus, we see the same enmity as was manifested in the days of Christ. Of the remnant people of God it is written, "The dragon was wroth with the woman, and went to make war with the remnant of her seed, which keep the commandments of God, and have the testimony of Jesus Christ." Revelation 12:17.

But "every plant which My Heavenly Father hath not planted, shall be rooted up." In place of the authority of the so-called fathers of the church, God bids us accept the word of the eternal Father, the Lord of heaven and earth. Here alone is truth unmixed with error. David said, "I have more understanding than all my teachers; for Thy testimonies are my meditation. I understand more than the ancients, because I keep Thy precepts." Psalms 119:99, 100. Let all who accept human authority, the customs of the church, or the traditions of the fathers, take heed to the warning conveyed in the words of Christ, "In vain they do worship Me, teaching for doctrines the commandments of men."

Barriers Broken Down

After the encounter with the Pharisees, Jesus withdrew from Capernaum, and crossing Galilee, repaired to the hill country on the borders of Phenicia. Looking westward, He could see, spread out upon the plain below, the ancient cities of Tyre and Sidon, with their heathen temples, their magnificent palaces and marts of trade, and the harbors filled with shipping. Beyond was the blue expanse of the Mediterranean, over which the messengers of the gospel were to bear its glad tidings to the centers of the world's great empire. But the time was not yet. The work before Him now was to prepare His disciples for their mission. In coming to this region He hoped to find the retirement He had failed to secure at Bethsaida. Yet this was not His only purpose in taking this journey.

"Behold, a Canaanitish woman came out from those borders, and cried, saying, Have mercy on me, O Lord, Thou Son of David; my daughter is grievously vexed with a devil." Matthew 15:22, R. V. The people of this district were of the old Canaanite race. They were idolaters, and were despised and hated by the Jews. To this class belonged the woman who now came to Jesus. She was a heathen, and was therefore excluded from the advantages which the Jews daily enjoyed. There were many Jews living among the Phenicians, and the tidings of Christ's work had penetrated to this region. Some of the people had listened to His words and had witnessed His wonderful works. This woman had heard of the prophet, who, it was reported, healed all manner of diseases. As she heard of His power, hope sprung up in her heart. Inspired by a mother's love, she determined to present her daughter's case to Him. It was her resolute purpose to bring her affliction to Jesus. He must heal her child. She had sought help from the heathen gods, but had obtained no relief. And at times she was tempted to think, What can this Jewish teacher do for me? But the word had come, He heals all manner of diseases, whether those who come to Him for help are rich or poor. She determined not to lose her only hope.

Christ knew this woman's situation. He knew that she was longing to see Him, and He placed Himself in her path. By ministering to her sorrow, He could give a living representation of the lesson He designed to teach. For this He had brought His disciples into this region. He desired them to see the ignorance existing in cities and villages close to the land of Israel. The people who had been given every opportunity to understand the truth, were without a knowledge of the needs of those around them. No effort was made to help souls in darkness. The partition wall which Jewish pride had erected, shut even the disciples from sympathy with the heathen world. But these barriers were to be broken down.

Christ did not immediately reply to the woman's request. He received this representative of a despised race as the Jews would have done. In this He designed that His disciples should be impressed with the cold and heartless manner in which the Jews would treat such a case, as evinced by His reception of the woman, and the compassionate manner in which He would have them deal with such distress, as manifested by His subsequent granting of her petition.

But although Jesus did not reply, the woman did not lose faith. As He passed on, as if not hearing her, she followed Him, continuing her supplications. Annoyed by her importunities, the disciples asked Jesus to send her away. They saw that their Master treated her with indifference, and they therefore supposed that the prejudice of the Jews against the Canaanites was pleasing to Him. But it was a pitying Saviour to whom the woman made her plea, and in answer to the request of the disciples, Jesus said, "I am not sent but unto the lost sheep of the house of Israel." Although this answer appeared to be in accordance with the prejudice of the Jews, it was an implied rebuke to the disciples, which they afterward understood as reminding them of what He had often told them,—that He came to the world to save all who would accept Him.

> **"Caste is hateful to God. He ignores everything of this character. In His sight the souls of all men are of equal value. . . . Without distinction of age, or rank, or nationality, or religious privilege, all are invited to come unto Him and live."**

The woman urged her case with increased earnestness, bowing at Christ's feet, and crying, "Lord, help me." Jesus, still apparently rejecting her entreaties, according to the unfeeling prejudice of the Jews, answered, "It is not meet to take the children's bread, and to cast it to dogs." This was virtually asserting that it was not just to lavish the blessings brought to the favored people of God upon strangers and aliens from Israel. This answer would have utterly discouraged a less earnest seeker. But the woman saw that her opportunity had come. Beneath the apparent refusal of Jesus, she saw a compassion that He could not hide. "Truth, Lord," she answered, "yet the dogs eat of the crumbs which fall from their master's table." While the children of the household eat at the father's table, even the dogs are not left unfed. They have a right to the crumbs that fall from the table abundantly supplied. So while there were many blessings given to Israel, was there not also a blessing for her? She was looked upon as a dog, and had she not then a dog's claim to a crumb from His bounty?

Jesus had just departed from His field of labor because the scribes and Pharisees were seeking to take His life. They murmured and complained. They manifested unbe-

lief and bitterness, and refused the salvation so freely offered them. Here Christ meets one of an unfortunate and despised race, that has not been favored with the light of God's word; yet she yields at once to the divine influence of Christ, and has implicit faith in His ability to grant the favor she asks. She begs for the crumbs that fall from the Master's table. If she may have the privilege of a dog, she is willing to be regarded as a dog. She has no national or religious prejudice or pride to influence her course, and she immediately acknowledges Jesus as the Redeemer, and as being able to do all that she asks of Him.

The Saviour is satisfied. He has tested her faith in Him, By His dealings with her, He has shown that she who has been regarded as an outcast from Israel, is no longer an alien, but a child in God's household. As a child it is her privilege to share in the Father's gifts. Christ now grants her request, and finishes the lesson to the disciples. Turning to her with a look of pity and love, He says, "O woman, great is thy faith. Be it unto thee even as thou wilt." From that hour her daughter became whole. The demon troubled her no more. The woman departed, acknowledging her Saviour, and happy in the granting of her prayer.

This was the only miracle that Jesus wrought while on this journey. It was for the performance of this act that He went to the borders of Tyre and Sidon. He wished to relieve the afflicted woman, and at the same time to leave an example in His work of mercy toward one of a despised people, for the benefit of His disciples when He should no longer be with them. He wished to lead them from their Jewish exclusiveness to be interested in working for others besides their own people.

Jesus longed to unfold the deep mysteries of the truth which had been hid for ages, that the Gentiles should be fellow heirs with the Jews, and "partakers of His promise in Christ by the gospel." Ephesians 3:6. This truth the disciples were slow to learn, and the divine Teacher gave them lesson upon lesson. In rewarding the faith of the centurion at Capernaum, and preaching the gospel to the inhabitants of Sychar, He had already given evidence that He did not share the intolerance of the Jews. But the Samaritans had some knowledge of God; and the centurion had shown kindness to Israel. Now Jesus brought the disciples in contact with a heathen, whom they regarded as having no reason above any of her people, to expect favor from Him. He would give an example of how such a one should be treated. The disciples had thought that He dispensed too freely the gifts of His grace. He would show that His love was not to be circumscribed to race or nation.

When He said, "I am not sent but unto the lost sheep of the house of Israel," He stated the truth, and in His work for the Canaanite woman He was fulfilling His commission. This woman was one of the lost sheep that Israel should have rescued. It was their appointed work, the work which they had neglected, that Christ was doing.

This act opened the minds of the disciples more fully to the labor that lay before them among the Gentiles. They saw a wide field of usefulness outside of Judea. They saw souls bearing sorrows unknown to those more highly favored. Among those whom they had been taught to despise were souls longing for help from the mighty Healer, hungering for the light of truth, which had been so abundantly given to the Jews.

Afterward, when the Jews turned still more persistently from the disciples, because they declared Jesus to be the Saviour of the world, and when the partition wall between Jew and Gentile was broken down by the death of Christ, this lesson, and similar ones which pointed to the gospel work unrestricted by custom or nationality, had a powerful influence upon the representatives of Christ, in directing their labors.

The Saviour's visit to Phenicia and the miracle there performed, had a yet wider purpose. Not alone for the afflicted woman, nor even for His disciples and those who received their labors, was the work accomplished; but also "that ye might believe that Jesus is the Christ, the Son of God; and that believing ye might have life through His name." John 20:31. The same agencies that barred men away from Christ eighteen hundred years ago, are at work today. The spirit which built up the partition wall between Jew and Gentile is still active. Pride and prejudice have built strong walls of separation between different classes of men. Christ and His mission have been misrepresented, and multitudes feel that they are virtually shut away from the ministry of the gospel. But let them not feel that they are shut away from Christ. There are no barriers which man or Satan can erect but that faith can penetrate.

In faith the woman of Phenicia flung herself against the barriers that had been piled up between Jew and Gentile. Against discouragement, regardless of appearances that might have led her to doubt, she trusted the Saviour's love. It is thus that Christ desires us to trust in Him. The blessings of salvation are for every soul. Nothing but his own choice can prevent any man from becoming a partaker of the promise in Christ by the gospel.

Caste is hateful to God. He ignores everything of this character. In His sight the souls of all men are of equal value. He "hath made of one blood all nations of men for to dwell on all the face of the earth, and hath determined the times before appointed, and the bounds of their habitation; that they should seek the Lord; if haply they might feel after Him and find Him, though He be not far from every one of us." Without distinction of age, or rank, or nationality, or religious privilege, all are invited to come unto Him and live. "Whosoever believeth on Him shall not be ashamed; for there is no difference." "There is neither Jew or Greek, there is neither bond nor free." "The rich and poor meet together; the Lord is the Maker of them all." "The same Lord over all is rich unto all that call upon Him. For whosoever shall call upon the name of the Lord shall be saved." Acts 17:26, 27; Galatians 3:28; Proverbs 22:2; Romans 10:11-13.

The True Sign

"Again He went out from the borders of Tyre, and came through Sidon unto the Sea of Galilee through the midst of the borders of Decapolis." Mark 7:31, R. V.

It was in the region of Decapolis that the demoniacs of Gergesa had been healed. Here the people, alarmed at the destruction of the swine, had constrained Jesus to depart from among them. But they had listened to the messengers He left behind, and a desire was aroused to see Him. As He came again into that region, a crowd gathered about Him, and a deaf, stammering man was brought to Him. Jesus did not, according to His custom, restore the man by a word only. Taking him apart from the multitude, He put His fingers in his ears, and touched his tongue; looking up to heaven, He sighed at thought of the ears that would not be open to the truth, the tongues that refused to acknowledge the Redeemer. At the word, "Be open," the man's speech was restored, and, disregarding the command to tell no man, he published abroad the story of his cure.

Jesus went up into a mountain, and there the multitude flocked to Him, bringing their sick and lame, and laying them at His feet. He healed them all; and the people, heathen as they were, glorified the God of Israel. For three days they continued to throng about the Saviour, sleeping at night in the open air, and through the day pressing eagerly to hear the words of Christ, and to see His works. At the end of three days their food was spent. Jesus would not send them away hungry, and He called upon His disciples to give them food. Again the disciples revealed their unbelief. At Bethsaida they had seen how, with Christ's blessing, their little store availed for the feeding of the multitude; yet they did not now bring forward their all, trusting His power to multiply it for the hungry crowds.

Moreover, those whom He fed at Bethsaida were Jews; these were Gentiles and heathen. Jewish prejudice was still strong in the hearts of the disciples, and they answered Jesus, "Whence can a man satisfy these men with bread here in the wilderness?" But obedient to His word they brought Him what they had, — seven loaves and two fishes. The multitude were fed, seven large baskets of fragments remaining. Four thousand men, besides women and children, were thus refreshed, and Jesus sent them away with glad and grateful hearts.

Then taking a boat with His disciples He crossed the lake to Magdala, at the southern end of the plain of Gennesaret. In the border of Tyre and Sidon His spirit had been refreshed by the confiding trust of the Syro-Phenician woman. The heathen people of Decapolis had received Him with gladness. Now as He landed once more in Galilee, where His power had been most strikingly manifested, where most of His works of mercy had been performed, and His teaching given, He was met with contemptuous unbelief.

A deputation of Pharisees had been joined by representatives from the rich and lordly Sadducees, the party of the priests, the skeptics and aristocracy of the nation. The two sects had been at bitter enmity. The Sadducees courted the favor of the ruling power, in order to maintain their own position and authority. The Pharisees, on the other hand, fostered the popular hatred against the Romans, longing for the time when they could throw off the yoke of the conqueror. But Pharisee and Sadducee now united against Christ. Like seeks like; and evil, wherever it exists, leagues with evil for the destruction of the good.

Now the Pharisees and Sadducees came to Christ, asking for a sign from heaven. When in the days of Joshua, Israel went out to battle with the Canaanites at Bethhoron, the sun had stood still at the leader's command until victory was gained; and many similar wonders had been manifest in their history. Some such sign was demanded of Jesus. But these signs were not what the Jews needed. No mere external evidence could benefit them. What they needed was not intellectual enlightenment, but spiritual renovation.

"O ye hypocrites," said Jesus, "ye can discern the face of the sky," — by studying the sky they could foretell the weather, — "but can ye not discern the signs of the times?" Christ's own words, spoken with the power of the Holy Spirit that convicted them of sin, were the sign that God had given for their salvation. And signs direct from heaven had been given to attest the mission of Christ. The song of the angels to the shepherds, the star that guided the wise men, the dove and the voice from heaven at His baptism, were witnesses for Him.

"And He sighed deeply in His spirit, and saith, Why doth this generation seek after a sign?" "There shall no sign be given unto it, but the sign of the prophet Jonas." As Jonah was three days and three nights in the belly of the whale, Christ was to be the same time "in the heart of the earth." Matthew 12:40,41. And as the preaching of Jonah was a sign to the Ninevites, so Christ's preaching was a sign to His generation. But what a contrast in the reception of the word. The people of the great heathen city trembled as they heard the warning from God. Kings and nobles humbled themselves; the high and the lowly together cried to the God of heaven, and His mercy was granted unto them. "The men of Nineveh shall rise in judgment with this generation," Christ had said, "and shall condemn it; because they repented at the preaching of Jonas; and, behold, a greater than Jonas is here." Matthew 12:40, 41.

Every miracle that Christ performed was a sign of His divinity. He was doing the very work that had been foretold of the Messiah; but to the Pharisees these works of mercy were a positive offense. The Jewish leaders looked with heartless indifference on human suffering. In many cases their selfishness and oppression had caused the affliction that Christ relieved. Thus His miracles were to them a reproach.

That which led the Jews to reject the Saviour's work, was the highest evidence of His divine character. The greatest significance of His miracles is seen in the fact that they were for the blessing of humanity. The highest evidence that He came from God is, that His life revealed the character of God. He did the works and spoke the words of God. Such a life is the greatest of all miracles.

When the message of truth is presented in our day, there are many who, like the Jews, cry, "Show us a sign. Work us a miracle." Christ wrought no miracle at the demand of the Pharisees. He wrought no miracle in the wilderness in answer to Satan's insinuations. He does not impart to us power to vindicate ourselves or to satisfy the demands of unbelief and pride. But the gospel is not without a sign of its divine origin. Is it not a miracle that we can break from the bondage of Satan? Enmity against Satan is not natural to the human heart; it is implanted by the grace of God. When one who has been controlled by a stubborn, wayward will is set free, and yields himself wholeheartedly to the drawing of God's heavenly agencies, a miracle is wrought; so also when a man who has been under strong

---

66The gospel is not without a sign of its divine origin. Is it not a miracle that we can break from the bondage of Satan? . . . When one who has been controlled by a stubborn, wayward will is set free, and yields himself wholeheartedly to the drawing of God's heavenly agencies, a miracle is wrought.99

---

delusion, comes to understand moral truth. Every time a soul is converted, and learns to love God and keep His commandments, the promise of God is fulfilled, "A new heart also will I give you, and a new spirit will I put within you." Ezekiel 36:26. The change in human hearts, the transformation of human characters, is a miracle that reveals an ever-living Saviour, working to rescue souls. A consistent life in Christ is a great miracle. In the preaching of the word of God, the sign that should be manifest now and always, is the presence of the Holy Spirit, to make the word a regenerating power to those that hear. This is God's witness before the world to the divine mission of His Son.

Those who desired a sign from Jesus had so hardened their hearts in unbelief that they did not discern in His character the likeness of God. They would not see that His mission was in fulfillment of the Scriptures. In the parable of the rich man and Lazarus, Jesus said to the Pharisees, "If they hear not Moses and the prophets, neither will they be persuaded, though one rose from the dead." Luke 16:31. No sign that could be given in heaven or earth would benefit them.

Jesus "sighed deeply in His spirit," and, turning from the group of cavilers, reentered the boat with His disciples. In sorrowful silence they again crossed the lake. They did not, however, return to the place they had left, but directed their course toward Bethsaida, near where the five thousand had been fed. Upon reaching the farther side, Jesus said, "Take heed and beware of the leaven of the Pharisees and of the Sadducees." The Jews had been accustomed since the days of Moses to put away leaven from their houses at the Passover season, and they had thus been taught to regard it as a type of sin. Yet the disciples failed to understand Jesus. In their sudden departure from Magdala they had forgotten to take bread, and they had with them only one loaf. To this circumstance they understood Christ to refer, warning them not to buy bread of a Pharisee or a Sadducee. Their lack of faith and spiritual insight had often led them to similar misconception of His words. Now Jesus reproved them for thinking that He who had fed thousands with a few fishes and barley loaves could in that solemn warning have referred merely to temporal food. There was danger that the crafty reasoning of the Pharisees and the Sadducees would leaven His disciples with unbelief, causing them to think lightly of the works of Christ.

The disciples were inclined to think that their Master should have granted the demand for a sign in the heavens. They believed that He was fully able to do this, and that such a sign would put His enemies to silence. They did not discern the hypocrisy of these cavilers.

Months afterward, "when there were gathered together an innumerable multitude of people, insomuch that they trod one upon another," Jesus repeated the same teaching. "He began to say unto His disciples first of all, Beware ye of the leaven of the Pharisees, which is hypocrisy." Luke 12:1.

The leaven placed in the meal works imperceptibly, changing the whole mass to its own nature. So if hypocrisy is allowed to exist in the heart, it permeates the character and the life. A striking example of the hypocrisy of the Pharisees, Christ had already rebuked in denouncing the practice of "Corban," by which a neglect of filial duty was concealed under a pretense of liberality to the temple. The scribes and Pharisees were insinuating deceptive principles. They concealed the real tendency of their doctrines, and improved every occasion to instill them artfully into the minds of their hearers. These false principles, when once accepted, worked like leaven in the meal, permeating and transforming the character. It was this deceptive teaching that made it so hard for the people to receive the words of Christ.

The same influences are working today through those who try to explain the law of God in such a way as to make it conform to their practices. This class do not attack the law openly, but put forward speculative theories that undermine its principles. They explain it so as to destroy its force.

The hypocrisy of the Pharisees was the product of self-seeking. The glorification of themselves was the object of their lives. It was this that led them to pervert and misapply the Scriptures, and blinded them to the purpose of Christ's mission. This subtle evil even the disciples of Christ were in danger of cherishing. Those who classed themselves with the followers of Jesus, but who had not left all in order to become His disciples, were influenced in a great degree by the reasoning of the Pharisees. They were often vacillating between faith and unbelief, and they did not discern the treasures of wisdom hidden in Christ. Even the disciples, though outwardly they had left all for Jesus' sake, had not in heart ceased to seek great things for themselves. It was this spirit that prompted the strife as to who should be greatest. It was this that came between them and Christ, making them so little in sympathy with His mission of self-sacrifice, so slow to comprehend the mystery of redemption. As leaven, if left to complete its work, will cause corruption and decay, so does the self-seeking spirit, cherished, work the defilement and ruin of the soul.

Among the followers of our Lord today, as of old, how widespread is this subtle, deceptive sin. How often our service to Christ, our communion with one another, is marred by the secret desire to exalt self. How ready the thought of self-gratulation, and the longing for human approval. It is the love of self, the desire for an easier way than God has appointed, that leads to the substitution of human theories and traditions for the divine precepts. To His own disciples the warning words of Christ are spoken, "Take heed, and beware of the leaven of the Pharisees."

The religion of Christ is sincerity itself. Zeal for God's glory is the motive implanted by the Holy Spirit; and only the effectual working of the Spirit can implant this motive. Only the power of God can banish self-seeking and hypocrisy. This change is the sign of His working. When the faith we accept destroys selfishness and pretense, when it leads us to seek God's glory and not our own, we may know that it is of the right order. "Father, glorify Thy name," (John 12:28.) was the keynote of Christ's life, and if we follow Him, this will be the keynote of our life. He commands us to "walk even as He walked;" and "hereby we do know that we know Him, if we keep His commandments." 1 John 2:6,3.

The Foreshadowing of the Cross

The work of Christ on earth was hastening to a close. Before Him, in vivid outline, lay the scenes whither His feet were tending. Even before He took humanity upon Him, He saw the whole length of the path He must travel in order to save that which was lost. Every pang that rent His heart, every insult that was heaped upon His head, every privation that He was called to endure, was open to His view before He laid aside His crown and royal robe, and stepped down from the throne, to clothe His divinity with humanity. The path from the manger to Calvary was all before His eyes. He knew the anguish that would come upon Him. He knew it all, and yet He said, "Lo, I come; in the volume of the book it is written of Me, I delight to do Thy will, O My God; yea, Thy law is within My heart." Psalms 40:7,8.

Ever before Him He saw the result of His mission. His earthly life, so full of toil and self-sacrifice, was cheered by the prospect that He would not have all this travail for naught. By giving His life for the life of men, He would win back the world to its loyalty to God. Although the baptism of blood must first be received; although the sins of the world were to weigh upon His innocent soul; although the shadow of an unspeakable woe was upon Him; yet for the joy that was set before Him, He chose to endure the cross, and despised the shame.

From the chosen companions of His ministry the scenes that lay before Him were as yet hidden; but the time was near when they must behold His agony. They must see Him whom they had loved and trusted, delivered into the hands of His enemies, and hung upon the cross of Calvary. Soon He must leave them to face the world without the comfort of His visible presence. He knew how bitter hate and unbelief would persecute them, and He desired to prepare them for their trials.

Jesus and His disciples had now come into one of the towns about Caesarea Philippi. They were beyond the limits of Galilee, in a region where idolatry prevailed. Here the disciples were withdrawn from the controlling influence of Judaism, and brought into closer contact with the heathen worship. Around them were represented forms of superstition that existed in all parts of the world. Jesus desired that a view of these things might lead them to feel their responsibility to the heathen. During His stay in this region, He endeavored to withdraw from teaching the people, and to devote Himself more fully to His disciples.

He was about to tell them of the suffering that awaited Him. But first He went away alone, and prayed that their hearts might be prepared to receive His words. Upon joining them, He did not at once communicate that which He desired to impart. Before doing this, He gave them an opportunity of confessing their faith in Him that they might be strengthened for the coming trial. He asked, "Whom do men say that I the Son of man am?"

Sadly the disciples were forced to acknowledge that Israel had failed to recognize their Messiah. Some indeed, when they saw His miracles, had declared Him to be the Son of David. The multitudes that had been fed at Bethsaida had desired to proclaim Him king of Israel. Many were ready to accept Him as a prophet; but they did not believe Him to be the Messiah.

Jesus now put a second question, relating to the disciples themselves: "But whom say ye that I am?" Peter answered, "Thou art the Christ, the Son of the living God."

From the first, Peter had believed Jesus to be the Messiah. Many others who had been convicted by the preaching of John the Baptist, and had accepted Christ, began to doubt as to John's mission when he was imprisoned and put to death; and they now doubted that Jesus was the Messiah, for whom they had looked so long. Many of the disciples who had ardently expected Jesus to take His place on David's throne, left Him when they perceived that He had no such intention. But Peter and his companions turned not from their allegiance. The vacillating course of those who praised yesterday and condemned today did not destroy the faith of the true follower of the Saviour. Peter declared, "Thou art the Christ, the Son of the living God." He waited not for kingly honors to crown his Lord, but accepted Him in His humiliation.

Peter had expressed the faith of the TWelve. Yet the disciples were still far from understanding Christ's mission. The opposition and misrepresentation of the priests and rulers, while it could not turn them away from Christ, still caused them great perplexity. They did not see their way clearly. The influence of their early training, the teaching of the rabbis, the power of tradition, still intercepted their view of truth. From time to time precious rays of light from Jesus shone upon them, yet often they were like men groping among shadows. But on this day, before they were brought face to face with the great trial of their faith, the Holy Spirit rested upon them in power. For a little time their eyes were turned away from "the things which are seen," to behold "the things which are not seen." 2 Corinthians 4:18. Beneath the guise of humanity they discerned the glory of the Son of God.

Jesus answered Peter, saying, "Blessed art thou, Simon Barjona; for flesh and blood hath not revealed it unto thee, but My Father which is in heaven."

The truth which Peter had confessed, is the foundation of the believer's faith. It is that which Christ Himself has declared to be eternal life. But the possession of this knowledge was no ground for self-glorification. Through no wisdom or goodness of his own had it been revealed to Peter. Never can humanity, of itself, attain to a knowledge of the divine. "It is a high as heaven; what canst thou do? deeper than hell; what canst thou know?" Job 11:8. Only the spirit of adoption can reveal to us the deep things of God, which "eye hath not seen, nor ear heard, neither have entered into the heart of man." "God hath revealed them unto us by His Spirit; for the Spirit searcheth all things, yea, the deep things of God." 1 Corinthians 2:9 10. "The secret of the Lord is with them that fear Him;" and the fact that Peter discerned the glory of Christ was an evidence that he had been "taught of God." Psalms 25:14; John 6:45. Ah, indeed, "blessed art thou, Simon Barjona; for flesh and blood hath not revealed it unto thee."

Jesus continued: "I say also unto thee, That thou art Peter, and upon this rock I will build My church; and the gates of hell shall not prevail against it." The word Peter signifies a stone, — a rolling stone. Peter was not the rock upon which the church was founded. The gates of hell did prevail against him when he denied his Lord with cursing

and swearing. The church was built upon One against whom the gates of hell could not prevail.

Centuries before the Saviour's advent, Moses had pointed to the Rock of Israel's salvation. The psalmist had sung of "the Rock of my strength." Isaiah had written, "Thus saith the Lord God, Behold, I lay in Zion for a foundation a stone, a tried stone, a precious cornerstone, a sure foundation." Deuteronomy 32:4; Psalms 62:7; Isaiah 28:16. Peter himself, writing by inspiration, applies this prophecy to Jesus. He says, "If ye have tasted that the Lord is gracious; unto whom coming, a living stone, rejected indeed of men, but with God elect, precious, ye also, as living stones, are built up a spiritual house." 1 Peter 2:3-5, R. V.

"Other foundation can no man lay than that is laid, which is Jesus Christ." 1 Corinthians 3:11. "Upon this rock," said Jesus, "I will build My church." In the presence of God, and all the heavenly intelligences, in the presence of the unseen army of hell, Christ founded His church upon the living Rock. That Rock is Himself,—His own body, for us broken and bruised. Against the church built upon this foundation, the gates of hell shall not prevail.

How feeble the church appeared when Christ spoke these words! There was only a handful of believers, against whom all the power of demons and evil men would be directed; yet the followers of Christ were not to fear. Built upon the Rock of their strength, they could not be overthrown.

For six thousand years, faith has builded upon Christ. For six thousand years the floods and tempests of Satanic wrath have beaten upon the Rock of our salvation; but it stands unmoved.

Peter had expressed the truth which is the foundation of the church's faith, and Jesus now honored him as the representative of the whole body of believers. He said, "I will give unto thee the keys of the kingdom of heaven; and whatsoever thou shalt bind on earth shall be bound in heaven; and whatsoever thou shalt loose on earth shall be loosed in heaven."

"The keys of the kingdom of heaven" are the words of Christ. All the words of Holy Scripture are His, and are here included. These words have power to open and to shut heaven. They declare the conditions upon which men are received or rejected. Thus the work of those who preach God's word is a savor of life unto life or of death unto death. Theirs is a mission weighted with eternal results.

The Saviour did not commit the work of the gospel to Peter individually. At a later time, repeating the words that were spoken to Peter, He applied them directly to the church. And the same in substance was spoken also to the Twelve as representatives of the body of believers. If Jesus had delegated any special authority to one of the disciples above the others, we should not find them so often contending as to who should be the greatest. They would have submitted to the wish of their Master, and honored the one whom He had chosen.

Instead of appointing one to be their head, Christ said to the disciples, "Be not ye called, Rabbi;" "neither be ye called masters; for one is your Master, even Christ." Matthew 23:8, 10.

"The head of every man is Christ." God, who put all things under the Saviour's feet, "gave Him to be the head over all things to the church, which is His body, the fullness of Him that filleth all in all." 1 Corinthians 11:3; Ephesians 1:22, 23. The church is built upon Christ as its foundation; it is to obey Christ as its head. It is not to depend upon man, or be controlled by man. Many claim that a position of trust in the church gives them authority to dictate what other men shall believe and what they shall do. This claim God does not sanction. The Saviour declares, "All ye are brethren." All are exposed to temptation, and are liable to error. Upon no finite being can we depend for guidance. The Rock of faith is the living presence of Christ in the church. Upon this the weakest may depend, and those who think themselves the strongest will prove to be the weakest, unless they make Christ their efficiency. "Cursed be the man that trusteth in man, and maketh flesh his arm." The Lord "is the Rock, His work is perfect." "Blessed are all they that put their trust in Him." Jeremiah 17:5; Deuteronomy 32:4; Psalms 2:12.

After Peter's confession, Jesus charged the disciples to tell no man that He was the Christ. This charge was given because of the determined opposition of the scribes and Pharisees. More than this, the people, and even the disciples, had so false a conception of the Messiah that a public announcement of Him would give them no true idea of His character or His work. But day by day He was revealing Himself to them as the Saviour, and thus He desired to give them a true conception of Him as the Messiah.

The disciples still expected Christ to reign as a temporal prince. Although He had so long concealed His design, they believed that He would not always remain in poverty and obscurity; the time was near when He would establish His kingdom. That the hatred of the priests and rabbis would never be overcome, that Christ would be rejected by His own nation, condemned as a deceiver, and crucified as a malefactor, — such a thought the disciples had never entertained. But the hour of the power of darkness was drawing on, and Jesus must open to His disciples the conflict before them. He was sad as He anticipated the trial.

Hitherto He had refrained from making known to them anything relative to His sufferings and death. In His conversation with Nicodemus He had said, "As Moses lifted up the serpent in the wilderness, even so must the Son of man be lifted up; that whosoever believeth in Him should not perish, but have eternal life." John 3:14, 15. But the disciples did not hear this, and had they heard, would not have understood. But now they have been with Jesus, listening to His words, beholding His works, until, notwithstanding the humility of His surroundings, and the opposition of priests and people, they can join in the testimony of Peter, "Thou art the Christ, the Son of the living God." Now the time has come for the veil that hides the future to be withdrawn. "From that time forth began Jesus to show unto His disciples, how that He must go unto Jerusalem, and suffer many things of the elders and chief priests and scribes, and be killed, and be raised again the third day."

Speechless with grief and amazement, the disciples listened. Christ had accepted Peter's acknowledgment of Him as the Son of God; and now His words pointing to His suffering and death seemed incomprehensible. Peter could not keep silent. He laid hold upon his Master, as if to draw Him back from His impending doom, exclaiming, "Be it far from Thee, Lord; this shall not be unto Thee."

Peter loved his Lord; but Jesus did not commend him for thus manifesting the desire to shield Him from suffering. Peter's words were not such as would be a help and solace to Jesus in the great trial before Him. They were not in harmony with God's purpose of grace toward a lost world, nor with the lesson of self-sacrifice that Jesus had come to teach by His own example. Peter did not desire to see the cross in the work of Christ. The impression which his words would make, was directly opposed to that which Christ desired to make on the minds of His followers, and the Saviour was moved to utter one of the sternest rebukes that ever fell from His lips: "Get thee behind Me, Satan; thou art an offense unto Me; for thou savorest not the things that be of God, but those that be of men."

Satan was trying to discourage Jesus, and turn Him from His mission; and Peter, in his blind love, was giving voice to the temptation. The prince of evil was the author of the thought. His instigation was behind that impulsive appeal. In the wilderness, Satan had offered Christ the dominion of the world on condition of forsaking the path of humiliation and sacrifice. Now he was presenting the same temptation to the disciple of Christ. He was seeking to fix Peter's gaze upon the earthly glory, that he might not behold the cross to which Jesus desired to turn his eyes. And through Peter, Satan was again pressing the temptation upon Jesus. But the Saviour heeded it not; His thought was for His disciple. Satan had interposed between Peter and his Master, that the heart of the disciple might not be touched at the vision of Christ's humiliation for him. The words of Christ were spoken, not to Peter, but to the one who was trying to separate him from his Redeemer. "Get thee behind Me, Satan." No longer interpose between Me and My erring servant. Let me come face to face with Peter, that I may reveal to him the mystery of My love.

It was to Peter a bitter lesson, and one which he learned but slowly, that the path of Christ on earth lay through agony and humiliation. The disciple shrank from fellowship with his Lord in suffering. But in the heat of the furnace fire he was to learn its blessing. Long afterward, when his active form was bowed with the burden of years and labors, he wrote, "Beloved, think it not strange concerning the fiery trial which is to try you, as though some strange thing happened unto you; but rejoice, inasmuch as ye are partakers of Christ's sufferings; that, when His glory shall be revealed, ye may be glad also with exceeding joy."

Jesus now explained to His disciples that His own life of self-abnegation was an example of what theirs should be. Calling about Him, with the disciples, the people who had been lingering near, He said, "If any man will come after Me, let him deny himself, and take up his cross daily, and follow Me." The cross was associated with the power of Rome. It was the instrument of the most cruel and humiliating form of death. The lowest criminals were required to bear the cross to the place of execution; and often as it was about to be laid upon their shoulders, they resisted with desperate violence, until they were overpowered, and the instrument of torture was bound upon them. But Jesus bade His followers take up the cross and bear it after Him. To the disciples His words, though dimly comprehended, pointed to their submission to the most bitter humiliation,—submission even unto death for the sake of Christ. No more complete self-surrender could the Saviour's words have pictured. But all this He had accepted for them. Jesus did not count heaven a place to be desired while we were lost. He left the heavenly courts for a life of reproach and insult, and a death of shame. He who was rich in heaven's priceless treasure, became poor, that through His poverty we might be rich. We are to follow in the path He trod.

Love for souls for whom Christ died, means crucifixion of self. He who is a child of God should henceforth look upon himself as a link in the chain let down to save the world, one with Christ in His plan of mercy, going forth with Him to seek and save the lost. The Christian is ever to realize that he has consecrated himself to God, and that in character he is to reveal Christ to the world. The self-sacrifice, the sympathy, the love, manifested in the life of Christ, are to reappear in the life of the worker for God.

"Whosoever will save his life shall lose it; but whosoever shall lose his life for My sake and the gospel's, the same shall save it." Selfishness is death. No organ of the body could live, should it confine its service to itself. The heart, failing to send its lifeblood to the hand and the head, would quickly lose its power. As our lifeblood, so is the love of Christ diffused through every part of His mystical body. We are members one of another, and the soul that refuses to impart will perish. And "what is a man profited," said Jesus, "if he shall gain the whole world, and lose his own soul? or what shall a man give in exchange for his soul?"

Beyond the poverty and humiliation of the present, He pointed the disciples to His coming in glory, not in the splendor of an earthly throne, but with the glory of God and the hosts of heaven. And then, He said, "He shall reward every man according to His works." Then for their encouragement He gave the promise, "Verily I say unto you, There be some standing here, which shall not taste of death, till they see the Son of man coming in His kingdom." But the disciples did not comprehend His words. The glory seemed far away. Their eyes were fixed upon the nearer view, the earthly life of poverty, humiliation, and suffering. Must their glowing expectations of the Messiah's kingdom be relinquished? Were they not to see their Lord exalted to the throne of David? Could it be that Christ was to live, a humble, homeless wanderer, to be despised, rejected, and put to death? Sadness oppressed their hearts, for they loved their Master. Doubt also harassed their minds, for it seemed incomprehensible that the Son of God should be subjected to such cruel humiliation. They questioned why He should voluntarily go to Jerusalem to meet the treatment which He had told them He was there to receive. How could He resign Himself to such a fate, and leave them in greater darkness than that in which they were groping before He revealed Himself to them?

In the region of Caesarea Philippi, Christ was out of the reach of Herod and Caiaphas, the disciples reasoned. He had nothing to fear from the hatred of the Jews or from the power of the Romans. Why not work there, at a distance from the Pharisees? Why need He give Himself up to death? If He was to die, how was it that His kingdom was to be established so firmly that the gates of hell should not prevail against it? To the disciples this was indeed a mystery.

They were even now journeying along the shores of the Sea of Galilee toward the city where all their hopes were to be crushed. They dared not remonstrate with Christ, but they talked together in low, sorrowful tones in regard to what the future would be. Even amid their questionings they clung to the thought that some unforeseen circumstance might avert the doom which seemed to await their Lord. Thus they sorrowed and doubted, hoped and feared, for six long, gloomy days.

"He Was Transfigured"

Evening is drawing on as Jesus calls to His side three of His disciples, Peter, James, and John, and leads them across the fields, and far up a rugged path, to a lonely mountainside. The Saviour and His disciples have spent the day in traveling and teaching, and the mountain climb adds to their weariness. Christ has lifted burdens from mind and body of many sufferers; He has sent the thrill of life through their enfeebled frames; but He also is compassed with humanity, and with His disciples He is wearied with the ascent.

The light of the setting sun still lingers on the mountain top, and gilds with its fading glory the path they are traveling. But soon the light dies out from hill as well as valley, the sun disappears behind the western horizon, and the solitary travelers are wrapped in the darkness of night. The gloom of their surroundings seems in harmony with their sorrowful lives, around which the clouds are gathering and thickening.

The disciples do not venture to ask Christ whither He is going, or for what purpose. He has often spent entire nights in the mountains in prayer. He whose hand formed mountain and valley is at home with nature, and enjoys its quietude. The disciples follow where Christ leads the way; yet they wonder why their Master should lead them up this toilsome ascent when they are weary, and when He too is in need of rest.

Presently Christ tells them that they are now to go no farther. Stepping a little aside from them, the Man of sorrows pours out His supplications with strong crying and tears. He prays for strength to endure the test in behalf of humanity. He must Himself gain a fresh hold on Omnipotence, for only thus can He contemplate the future. And He pours out His heart longings for His disciples, that in the hour of the power of darkness their faith may not fail. The dew is heavy upon His bowed form, but He heeds it not. The shadows of night gather thickly about Him, but He regards not their gloom. So the hours pass slowly by. At first the disciples unite their prayers with His in sincere devotion; but after a time they are overcome with weariness, and, even while trying to retain their interest in the scene, they fall asleep. Jesus has told them of His sufferings; He has taken them with Him that they might unite with Him in prayer; even now He is praying for them. The Saviour has seen the gloom of His disciples, and has longed to lighten their grief by an assurance that their faith has not been in vain. Not all, even of the Twelve, can receive the revelation He desires to give. Only the three who are to witness His anguish in Gethsemane have been chosen to be with Him on the mount. Now the burden of His prayer is that they may be given a manifestation of the glory He had with the Father before the world was, that His kingdom may be revealed to human eyes, and that His disciples may be strengthened to behold it. He pleads that they may witness a manifestation of His divinity that will comfort them in the hour of His supreme agony with the knowledge that He is of a surety the Son of God, and that His shameful death is a part of the plan of redemption.

His prayer is heard. While He is bowed in lowliness upon the stony ground, suddenly the heavens open, the golden gates of the city of God are thrown wide, and holy radiance descends upon the mount, enshrouding the Saviour's form. Divinity from within flashes through humanity, and meets the glory coming from above. Arising from His prostrate position, Christ stands in Godlike majesty. The soul agony is gone. His countenance now shines "as the sun," and His garments are "white as the light."

This chapter is based on Matthew 17:1-8; Mark 9:2-8; Luke 9:28-36.

The disciples, awaking, behold the flood of glory that illuminates the mount. In fear and amazement they gaze upon the radiant form of their Master. As they become able to endure the wondrous light, they see that Jesus is not alone. Beside Him are two heavenly beings, in close converse with Him. They are Moses, who upon Sinai had talked with God; and Elijah, to whom the high privilege was given— granted to but one other of the sons of Adam—never to come under the power of death.

"As they heard the voice of God speak in awful majesty . . . the disciples fell smitten to the earth. They remained prostrate, their face hidden, till Jesus came near, and touched them, dispelling their fears with His well-known voice, 'Arise, and be not afraid.'"

Upon Mount Pisgah fifteen centuries before, Moses had stood gazing upon the land of promise. But because of his sin at Meribah, it was not for him to enter there. Not for him was the joy of leading the host of Israel into the inheritance of their fathers. His agonized entreaty, "I pray Thee, let me go over, and see the good land that is beyond Jordan, that goodly mountain, and Lebanon," (Deuteronomy 3:25.) was refused. The hope that for forty years had lighted up the darkness of the desert wanderings must be denied. A wilderness grave was the goal of those years of toil and heart-burdening care. But He who is "able to do exceeding abundantly above all that we ask or think," (Ephesians 3:20.) had in this measure answered His servant's prayer. Moses passed under the dominion of death, but he was not to remain in the tomb. Christ Himself called him forth to life. Satan the tempter had claimed the body of Moses because of his sin; but Christ the Saviour brought him forth from the grave. Jude 9.

Moses upon the mount of transfiguration was a witness to Christ's victory over sin and death. He represented those who shall come forth from the grave at the resurrection of the just. Elijah, who had been translated to heaven without seeing death, represented those who will be living upon the earth at Christ's second coming, and who will be "changed in a moment, in the twinkling of an eye, at the last trump;" when "this mortal must put on immortality," and "this corruptible must put on incorruption." 1 Corinthians 15:51-53. Jesus was clothed with the light of heaven, as He will appear when He shall come "the second time without sin unto salvation." For He will come "in the glory of His Father with the holy angels." Hebrews 9:28; Mark 8:38. The Saviour's promise to the disciples was now fulfilled. Upon the mount the future kingdom of glory was represented in miniature,—Christ the King, Moses a representative of the risen saints, and Elijah of the translated ones.

The disciples do not yet comprehend the scene; but they rejoice that the patient Teacher, the meek and lowly One, who was wandered to and fro a helpless stranger, is honored by the favored ones of heaven. They believe that Elijah has come to announce the Messiah's reign, and that the kingdom of Christ is about to be set up on the earth. The memory of their fear and disappointment they would banish forever. Here, where the glory of God is revealed, they long to tarry. Peter exclaims, "Master, it is good for us to be here; and let us make three tabernacles; one for Thee, and one for Moses, and one for Elias." The disciples are confident that Moses and Elijah have been sent to protect their Master, and to establish His authority as king.

But before the crown must come the cross. Not the inauguration of Christ as king, but the decease to be accomplished at Jerusalem, is the subject of their conference with Jesus. Bearing the weakness of humanity, and burdened with its sorrow and sin, Jesus walked alone in the midst of men. As the darkness of the coming trial pressed upon Him, He was in loneliness of spirit, in a world that knew Him not. Even His loved disciples, absorbed in their own doubt and sorrow and ambitious hopes, had not comprehended the mystery of His mission. He had dwelt amid the love and fellowship of heaven; but in the world that He had created, He was in solitude. Now heaven had sent its messengers to Jesus; not angels, but men who had endured suffering and sorrow, and who could sympathize with the Saviour in the trial of His earthly life. Moses and Elijah had been colaborers with Christ. They had shared His longing for the salvation of men. Moses had pleaded for Israel: "Yet now, if Thou wilt forgive their sin;—and if not, blot me, I pray Thee, out of Thy book which Thou hast written." Exodus 32:32. Elijah had known loneliness of spirit, as for three years and a half of famine he had borne the burden of the nation's hatred and its woe. Alone he had stood for God upon Mount Carmel. Alone he had fled to the desert in anguish and despair. These men, chosen above every angel around the throne, had come to commune with Jesus concerning the scenes of His suffering, and to comfort Him with the assurance of the sympathy of heaven. The hope of the world, the salvation of every human being, was the burden of their interview.

Through being overcome with sleep, the disciples heard little of what passed between Christ and the heavenly messengers. Failing to watch and pray, they had not received that which God desired to give them, — a knowledge of the sufferings of Christ, and the glory that should follow. They lost the blessing that might have been theirs through sharing His self-sacrifice. Slow of heart to believe were these disciples, little appreciative of the treasure with which Heaven sought to enrich them.

Yet they received great light. They were assured that all heaven knew of the sin of the Jewish nation in rejecting Christ. They were given a clearer insight into the work of the Redeemer. They saw with their eyes and heard with their ears things that were beyond the comprehension of man. They were "eye-witnesses of His majesty," (2 Peter 1:16) and they realized that Jesus was indeed the Messiah, to whom patriarchs and prophets had witnessed, and that He was recognized as such by the heavenly universe.

While they were still gazing on the scene upon the mount, "a bright cloud overshadowed them; and behold a voice out of the cloud, which said, This is My beloved Son, in whom I am well pleased; hear ye Him." As they beheld the cloud of glory, brighter than that which went before the tribes of Israel in the wilderness; as they heard the voice of God speak in awful majesty that caused the mountain to tremble, the disciples fell smitten to the earth. They remained prostrate, their faces hidden, till Jesus came near, and touched them, dispelling their fears with His well-known voice, "Arise, and be not afraid." Venturing to lift up their eyes, they saw that the heavenly glory had passed away, the forms of Moses and Elijah had disappeared. They were upon the mount, alone with Jesus.